# RAF
# ACKLINGTON

# RAF ACKLINGTON

## GUARDIAN OF THE NORTHERN SKIES

MALCOLM FIFE

FONTHILL

*In memory of my grandmother, Edith V. Zienkiewicz*

Fonthill Media Language Policy

Fonthill Media publishes in the international English language market. One language edition is published worldwide. As there are minor differences in spelling and presentation, especially with regard to American English and British English, a policy is necessary to define which form of English to use. The Fonthill Policy is to use the form of English native to the author. Malcolm Fife was born and educated in Edinburgh, and therefore British English has been adopted in this publication.

Fonthill Media Limited
Fonthill Media LLC
www.fonthillmedia.com
office@fonthillmedia.com

First published in the United Kingdom and the United States of America 2017

British Library Cataloguing in Publication Data:
A catalogue record for this book is available from the British Library

Copyright © Malcolm Fife 2017

ISBN 978-1-78155-622-1

Typeset in 10pt on 13pt Sabon
Printed and bound in England

MIX
Paper from responsible sources
FSC® C013056

# Acknowledgements

Ross Dimsey for assistance with editing and layout of text.
Aldon Ferguson for photographs.
Bob O'Hara for research in National Archives.
The late Don Aris for information on 141 Squadron.
Andrew Dennis, Assistant Curator, RAF Museum.
Roger Lindsay for his photographs of RAF Acklington.
Paul Johnson, Image Manager for the National Archives, Kew.
Nigel Denchfield for his father's memoir on RAF Acklington.
Jim Jobe for his record on air displays.
Wilhelm Ratuszynski for photographs of 315 Squadron.
Eric Mannings for photographs of 72 Squadron.
Brian Pickering for photographs.
Mark Postlethwaite, ww2images.
Richard Flagg for list of based squadrons and units.

The Station Badge for RAF Acklington, designed in 1957. The Latin motto translates as 'Yesterday it had to be taught, today it has to be carried out'. (*The National Archives*)

# Contents

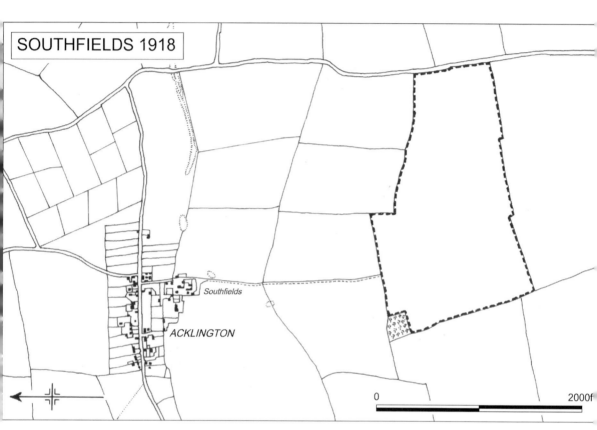

A plan of the First World War landing ground, Southfields. Acklington airfield was constructed on the site in the late 1930s. (*Mick Davis*)

# Introduction

Acklington Airfield was Fighter Command's most northerly airfield in England during the Battle of Britain. It was also one of the most important in the region throughout the Second World War. This came about more by accident than design. Shortly before the outbreak of hostilities, it had opened as a training station where pilots were given the opportunity to fire live weapons and drop bombs on the nearby ranges at Druridge Bay. With the declaration of war, it was transferred to Fighter Command, as military airfields in north-east England were few and far between.

The fighter aircraft of Acklington were tasked to defend what was one of Britain's most important industrial conurbations. Acklington airfield was situated on the edge of the Northumberland and Durham coalfield. There were coal mines and slag heaps in its vicinity, but much of the area was still farmland. Further south, industry dominated the landscape. The large cranes of the shipbuilding industry lined the rivers Tyne and Wear, and there were numerous other industries including iron and steel production and armaments manufacturing that acted as a magnet for German bombers for most of the war.

Northumberland was no stranger to conflict, being one of the most heavily fought-over areas in Britain. In Roman times, there was a large garrison to defend 'civilisation' against the wild tribes to the north. Supplies for the legions were delivered by sea to a number of ports in the region, one of which was at Druridge Bay, the bombing and gunnery range for Acklington Airfield.

During the Dark Ages, a small village—known as Aecceley or Acley, after the sons of its Anglo Saxon founder Aeccel—was established on rising ground a short distance to the north of the airfield's location. Eventually becoming known as Acklington, it experienced considerable strife during its history. During the Middle Ages, the residents would often take refuge in Warkworth Castle when Northumberland suffered one of the frequent raids from the Scots. In 1316, the village was devastated by Robert the Bruce and again in 1342 by King David II. As Scotland moved towards union with England, conflict along the border came to an end.

The north of England became a military backwater in the eighteenth and nineteenth centuries when the main threat was perceived as emerging from over the English Channel. However, with the rise of Germany, there was now a threat across the North

Sea. With the outbreak of the First World War, the danger was not only by sea but from the air in the form of Zeppelins. It was thought, however, that London would be the main focus of attack from the air and little had been done to protect other parts of Britain. It was not long before Zeppelins began to raid further afield. In April 1915, the second Zeppelin raid on Britain was on Tyneside. A few weeks later, there was a further attack when Zeppelin *L10* crossed the coast at Blyth and dropped bombs on a colliery and a shipyard at Jarrow. To counter this menace, a network of airfields was established along the east coast.

Cramlington became the base for the newly formed 36 Home Defence Squadron in March 1916. It was during this year that Zeppelin raids on north-east England reached a peak. In the autumn, 77 Home Defence Squadron was established at Turnhouse, Edinburgh, to defend the Firth of Forth. It operated from a number of airfields including one at New Haggerston in Northumberland. Both Squadrons had only around a dozen aircraft on strength. In an attempt to plug gaps in the air defences, 36 Home Defence Squadron deployed flights of aircraft at Ashington, Hylton and Seaton Carew airfields, despite the lack of machines. In addition, numerous night landing grounds were established in Northumberland and around Newcastle with the intention of providing alternative landing grounds for the aircraft of the Home Defence Squadrons. Generally, they were little more than grass fields with a windsock and a tent or a shed. To illuminate the landing area at night, buckets filled with petrol were set alight and could be seen from about eight miles away. One such night landing ground was at Southfields, just to the south of Acklington Village.

When the First World War came to an end, many of these airfields were rapidly abandoned. Cramlington Airfield stayed open until 1935 in a civil capacity. Flying at Southfields was resurrected when the site was selected for the construction of a new airfield to be known as RAF Acklington.

# 1

# Recollections of a Spitfire Pilot at Acklington

H. David Denchfield was posted to RAF Acklington to join 610 Squadron in 1940 as a sergeant pilot. His account of his stay at this station gives an interesting insight both to life there at that time as well as Spitfire operations:

By 11 a.m. the next day a local train deposited us on the wayside halt at Acklington from where we could see the lean Spitfire shapes about 500 yards away. Whilst waiting for the requested transport, we amused ourselves by putting halfpenny pieces on the rails to be flattened and enlarged in diameter by passing trains. The porters thought we were sublimely potty! For a change we were not greeted with an air of surprise at our appearance—as Ollie said, that was a plus straight away! The CO— Sqn Ldr Ellis— welcomed us and told us a little of what we would be doing and of the squadron itself and then for the rest of the day we were settling in.

No. 610 (County of Chester) Squadron was a pre-war Royal Auxiliary Air Force unit with affiliations to the City of Chester and its environs, formed in 1936 as a bomber unit, flying Hawker Harts. In 1938 it was redesignated as a fighter unit. Mobilised on 31 August 1939, it had then one Hurricane but later became all Spitfire and flew over the Dunkirk evacuation. Until coming to Acklington on rest on 31 August, it had flown in the Battle of Britain at Hornchurch, Rochford and Biggin Hill. I think the original pilots were all gone, one way or the other but the ground staff as usual with Auxiliary squadrons remained. They could not be posted to another unit against their wishes, hence spent most of the war with their original units. A great spirit resulted.

Bill Ballard and myself were allocated a small room at the end of a communal block holding some thirty airmen—it was small indeed but warm and cozy. The ablutions were a mere 100 yards walk away, all outside and on a freezing morning at 6 a.m. a jaunt to wash and shave before readiness at 6.30 a.m. daunted the bravest. We started flying the following day in between rain showers, the visibility was atrocious but I think the six remaining pilots of 610 Squadron were anxious to see how we would all shape. Even at this late stage we found a pressure to succeed. Those who were thought not to come up to expectations were posted away—to Bomber Command, there to undergo a conversion course on to twins. Some who even Bomber Command wouldn't have, ended up on target towing units!

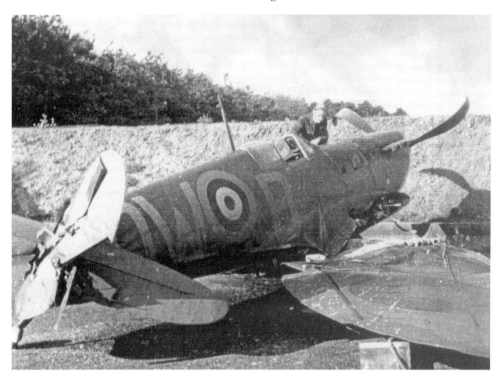

Joe Doley of 610 Squadron with his damaged Spitfire. He landed too fast and ended up in his CO's dispersal pen. (*HD Denchfield*)

We had one 'incident' in the first two days. Cranwell, who set off early in the morning before the rest of us arrived, achieved the unique. He taxied straight up to the nose of a visiting Blenheim, his prop chopping away metal, perspex and Lord knows what else until he stopped his prop-blades in the region of the pilot's seat! The all-NCO crew were not amused and grew less amused as the weeks went by. Thereafter they spent every day in the Mess and were in an awful fix. Their base was in East Anglia from where they were instructed to stay at RAF Acklington until their aircraft could be flown home. They were not attached to us and could get no pay from Acklington—in fact I'm not sure just how they were paid. They were still there in December when we flew south and the relations with us had not improved a jot.

Our second day came with weather so vile we had a glorious day in the Mess— perfect 'airman's' weather! After Hawarden [on the Welsh border, near Chester], the Mess was sheer luxury—solid brick-built with a billiard room, large ante-room filled with leather arm chairs and a large quiet dining room in which we were served by white-coated mess waiters. The food was good and perhaps best of all there was no 'atmosphere' between the pilots and ground staff.

Bill, myself and Cranwell were in A-Flight with Flt Lt Pegge, whilst Ollie and another newcomer, Billy Raine (proper Christian name: Woodrow!) were in B-Flight with Flt Lt Norris. The other two originals were Fg Off. Douglas and Sgt Hamlyn (whose aircraft bore a Walt Disney Pied Piper and 15 rats each with a swastika collar).

On our third morning, Hamlyn led Bill and myself to Usworth (just south of the Tyne and surrounded on three sides by the Newcastle balloon barrage), where we were shown the 'sector ops room' from which our movements would be controlled. All most interesting except I hoped never to have to rely on the radio direction finding system. Three widely separated receivers plotted the bearing of one's transmission and these three bearings were transferred to a vertical map board of the area via three lengths of wire, each pivoting about on a spot on the map corresponding to the position of one of the receivers. The three wires crossed making a shape of a small triangle or 'cocked hat'. What with 'out of the true' of each wire the area inside the cocked hat looked to be some 20 square miles—we were somewhere in that! Bill and myself thought it a bit much. Still, as we were not allowed to go out over the sea unless after something, we ought to be able to get a pinpoint within the area.

It was with this opps room that our only radio contact was made (we had none with our base). We were ordered off, given courses, ordered to return, etc., by ops and gave our replies to them, but we were still not controlled, as later, in our circuits in flight or on the ground. We still had only the ubiquitous duty pilot and his ever ready Very signal flare pistol. Back at base, Hamlyn told us to aerobat for half an hour. On landing, my starboard oleo leg slowly but irretrievably retracted during the latter part of the landing run until the Spitfire nestled shyly on the port main wheel, tail wheel and starboard wing tip. I had landed heavier than I should have done, resulting in a bent out of engagement locking pin. It was my first ever accident and brought home that the Spitfire was a thoroughbred, not a plodding Harvard!

Two days later we had a swine of a day. It all started in mid-morning. I was at about 20,000 feet over Berwick aerobatting when opps sent out a general recall to base. Thinking 'good', they've got wind of something coming over, I went down and to the south very fast. From halfway back at 200 feet, I thought the strange looking white blanket to the south couldn't possibly [be] fog, could it? It was sea mist which up there used to come and go with great suddenness and although this one was thin enough to see through vertically with some success, the forward vision was of blinding white opaqueness. I missed the field on the first attempt and turned back when the Newcastle barrage balloons appeared! Picking up on a pinpoint in the clear north, I followed the Newcastle/Berwick railway down to the bifurcation around the airfield and also managed to align with the 400 feet slag heap poking through the muck 1½ miles east of the airfield.

Spotting a hanger below, I dropped to about 100 feet and succeeded in orbiting the perimeter, watching for trees, huts, etc., that could be a hazard. After the 2nd orbit I decided on my east/west approach and was on a dummy run from near the slag heap when opps called up and said all aircraft were to land north to south and whilst positioning myself heard Cranwell call to ask opps to get a starter truck to him as he'd stopped his engine in the middle of the airfield. So consigning him to the devil for his lack of public spirit, I then flew two dummy runs to make sure my proposed run was clear—these at 60 feet over this mist bedevilled landscape, seeing the somewhat ghostly shapes of hangers, buildings flash past in the murk below made for great address of the problem. Anyway two runs and then for real.

The Spitfire touched down just about 100 yards inside the boundary, ran up the slope and rolled down the other side. She was almost stopped—when she did! Very abruptly too. The propeller stopped very violently amid a veritable Devil's chorus of sound! Looking around the right-hand side of the windshield I was horrified to see my starboard wing embedded in a Spitfire's rudder and one blade of my propeller stuck firmly down into the Spitfire's fuselage just behind the armour plate and at the front of a trail of rear fuselage damage. Unstrapping, I leapt out to the front, kicked my tyre, called the other aircraft a revolting word—and then stood in horrified wonderment as the other apparently unoccupied cockpit suddenly spawned a very white and frightened face. Yes, it was Cranwell still in his aircraft. He later said he sat waiting for his trolley acc (starting batteries on wheels) which came along two minutes later with a crowd from dispersal who from 150 yards away had just been able to see what had happened) when he heard a gentle 'pop-pop-pop' and turned to watch the inexorable arrival of my aircraft. My propeller had hit the rear of his armour plate, knocking it, the seat and him forward about 6 inches.

Just after a Beaufighter had landed, a Spitfire which had been endlessly orbiting, finally came into land. He seemed to float an awful long way and to be travelling too fast. We had all, I guess, thought he was about to blast through the windward hedge (if he missed our dispersal hut!) when he obviously came to the same conclusion, for he opened up the engine and started a new circuit. Sadly, whilst retracting flaps, he left the wheels down—the starboard undercarriage leg blanked across the front of the radiator to prevent proper cooling, so we were instructed to retract wheels as soon as possible after take-off to ensure the engine would not overheat. From the aircraft identification we saw it was Joe Doley, who went off only five minutes before the recall and so with plenty of fuel to spare was able to orbit, if need be, for 1.5 hours with a good chance the mist would go as suddenly as it had come.

In all he made nine abortive attempts to land—each time floating in very flat and fast indeed. And each time he opened up to drive on up with wheels down. Someone said the bloody Merlin must be red-hot by now. On his tenth attempt, he obviously decided this was it. Again flat and fast he touched down, main wheels only, a good half way across the airfield and thundered on, his tail wheel touched down some 250 yards from the perimeter and by now we could all see he was set to blast through, first the ground staff hut (which was disgorging folk out of every hole) and if that didn't stop him, then secondly he would tear a hole in the hedge. However, with about 100 yards to go, Joe slanted left, then immediately back right, missing the hut, took his aircraft at about 40 mph clean as a whistle into Sqn Ldr Ellis's dispersal bay in which sat his aircraft, secure behind its sandbagged blast walls. The aircraft was tucked within the confines of three walls out of the safety of which it could trundle forward to swing left out through a wingspan wide gap between 1st and 4th walls—this gap was tight and gave only about 18 inches clear each side. Anyway Joe entered the gap and was immediately blanketed from view by an eruption of dust, steam and corruption.

As we drew near the mess we could hear two angry voices and one was clearly Joe's. Don't you shout at me. I've just had an accident and don't feel like being shouted at! When the dust and tempers had settled, we could see that Joe's aircraft was pointing back the way it had come, both wings were torn off, the fuselage was on its side with the tail assembly twisted through ninety degrees. One undercarriage leg was torn off and the other barely attached. Smoke and steam tendrilled gaily away and lots of little tinkling noises came from an extremely hot engine. Miraculously, the CO's aircraft had just one penny-sized dent in the front of the propeller spinner! The CO wanted to know why Joe repeatedly come in so fast and why his undercarriage was left down. Joe said his throttle had stuck so he couldn't throttle right back and maybe 'he'd forgotten his wheels'. Joe got a red endorsement and was, I think, from then on permanent flying control duties—it must have been a life of purgatory!

Apart from this, I suffered only a couple of minor mishaps when manoeuvring violently during mock dogfights—in each case, not only did I crick my neck but my cockpit hood completely disintegrated. Chiefy said the cause was likely the small soft riveted-on panel on the right side tearing free and taking the hood with it.

The days settled to a routine. Most days we had one flight on training flights with the other on readiness in case anything hostile came over. Those on readiness sat in the pilot's hut reading, chatting, listening to the radio or more usually the gramophone or just plain dozing (certainly on the 7 a.m. turn). Helmets were in the aircraft draped over the gunsight (against all authority) with the wireless lead plugged in up on the right side of the cockpit.

Normally one flight went on readiness at 7 a.m., then being replaced by the other flight from 9-10 a.m. while it breakfasted. Usually then one flight took over from 10 a.m. till 1 p.m., when the other replaced it until dusk (about 4 p.m.) and as Spitfires at that time were non-operational at night, we were then stood down until 7 a.m. the following day. While one flight (six aircraft) was on duty, all other pilots were able to fly training exercises and these exercises went on to an obviously lesser extent when the whole squadron was at readiness (twelve aircraft in two flights—the squadron pilot strength was around twenty).

I think the whole squadron was released for the whole day one day in four and training was utilising all eighteen of our aircraft. We practised formation flying in sections of three, in flights of six and the squadron of twelve at all heights from low level to 30,000 feet. Also on the list were steep turns, high and low, forced landings, spinning and aeronautics, low flying, flying through cloud, radio homing and a certain amount of stooging up and down the coast watching to seaward. When on readiness, we had to be within an easy run of our aircraft and usually spent the time in the pilot's huts in wicker armchairs in a circle round the cast iron stove with our feet on it! We did once come to 'standby' which meant pilots strapped in the aircraft with trolly accs plugged in and ground crew at the ready. Nothing came of this and we all came to think it had just been a simulation.

One day in eight pilots were allowed off station for twenty-four hours. My schedule was—as for the others—to catch the Newcastle train at 9 a.m. and once in Newcastle straight over to the Sally Ann [Salvation Army] hostel to book a bed for the night, across to the municipal baths for a steaming hot soak (ours at the station were never more than lukewarm and the bathrooms ice cold) and a change of underwear. The day was spent in town and the night at the Sally Ann, from whence at 5 a.m. next morning I sallied out to catch the 5.30 a.m. train back to Acklington. By nipping through the hedge next to the station it was possible to check in the pilot's hut if some unsympathetic soul had listed one for early morning readiness. If so, well it was now nearly 7 a.m., so one stopped in the hut and got the duty clerk to phone the guard room to say one was on duty and the pass would be surrendered at the breakfast stand down. If not on duty, one handed the pass in directly to the guardroom and then went for a good clean up and a leisurely breakfast.

As the winter of 1940 developed, the area of our dispersal became a morass and with the consequent moving of our aircraft further out on to firmer ground the morass area grew and grew. Eventually, our aircraft were out a good 100 yards from the dispersal site and trudging through the gooey mess was a pain and very mucky. Later on everywhere froze solid so although walking was less mucky, it was still tricky. In fact, the temperature was always bitingly cold and just how the ground crews kept so even tempered and cheerful is beyond me. Quite apart from their daily maintenance work—in the open with ice cold tools—they were caught for yet another pleasant duty. The Spitfire always liked to lift her tail at the least provocation with the risk of using her propeller as a rotovator and as the bad muddy/frozen conditions increased this risk, we were not allowed to taxy unless a ground crew was squatted on each tailplane. I just cannot imagine the sheer awfulness of the experience—the slipstream from the prop threw a spray of freezing muddy goo at them and only too often they no sooner got from one aircraft than another wanted its human ballast. At the very least they were only too often faced with a cold wet trudge from one side of the airfield to another.

In mid-November airfield conditions were so bad we were ordered to use the one and only runway—itself under construction with a bank of earth about 18 inches high running down the full length of each side. At the west (dispersal) end the bank had been flattened over some 30 yards for an entry/exit and something or other used to make a relatively firm taxiway through the mud. The runway state meant that only one aircraft could use it throughout the time it took to, say, approach, land and taxy all the way back down the runway again.

We weren't too impressed, as most of us had never used a runway before and had to sort out our own technique [most airfields did not have runways at this time and were nothing more than grass fields]. I well remember the bloody thing see-sawing too and fro across my windscreen as I attempted to sort out the drift—it was never truly into wind and if the Spitfire's under carriage disliked anything it was to be touched down with drift on!

Happily there was one diversion. Across the eastern end extended a bank of earth some eight feet high with planked runs for wheelbarrows feeding down from the top at both ends. A bunch of Irish labourers seemed to spend all day humping loads of dirt up at one end, what time another bunch humped it all down again from the other end. For about two days after we began using the runway they used to stand leaning back on their shovels watching us approach to land and clearly believing we would miss them! Oh thee of too much faith, woe unto thee for HM pilots are not as other men! Quite apart from the shortness of the runway causing us to touch down as close to it as humanly possible and therefore to skim the bank as close as we dared, we also used to do so for the sheer pleasure of seeing that rapidly approaching mass of humanity suddenly go tumbling and rolling wheel barrows and all in a higgledy, piggeldy mess down the sides of the bank! After two days the merest sniff of an aircraft on the circuit caused an immediate evacuation of the bank.

We didn't care much for runway operation in general and in particular the number of burst tyres wasn't confidence building. Billy Raine had a shocker. As his wheels touched so a tyre went off with a crack and within a split second was sliding along the concrete, his aircraft on its side, both wings off and the tail twisted through about ninety degrees. He was shaken but unhurt and was flying again that afternoon—we didn't have time in those days for 'trauma' to appear! Still I suppose our runway with its failings was preferred to that at Usworth, with its two runways and perimeter, where to move off the concrete more or less anywhere was to give one's aircraft an open invitation to become bogged down. Additionally, the grassed area of the airfield in my recollection resembled a the First World War landscape—certainly no one in his right mind would consider attempting to taxy over it.

Unhappily 'opps' (which were at Usworth) decreed that a section from Usworth could reach operational height over Newcastle quicker than from Acklington 25 miles away. It was a complete misconception, as quite apart from the fact that we could, if the wind allowed, take off direct from the dispersal, we did at Acklington have the full panoply of the 610 ground facilities at our disposal. I believe Usworth did not have enough trolly accs to start three aircraft simultaneously and having once started one faced, possibly, a long taxy in line astern round the perimeter track before turning carefully on to the runway to take off individually and form up when airborne. The assumption was fallacious and I believe it to be far from impossible that if sections at Usworth and Acklington began to start up at the same time, the Acklington section would be in position before the last aircraft became airborne at Usworth! However, on many days we had to have a section at Usworth and unhappily broke a number of aircraft in doing so.

Life was very enjoyable at Acklington—we were treated as adult fully trained pilots and although we went to bed normally tired, it was not the brain dulled torpor so usual throughout our training. We spent most evenings in the mess as the nearby towns of Ashington and Morpeth were just too far away to reach easily after standing down, so we became fairly adept at darts, billiards and snooker! The sequence of readiness, practise flying, life in the mess and the eighth day in Newcastle was more satisfying and one rapidly became aware that this was the life. Training seemed so long ago and civilian life just a rare interlude. We scrambled on quite a number of occasions but having since seen the 610 Operations Record Book in which only few are recorded, I would guess opps must have thrown in a number of simulated ones with no prior warning.

We lost two pilots during my period at Acklington. Flt Lt Smith—returned from injuries received at Biggin Hill—tried to take off one night with his pitch lever left in 'coarse' and not unnaturally did not leave the ground and was killed when he hit a Bofors gun pit. Then our RAFVR badminton playing friend Kim Miller, who joined us in late October, went vertically into marshland north of the airfield and clearly did so from a great height. Hardly any wreckage was visible but the boggy surface was discoloured from the yellow dye carried in our Mae Wests (life jackets named after the American film actress). The dye was meant to give a patch of yellow on the sea to aid in air/sea rescue. Kim's parents came up two days later, although there was nothing to see or do as it was impossible to recover Kim. Ollie and myself spoke with them for they were terribly upset and I suppose it probably helped to speak with his few local friends at the station but I hope I don't sound unfeeling or callous if I say we were relieved when they had set off for home.

We seemed to break aircraft regularly, although after my disastrous two days at the beginning appeared to be lucky. We didn't suffer any engine failures but did have a number of internal glycol leaks which normally caused the aircraft to be partially enveloped to varying extents in their own private little clouds. One day Bill Ballard at No. 2 had a swine. Climbing out in vic at about 100 feet there suddenly appeared a cloud instead of his gently undulating aircraft! Out of this cloud poked a Spitfire nose and half a wing. No. 1 and No. 3 (myself) slid away to port just in case and then suddenly as it had come, the cloud had gone and there sat dear old Bill wondering how he had suddenly drifted 200 yards away from us and we didn't tell him!

I did have a bad oil leak from the propeller hub whilst on one and for good measure lost glycol as well. The whole lot froze in a blue/black mess over my windscreen so I could see 10/10th of sweet dawn all to the front. I left the formation and went home. Approaching to land I had the hood open and had opened the door to give me a chance of peering round the windscreen frame. Taxiing back to dispersal we left a spume of thick black smoke in our wake. That part of my face unprotected by helmet or goggles was as black as Satan and I had a spitting headache. The latter went after taking some aspirin but the oily face took some cleaning! I seem to remember we did often suffer headaches, possibly as a result of strain or of flying high all encumbered with oxygen and maybe of not wearing goggles as a normal practise.

Later in November the CO gave us all an ear bashing he'd had from the station commander who had it from Group, who'd had it from the C-in-C, Fighter Command. It was to the effect Fighter Command were breaking more aircraft than were lost in action and that we'd better get our act together or else (610 by this time had broken about twenty aircraft since we'd arrived at Acklington).

Quite a number had been when operating from Woolsington (the Newcastle municipal airport just north of the Tyne base). It was a reasonably large grass aerodrome. Opps decided each pilot should carry out one hour of circuits and bumps (landings) so all could be conversant with the field. I went first—on our oldest aircraft and all went well. My first three circuits were carried out in competition with a Hawker Hart trainer and it was thought provoking to take off in parallel, 200 yards apart and then glide in in similar positions but to realise my circuit at its tightest was a good half mile outside his.

Cruising home, I was not too happy to see an outboard running panel edge lift undulating as I used aileron—a line of rivets had popped! When I reported it to

Chiefy he just laughed—'we hoped you wouldn't bring the swine back. We want rid of it'. Ironically, two days later when trying to push up my hours, I was to leave my starboard wheel and oleo leg complete behind me while I cavorted in a gradually tightening turn across the airfield on one wingtip, one main wheel and the tail wheel. Chiefy did not laugh! So again a visit to the station commander and a carefully worded accident report and this time a red endorsement in my flying logbook. But four days later I had piled up fifty-two Spitfire hours so could at last have seven days of leave—my first since pre-Redhill leave in April. Back at Acklington, we had a section over a north running convoy all day long. From 2,000 feet the sea looked awful. It was winter slate grey with a swell that repeatedly buried the front half of most of the ships and I bet most thought as I did 'why do idiots go to sea'. Then followed a short instruction to the Almighty to keep the fan in front turning over!

I also managed some night flying, taking off at dusk. It was great and strange to climb up into the sunlight and then return to the dark. We were starting to hear that Spitfires had now to be night operational after all. As we now know our night fighting arrangements had proved next to useless and supposedly the only remedy at that time was to be able to put as many fighters in the air as could be handled in the hope that more eyes up would result in more interceptions being made. The Spitfire was a bit delicate for night work, its undercarriage not liking side-load or heavy landings.

On 13 December we learned 602 Squadron were flying their aircraft up for us to take back down to their present home at Westhampnett (a satellite of Tangmere) while they flew our aircraft up to I think Lossiemouth. So we were off at last—the culmination of twelve months arduous work. I for one had happy and other memories of Acklington and some pictures flash into mind even after all these years. I recall Bill and myself tucked in tight to PO Drever orbiting at 1,200 feet, some 2 miles away from what, no doubt was Bilton railway halt awaiting the train bringing Joe Pegge back from honeymoon. And then the view of the train swiftly growing in the windscreen as we swept down on it. The next five minutes is a confused medley of very low flying by three now completely individual aircraft, as we each shot up the train from each and every direction. What with the concentration to avoid two other maniacs who at times seemed within spitting distance and oblivious of one's proximity, to miss the track side wires slung at about 20 feet and to get one's aircraft down as close to the carriages as was possible, it was an exhilarating session! And as I straightened up with the train about half a mile away and broadside on, all the black rectangles of its windows amazingly and suddenly turned white with the faces of the passengers who'd shot from one side to the other! I think my face is perhaps white as I think of it. And with what tact did the returned Joe Pegge check the pilots flying order book to see what idiots had been ostensibly on a formation exercise before, with no CO present thanking us for putting his wife completely off flying—said with a grin.

H. David Denchfield was shot down over St Omer, France on 5 February 1941 and spent the rest of the war as a prisoner in Germany and Poland.

# 2
# The Armament Training Station
# 1938–1939

In 1932, the RAF had aircraft based at just over forty airfields scattered throughout Britain. Many of its aircraft were deployed in far flung parts of the Empire to subdue 'restless elements'. The following year, Hitler became Chancellor of Germany and it became apparent that the main threat now lay closer to home. The British government drew up plans to expand the RAF and construction on new frontline airfields commenced in 1935. For the first time since the First World War, it was planned to have a continuous system of fighter defence to cover the entire country. With an increase in frontline squadrons, new training facilities would be needed to train aircrew for them. It was announced in Parliament on 22 May 1935 that a Metropolitan Air Force of 123 squadrons would be provided with 1,500 aircraft. The following year, this was increased to 124 squadrons with 1,750 aircraft. New Armament Training Camps and Air Observer Schools were to be built at Acklington, Evanton, Penrhos, and West Freugh, each able to accommodate 500 personnel. For what were to become permanent airfields, it was perhaps a somewhat retrograde step that most of the buildings at each site were to be no more substantial than wooden huts. However, they could be constructed quickly and at a low cost. The locations selected were all in relatively remote locations where there would be few other aircraft in the surrounding airspace. In addition, they were next to the coast, so practice targets could be placed in the sea.

Objections were lodged during 1936 by local fishermen against the proposed bombing range in Druridge Bay for the planned airfield at Acklington. The Coquet Fishery Board was invited to send a representative to a meeting at Adastral House, London:

> The Air Ministry do not wish to hear any more opinions from the Fishing Board but are anxious to have their representatives present when the subject is re-opened and discussed, so that they may be able to answer any questions as they arise.

The local council was more enthusiastic about having a new air station in the area as it would boost the local economy.

It had been hoped that the airfield would be ready for use at the beginning of 1938, but the complex had yet to be connected to the mains water supply. The Air Ministry were less than happy with the situation, and wrote an abrupt letter to the local council requesting that this matter should be given immediate attention. It was stated that the opening of the Station would not be delayed beyond 1 April 1938. The council responded by arranging a temporary water supply pending connection to the mains.

No. 7 Armament Training Station was formed as intended on the first day of the month. Initially, it had been referred to as 'No. 7 Armament Training Camp'. The two steel hangars and many of the wooden buildings and were still incomplete at that time. Wg Cdr J. Payne arrived to take command along with Sqn Ldr D. H. Carey, the senior armament officer. The first three aircraft for No. 7 Armament Training Station were delivered from 24 Maintenance unit on 29 April. They were Fairey Seals—obsolete biplanes. The Seal had originally been designed as a three-seat spotter-reconnaissance aircraft for service on board aircraft carriers. There was also a twin-float seaplane version which was launched by catapult from large warships. By 1938, most of the Seals had been replaced in frontline service by the Fairy Swordfish.

*The Yorkshire Post* and *Leeds Intelligencer* featured an article on the opening of the airfield at Acklington on 28 April 1938. It has been quoted at length as it probably one of the best descriptions of the early airfield:

On the first of May, very early in the morning, three squadrons of military aeroplanes will fly up the coast of Northumberland, circle and land at Acklington Aerodrome. The eighth and in some respects the largest RAF training centre in the British Islands may be considered officially opened. A year ago the Air Ministry acquired a strip of land eight miles long round the edge of Druridge Bay. It was and still is a pleasant place with a wide stretch of sand at low tide and grassy dunes shutting off the shore from the fields. Nature lovers and holiday makers were indignant at the acquisition but the bay though no longer free to the public, remains almost as pretty as formerly.

A mile or so inland is the huge training camp covering three hundred acres. Rows of neat huts and workshops have shot up in the last six months. A staff of 200, most of them technical experts, will be stationed there permanently. Three visiting squadrons (with nine planes per squadron) will arrive every month of the year and every month fifty pilots will receive training in bombing and gunnery. To some it will be new, to others a refresher course.

The first batch of squadrons from Wiltshire, Lincolnshire and Driffield will be met on 1st May by Squadron Leader D. H. Carey, chief armaments officer. He will take the pilots round the station and over the targets explaining the routine and signalling systems. Practice will begin the following day.

After 22 years of flying, Mr. Carey is as enthusiastic over his camp as though he had just grown his 'wings.' Each month he will act as supervisor to a new lot of eager young men—inevitably known as 'Mother Carey's Chickens.' The joke is old but he still smiles. A visiting squadron is housed in a detached block of buildings with its own workshops. The men in each squadron are under their own officers and instructors with Mr. Carey as umpire or referee. He himself says amiably, 'We are really a hotel offering shooting to visitors with me the head gamekeeper.'

The shooting is extensive. Out in the Bay and spaced well apart are three triangular rafts, the bombing targets. They are armoured plated and firmly anchored. Bombing will take place from as high as 15,000 feet and as low as 250 feet. When the white puff of smoke goes up from the sea its bearings are taken and telephoned to the camp. In the plotting office the position of each hit is drawn as it comes in.

Gunnery with air towed targets is a different business. The towing pilot flies a long determined course over the Bay, with a 'sausage' of the wind indicator type trailing behind its tail. The attacking plane shoots at the sausage and the hits are afterwards registered by the number of bullet holes. Two machines can attack at the same time, one pilot using painted ammunition to distinguish his own hits. Night bombing has been tried out at other stations but Acklington is the first where it will be a regular part of the training. A powerful searchlight unit has been built on the shore to illuminate targets during this work. The boundary of the strip of land in the danger zone is thick with warning notices but so far it has not been shut in by fences or barbed wire. The danger is real. To appreciate it one need only look at the markers huts. Their hollow walls are stuffed with sand, the inner wall is armoured plated and the roof is piled high with sandbags. From the central control tower where there is a telephone switchboard in touch with every part of the range and the aerodrome, the full length of the shore visible. Sentries are posted at both ends of the beach to keep people away. But the approach from the landward side is more difficult to patrol. For years the little hills and hollows of the dunes have been a popular camping and picnic ground. The notices say that approach is 'dangerous' but do not use the word 'forbidden.' It should mean the same thing.

When Druridge Bay was taken over there was some public concern for the future of the fishermen in the district. Sympathisers drew moving pictures of jersied, sunburnt figures standing on the shore and gazing wistfully at their lost living. It was said perversely that number one bombing target floated over the best bit of lobster fishing on the coast. The truth is that recently no more than seven men with three cobles [a type of open fishing boat] have fished the Bay. Two fishing grounds are still open for use and beyond that there are compensations. At Hauxley, the northern point of the Bay, the RAF are setting up a motor boat patrol to warn shipping away from the danger area. The patrol offers permanent work for 40 men all fishermen or other men with local knowledge.

The main contractor for the construction of the airfield was Henry Kelly of Newcastle but around seven other firms were also involved in the construction of the hangars, recreation and mess buildings. Four large bombing rafts for the range were fabricated by Clelands Ltd, at Willington Quay.

On 2 May 1938, 88 Squadron with Fairey Battles, 148 Squadron with Vickers Wellesleys and 215 Squadron with Handley Page Harrows arrived for training. The same day, the Inspector General, Sir Edward Ellington, paid a visit to the Station. A less notable event occurred when a Miles Magister (L8141) being flown by Fg Off. G. Fothergill was forced to land on its delivery flight to RAF Acklington. The aircraft was severely damaged but the pilot was unhurt. A replacement machine was delivered in July. It would be the first of many crashes on this airfield.

By the end of May, 88, 148, and 215 Squadrons had completed their training and departed. Their place had been taken by 75 and 77 Squadrons, the former flying

Handley Page Harrows and the latter Vickers Wellesleys. A few days later, 103 squadron with Fairey Battles arrived. A further six Fairey Seals were delivered to RAF Acklington in June. By then, the number of personnel based on the station had risen to eleven officers, twelve senior NCOs and 100 corporals and airmen.

Towards the end of June, two young men were sailing along the coast from Blyth to Holy Island to participate in a regatta. Col. Sprot, the father of one of the men, had followed the yacht along the coast, but lost sight of it near Cresswell, when it was engulfed by a squall. When it did not arrive at its destination, Col. Sprot contacted the Admiralty requesting a search be organised. Ships were informed to look out for the missing men and aircraft took off from RAF Acklington to scour the coast. It was all to no avail. There was no trace of either Alexander Sprot or his cousin Charles Stirling, the son of the keeper of Dumbarton Castle in Scotland. The only clue to their disappearance was the discovery by the lightship off Ostend of the wreckage of a small yacht fitting the description. Although RAF Acklington was unsuccessful in what was its first search and rescue mission, it would in time develop a long legacy of rescuing many lives.

In early July, 38 Squadron with Fairey Hendon IIs and 215 Squadron with Handley Page Harrows were detached to the airfield for training. During August, advanced training squadrons from No. 2 and No. 9 FTS underwent instruction.

In an ominous sign, civilian labourers began preparing ARP (Air Raid Precautions) trenches in October. The procession of antiquated bombers through RAF Acklington

Handley Page Harrow II (K6994) of 75 Squadron at RAF Acklington in May 1938. By the time war broke out, this type of bomber was obsolete but many examples continued to serve as transport aircraft. (*RAF Museum*)

continued with 18 Squadron (Hawker Hinds) and 37 Squadron (Harrows) being present at that time. On 11 November, a Harrow (K6956), which a just completed a practice flight, crashed on landing. Three days later, the first fatal accident to an Acklington-based aircraft occurred. A Fairey Seal (K4780), used for target towing and flown by FS W. A. Curl with AC I. J. Milligan as a passenger, crashed into the sea to the east of Alnmouth. At the inquest into the death of the latter man, Robert Hogg, a solicitor, stated that he saw an aeroplane approaching from the direction of Acklington Aerodrome:

> The machine circled overhead twice and then proceeded eastwards in the direction of Coquet Island. It appeared to be gaining altitude and the engine appeared to be functioning normally. The next time I saw it a few minutes afterwards, it was in what I took to be a vertical spin at 1,500 feet and in the same direction of Boulmer Point. It did not give me the impression that it was out of control. I have frequently seen similar manoeuvres or something similar carried out. I do not think the engine was actually running when I first saw the spin but it started again. I fully expected to see the aeroplane flatten out again but for some reason it did not and crashed into the sea. After the plane struck the water it was visible for about two minutes before it disappeared under the water.

Another witness, Benjamin Brown, also gave evidence at the inquest. He added that he saw the aeroplane overhead at a height which he estimated to be 3,000 feet:

> It seemed to be flying in a hesitant way, as if it were preparing some stunt. Then it began to fall head first with the engine not then running. After falling about half way down to the sea, the engine started again and was pulling quite well. The part before was obviously done on purpose and was a perfectly good spin. Instead of flattening out the plane continued on its course, faster and faster towards the sea.

The wreckage of the Fairey Seal was raised from the sea on 20 November. The body of J. Milligan was recovered at the same time. Sqn Ldr Carey related that a detailed examination of the remains of the aircraft had been carried out. It indicated that the Fairey Seal had hit the water in a steep dive. The flying controls were serviceable at that time. The conclusion was that the aircraft was recovering from the spin when it hit the water. Carey stated that the accident was probably caused by the pilot leaving it too late to recover from the spin.

On a less serious note, eighteen airmen from RAF Acklington were arrested for trespassing on the Chevington to Amble railway line that ran near the southern edge of the airfield. Despite repeated warnings, they had been taking a short cut to catch a bus. For this misdemeanour, they were each fined two shillings and six pence (about £20 in 2016). During November 1938, No. 7 Armament Training Station was redesignated No. 2 Air Observers School to train direct entry air observers. All personnel at RAF Acklington were transferred to this new unit. The first course commenced early the following year. Each course could train up to sixty observers and lasted six weeks.

On 31 December 1938, the following aircraft were based at RAF Acklington:

Six Boulton Paul Overstrands
Seventeen Fairy Seals
One Hawker Hind

The number of personnel on the Station was:

Twenty-four Officers
Twenty-nine Senior NCOs
337 Corporals and Airmen

During March, two searchlights were installed on the north and south ranges. The No. 4 Course for Air Observers commenced with the training of twenty-six airmen. Among those that arrived for training in the spring was Lawrence Wheatley, who recorded his impressions of the station in his book *An Erksome War* (an erk was slang for an aircraftsman from the cockney 'erkraft'):

In May 1939 RAF Station Acklington was an aerodrome without runways [like most pre-war establishments] and with rather ancient hangars which matched the

Although Bolton Paul Overstrand bombers were delivered to the RAF in the mid-1930s they already looked antiquated compared to many other aircraft of the time. Most were withdrawn from front line service a few years later and relegated to training purposes with RAF Acklington operating a small number of the type in the years before the Second World War. (*ww2 images*)

aircraft: all biplanes, single engine, open cockpit Hawker Hinds and Fairey Seals and twin-engined Boulton Paul Overstrands which had a pneumatically operated enclosed perspex gun turret in the nose, the pilot's cockpit and the upper and lower rear gun positions all being open. There was one Sidestrand, a forerunner of the Overstrand with all cockpits open. These last aircraft were popularly supposed to have been built just too late for the Great War.

We were accommodated in wooden huts with an ablutions hut between each pair of huts. Our beds were still iron, in two sections and made up into a sort of large chair but the chain link was secured to the frame by springs all round and with three 'biscuits' were reasonably comfortable with canvas sheets and pillowcases. We were required to wear uniform at all times but were allowed out until 1 a.m. each night apart from the occasional guard duties. However, since reveille was at 6 a.m. I went out only every other night to avoid falling asleep during lectures.

The pupils were divided into two groups, one flying while the other was at lectures. Lawrence Wheatley's first practical lesson was to find the wind speed and direction by using the course setting bomb site. This instrument was located in the Hawker Hind beneath the pilot's seat where there was a square opening in the fuselage. The pupil had to lie on the floor of the aircraft, feet towards the tail, to operate it. He would then direct the pilot to the target and drop the bomb. Such exercises were usually undertaken at an altitude of 6,000 feet. The bomb aimer had to also take into account the diurnal wind changes along the coast in warm weather. During the day the wind blows towards the shore as the land warms up. The direction is reversed at night.

Pupils were also instructed in air gunnery. This started with lessons in how to strip down and re-assemble Browning, Lewis, and gas-operated Vickers 'K' machine guns. In the air, a camera gun was used to assess the accuracy of the pupil's marksmanship on an enemy aircraft. Live ammunition was used on some exercises:

We began by firing at a two feet square yellow painted wooden target lying on the beach. The pilot would fly the Hawker Hind parallel to the beach on the landward side and the observer would stand with his weapon pointed over the side and watch for the target, which looked about the size of a postage stamp, to appear from below the trailing edge of the lower wing, hoping to get off half a dozen shots before the leading edge of the tailplane appeared in his view.

Then, pupils progressed to firing at moving targets. These were drogues, resembling a wind sock, which were towed behind a tug aircraft. Some of the ammunition was dyed red so two pupils could fire on the same target simultaneously and the accuracy of each could then be assessed.

The highlight of activity at the station early in 1939 was the staging of Empire Air Day. Although this was the first air display to be held at RAF Acklington, Empire Air Days had become an annual event at other RAF airfields since 1934. The idea was to open as many RAF stations as possible to the public to give them an insight into the role carried out by the RAF. On 20 May 1939, Acklington threw open its gates along with seventy-eight other airfields including sixty-two RAF stations and eighteen civil airfields. On 12 May, a journalist from the 'Alnwick Mercury' was treated to a preview of the air display as well as a flight in one of RAF Acklington's aircraft:

There will be solo aerobatics, message picking up, dummy parachute drops, balloon bursting, a flypast of the latest types of RAF machine, etc., and what is succinctly described as a 'low flying attack on a tank.' This consists of machines dive bombing from about 250–300 feet with a tank as its target. I am going to Acklington to see what it feels like. We took off in a formation flight of five Hawker Hinds in line abreast and immediately rushing over the ground until the tails came up and the machines were airborne and climbing well. We missed the top of Broomhill Colliery pit heap adequately and were heading out to sea.

We passed over familiar landmarks and skirting Druridge Bay, the fine stretch of sand looked properly golden. Up we went and I had a quiz round to see what I could recognize below. I didn't know it but just about then the real business of the flight began. It was what was known as 'dive bombing.' The technical description of this type of attack is quite interesting. An authoritative work on the subject states 'it is perhaps the outstanding tactical innovation of the past ten years. It has been developed from a crude form of attack to a most efficient and certain form. It consists in approaching the target to be bombed, not flying level at a predetermined height so that ordinary bomb sights can be used but in a steep dive. The aeroplane itself is aimed at the target and dived down until it is fairly close to the ground. The bomb is then released and the aeroplane zooms upward again.'

We were followed over the target by the other machines in line astern and in the language of an official communiqué the enemy object of attack was destroyed and our forces returned without loss.

The intended Empire Air Display Programme was as follows:

2 p.m. Demonstration by Westland Lysander.
2.20 p.m. Attack on a Towed Target by a Hawker Hind and Fairey Seal.
2.32 p.m. Solo Aerobatics by a Hawker Hind.
2.40 p.m. Message Pick Up from Ground by a Fairey Seal.
2.53 p.m. Dummy Parachute Drop from a Fairey Seal.
3.05 p.m. Formation of Armstrong Whitworth Whitley bombers (some sources state this was to be Fairey Battles).
3.15 p.m. Formation Drill with Hawker Hinds and Fairey Seals
3.55 p.m. Flypast by a Supermarine Spitfire.

Break and Flying by Civil Aircraft.

5 p.m. Demonstration of speed by a Supermarine Spitfire.
5.05 p.m. Attack on a Boulton Paul Overstrand by a Hawker Hind.
5.15 p.m. Low Flying Attack on tank by Hawker Hinds.
5.30 p.m. Pupil and Instructor in Hawker Hind.

5.45 p.m. Flypast by crowd exhibits—Miles Magister, Boulton Paul Overstrands, Boulton Paul Sidestrands, Fairey Seal, Hawker Hinds.

5.55 p.m. Balloon Busting by a Miles Magister.

6.15 p.m. Set Piece Demonstration—An Attack on a Village.

The air display was a great success, with an attendance of around 20,000—far higher than many other RAF Stations. RAF Usworth at Sunderland had a crowd of 17,000. There were long lines of cars on the Great North Road with all the routes around the airfield almost at a standstill. Vehicles were still arriving at 3 p.m., long after the flying display had commenced. Many visitors arrived by train, with the rail companies offering a special half-price excursion fare.

For the major part of the afternoon, fine weather prevailed, but a heavy rain shower conveniently occurred during the break in the flying programme. The highlight of the display for many was a Supermarine Spitfire which performed high-speed runs. In contrast, the high-winged Westland Lysander displayed its ability to perform short take-offs and landings at a very low rate of knots. A wood and canvas fort was bombed by Hawker Hinds who were then driven off by Fairey Seals. In an ominous sign, some of the bombs were supposed to have contained gas. The occupants of the 'fort' donned masks and protective clothing and used stirrup pumps and brooms to disperse the gas.

Not all spectators were impressed by the RAF aircraft on show. Some complained about the age of the aircraft participating in the flying display. Many were biplanes such as Hawkers Hinds with open cockpits. There were examples of modern bombers, such as the Armstrong Whitworth Whitley, on show in the static display but they were at that time so secret that the public were kept at a distance of 150 yards. This was to be the first and last Air Show to be held at RAF Acklington before the outbreak of the Second World War. It would again become a major event in Northumberland in the post-war years.

On 2 March 1939, three lorries full of airmen from RAF Acklington set off from Edlingham near Alnwick to attend the funeral of Fg Off. Lupton, who had been killed when his Bristol Blenheim crashed at RAF Wyton. Later the same year, RAF Acklington suffered a fatal aircraft accident of its own. Four Fairey Seals took off on the afternoon of 17 August on a routine practice flight to Scotland. Close to Beal on the coast opposite Holy Island, two of the aircraft—K3579 and K4783—collided while changing formation at 5,000 feet. The crew of the former aircraft attempted to parachute to safety. The pilot, Flt Lt J. Bodham, landed safely but the observer, J. Prudhoe, was found dead next to the burning wreckage of his Fairey Seal, close to Low Lynn Farm. His parachute was unopened.

The pilot of the other plane, Plt Off. Lindsay, had two passengers on board, aircraftsman William Fletcher and Alex Armour. He decided not to abandon his damaged machine and told them 'stick tight and I'll get you down'. The Fairey Seal crash-landed in a field about a mile from the other aircraft. It struck a number of trees on the edge of a plantation, smashing the wings and wrecking the engine. The passengers survived the experience unscathed but Plt Off. Lindsay broke his leg.

Sqn Ldr Hawkins then landed his Fairey Seal (K3535) within a few yards of the burning wreckage of K3579 to render assistance. While attempting to avoid haystacks in the field, his plane tilted forward and the propeller struck the ground. Dr L. McNabb, the Station medical officer who was flying with Sqn Ldr Hawkins, administered first aid to Plt Off. Lindsay. Another doctor arrived at the scene shortly afterwards. The fourth aircraft in the formation headed back to RAF Acklington to alert the station to the situation. Three of the Fairey Seals involved in the incident were later written off.

At the inquiry, a Mr J. White stated he noticed four planes flying overhead in formation at 3.30 p.m.:

> All at once, one of them at the back seemed to change position and went over from the left to the right. It appeared to touch the wing of another and both momentarily shuddered. One—that which is now lying burnt out—nosedived with a terrific swoop but the pilot got it back on a level keel. I saw one occupant climb out onto the wing and jump. His parachute opened perfectly and he landed in a field near Kentstone Farmhouse on the other side of the road from the field in which the plane crashed. The next instant the plane seemed to dive again but soon after the pilot again managed to straighten out. I then saw him try to get off in his parachute ... he had rapidly lost height and I don't know what exactly happened but he was never able to jump from the plane and as it hit the ground he was thrown clear of the wreckage which immediately burst into flames. In ten minutes the machine was a heap of tangled metal.

Another eye witness, Mr Thomas Wake of Embleton, said:

> After one man had jumped clear, another climbed out onto the wing and it seemed as if he was caught by one obstruction as he accompanied the plane to within fifty feet of the ground. He apparently managed to extricate himself and jumped but his parachute had no time to open. He was dead when they reached him.

Cpl John Prudoe was given a military funeral in his home town of Washington, County Durham. Hundreds of people lined the streets and RAF personnel from both RAF Acklington and RAF Usworth attended. He was aged twenty-seven and had been in the RAF for seven years.

Accidents were not confined to the air. AC John Sanderson, who was driving a military vehicle in connection with his duties at Cresswell Bombing Range, was struck by a lorry driven by William Stirling when emerging from a side road near Broomhill Church on 7 February. The impact lifted the military vehicle off the ground and its fire extinguisher was wrenched from its holder, striking the driver in his face. William Stirling was charged with driving a lorry without due care and attention. The police stated it was travelling at a considerable speed when it struck the other vehicle. The defendant had several previous convictions for driving offences. The magistrates imposed a fine of 10 shillings (equivalent to £80 in 2016) and ordered the defendant to pay 25 shillings (£200) in costs including £1 (£160) for photographs of the scene of the accident. The pictures were taken by Sqn Ldr Carey at the request of the police and several of them were aerial views.

With the storm clouds gathering over Europe all officers and airmen were recalled from leave on 24 August 1939. The following day, soldiers from the Durham Light Infantry arrived to guard the Station. They did not linger long and departed on the 28th. Their place was taken by the Royal Northumberland Fusiliers. With war only days away, 2 Air Observers School was ordered to move to RAF Warmwell on 1 September 1939. Its aircraft departed on the 4th, the day after war was declared.

RAF Acklington was left with just over 160 officers and other ranks. Fighter Command took over control of the airfield on the 9th, and it became part of 13 Group. Initially it was designated a satellite airfield to RAF Usworth with Wg Cdr Adams becoming responsible for both airfields. At the end of September, Armstrong Whitworth Whitley bombers landed at RAF Acklington to use the bombing ranges. On 1 October, the airfield got its first fighter squadron with the formation of 152 Squadron of Gloster Gladiators. Throughout the war, RAF Acklington and its ranges would be continued to be used for firing practice although it was now a frontline airfield and no longer a training facility.

The fourth production Gloster Gladiator (K6132), which first flew in 1937. It was the RAF's last biplane fighter. In the first few months of the war, squadrons operated the type from RAF Acklington. (*ww2 images*)

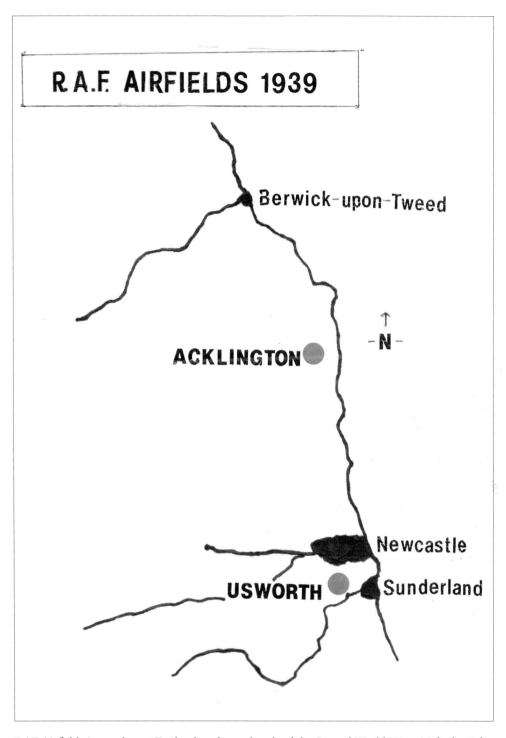

RAF Airfields in north-east England at the outbreak of the Second World War. (*Malcolm Fife*)

# 3

# Gloster Gladiator Squadrons

152 Squadron: October 1939–April 1940, Gladiator I and II
(also Spitfires from January 1940)
607 Squadron: October 1939–November 1939, Gladiator I
72 Squadron: March 1940, Gladiator I and II

When war was declared on 3 September 1939, the people of north-east England would have been less than re-assured to know that their defence from enemy bombers depended on a handful of Gloster Gladiator biplanes. When the Gladiator was first ordered for the RAF in 1935, it was a state of the art fighter, with an enclosed cockpit (instead of one exposed to the elements) and forward-firing machine guns. On Tuesday, 10 October 1939, shortly after dawn, sixteen Gloster Gladiators of 607 County Durham Squadron touched down at RAF Acklington. They had been forced to move from their home base—RAF Usworth near Sunderland—as it was undergoing major reconstruction work. There was a problem with the accommodation in their first week there as there were already two squadrons, 152 and 609, as well as numerous soldiers at the airfield. Every available building in the camp was occupied.

For some days, there was no activity other than practice flying and occasional air firing on sea markers at Druridge Bay. Suddenly, on 16 October, orders were received that the entire Squadron was to proceed to RAF Drem. Royal Navy ships in the Firth of Forth had come under a surprise attack by Junkers Ju 88s. There had been no warning of their approach as the radar was not functioning at that time because of a power failure. Two of the enemy bombers were shot down, one crashing into the sea off Port Seton. The Gloster Gladiators flew four patrols but did not encounter any German aircraft. The ground crews had followed them by road but their arrival was delayed by a road accident between two tankers not far from RAF Drem.

The following day, 607 Squadron was ordered to return to RAF Acklington. The Germans had dispatched two Dornier Do 18 flying boats (8L+DK and 8L+AK) to search for their colleagues who had not returned from the raid. On reaching the mouth of the Firth of Forth, they were fired on by the destroyer HMS *Juno*. The Dorniers decided that discretion was the better part of valour and flew south towards Northumberland. Three Gloster Gladiators were dispatched from RAF Acklington

A Dornier Do 18 forced-landed in the sea. The Germans used this type of seaplane to rescue crashed aircrew. Gloster Gladiators of 607 Squadron damaged an aircraft of this type on 17 October 1939, which was forced to put down in the North Sea. (*ww2 images*)

to investigate enemy seaplane activity. Flying at 10,000 feet some 25 miles off Blyth, they were about to return to base when they caught sight of Dornier 8L+DK flying far below them. The Germans, realising they were about to be attacked, had descended to a height of just 50 feet above the sea. The Gladiators opened fire, making three passes, but were then forced to abandon their attack, having expended all their ammunition and being short of fuel. Although pieces were seen to fall off the Dornier, it remained airborne. One of its crew had been killed and its pilot, *Feldwebel* (staff sergeant) Grabbet, had been wounded in the arm. He contacted the second Dornier with the intention of abandoning his aircraft and being rescued by the other aircraft. HMS *Juno*, now some forty miles north of Berwick-upon-Tweed, picked up the distress call. The destroyer headed at full speed towards the two Do 18s sitting on the sea. The crew of the damaged machine could not inflate their dinghy to transfer to the other seaplane. Their would-be rescuers aborted their attempt in the knowledge that its crew would be picked up by the Royal Navy and took to the air again. The 8L+DK was taken in tow by the *Juno* but sunk some time later. Three of the crew were taken prisoner, but the pilot had to have his arm amputated. When later questioned as to the purpose of their mission, he stated they were out 'joy riding'!

The encounter for 607 Squadron with enemy flying boats was not over. At 1.30 p.m., three Gladiators of 'B' Flight were scrambled to investigate a further report of German seaplanes off the coast. This time, contact was made with four Heinkel 115s, three of which were flying in 'V' formation at about 6,000 feet with the fourth following behind. The Gladiators attacked, but the Heinkels escaped by diving into the clouds below and disappearing. On returning to RAF Acklington, it was discovered that one of the Gladiators had two bullet holes through the fabric of the main plane. For the rest of October, 607 Squadron did not have any further encounters with German aircraft. However, disaster struck the squadron on the 29th. While practising attacks at a height of about 3,000 feet, a Gladiator (K7997), flown by Fg Off. A. Glover, went into a spin and crashed at Swarland Dene, a short distance to the west of RAF Acklington. He perished in the accident.

At the beginning of November, 111 Squadron arrived to share operational duties with 607 Squadron. Still undergoing training, 152 Squadron was also at RAF Acklinton. At that time, rumours began to circulate that 607 Squadron was going to move to France. On 10 November, an Armstrong Whitworth Ensign airliner arrived at the airfield, confirming the imminent departure. A further two Ensigns arrived over the next few days along with four De Havilland DH.86s and a Fokker airliner. They transported the squadron's equipment and ground crew south to London before moving to Merville Airfield in France. In June 1940, 607 'County of Durham' Squadron returned to its home base at RAF Usworth.

The only other Gloster Gladiator squadron to be based at RAF Acklington was 152 Squadron. It was one of a small number of RAF squadrons to be actually formed at RAF Acklington during the Second World War. The official date of its establishment was 1 October 1939, with an intended strength of sixteen aircraft. Over the new few days, pilots and ground crew began arriving at the airfield to report for duty. Three Avro Tutors and a Hawker Hart Trainer were handed over from 607 Squadron for training purposes. On the 10th, four Gloster Gladiators and a Hawker Hart were collected from RAF Turnhouse, Edinburgh. The latter aircraft (K6482), flying in low cloud, crashed and burst into flames on the northern slopes of The Cheviot. Its pilot, Sgt Thomas Mycroft, perished in the accident.

By the 13th, 152 Squadron had eight Gloster Gladiators, three Avro Tutors and one Hawker Hind on strength. Over the next few days it also received a Fairey Battle and North American Harvard. A letter was received from 13 Group Fighter Command informing the personnel that from now on they would be known as 152 Hyderabad Squadron. This was in appreciation of £100,000 (approximately £6 million in 2016) donated to the Air Ministry by the Nizam of Hyderabad, India. Early in November, the squadron was declared ready for day operations. By the end of that month it was brought to readiness and was flying its first operational patrols. On 21 November, Red and Yellow sections of A-Flight searched for an enemy bomber, but without success. As a consequence of this failure, intensive interception exercises were carried out with the Sector Controller. Three days later, Plt Off. N. Doughty was flying over Newcastle at 7,000 feet on a searchlight calibration patrol when his Gloster Gladiator (N5640) got into difficulties. He parachuted to safety while his aircraft crashed six miles west of the city at Walbottle Farm.

On the 25th, two De Havilland DH.89s arrived at RAF Acklington to transport the ground crews of Blue Section north to defend the Royal Navy anchorage at Scapa Flow in the Orkney Islands. Some of the pilots and their Gloster Gladiator aircraft remained there, being transferred to Coastal Command. Throughout December, 152 Squadron flew patrols from RAF Acklington. The Squadron's first Spitfire arrived in

January 1940, but for the immediate future, the Gloster Gladiators were still tasked with the front line duties.

From the outbreak of the war, the aircraft at RAF Acklington had the responsibility for protecting the numerous convoys navigating along the east coast. Many were merchant ships carrying cargoes, such as coal and wheat, from Scotland to London and south-east England, thus relieving the burden on the already overworked railway network. Two sections of Gladiators were carrying out one such patrol on 20 January 1940, when, on their return flight to the airfield, one of the pilots caught sight of a black shape travelling in a westerly direction near the Farne Islands. He set out in pursuit and as he closed in became convinced it was an enemy aircraft. Due to the relatively slow speed of the Gladiator, the intruder managed to make good its escape. There was a further encounter with a German aircraft on the 29th. Red Section had been patrolling over the sea near Whitby when they saw an aircraft circling two ships. Establishing it to be hostile, the Gladiators immediately got onto its tail, closing to within 600 feet. They were buffeted by a strong slipstream and the German machine got away, disappearing into cloud. Back at RAF Acklington, it was found that two of the Gladiators had been struck by enemy bullets.

There was better luck for 152 Squadron early the following month. The entry for their record book for 3 February opens with the following statement: 'This was without question the most exciting day the squadron had experienced.' At 10.17 a.m., a trawler sent out an SOS message. Yellow Section lead by Sqn Ldr Shute was scrambled and within a few minutes they encountered a Heinkel He 111 over Druridge Bay. What happened next was described in Shute's report:

> Fighters flying in open vic formation from Druridge Bay sighted enemy aircraft flying north-east. Yellow Leader turned to port and carried out quarter attack at 250 yards, gradually coming to No. 1 attack. Yellow 2 carried out similar attack with a continuous burst of 500 rounds and broke away. By this time Yellow Leader was carrying out astern attack, its continuous burst of fire closing to about 50 yards. Enemy aircraft started to fire but no damage was sustained. By the time enemy aircraft entered cloud with undercarriage down, dense black smoke emitted from enemy aircraft and when was seen to turn south, it appeared to be in difficulty.

Three days later, No. 13 Group informed 152 Squadron that the Heinkel He 111 had crashed in Druridge Bay and the squadron was credited with its destruction. There was some confusion about this claim as 43 Squadron also stated it had destroyed a He 111 over Druridge Bay, but at a different time. It seems, however, that 607 Squadron was most probably responsible.

During February 1940, 152 Squadron prepared for operations with Spitfires, but Gloster Gladiators still remained in use. On the 29th, the Squadron Record Book bemoans: 'This is probably the most unfortunate day the Squadron has known.' Sqn Ldr Shute had taken off in the afternoon in a Gloster Gladiator (N5646) to look for an aircraft that was believed to have come down off the coast. The last message received from Shute was that his engine had failed and that he was going to land in

# Chart of 72 Nazi Raids on Britain in Six Months

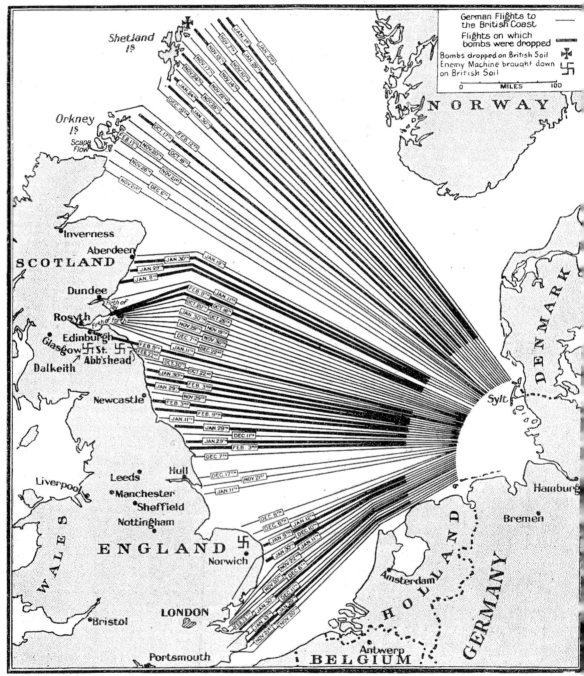

This contemporary map shows all German air raids on Britain between September 1939 and 22 February 1940. There had been twenty-five bombing raids (mostly on shipping) and forty-seven reconnaissance flights, but few enemy aircraft crossed the coastline and those that did so dropped no bombs inland. (*Evening Standard*)

the sea. Two further Gladiators took off to look for him, but there was no trace of either him or his aircraft.

During its time at RAF Acklington, 152 Squadron had operated around thirty-four examples of the Gloster Gladiator. The unit remained at the airfield for several more months with the newly delivered Spitfire Mk I, mentioned elsewhere in this book under the chapter on the type. This was not quite the end of Gloster Gladiator operations at RAF Acklington; 72 Squadron arrived at the beginning of March with the Spitfire I. At that time, RAF Acklington was badly waterlogged, which hindered the ability of its aircraft to operate. In the air, the Spitfire was very agile but on the ground it was a different story. Its large heavy engine made it particularly awkward to taxi over grass with it sometimes ending up on its nose after becoming bogged. As a consequence, a number of Gloster Gladiators were issued to 72 Squadron so that it could continue to operate from the airfield during March 1940. By the following month, conditions had improved and the squadron reverted to the Spitfire. Gloster Gladiators continued to be seen in the skies over Northern England until the end of the war, with small numbers employed in weather, reconnaissance and communications roles.

# 4

# Hawker Hurricane Squadrons

111 Squadron: October–December 1939, Hurricane I
43 Squadron: November 1939–February 1940, Hurricane I
46 Squadron: December 1939–1940, Hurricane I
79 Squadron: July–August 1940, Hurricane I
32 Squadron: August–December 1940, Hurricane I
258 Squadron: December 1940–February 1941, Hurricane 1
43 Squadron: October 1941–June 1942, Hurricane IIB and 11C
1 Squadron: July 1942–February 1943, Hurricane IIB and Typhoon IB (see chapter on Typhoons)

At the outbreak of the Second World War, the Hawker Hurricane was held in the same esteem by the general public as the Supermarine Spitfire; however, with the passage of time, the Spitfire stole the limelight. A number of factors contributed to this, the principal being the decision by the RAF to concentrate on developing the Spitfire as its main fighter, ensuring a long career in service. Propaganda also played a part in boosting the aircraft's image as Britain wanted to impress the Americans with its technological achievements, of which the Spitfire was one.

The Hawker Hurricane—the first operational RAF aircraft capable of exceeding 300 mph—could not match the Spitfire for speed and rate of climb. However, unlike the Spitfire, it was a wholly operational 'go anywhere do anything' fighter. It was robust and manoeuvrable as well as being capable of sustaining massive combat damage. During the Second World War it shot down more enemy aircraft than any other allied fighter. By the outbreak of war, 497 aircraft had been completed out of an order for 3,500.

The first Hawker Hurricane unit to be deployed to RAF Acklington was 111 Squadron, which arrived on 27 October 1939. The unit had received its Hurricanes in January 1938 and had the distinction of being the first RAF Squadron to be equipped with the type. When it arrived, there were already two other fighter squadrons at RAF Acklington, namely 152 and 607, both of which flew Gloster Gladiator biplanes. The day after the Hurricanes arrived, they were instructed to patrol over Alnwick at 10,000 feet. German aircraft were reported in the Sector, but none were seen by

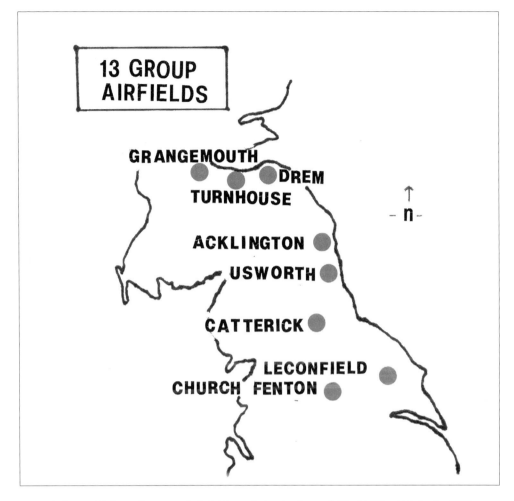

No. 13 Group Fighter Command airfields early in the Second World War. (*Malcolm Fife*)

111 Squadron's pilots. On the 30th, Green Section's Hurricanes were ordered to patrol Acklington at 1,000 feet at 8.30 a.m., as information had been received that there were enemy aircraft in the immediate area; very bad weather made their interception impossible. More German bombers were reported to be approaching Newcastle and Red Section were ordered to investigate. The Germans then headed north, but again the Hawker Hurricanes could do little because of the dense cloud.

Target practice was undertaken at the beginning of November using sea markers on the nearby ranges. Although RAF Acklington was no longer a training station, its ranges continued to be used throughout the war, both by squadrons based at the airfield as well as those from further afield. No. 111 Squadron flew a Hurricane to RAF Grangemouth in order that ground crews there could be instructed in the re-arming of the type. The unit further assisted with training by dispatching another aircraft to take part in a 'recognition of types' flypast for the Royal Navy and shore guns. Other types included an Anson, a Blenheim, and a Gladiator. A similar exercise was carried out on 18 November for the anti-aircraft guns on the coast between Blyth and Middlesbrough. The Edinburgh and Glasgow Balloon Barrage was also inspected from the air by the section leaders of 111 Squadron.

Bad weather at the end of November limited flying, and the grass airfield was by this time becoming very waterlogged. There was sea mist and fog with visibility down to 300 feet. This not deter Sqn Ldr H. Broadhurst from taking off on patrol in the morning of the 29th. Heading north along the coast, he caught sight of a Heinkel He 111 near Alnwick. Using the clouds as cover, he closed in on it. When he emerged from the cloud, the enemy aircraft was immediately above him. As the Hurricane closed, the enemy aircraft took evasive action, diving towards a bank of cloud below. Sqn Ldr Broadhurst, now being shot at by the crew of the Heinkel, followed close behind. Once he had closed to about 450 feet, he opened fire. Within seconds the German bomber turned onto its side and plunged towards the sea. Broadhurst lost sight of it but it was later confirmed that it had crashed some miles off the coast, not far from Amble. *The Berwick Journal* published the following account of the action:

> A German plane was shot down in a thrilling duel with a RAF fighter off the Northumberland coast. People in the coastal town of Amble watched the aerial battle and saw the beaten German plane fall into the sea. No air raid warning was sounded. A lifeboat was launched with a scratch crew headed by the local vicar. It returned after a three hour search where the raider was thought to be shot down but no trace was found. RAF planes also took part in the search.

Early in December 1939, 111 Squadron departed for RAF Drem where it joined 602 and 609 Squadrons. During the same month, 46 Squadron was ordered to head north from its base at RAF Digby to reinforce 43 Squadron, which had arrived at RAF Acklington the previous month. The ground crew were to have been transported by civilian airliners, but these became unavailable, so they made the trip by road.

The first patrol was flown on 10 December over South Shields to investigate a raid, but no German bombers were seen. The next day, 46 Squadron's Hurricanes were ordered to patrol over RAF Acklington, first at a height of 2,000 feet and later at 15,000 feet. Over the next few days, there was little flying because of bad weather. Flt Lt C. Stewart was sent to investigate an unidentified aircraft on the afternoon of the 17th. It turned out to be a Heinkel He 111, which he attacked. It disappeared into cloud, but not before putting a bullet through the wing of Stewart's Hurricane. Further patrols were flown on most days for the remainder of the month but no more enemy aircraft were seen. On 19 December, Red Section patrolled over Berwick-upon-Tweed and Green Section over Alnwick. A dusk patrol was flown between Alnwick and Blyth on the 22nd. Night flying was undertaken over Druridge Bay a couple of days later, followed by circuits and landings. Further night flying was carried out on the 30th, this time some 10 miles out to sea.

During January 1940, 46 Squadron's Spitfire pilots practised mock attacks on each other's aircraft in addition to flying patrols. Numerous sorties were flown on the 11th. Red Section was ordered to patrol Acklington at 10,000 feet. In the afternoon, Blue Section, and later Yellow Section, patrolled between Alnwick and Seaham Harbour. At 3.30 p.m., Red Section was instructed to patrol over the airfield at 2,000 feet.

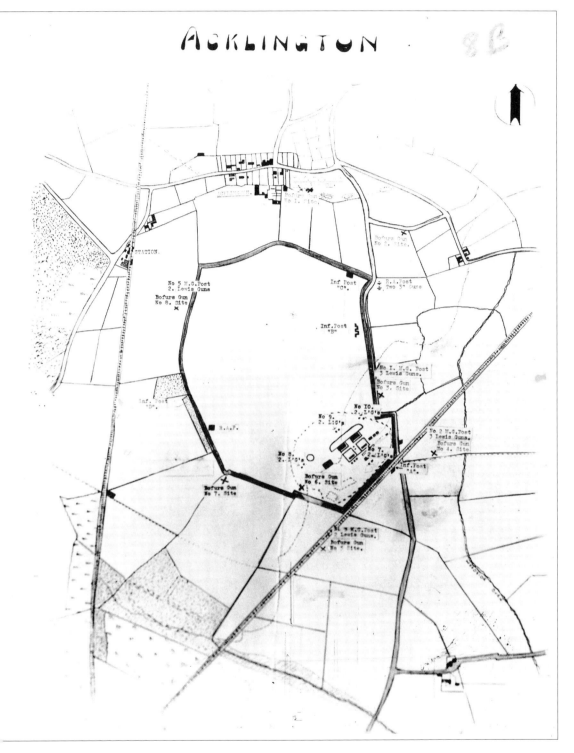

A plan of RAF Acklington airfield in 1940 showing the positions of Bofors and Lewis guns. The London to Edinburgh railway line is depicted on the left side of the plan and the branch line to Amble skirts the southern edge of the airfield. (*The National Archives*)

Later, a single Hurricane took over this duty. On the 17th, the Hurricanes returned to RAF Digby. Four aircraft had to be left behind with their pilots as they were unserviceable. It had originally been intended that 46 Squadron's deployment to RAF Acklington would be for a week but, in fact, it lasted for over five weeks.

Since 18 November 1939, 43 Squadron had been at RAF Acklington. It was one of the RAF's oldest squadrons, having been formed in 1916 as part of the Royal Flying Corps. Its distinct emblem was the Fighting Cock, the name by which the squadron was sometimes known. At the outbreak of the Second World War, it was based at RAF Tangmere on the south coast of England. During the first months of the conflict, most of the enemy raids were concentrated on Scotland and north-east England. France had not been invaded yet and there was no threat from the opposite side of the English Channel. Hence, on 16 November 1939, 43 Squadron was ordered to reinforce 13 Group. Two days later, twelve Hurricanes flew north to RAF Acklington. Most of the ground crew and equipment were transported on two Armstrong Whitworth Ensigns and a single De Havilland DH.86.

James Beedle's book *43(F) Squadron: History of the Fighting Cocks, 1916-84* conveys the impression that they were less than enthusiastic about their new surroundings:

> There were no runways, a scarcity of hangar accommodation and living space was tight, for 111 Squadron were already installed there and when they subsequently left, 152 Squadron arrived. Yet none of these inconveniences were as troublesome as the weather and the most abiding memory of Acklington is that it was always cold. The Northumbrian climate, superimposed upon the basic severity of the winter of 1939–1940, added up to utter discomfort. Coldest of all was the last dark hour before dawn, when the eternal east wind that flew in from the dull grey seas a mile away sharpened its cutting edge of iceness to an extra keenness. Just at that hour on most days the Squadron prepared to come to readiness. For the mechanic, 'warming up' his engine, life held promise, for he could shut tight the sliding hood and receive the full benefit of the main coolant pipes which ran between and beside his feet to the radiator amidships and below and produced a heat that rose rapidly to sub-tropical levels so that all life was lost in desire to stay forever in that one small space, insulated from the frozen world outside and to drift back into the sleep from which he had been so rudely awakened.

So that the aircraft could take off at first light, the pilots on alert had to sleep at the dispersals next to the Hurricanes. Breakfast was delivered from the mess by van, and often, the bacon was cold by the time it had reached them.

For the remainder of 1939, the guns of 43 Squadron's Hurricanes remained silent. The days were passed carrying out practice flights or convoy patrols. Although merchant ships had ceased trading with countries across the North Sea, coal and foodstuffs were carried from Scotland and north-east England to London by convoys hugging the coast. While carrying out practice formation flying above the clouds, Hurricane (L1725), piloted by Sgt J. Arbuthnott, got into difficulties and broke away in a spin. When he managed to recover from the spin, the aircraft had reached a speed of 330 mph. Not having enough time to pull up and still being in thick cloud, he abandoned his machine and parachuted to safety. What little was left of the aircraft was found in a hole twelve feet deep in the peat moorland.

On the evening of 21 December, there was a report that several German mine-laying aircraft were approaching the coast. The Hurricanes intercepted them at 1,000 feet above Alnwick. They were discovered not to be hostile aircraft but Hampdens returning from a raid on Germany that had lost their way. They were escorted to RAF Acklington by the Hurricanes. One aircraft crashed a short time later; this incident is mentioned in the chapter 'Diversion Airfield'. This was the first operational mission flown by 43 Squadron from RAF Acklington.

The Squadron suffered a serious blow early in 1940. On 18 January, two of its Hurricane Is (L1734 and L2066) crashed at Longhoughton while carrying out practice attacks. Both the airmen, Pilot Sgt E Mullinger and Pilot Sgt Steeley, who were close friends, were killed. L2066 was 43 Squadron's first Hurricane equipped with the De Havilland two-pitch propeller and metal wings. Three days later, another Hurricane I (L1729) was destroyed when in crashed into a haystack while taking off at night for a convoy patrol. By now, there was some concern in 13 Group about the number of aircraft the squadron was losing to accidents. Flying was restricted in any event on 21 January, as snow covered the airfield.

The Squadron redeemed itself on the 30th with the downing of a Heinkel He 111 (1H+KM of 4/KG26). Flt Lt Hull and Sgt Carey incepted two He 111s off Coquet Island. It was thought that the enemy aircraft were about to attack some fishing boats. One of the Heinkels made good its escape while the Hurricanes closed in to attack the other. After the first burst of gun fire, smoke began streaming behind one of its engines. The rear gunner fired back at the two fighters. The Hurricanes made a total of

Heinkel He 111s frequently took part in raids on shipping off the east coast in the early part of the Second World War. This example, 1H+EN, was forced down at North Berwick at the mouth of the Firth of Forth on 9 February 1940 by Spitfires of 602 Squadron based at RAF Drem. (*ww2 images*)

six synchronized passes on the He 111 before it plunged into the sea, some ten miles to the east of Coquet Island. There was no sign of its crew of four.

At the beginning of February, 43 Squadron was in action again. Although much of the north of England was under a blanket of snow, the initiative of the ground crews kept RAF Acklington operational. A door was torn off one of the huts and towed behind a tractor to clear the landing ground. Airmen sat on the door to give it extra ballast. Shortly after 9.30 a.m. on the 3rd, Fg Off. Simpson and Fg Off. Edmonds witnessed two enemy aircraft attacking shipping five miles south-east of the Farne Islands. The cloud base was only 900 feet. Simpson climbed up from sea level to attack and fired a burst of 260 rounds as the Heinkel He 111 made for the clouds. Edmonds then opened fire. The enemy aircraft entered cloud with black smoke pouring from its starboard engine. According to the squadron's operational record book, it was recorded as having crashed some 50 miles off the Farne Islands. AVM telephoned the squadron to confirm it had been destroyed. There is some confusion as to where it came down as some sources state it landed in Druridge Bay. The convoy that was attacked suffered several losses including the Norwegian steamer, the *Tempo*, which sunk off St Abbs Head. It was estimated by the Admiralty that over twenty Heinkel He 111s were involved in anti-shipping strikes off the north-east coast that day. An hour later Red Section encountered a further enemy aircraft in the vicinity of the Farne Islands. A Hurricane flown by Fg Off. Carswell managed to briefly fire at it before the bomber disappeared into a murky sky.

A third He 111 was engaged by Sgt Carey and Sgt Ottewill, 15 miles east of the mouth of the River Tyne. They were on patrol when they caught sight of anti-aircraft fire from a cargo ship. On investigation, they caught sight of a Heinkel He 111 of 1H+GK, which on the approach of the Hurricanes headed for the low cloud covering much of the North Sea at the time. Carey and Ottewill were close on its tail and opened fire, closing to within 450 feet. Pieces began to fall off the enemy aircraft, with its starboard engine failing followed by the port engine. It put down in the sea, remaining afloat for about a minute. Four of its five crew were picked up by the trawler the *Harlech Castle*. The fifth appeared to have drowned before being rescued; another of the crew died of his injuries while on board the trawler. A search of the airmen's uniforms uncovered a book of the wireless frequencies and call signs for their unit, KG26.

Further to the south, Flt Lt Townsend, Fg Off. Folkes and Sgt Hallowes intercepted another Heinkel He 111, 3 miles out to the sea, not far from Whitby. Townsend attacked using deflection, while Hallowes headed the enemy aircraft from the cloud. Folkes attacked from astern. The enemy aircraft was badly damaged; it turned inland and crash-landed at Sneaton Castle Farm, near Whitby. It was the first enemy aircraft to be brought down on English soil in the Second World War. A Heinkel He 111 had previously been shot down by fighters based at Drem and force-landed on the Lammermuir Hills in Southern Scotland. An article in *The War Illustrated*, 16 February 1940, carried a detailed description of the incident entitled 'I Saw the First Raider Down in England':

The first German raider to be brought down in England in the present war crashed near the Yorkshire farmhouse of Mr P. A. Smales. Two of the crew were killed and two injured. The machine was first sighted at 9.40 a.m. flying low over the sea, five miles off Whitby. The fighter patrol which gave chase caught the enemy as he tried to climb up to the clouds. As they swept past, firing bursts at close range, the German rear gunner fought back, then the Heinkel's starboard engine stopped, its undercarriage fell down and the German pilot, his aircraft disabled, began to look for a landing place. One of the three Fighter Command pilots who attacked him, on returning to his station, said, 'I saw the enemy aircraft crash through a hedge and stop 50 yards from a farmhouse.' Mr George Jackson, a member of the Whitby Urban Council, was one of the first on the scene. 'When I got to the 'plane the rear gunner stumbled out, fell and crawled across the ground,' he said. 'I ran to help him but he seemed to resent my offer. At that moment there were four flashes in various parts of the machine. Mr Smales arrived with bundles of first aid equipment. There was a repetition of the flashes and it occurred to me that someone was setting the 'plane on fire.'

Mr H. Steele, the occupant of a nearby cottage said, 'I saw two or three occupants of the machine rushing in and out of the cockpit as though trying to pull someone out. There was a loud explosion and I took cover, expecting the machine to blow up. Our fighter machines were overhead all the time.' Miss Ruth Smales said that when the machine came down telephone wires were cut and the 'plane crashed through a hedge and cut down a large tree. Mr Smales, to whose house the injured men were taken, said, 'Although badly shot about the legs, the first thing they asked for was a cigarette. They were supplied and also with tea. We put them on a mattress in front of the fire and rendered first aid.'

Blue section was airborne shortly after midday on 9 February when two enemy aircraft were sighted flying in a north-east direction below clouds at 1,000 feet near Coquet Island. Two of the Hurricanes managed to fire short bursts at a Heinkel He 111, while Flt Lt Townsend went after the second aircraft, which fired back at him. A second Hurricane came to his assistance and also attacked. Pieces were seen to come off the Heinkel before it vanished into cloud. A short time later, Hurricane 1 (L1744) flown by Fg Off. M. Carswell suffered engine failure while flying near Blyth. He thought he was too low to use his parachute, so he ditched near a Swedish ship. Carswell managed to escape from the sinking aircraft but had difficulty in inflating his life jacket. He was pulled from the sea unconscious and had to be given artificial respiration by his rescuers.

The Heinkel He 111 was claimed as damaged but around a year later it was confirmed destroyed. An entry in the diary of a captured German airmen who was on board the aircraft at that time stated that after the attack by 43 Squadron Hurricanes it flew on until it crashed around 150 miles off the Dutch coast. There was a further accident on 21 February when Fg Off. Simpson crashed shortly after take-off for night flying practice when his engine failed. His aircraft (L1729) bounced off the top of a haystack and felled thirty-six larch trees before it came to rest. He luckily escaped with only minor injuries.

The next day, Flt Lt Townsend, Plt Off. Christie, and Sgt Ayling were ordered to patrol over the Farne Islands at 2,000 feet. Flying high above them, they saw the contrails of a Heinkel He 111 on a long-range reconnaissance mission to Carlisle. The Hurricanes climbed up after it but Christie's engine began overheating and he had to give up the pursuit. The other two aircraft reached an altitude of nearly 20,000 feet. The Heinkel then commenced a dive, with its rear gunner firing at Townsend's aircraft. Now some twenty-five miles east of Blyth, and having closed to a range of around 750 feet, the Hurricane opened fire. Smoke began pouring from the enemy aircraft which lowered its undercarriage. At 15,000 feet, Townsend opened fire again as the Heinkel dived at high speed towards the sea with smoke billowing from both engines. The outer sections of its wings then broke off before it turned on its back and hit the sea. Flt Lt Peter Townsend, who later achieved fame through his association with the Royal Family recalled: 'as the fuselage disappeared, followed by a trail of fluttering debris. Only at that moment did I realise what I had done to the men inside. I felt utterly nauseated.'

He later expressed remorse for the crews of other German bombers he had shot down. In his autobiography, Townsend made some disparaging comments about RAF Acklington as well:

> We in 43 northwards to Acklington, a bleak windswept terrain near Newcastle. Our Hurricanes were formidable weapons, but we and they were ill-provided. Our dispersal points were concrete slums, poorly heated, sparsely furnished. Mobile starter batteries were few and often flat. Transport was a rare luxury. At dawn, each day of that bitter winter of 1939–40, the ground crews and we would trudge across the airfield to our dispersed aircraft with the starting handles. But our lack of equipment was compensated for by our passion for the chase. Though for months the enemy never showed up, we kept our senses sharpened with wild aerial escapades.

In an interview after the war, he also remarked: 'Acklington, yes it was tough but it was easier to die from a place like that!' At the end of February 1940, 43 Squadron was sent north to RAF Wick. The ground crew followed by train. A typical comment: 'Wick was like Acklington but 400 miles nearer the North Pole.'

Unlike most other units, 43 Squadron returned for a second stay in autumn 1941. During its first stay at RAF Acklington, 43 Squadron was accompanied by 152 Squadron. The summer of 1940 saw the arrival of a further two Hawker Hurricane Squadrons—32 Squadron which remained at RAF Acklington until the end of the year, and 79 Squadron which was there for just over a month. No. 79 Squadron was the first to arrive on 13 July 1940. It had been involved in combat, first in France and then at RAF Biggin Hill. Like several other fighter squadrons in the early part of the war, it had been sent north away from the front line for a rest. While on its way to RAF Acklington, it suffered a further loss. At RAF Sealand, two Miles Masters ran into three of its Hurricanes, damaging two beyond repair.

Twelve of 79's Hurricanes touched down at RAF Acklington on 13 July. For the remainder of the month, the squadron's aircraft carried out night flying ,which ceased shortly after 11 p.m. Air Commodore Nicholas visited RAF Acklington on the 31st, to pass out the squadron operationally.

At the beginning of August, several convoy patrols were undertaken and as the month progressed, activity by German aircraft increased. On the 9th, Yellow Section's Hurricanes were vectored to make an interception, when at 12,000 feet over Newcastle they caught sight of a Heinkel He 111, around five miles to the south. The Hurricanes flew after it and opened fire. The German bomber fought back, hitting one of the Hurricanes. Not deterred, the fighters pressed home their attack. The Heinkel (1H+ER) from KG26 turned and headed towards the clouds with white smoke coming from both engines. Its pilot managed to ditch in the sea close to Whitburn, much to the delight of numerous spectators on the shore. The four crew members were rescued from their rubber dinghy a short time later by a Royal Navy vessel. At 10.30 p.m., Flt Lt G. Hayson was ordered on patrol. An enemy aircraft had been reported at 20,000 feet, but nothing was seen by Hayson. A short time later, Plt Off. Laycock took off in a second Hurricane. Searchlights were active in the Blyth and Tyne area with flashes over Tynemouth. A third aircraft from 79 Squadron joined them but none of them encountered hostile aircraft.

The 15th saw the largest raid of the war by German bombers on north-east England. It is described in the chapter 'Supermarine Spitfire Squadrons'. The part played by 79 Squadron is narrated in its record book:

> The Squadron were called to readiness from released and at 12.42 hours were ordered to patrol Farne Island at 20,000 feet but whilst in the air, Controller reported a large raid approaching base. About 60 bombers were seen flying south over the sea off Amble and several Me. 110s which were attacked two being shot down and one probable. (Flt Lt Hayson accounted for one of them which crashed into the sea off Blyth and Plt Off. D. Clift the other which came down some 20 miles east of Coquet Island). The Squadron split up but rejoined over Blyth and when ordered to patrol Usworth at 10,000 feet about 60 Dornier 215s were seen approaching Newcastle and two Squadrons of Me 110s. Our fighters attacked and one Dornier Do 215 was believed to have been shot down near Newcastle. Plt Off. Millington attacked a formation of 60–80 He 111 alone and shot down three. The Squadron had all landed by 14.25 hours and our only casualty was one aircraft which was badly shot up. It may be noted that R/T was very bad due to German interference which was present during the whole of the engagement.

Some of the claims regarding the destruction of German bombers were not confirmed. On the 17th, two 79 Squadron Hurricanes shot down an escaped barrage balloon about 12–15 miles east of Blyth. There were further scrambles during the second part of the month. On the 19th, there was a report of a German bomber off the Farne Islands, but after a search of the area, nothing was seen. Yellow Section was vectored onto an unidentified aircraft on the 22nd, but it turned out to be 'friendly'. Several of the Squadron's Hurricanes were deployed to a forward base at West Hartlepool which was little more than a grass airstrip.

No. 79 Squadron was ordered back south to RAF Biggin Hill on 27 August. This move was implemented immediately with fifteen Hurricanes leaving RAF Acklington shortly after midday the same day. Heading in the opposite direction was 32 Squadron, which was relieved by the arrival of 79 Squadron at RAF Biggin Hill. Its motto was 'Rally Round Comrades'. Before it could move north, its Miles Magister was destroyed in a bombing raid on the airfield.

Throughout September 1940, 32 Squadron Hurricanes participated in numerous scrambles in defence of north-east England. On the 16th, three Hurricanes of Red Section were ordered to patrol over Usworth. Three days later they patrolled over the airfield, but again no enemy aircraft were seen. Three Hurricanes were ordered to investigate an X-raid 2 miles east of Newcastle on the 26th. In this case a Heinkel He 111 was attacked, but disappeared into clouds. Later that day, three Hurricanes took off to investigate an aircraft flying near the Farne Islands. In this case it turned out to be 'friendly'.

Throughout October, numerous patrols were flown but enemy aircraft again were elusive. Protection was provided to a cable-laying vessel in the River Tyne on the 11th. Yellow Section flew a dusk patrol on the 15th and, three days later, 32 Squadron Hurricanes operated over Acklington airfield itself. On the last day of the month, Blue and Green Sections with a total of six aircraft were ordered to patrol over Berwick-upon-Tweed at 10,000 feet. There was one incident when Hurricane (P3679) made a forced landing at Boulton, near Alnwick, due to a glycol leak.

During November, 32 Squadron lost several more aircraft, all attributable to accidents and none to enemy action. A Hurricane (P3351), flown by Plt Off. Sniechouwski, crashed at RAF Acklington on the 3rd. The aircraft was repairable. There was a further incident on the airfield the same day when a Hurricane (V6552) overshot on a night landing, damaging the aircraft. Plt Off. Waszkiewicz damaged his Hurricane (R4216) in a forced landing at Newbrick Farm, Wooperton. A few days later, Plt Off. Sniechouwski was involved in a further accident when his Hurricane (P3460) crashed on the airfield. He again survived the experience unhurt. There was another accident that day when Hurricane (P3122) taxied into a stationery Hurricane (P3469) while being run up. On the 18th, Plt Sgt Gardiner in a Hurricane I (V6724) was on patrol 6 miles west of Morpeth when its engine failed. He parachuted to safety and his aircraft plunged to the ground at Buckshaw Farm. There were a further two accidents on the 22nd. A Hurricane (V6602) crashed on the airfield. Its pilot was uninjured and the aircraft was repairable. More seriously, Plt Sgt J. Lowndes' Hurricane (N2587) caught fire and was abandoned by him. It crashed 5 miles to the north of Berwick. The pilot was taken to the hospital in the town, having sustained a number of injuries.

In early December, patrols were flown over the Farne Islands as well as the airfield itself. No. 32 Squadron was ordered to return south and departed RAF Acklington on the 15th. Sgt Wright was flying Hurricane (N2468) to the squadron's new base at RAF Middle Wallop on the 27th when it suffered engine failure near Dunchurch, Rugby. The aircraft crashed and burst into flames, killing Sgt Wright. No. 258 Squadron arrived at the end of the year from RAF Drem. Twenty-one aircraft took off and flew towards

RAF Acklington on the 16th, but five were forced back because of bad weather. They arrived the following day when the Squadron was ordered to supply a section at thirty minutes readiness for night-time duties. The only two pilots qualified for operational flying after dark were allocated this duty. On the 18th, intensive training was undertaken as 258 Squadron had been formed only the previous month and was not ready to undertake front line duties. Snow was falling thickly as the year drew to a close, restricting flying, but this was not before Plt Off. Bush had crash landed his Hurricane near the colliery on the 28th. The next day, Plt Off. Shaw had to make a forced landing because of engine failure. Both the pilots were none the worse for their experience.

At the beginning of 1941, a Miles Magister I was delivered to 258 Squadron to assist with the training of its pilots. The first operational flight by the unit was flown on 6 January when it patrolled over the Farne Islands. Three days later, several Hurricanes took off in an attempt to locate a Heinkel He 111, but it evaded detection. Further heavy falls of snow disrupted flying on a number of days with Army personnel being used to clear the runways. The weather also delayed the departure of 258 Squadron, which had been ordered to move to RAF Jurby on the Isle of Man. Two officers and 137 men of other ranks left by rail in icy weather on the 21st, but the Hurricanes remained stuck on the ground. Three of the aircraft took to the air on the 26th to provide protection to a convoy in the vicinity of the Farne Islands. At one stage, red flares were dropped on it from an enemy aircraft. The pilots of 258 Squadron remained with the convoy until it had passed south of Newcastle, landing at RAF Usworth to refuel.

There was a blizzard on 1 February 1941, but not wanting to be delayed at RAF Acklington any longer, seventeen of the squadron's Hawker Hurricanes took off for RAF Jurby on the Isle of Man. A-Flight reached their destination without incident, but B-Flight was forced to return to RAF Acklington. They made a second attempt in the afternoon. *En route* one of its Hurricanes made a forced landing in Cumberland and two other aircraft diverted to Blackpool. The two then made a second attempt to reach RAF Jurby but returned to the mainland and force landed at Aberfraw where one of the Hurricane's suffered propeller damage. The remaining aircraft in B-Flight made it to RAF Jurby without incident. On the 4th, a Hurricane I (L1968), flown by Sgt Stoker of 43 Squadron crashed into the sea while carrying out air firing practice. A search could find no trace of him or his aircraft.

No. 43 Squadron returned to RAF Acklington in October 1941 after spending ten months at RAF Drem, where it was responsible for destroying no less than eleven enemy aircraft. While based there, like other squadrons, it sometimes sent small numbers of aircraft to RAF Acklington to use the local ranges. The main reason for the move back to RAF Acklington was for its Hurricanes to work in conjunction with No. 1460 Flight Turbinlite Douglas Havocs mentioned in a separate chapter. Shortly after its arrival, the squadron suffered its first accident. On 12 October, Sgt J. Meredith's aircraft was damaged on the airfield when it stuck a patch of rough ground. There was a far more serious accident on the same day when two Hurricanes were carrying out practice attacks on each other. Flt Lt Hutchison's aircraft (Z3270) was acting as the target and Sgt Turner, a Canadian, was chasing it in Z2807. He misjudged the attack and overshot Hutchison. The propeller of Hutchison's aircraft cut off the tail of Turner's aircraft, sending it spinning out of control. It hit the ground near Alnwick; Turner died in the crash. Hutchison temporarily lost consciousness but soon came round and regained control of his aircraft. He made a successful forced landing near Embleton, despite his instruments not working and having lost his propeller blades.

The Squadron suffered a further fatality on 3 November. Plt Off. Hukam Chand Mehta, an Indian, had taken off on a training flight with another Hurricane, which eventually returned safely to base. Mehta appeared to have got lost and asked for a homing. Shortly after this message his Hurricane II (Z3150) crashed into a slope of Peel Fell, a 2,000 foot hill near Kielder Water, which was covered in cloud at the time. It was several days before the wreckage was found. Plt Off. Mehta's body was cremated at West Road Crematorium, Newcastle upon Tyne, in accordance with Hindu rites.

It was not long before another Hurricane was lost. Sgt J. Pipa, a Czech, was leading an operational patrol when 10 miles east of Blyth, Sgt Williams, an Australian, had to ditch in the sea when the engine of his Hurricane II (Z2968) failed. Whilst escaping from his aircraft he became separated from his dinghy. Sgt Pipa, orbiting overhead, became aware of Sgt Williams' plight. He inflated his own dinghy in his cockpit and dropped it close to where his colleague was floating. Unfortunately, Sgt Williams was unable to reach it and remained clinging onto a piece of wreckage until he was picked up by a naval launch. He was taken to hospital with severe shock and a wound in his leg. Sgt Pipa was later awarded a Bar to his Czech War Cross for his actions.

No. 43 Squadron lost another of its pilots when Sgt O'Brady was killed in an accident in Scotland whilst carrying out ferrying duties with No. 4 Delivery Flight. Sgt Bower died later the same month. He crashed near Swinderby while ferrying an aircraft to Walsall. The first enemy aircraft encountered since 43 Squadron's second deployment to RAF Acklington took place on 9 December 1941. Black section took off at 10.50 a.m. to patrol over the Farne Islands. It was then ordered to proceed to Blyth, where anti-aircraft fire was seen to the south of the Tyne. An enemy aircraft was spotted 10 miles east of Seaham, flying at 7,500 feet. The Hurricanes flying at the same height identified it as a Junkers Ju 88 and commenced an attack. The German bomber responded by weaving in and out of clouds. Further shots were fired by the Hurricanes and black smoke began trailing from the starboard engine of the Junkers, which responded by returning fire. After the fourth attack, the enemy aircraft dived steeply and crashed into the sea. The Ju 88D's identity was thought to be F6+CL.

In the New Year of 1942, Flt Lt du Vivier, a Belgian, was promoted to command 43 Squadron. He had little interest in administration and devoted most of his effort to chasing radar plots of enemy aircraft. As well as operational patrols, training flights were flown on most days. For example, on 14 February six Hurricanes carried out mock attacks on each other with the results being recorded on cine-camera guns, four more performed landings using radio beam for approaches, and another took part in a co-operation exercise with a Turbinlite Douglas Havoc. Shortly before 5 p.m. on the 25th, Plt Off. F. Lister took off in a Hurricane on an air firing exercise. When he retracted his undercarriage there was an explosion and a blast of air in the cockpit. His Flight Commander took off to investigate. When Lister lowered his undercarriage he was informed that his port tyre had burst. His Flight Commander told him to make a normal approach and on touching down to hold off the port wheel as long as possible. Lister did this and as his aircraft slowed it swung off the runway and hit a bank of snow accumulated on the edge. The aircraft tipped onto its nose but Lister was unhurt.

In the spring of 1942, 43 Squadron undertook trials of an anti-G suit. It was an invention of Sqn Ldr Franks, a Canadian specialist in aviation medicine. Pilots found that they no longer experienced any gravitational forces when flying in it, but in some ways this was a disadvantage as they had no feeling as to how their aircraft was behaving. FS Harvey Helbock, an American, was killed flying a Hurricane II (Z2983) on 5 April when it crashed due to a low-level high speed stall at South Side Farm, near Belford. At the time he was wearing a 'Franks Suit', after which tests were temporarily suspended. Helbock was buried locally in Chevington Cemetery. On the 17th, there was yet another fatal accident involving 43 Squadron. FS A. Reed, a Canadian, was killed at Whittingham, west of Alnwick, while taking part in an exercise with the Army. His Hurricane II (Z3068) struck an electrical cable, which caused the aircraft to crash and disintegrate next to a road. FS Reed 'had shown himself to be a keen and sensible pilot and had only recently been promoted to the rank of Flight Sergeant.'

The following day, there was a further, albeit less serious, accident at RAF Acklington. Sgt Webster had just touched down on the runway when he found his aircraft was drifting to the right. He attempted to correct this, but the wing of his Hurricane touched the ground and his undercarriage collapsed. The machine was not seriously damaged. Shortly after midday on 25 April, a lone Junkers Ju 88 approached the coast to photograph the shipyards on the River Tyne. 43 Squadron was not at readiness, and Spitfires from RAF Ouston were sent to intercept it. Squadron Commander Du Vivier overheard the transmissions and took off in a 43 Squadron Hurricane with the excuse that he was going to air-test the machine. The Junkers Ju 88 flew an arc over Newcastle then headed back out to sea with its mission completed. The Spitfires of 81 Squadron from RAF Ouston were far below and could not catch the enemy aircraft, now flying at around 30,000 feet. Du Vivier, determined it would not get away, pushed his Hurricane to the limits of its performance. Other German aircraft had escaped because the ageing Hurricane could not match their performance. Some 50 miles out to sea, Du Vivier caught up with the Junkers and opened fire from behind. As the range closed the enemy aircraft fired back. A bullet shattered the Hurricane's windscreen, lacerating du Vivier's face. A second bullet then passed through his life jacket. Not deterred, he opened fire again as the Junkers began to lose speed. Its starboard engine began emitting smoke and then burst into flames. One of the crew parachuted from the doomed machine, but the other three perished when it struck the sea and exploded.

Training continued, with low flying attacks and simulated ground strafing on Army units. Members of the King's Own Scottish Borderers visited 43 Squadron at RAF Acklington to discuss how both services could best co-operate with each other. In

Don Whitten, a New Zealander in 43 Squadron, in front of a Hawker Hurricane. (*ww2 images*)

No. 43 Squadron pilots ready to scramble in 1942. (*ww2 images*)

*Right:* Sgt 'Joe' Pipa, a Czech pilot in 43 Squadron, poses in front of a Hawker Hurricane in May 1942. (*ww2 images*)

*Below:* A group of 43 Squadron pilots sticking the unit's emblem, a fighting cock, onto the nose of one of their Hawker Hurricanes 1942. (*ww2 images*)

May, tests with the anti-*g* suit resumed, and training with the Army continued. Flying accidents continued to take their toll. Sgt Lewis, on a practice flight, was informed by his Section Leader that a white vapour was coming from his exhaust. The Section leader told him that he would inspect Brunton Airfield to see if it would be possible to land there. Immediately, the cockpit of Sgt Lewis's Hurricane I (P5197) began filling with smoke. He responded by climbing steeply on full throttle, disconnecting his radio lead and oxygen tube, half rolling his aircraft and bailing out. He made a successful parachute descent and his aircraft crashed in a field near Chathill. Five days later, Flt Lt Hutchison was killed in a flying accident. He had just taken off on a flight in co-operation with a Havoc Turbinlite, but found he could not retract the undercarriage of his Hurricane II (BD954). This caused his aircraft to stall and spin into the ground, bursting into flames close to RAF Eshott.

On 23 May, seven aircraft of 43 Squadron flew south to RAF Ford to participate in exercises with the Army. Four Hurricanes remained behind for operations with the Havoc Turbinlites. In mid-June, 43 Squadron departed for RAF Tangmere on the south coast. Here, it undertook intensive training, particularly the strafing of ground targets. Four aircraft flew on a mission to attack German destroyers off Le Harve, but the ships could not be located. By now, the Hurricane was increasingly being withdrawn from the fighter role in Britain and replaced by the Spitfire.

In July 1942, 1 Squadron arrived with its Hawker Hurricanes. Over the next few months, they were replaced with Hawker Typhoons. This is covered in the chapter 'Hawker Typhoon Squadrons'.

## Polish Hawker Hurricane Squadrons

315 (Polish) Squadron: January–March 1941, Hurricane I
317 (Polish) Squadron: February–April 1941, Hurricane I
309 (Polish) Squadron: July–September 1944 (detachment only), Hurricane IIC

During the Second World War, three Polish squadrons were based at RAF Acklington—two for only a very short time. When Germany invaded Poland in September 1939, the Polish Air Force, despite being heavily outnumbered, fought with great distinction. Towards the end of that year, Britain agreed to accept over 2,000 Polish airmen into the Royal Air Force Volunteer Reserve. In the meantime, the Polish Air Force had reformed in France and had on strength about ninety operational aircraft and 7,000 personnel. When Germany overran France, many Poles fled to Britain to swell the ranks of their fellow countrymen in the Royal Air Force. With the signing of the Polish-British Military Agreement in early August 1940, the formation of the Polish Air Force under RAF operational control was permitted. There were a number of other nationalities from occupied Europe in the RAF, but the Poles were the most numerous. Large numbers of Poles also served as soldiers in British Army.

RAF Acklington would host squadrons of several nationalities during the Second World War, including three composed of Poles. The first—315 Squadron—was

A newly delivered Hawker Hurricane (P3635) for 315 Polish Squadron. (*Wilhelm Ratuszynski*)

Sqn Ldr S. Pietraszjewicz, the CO of 315 Squadron pictured in front of a Hawker Hurricane. (*Wilhelm Ratuszynski*)

formed on 21 January 1941. There were initially considerable difficulties in finding accommodation for its personnel. Sqn Ldr S. Pietraszkjewicz, who had been a fighter pilot since 1930, was its commander. Many of the other pilots who began arriving at the end of the month also had considerable experience. Sgt Kowalski had been a fighter pilot since 1936. Plt Off. Miksa had flown both in in France and England, already having one enemy aircraft to his credit.

The squadron's first Hurricane I (L1740) was delivered on 3 February 1941. Pressure was put on the Polish Depot at Blackpool to post ground crew with various skills to complete the manning of the unit. Fg Off. Molyneux, a qualified teacher, was given the task of teaching the Poles English. On the 26th, a Miles Magister was delivered, but was damaged on landing. There was a further accident two days later when a Hurricane (R4122) taxied into another Hurricane (V6582), both aircraft sustaining minor damage. A further nine Hurricanes from 145 Squadron arrived from RAF Tangmere to swell the ranks of the newly-formed Polish unit. There was a further mishap on 5 March when a Hurricane (V7188) landed on the runway and collided with a roller, resulting in slight damage to the aircraft. Over the next few days, heavy snow made flying impossible. After a brief stay at RAF Acklington, 315 Squadron departed on the 13th with eighteen Hurricanes for RAF Speke (Liverpool) to provide air defence for Merseyside.

On 15 February 1941, the official blessing was given by the Air Ministry to form another Polish fighter squadron within the RAF. This move was received with great enthusiasm by the many pilots still at the Polish Depot at Blackpool who had not been selected for the recently formed 315 and 316 Squadrons. Major Stanislaw Brzezina was appointed the co-commander of the new unit, designated 317 Squadron. It too was to be formed at RAF Acklington. On the 22nd, its first Hurricane I was ferried in. By the end of the month, fifteen aircraft had arrived but the formation of the squadron was hindered by the shortage of aircraft mechanics. There was also friction between some of the newly arrived pilots. Sgt Brzeski, for instance, refused to serve in the flight commanded by Flt Lt Wczelik.

A major milestone in the creation of the squadron took place on 24 March 1941 when one section of A- and B-Flights were declared operational. By April, this had increased to three sections at readiness, usually from 8.30 a.m. until dusk. During the month there were numerous operational scrambles. At 2.10 p.m. on 2 April, a Hurricane was vectored onto a Junkers Ju 88 which managed to escape. Over the next couple of days there were further alerts and Hurricanes took off to patrol over the airfield. Whilst on a practice formation on the 4th, three Hurricanes were sent to investigate the sighting of a Junkers Ju 88 by some trawlers. No contact was made with the enemy aircraft, and the Hurricanes were instructed to patrol over the Farne Islands. 317 Squadron also flew a number of night patrols over Blyth, as well as providing air cover for two convoys. At the end of April, it made the short hop to RAF Ouston, which was to be its home until June 1941.

Early in the morning of 22 June 1941, a Royal Observer Post near Amble reported a small aircraft approaching the coast. A section of Spitfires was sent to investigate what was thought to be a hostile machine. When the fighters had closed in on their target they were astonished to find it was a DH.87 Hornet Moth with Danish registration OY-DOK, displaying a white flag. The plane landed immediately it made landfall at Chevington Drift near RAF Acklington. On board were two men in Danish Naval officer's uniforms—Thomas Sneum and Kield Pedersen—who were immediately arrested. Their aircraft had run out of oil, necessitating the hasty landing. The men were placed in the sick quarters under guard as there was no other accommodation available. Members of MI5 later arrived to question the Danes who stated that they had been secretly planning their escape to England for many months. Although all civil aircraft had been immobilised, they had secretly managed to return the Hornet Moth, which they had found on a farm, to airworthy condition. They took off from Denmark and flew at low level to avoid detection by German radar. Half way through their six-hour flight they had to smash a hole in their fuel tank so that more petrol could be funnelled in from the cockpit. Convinced of the authenticity of their account, MI5 released the two Danes, who went on to serve in the RAF. Thomas Sneum had previously handed over information to the British Embassy in Stockholm on a network of German radar controlled searchlights. Their Hornet Moth was impressed into RAF service until it was destroyed in a collision with an Avro Tutor at RAF Bicester in June 1942.

By the latter stages of the Second World War, the Hawker Hurricane had been generally withdrawn from front line fighter squadrons. One exception was 309 Polish Squadron, which still had them on strength in April 1944. It is an indication of the low priority given at this time to air defence of the east coast that their Hurricanes were tasked with defending the skies from the Forth of Forth to as far south as Newcastle. The main contingent was based at RAF Drem near Edinburgh, with a detachment at RAF Acklington. Most of the Poles were less than thrilled with this deployment as many of their colleagues were in the process of taking the fight to the Germans on the Continent. To add insult to injury, not one enemy aircraft was encountered by either the pilots at RAF Drem or RAF Acklington during this time.

On 1 July 1944, 309 Squadron took over the state of readiness from 504 Squadron at RAF Acklington. One section was placed at immediate readiness, the second placed at fifteen minutes readiness, and the third at thirty minutes. They were released from this duty at dusk. A Hurricane II (LF.699) crashed on landing on the 7th, causing damage to its undercarriage leg and starboard wing tip. At the end of the month, the aircraft of B-flight flew to RAF Langham near Norwich for an exercise with 76 Division Royal Artillery. At the end of August, the Pole's association with RAF Acklington came to an end. The detachment of 309 squadron's nine Hurricane IIs and one Tiger Moth left for their new home at RAF Peterhead. The ground crew of 6309 Servicing Echelon were transported there in two Douglas Dakotas.

# 5

# Supermarine Spitfire Squadrons

609 Royal Auxiliary Air Force Squadron: October 1939, Spitfire I
152 Squadron: January–July 1940, Spitfire I
72 Squadron: March–August 1940, Spitfire I
610 Royal Auxiliary Air Force Squadron: September 1940–December 1940, Spitfire
72 Squadron: December 1940–July 1941, Spitfire I, Spitfire IIA and IIB
74 Squadron: July–October 1941, Spitfire IIA
167 Squadron: April–June 1942, Spitfire VB
130 Squadron: December 1943–January 1944, Spitfire VB
222 Squadron: February–March 1944, Spitfire LF IXB
504 Squadron: April–July 1944, Spitfire VB

The first Spitfire squadron to arrive at RAF Acklington was 609 (West Riding) Squadron. On 5 and 6 October 1939, two flights landed there, fully armed. From their arrival, they observed a 'state of readiness', with one section of Spitfires ready to be airborne within five minutes. During the first few days of their stay there were a number of operational patrols to investigate unidentified aircraft. On the 16th, 609 Squadron were told to patrol over Alnwick and then Berwick-upon-Tweed, as four enemy aircraft were believed to be heading south. Unbeknown to the RAF pilots at the time, the Germans had launched a raid on ships in the Firth of Forth, slightly damaging two cruisers and a light cruiser in what was the first major air attack of the war. The Germans lost two Junkers Ju 88s. RAF Acklington now was on a heightened state of alert in the belief that further raids by German aircraft were imminent. 609 Squadron was ordered north to RAF Drem the following day to deter further raids on the Home Fleet. The ground crews were transported there in Whitley bombers carrying twenty men or more at a time. The Squadron remained at Drem until May 1940 except for a brief deployment further north to RAF Kinloss.

Although 152 Squadron had been at RAF Acklington since autumn 1939, it did not begin to receive its Spitfires until early the following year. By March, they had replaced most of the Gloster Gladiators, although a few appeared to still be in the ranks of the Squadron in April 1940. Early that month, a Gladiator (N5646) was on an air-sea rescue patrol when its engine failed and it came down in the sea. In this case, its pilot was rescued.

During the spring, the Spitfires flew a number of operational patrols, including several to protect convoys off the Farne Islands. Due to melting snow in March, the airfield became very boggy. Plt Off. Falkson crashed on the boundary of the airfield, his Spitfire's wheels having sunk into the mud, resulting in the aircraft turning on its back. The pilot was not injured. On 11 April, Red Section took off to intercept an enemy aircraft some 15 miles east of the airfield, but no contact was made. The following day, Green Section took off to investigate two unidentified aircraft north-east of the Farne Islands. On many days there were no operational flights at all. Intense practice flying on the newly delivered Spitfires took place much of the time, which included many practice interceptions, as well as flight and squadron formations.

Throughout April and May, 152 Squadron pilots did a great deal of night flying. At that time the squadron was required to supply one flight at readiness every second day, with the remainder of the squadron available at fifteen to twenty minutes' notice. There was the occasional scramble to intercept an aircraft which may have been hostile but which usually escaped out to sea by the time the Spitfires arrived. On 20 April, there was a serious accident when three Spitfires were practicing formations. Two of the machines—flown by Plt Off. Inness and Plt Off. Atkinson—collided while flying in low cloud. Inness crashed his machine when making a forced landing, but unfortunately Atkinson hit the top of some trees on landing and his aircraft burst into flames. He was very badly burnt about the face and hands and was admitted to Alnwick Hospital.

On 23 May, the commanding officer of 152 Squadron received an unexpected phone call from Fighter Command inquiring if his aircraft were armour-plated. He replied they were not. The caller then remarked: 'what a pity as if they had you could have gone south to assist with the evacuation at Dunkirk.'

Within twelve hours, the ground crews of 152 Squadron had fitted armoured plating onto most of their Spitfires.

An Ensign airliner arrived and was loaded up with equipment. We were all set to have a hit at the Germans whom we had up to date only met singly. Half an hour before we were set to take off, No. 13 Group rang up to say it was all off … I think everyone was very disappointed as we were then into a very high state of training.

A-Flight was instructed to go to RAF Catterick at the beginning of June. While there, a Spitfire 'I' flown by Plt Off. Bell, a New Zealander, struck an aircraft pen and crashed. Bell was severely injured and died in hospital the following day. There were so many wreaths for his funeral that a Blenheim had to be borrowed from 219 Squadron to transport them from RAF Acklington to RAF Catterick. The whole squadron took off for RAF Prestwick on the 15th to protect ships with Canadian troops arriving in the Firth of Clyde. The Spitfires returned to Acklington the following day.

In July, 152 Squadron was ordered to move to RAF Warmwell (near Dorchester) from where it was to defend Portland, which was experiencing heavy attacks by German bombers. 152 Squadron was not the only Spitfire Squadron at RAF Acklington; it had been joined by 72 Squadron, which arrived from RAF Church

Fenton on 3 March 1940. The next day, it was flying convoy patrols off the coast at Tynemouth. On the 7th, its Spitfire Is were ordered to intercept two unidentified aircraft 16 miles north of the Farne Islands; they were found to be RAF Whitley bombers. The same day, a convoy patrol was flown off Holy Island. For much of the month, RAF Acklington—at that time a grass airfield—was waterlogged. In such conditions, Spitfires had a tendency to topple onto their nose when taxiing. In order to prevent this, ground crew often sat on the tails of the aircraft.

Tom King of 72 Squadron was at the centre of one of the more extraordinary incidents to take place at RAF Acklington during the War. He had just strapped Jimmy Elsdon into his cockpit and then went to hang onto the tailplane with Harris, another member of the ground crew. The pilot opened up his throttle. The aircraft, with the two mechanics hanging on tightly and holding their legs up along the bottom of the tail plane to keep them away from the ground, began to move across the field. Then, much to their horror of the two ground crew, the Spitfire was no longer taxiing but had begun to take off. The awful truth dawned on Harris who released his grip on the Spitfire. Turning three somersaults, he hit the grass on his shoulders at about 70 mph. Much to the surprise of those watching, Harris picked himself up from the ground and walked away.

Attention now turned to the Spitfire with Tom King still clinging on. The aircraft managed to get airborne and climbed to 300 feet. Elsdon now realised that something was wrong and decided to land. Port wing dropping and nose down, he made a jerky tail-first landing. The Spitfire touched down, and Tom King fell off and lay prostrate on the grass. As onlookers ran to his assistance, he got up and walked towards them. He then told the astonished pilot: 'I've just done a circuit with you, sitting on the tailplane.' Elsdon responded by stating he was glad he did not realise that he had a passenger, otherwise he would have probably spun in.

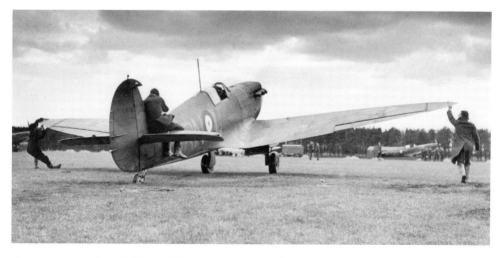

Ground crew assist a Spitfire of 72 Squadron taxiing from its dispersal in April 1940. One man is weighing the tail down which was standard practice on grass airfields to prevent the propeller from striking the ground. (*Imperial War Museum*)

On 19 March 1940, Fighter Group ordered that 72 Squadron was to fly all its Spitfires to RAF Thornaby at dusk each day for dispersal during the night, returning to RAF Acklington in the morning. This arrangement was cancelled a few days later.

At the beginning of April, a number of convoy patrols were flown in the vicinity of the Farne Islands. On a couple of occasions, unidentified aircraft were intercepted, but they turned out to be 'friendly'. Numerous convoy patrols were flown on 10 April, with sections of Spitfires taking it in turn to perform this duty. Later in the month, patrols were made over Blyth but again no enemy aircraft were encountered.

Coastguards reported that two aircraft were flying north over Blyth at 10.35 p.m. on 1 May. Weather was very poor over Acklington and it was not considered worthwhile risking pilots and aircraft in an attempt to intercept them. Around half an hour later, it was reported they were returning south and they could be heard from the airfield. It was then decided to scramble a single Spitfire to patrol the base at 6,000 feet. Mist and haze prevented any enemy aircraft being seen. Eight days later, 72 squadron was ordered to maintain a standing patrol between Seaham Harbour and Tynemouth from 7 p.m. to 10 p.m. A further mission was flown over Alnwick. On the 9th, Blue Section was instructed to patrol over the airfield at 5,000 feet. An aircraft was intercepted, but it turned out to be 'friendly'. Later in the month, further patrols were flown over Farne Islands and the Holy Island, but they also proved to be uneventful. There was an incident involving a Spitfire (K9925), which stalled on approach to RAF Woolsington. Its undercarriage collapsed, and the aircraft then cart-wheeled.

On 1 June 1940—with the fall of France imminent—72 Squadron was ordered south to Gravesend to provide air cover over Dunkirk for the evacuation of allied soldiers. Just as fifteen Spitfires were airborne and about to head south, Sqn Ldr Lees was ordered to return to RAF Acklington. This was so he could receive a personal message from AOC 13 Group, wishing 72 Squadron 'God Speed'. After an eventful few days, the squadron returned to RAF Acklington on the 6th. For the remainder of June, the Spitfires were split between Acklington and nearby RAF Woolsington. On the 18th, Blue Section was scrambled to intercept an X-raid which was approaching the coast. The plot faded and the Spitfires were recalled. The following day, there was a further alert and a single aircraft was scrambled, but no enemy was sighted.

There was a lull in activity until shortly before midnight on 26 June, when there was a considerable amount of activity by enemy aircraft. Three Spitfires—far from ideal as night fighters—were ordered on patrol. A Junkers Ju 88 was picked out by one of the searchlight beams illuminating the sky around Acklington and was attacked by Plt Off. Thomson. When he was at the same altitude as the bomber, Thomson was unable to see it, as it was in the apex of the cone of the searchlights, but when the Spitfire lost altitude, he could see the outline of the hostile aircraft above him. He positioned his aircraft 150 feet astern and 20 feet below; he then opened fire. After the first burst, smoke was seen to come from both engines of the Junkers. When Thomson fired his guns again, there was a blinding white flash and the Junkers appeared to explode, with fragments being sprayed in all directions. Some of them struck the Spitfire and a few of the smaller pieces lodged in its radiator cowling. At this point, the Spitfire broke off the attack and Thomson saw nothing more of the Ju 88.

Members of 72 Squadron pose for their photograph on a Spitfire. (*72 Squadron Archives*)

The whole of the action could be seen clearly by onlookers at Acklington. The enemy aircraft was first illuminated by about twelve searchlights, then made no attempt to evade the beams other than turn towards the sea. Although a number of the searchlights went out before Plt Off. Thomson attacked, the Junkers Ju 88 at 7,000 feet was well illuminated. After two bursts of gunfire, an explosion was clearly seen by a number of witnesses on the ground, and it was thought wreckage came down in the sea 3 miles east of Cambois. A search of the area found nothing. It was an unusual achievement for a Spitfire to succeed in downing a hostile aircraft during the hours of darkness. There was further enemy activity that night, but none of 72 Squadron's pilots caught sight of enemy planes.

On the night of 29 June 1940, several aircraft were heard close to RAF Acklington. At 3.30 a.m., Red Section was ordered on patrol and intercepted an Armstrong Whitley bomber, 'the identity of which appeared doubtful.' It was not unknown for Germans to repair captured RAF machines and use them in their air force. The Whitley was escorted to RAF Thornaby, where it was forced to land for identification. Later that morning, shortly after 8 a.m., 72 Squadron Spitfires were scrambled again. An unidentified aircraft was flying east at 20,000 feet about 10 miles north-east of Holy Island. At 8.30 a.m. the pilots could see an aircraft flying east and climbing. They ascended to 23,000 feet and followed it for about twenty minutes. When challenged to identify itself, the aircraft failed to give a satisfactory response. As the Spitfires closed in, it was identified as a Dornier Do 17 (it was in fact a Do 215). Aware that it was about to be attacked from the rear, the enemy aircraft performed violent stall turns and dives in an attempt to shake off the Spitfires. All three Spitfires took turns to fire at it from dead astern at a range of about 750 feet. After the first two attacks, smoke was seen pouring from both engines. As one of the Spitfires attacked, the Dornier stalled steeply and several bursts of fire hit the bomber's cockpit. The enemy aircraft pulled out of the stall but was hit again, causing its cockpit to break up. A Spitfire then closed in to a very short range and open fire again. The Dornier 215 went into a steep right hand spiral to about 2,000 feet, after which it dived vertically into the sea, bursting into flames and breaking up. The Spitfires landed back at RAF Acklington at 9.45 a.m. One had suffered a bullet hit to its engine. In the aftermath, Sir Archibald Sinclair, the Secretary State for Air, visited 72 Squadron and 'congratulated it on its magnificent achievements.'

On 1 July, 72 Squadron had a further encounter with an enemy aircraft, but this incident provoked some controversy rather than congratulations. A Heinkel He 115 had been lost in a mine-laying operation off the Yorkshire coast and an air-sea rescue Heinkel He 59 seaplane (D-ASAM) was dispatched from Germany to search for the crew. While flying off the coast, close to a convoy near Sunderland, it was attacked by three Spitfires of 72 Squadron. This was despite the fact that the seaplane was painted white with large Red Cross markings. The Spitfires shot more than 2,500 rounds at it. Within a matter of a few minutes, it was seen emitting smoke from its fuselage and landed on the sea off Hartlepool. Its four crew, one of whom was seriously injured, took to their dinghy and were soon picked up by the destroyer HMS *Black Swan*. The He 59, which had only partially sunk, was beached and salvaged. There was a belief that the Germans had been sometimes using search and rescue seaplanes for nefarious purposes. Two weeks after this incident, the British Government warned the Germans that seaplanes—even those marked with red crosses—would be shot down if they flew close to convoys.

No. 72 Squadron A-Flight ground crew members. (*72 Squadron Archives*)

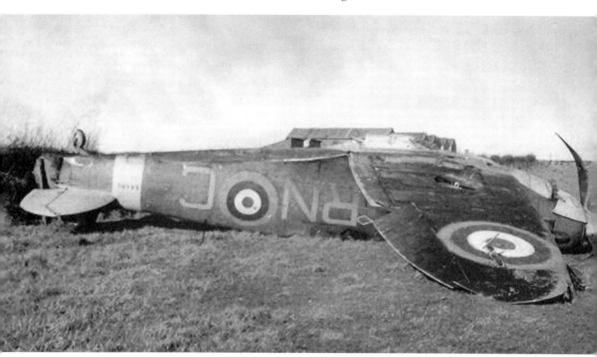

A 72 squadron Supermarine Spitfire after a landing accident, May 1941. (*72 Squadron Archives*)

72 Squadron pilots prepare for flying in summer 1940. (*ww2 images*)

On 2 July, twelve aircraft of 72 Squadron carried out practice attacks with 607 Squadron, which was also based at RAF Acklington. In the afternoon, there was considerable enemy activity towards the north and no less than four Sections—each with three Spitfires—were instructed to investigate. There was a brief glimpse of a Junkers Ju 88, but it was not intercepted. A few minutes after midnight on the 5th, enemy aircraft were reported off the coast, but the weather prevented the Spitfires from taking off. Shortly after 4 a.m., Blue Section was scrambled to intercept a raid off Blyth, but nothing was seen. A further patrol was made over Seaham Harbour, but with negative results. The following day, 72 Squadron Spitfires were ordered into the air to protect RAF Acklington, but poor weather again prevented any action against hostile aircraft. During this operation, Plt Off. Elliott became unconscious when he reached an altitude of 20,000 feet, as the oxygen tube was missing from the aircraft. After he passed out, his Spitfire dived some 17,000 feet over the Cheviots. Elliott regained consciousness 1,000 feet above the ground and managed to make it back to RAF Acklington. His Spitfire never flew again as it had been so badly stressed in the rapid descent. Later that day, the entire Squadron was placed at readiness to move to RAF Drem as an attack was expected in the vicinity of the Firth of Forth; this instruction was later cancelled.

Enemy aircraft were detected in the sector on 7 July. Spitfires from 72 Squadron flew over the airfield, but no German bombers were engaged. The next day, Red Section flew north to Berwick-upon-Tweed to intercept a raid. The pilots briefly caught sight of a Heinkel He 111 before it disappeared into dense cloud. There were several more scrambles over the next couple of weeks, but none resulted in visual sightings of German aircraft. On 21 July 1940, with invasion threatening, the edginess of the situation meant that an Avro Anson, which was thought to be suspicious, was escorted by Spitfires and forced to land at RAF Acklington for investigation. Two days later, Green Section was ordered to intercept an enemy aircraft shortly before midday. It turned out to be another Anson flying near Berwick-upon-Tweed. Even so, it was not taken for granted that it was being flown by an RAF aircrew and was instructed to land at RAF Acklington. A large number of enemy aircraft were again reported near the airfield on 24 July, but low cloud precluded action against them. On a number of occasions, they could be heard flying in the vicinity during the hours of darkness. Two mines were dropped at Guyzance; the explosions shook the airfield.

August 1940 began as July had ended—there were numerous scrambles, but enemy aircraft vanishing before contact could be made. Bombs fell on a number of towns in Northumberland during the night. On the 6th, a 72 Squadron Spitfire I (L1078) crashed on landing. Its pilot, Sgt R. C. Staples, was uninjured. On the 15th, 79 Squadron at RAF Acklington was on 'stand down' while the pilots of 72 Squadron were 'at readiness' in their huts or out on the grass. At that time, the south of England was experiencing heavy bombardment by large formations of German bombers, such actions were almost unheard of in the north. All this was about to change.

Shortly after midday, radar screens picked up around twenty aircraft heading towards the Firth of Forth. Hermann Goering, Commander of the Luftwaffe, believed that most of the RAF fighter squadrons had been deployed to the south coast to repel attacks mounted from France. By despatching bombers from Norway and Denmark, he planned to catch the RAF off guard and strike a blow where it was least expected. Fifty Junkers Ju 88s had been instructed to attack RAF Driffield in Yorkshire. A further sixty-three Heinkel He 111s were to attack RAF Disforth and RAF Linton-on-Ouse or attack towns in north-east England as alternatives. Thirty-four Messerschmitt Bf110s long range fighters provided protection for the Heinkels. The first radar plot picked up over the Forth was actually a formation of German seaplanes acting as decoys to make RAF Fighter Command think the attack was going to be on Edinburgh. At RAF Acklington, the controller rang 72 Squadron to warn them that 'a very large group of Huns was approaching.'

The whole squadron was called to readiness. Off-duty pilots also turned up, hoping to be given a chance to fly; they were to be disappointed. Only eleven Spitfires were serviceable, all of which took to the air. They were ordered to investigate a formation of between twenty-four and fifty enemy aircraft heading inland from the Farne Islands. Finding nothing there, the 72 Squadron Spitfires headed further out to sea. Some 30 miles beyond the Islands, they caught sight of what appeared to be hundreds of aircraft. The Germans had blundered. They should have made landfall much further down the coast near Sunderland. As they flew south, the Spitfires of 72 Squadron fell on the aerial armada, which was led by Heinkel He 111s and Junkers Ju 88s, with the Messerschmitt Me 110 fighters in the rear. When the attack commenced, many of the German aircraft jettisoned their bombs to fall harmlessly into the sea. The Me 110 fighters, aware of their inferior performance compared to the Spitfires, formed defensive circles. The German planes resembled a wagon train being attacked by Indians.

Although the Messerschmitt Me 110 usually had a crew of two, it was thought that for this operation there was only one on board, as the type was operating at the limit of its range. Fg Off. T. A. F. Elsdon found himself becoming encircled by Messerschmitt Me 110s, but succeeded in extraditing himself before they opened fire. He then positioned himself to attack the enemy fighters, which had now broken their formation. The Spitfire fired three bursts at one of the Messerschmitt Me 110s. Smoke came from the starboard engine, and it disappeared into the clouds in a spiral dive. A further Messerschmitt Me 110 crashed into the sea off Newcastle and was claimed by Fg Off. Desmond Sheen. It contained the Group Leader of ZG26. As it was hit, the long range fuel tank on the underside of the Me 110 exploded, destroying the German fighter. Sheen then searched for another enemy aircraft to attack. He unsuccessfully shot at another Messerschmitt Me 110, but then a Junkers Ju 88 appeared in his sights, approaching him head on. The Spitfire's guns opened fire and flames and smoke began spewing from the Junker's port engine. The crippled machine continued flying on a collision course with the Spitfire and Sheen had to take evasive action to avoid being rammed.

The enemy formation, flying west in numerous vic formations—line abreast and line astern—was then attacked by Flt Lt T. Graham. Along with the other Spitfires of Blue section, 72 Squadron, he attacked three Heinkel He 111s towards the rear. At a range of around 700 feet, Graham opened fire on one of the bombers. Its gunners replied

A Messerschmitt Bf 110G of the Luftwaffe. This type of German aircraft was a long-range fighter that escorted Heinkel He 111 bombers on their large day raid on north-east England on 15 August 1940. Hilter's deputy, Rudolf Hess, also piloted a Messerschmitt Bf 110 on his one-way flight to Scotland. (*ww2 images*)

An impressive formation of 72 Squadron Supermarine Spitfires over the coast, 1941. (*72 Squadron Archives*)

with an intense burst of fire, but this was to little avail. By now smoke was coming from the fuselage and one of the engines. Catching sight of a Messerschmitt Me 110 circling above him, Graham broke off the attack and dived towards the clouds to escape. The German fighter was hard on his tail but as it descended it gave the impression it may have been out of control. When Graham emerged from the clouds, there were no aircraft to be seen. Now 20 miles out to sea, he headed back towards RAF Acklington. Plt Off. D. Winter was acting as rear-guard to the Spitfires of Green Section. His combat report relates his experience of the air battle that day:

> Then I decided to attack myself, at the same time seeing a He 111 with its wheels down gliding seawards. I followed it for a while until I saw it hit the sea and disappear. Climbing up again I saw about 2,000 feet below me at 16,000 feet a circle of six Me 110s with a Spitfire in the circle. I waited until one Me 110 was detached a little from the circle on the Spitfire's tail and dived to attack. I waited until I was about 100 feet from it and opened fire. I saw bullets entering the pilot's cockpit. The enemy aircraft turned on its back and dived seawards, eventually crashing into the sea. I observed no return fire. Climbing up again I found another ring of six Me 110s with three Spitfires in a circle. One of the Me 110s flew to one side and I again dived to attack. In the first combat I fired at about 150 feet and the port engine started to smoke. I fired two more bursts which entered the pilot's cockpit. I followed it through the cloud and saw it crash into the sea. No return fire was observed and no markings on the second enemy aircraft.

A Heinkel He 111 was shot down by Fg Off. E. Wilcox, who gave the following account of the combat:

> On receipt of the order to attack I sighted a He 111 bomber and observed the rear gunner firing at me. As I was at a range of about 600 yards. I put my head a little above the rear gunner of the Heinkel. After a short burst I observed no more enemy fire from this machine. I closed to point blank range and fired at the port engine until black smoke poured from it and the undercarriage dropped. I then transferred my attention to the starboard engine and fired until black smoke appeared. The enemy glided down towards the water. My windscreen was splashed with oil from the engines of the Heinkel. As I had expended all my ammunition I returned to base.

By 2.39 p.m., all eleven Spitfires had landed back at RAF Acklington. The Hurricanes of 79 Squadron touched down a short time later. Along with 605 Squadron from RAF Drem, it had engaged the enemy formation as it flew close to Newcastle to the south of RAF Acklington. 607 Squadron at RAF Usworth and 41 Squadron at RAF Cattrick were also involved in the air battle. Further south, fighters from 12 Group had repulsed a formation of Junkers Ju 88s. The pilots of 72 Squadron claimed to have destroyed eleven enemy aircraft—one for every pilot who participated in the action. The figures proved widely optimistic. When all totals for it and the other squadrons were added they amounted to over seventy Heinkel He 111s and Messerschmitt Me 110s claimed by fighter squadrons of 13 Group along with anti-aircraft batteries. This figure did not include any of the Junkers Ju 88s engaged by 12 Group in Yorkshire. As most of the air battles took place over the sea, it was difficult to determine exactly how many German aircraft were destroyed. The probable total was thought to be around eight Heinkel He 111s, eight Messerschmitt Me 110s, and seven Junkers Ju 88s. The RAF's only losses were three fighters which had to make forced landings. Thirteen Whitley bombers were destroyed on the ground at RAF Driffield by the Junkers Ju 88s. Few of the other intended targets were hit, and the Luftwaffe never mounted a large scale raid on north-east England in daylight hours again.

The remainder of August was an anti-climax for the fighter squadrons at RAF Acklington. While there was frantic air activity over southern England, no further German aircraft were seen by 72 Squadron. At the end of a night patrol, the pilot of one of its Spitfire's misjudged his height on landing. The aircraft hit the ground just as the pilot was about to lower the flaps. It pitched back into the air and as it fell back to earth the right wing hit the ground and was torn off. The only damage to the pilot was a minor injury to his right kneecap. At the end of August, with the Battle of Britain at its height, 72 Squadron was ordered south to RAF Biggin Hill, but it would return at the end of the year to RAF Acklington for an eventful stay.

At the end of August 1940, 610 City of Chester Squadron became the second Royal Auxiliary Air Force Squadron with Spitfires to operate from Acklington. It had suffered severe casualties while based at RAF Biggin Hill during the Battle of Britain and had been withdrawn from the front line for a period of recuperation. Shortly after its arrival at RAF Acklington, all airmen were authorised to draw 'war pay'. Later that month, A. C. D. Evans died as a result of a bullet wound he accidently received while travelling by train from RAF Biggin Hill to RAF Acklington. During 610's stay, its Spitfires were involved in a number of operational patrols. On 19 September, Red and Yellow Sections were ordered to patrol 50 miles out to sea, but nothing was seen. Blue Section patrolled off the Farne Islands on the 23 September and Red Section orbited RAF Usworth on 29 September, where they encountered an RAF Fairey Battle.

A week later, the squadron suffered the first of several serious accidents during its stay at RAF Acklington. A Spitfire (K9818), flown by Fg Off. Charles Bacon, and a Spitfire (L1037), piloted by Sgt Henry Clarke, collided while practicing a head-on attack. The former aircraft had a wing severed and crashed on the beach near Alnmouth, killing Bacon. Henry Clarke was more fortunate; his Spitfire remained in the air but with its engine malfunctioning. He decided to abandon the aircraft, but as he jumped, the parachute caught on part of the cockpit and wrenched the parachute straps off. The next thing Clarke could remember was dangling upside down, suspended by one strap of his parachute entangled round his leg. As he approached the ground he pulled himself upright. Later, he recalled that when he bailed out he may have hit the tailplane, which had knocked him unconscious. His aircraft came to earth at Wildhope Hill, about 1 mile west of Alnmouth.

In October, patrols were flown over the Tyne and Farne Islands but they were again uneventful. On the 11th, Blue Section guarded the airspace between Woolsington and Acklington Airfields. There were also a number of night patrols.

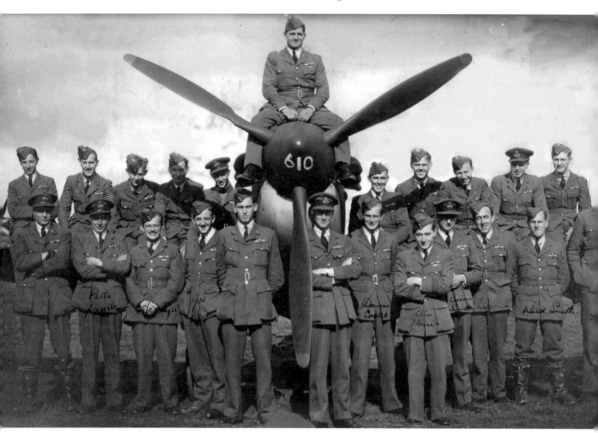

Pilots of 610 Squadron pose for their photo in 1940. (*610 Squadron Association*)

November was marred by several more flying accidents. A Spitfire I (L1094) crashed into boggy ground near Edlingham. Its pilot, Sgt I. M. Miller, had lost control of his machine and perished in the accident. The following day, Plt Off. Donald Gray lost his life when his Spitfire I (X4011) crashed while taking off at night. He was buried locally in Chevington Cemetery. 610 Squadron lost yet another Spitfire (R6891) on the 19th. This time its pilot managed to parachute to safety. The aircraft came off less well and smashed into the ground two miles south-east of Edlingham. As 610's stay was drawing to a close there was another mid-air collision involving a Spitfire (P9451) flown by Sgt H. McGregor and a Spitfire (X4649) flown by Plt Off. Ross. The latter bailed out successfully with his aircraft hitting the banks of Titlington Burn. Tragically, McGregor was killed in his Spitfire when it crashed near Kimmer Lough.

610 Squadron departed RAF Acklington on 19 December, when fifteen Spitfires took off for their new base in the south of England. Their place was taken by 72 Squadron which returned for a second deployment at RAF Acklington. The ground crew arrived on the 14 December but the arrival of the Spitfires was delayed by five days due to adverse weather conditions. The spare pilots were flown in aboard two Handley Page Harrows.

The first few days of January 1941 were cold and there were heavy falls of snow. The routine was much as before, with patrols over the Farne Islands and Blyth. The poor weather continued into the following month, restricting flying on a number of days. Snow began falling on 20 February and did not cease for fifty-two hours. The airfield was covered to a depth of a foot and half in what was said to be the heaviest snowfall in the area since 1886. Early in the war, there was no specialised snow clearing equipment and most of the work had to be undertaken by men wielding shovels.

During March, German bombers made a number of hit-and-run attacks on Northumberland towns. Usually only one or two aircraft were involved. In response, 72 Squadron flew several operational patrols each day. One patrol at the beginning of the month nearly ended in disaster. Flt Lt Sheen, an Australian, took off with two other aircraft shortly before 7 p.m. Soon after, the weather closed in and visibility was reduced to less than 1,000 yards. Control had little knowledge of the position of the three Spitfires and it was only that the pilots were familiar with the local topography that they were able to find their way back to RAF Acklington and land without incident.

In the evening of the 13th, Flt Lt Sheen was ordered to patrol over the airfield at an altitude of 6,000 feet. He was then instructed to climb to 12,000 feet. While ascending, he glimpsed an aircraft silhouetted against the moon-lit high cloud. He chased it in his Spitfire and, as he caught up, he recognised it as a Junkers Ju 88. As the enemy aircraft headed out to sea, he opened fire. The Ju 88's starboard engine burst into flames. Sheen broke off the attack and headed back to the airfield. Eyewitnesses on the ground reported seeing the crippled Junkers Ju88 (M2+JL) burst into flames and fall into the sea, about three miles north-east of Coquet Island. Its crew of four

A snowplough at work. (*Imperial War Museum*)

were killed. Shortly before midnight, several more Junkers Ju 88s, clearly visible from the ground, flew over RAF Acklington at around 6,000 feet.

Many of the patrols flown by 72 Squadron in early April were flown over the airfield itself. During one such sortie, at 6.44 p.m. on the 10th, Green Section intercepted a Junkers Ju 88A (F.6+NL) and opened fire. It ditched in the sea about a mile below the low-water mark. The aircraft sank so quickly that none of its four crew managed to escape. Three Spitfires of Blue Section were also ordered to patrol over RAF Acklington around the same time. They too claimed to have downed a Junkers Ju 88 about 10 miles north-east of Long Haughton. When last seen, its port engine was on fire and was disintegrating as it plunged towards the sea, but none of the pilots saw it crash. There was some speculation that only one Junkers Ju 88 was destroyed that evening by 72 Squadron, with both Green and Blue Sections having attacked the same aircraft.

The next encounter with a German aircraft took place in the afternoon of the 29th. Green Section was airborne at the time on a training flight. It was vectored towards an aircraft identified as a high-altitude reconnaissance Junkers Ju 86, off the coast near Blyth. Two of the Spitfires managed to open fire as it passed through a gap in the clouds before disappearing. Sgt Collyer gave chase but then radioed that the engine of his Spitfire II (P8231) had failed and he was going down in the sea. His two colleagues searched for him, but in vain. Later the same day Sgt Collyer's body was recovered. He was buried in Chevington Cemetery.

The following afternoon, Yellow Section of 72 Squadron was flying over RAF Acklington when it was informed that a Junkers Ju 88 was heading south from the Farne Islands. The two Spitfire pilots first caught sight of two explosions in the sea. This was thought to have been caused by the Junkers jettisoning its bomb load. Not long after, the enemy bomber was detected flying low over the water. The Spitfires gave chase and commenced their attack. After firing numerous bursts, they broke off the engagement, leaving the enemy bomber flying in cloud at 500 feet with smoke streaming from both engines. The 72 Squadron pilots claimed a Junkers Ju 88 (S4+JH) as damaged. It later became known that it had crashed off the Farne Islands with none of its crew of four surviving.

In May, a number of convoy patrols were undertaken as well as the usual ones over the airfield itself—most by sections consisting of only two Spitfires instead of three. At 7.34 p.m. on the 5th, there was a scramble to protect the base itself. Blue Section came across a Junkers Ju 88 which was attacked and damaged before it escaped. On the 18th, two Spitfires were flying a convoy patrol off Blyth during which they fought with a Dornier Do 17, but the enemy succeeded in evading the attack again.

A week earlier, another enemy aircraft had a close call. Late in the evening of the 10th, what was thought to be a German raid approaching the coast was detected by Ottercops Moss Chain Home Radar Station to the west of Newcastle. It was then detected by other radar stations in the region. What was unusual about the plot was that it appeared to be a single aircraft travelling at considerable speed. Two Spitfires of 72 Squadron were already airborne but due to an error by ground control they were vectored onto each other and not the target. A further attempt was made at interception by scrambling a single 72 Squadron Spitfire at 10.20 p.m. Had the Spitfire managed to down this enemy aircraft, it may have changed history. The target was a

Messerschmitt Me 110, flown by Hitler's deputy Rudolf Hess. As it crossed the coast to the north of RAF Acklington, the Spitfire gave chase but its pilot, Sgt Maurice Pocock, was unable to see it in the fading light. Rudolf Hess later related he was aware of being followed by a Spitfire some 3 miles behind him.

On reaching the west of Scotland, Hess abandoned his aircraft with some difficulty. He found he could not open the cockpit, so he had to fly inverted before he could escape and deploy his parachute. For the rest of his life, Hess was held prisoner of the Allied Powers. The intention of his mission was to contact the Duke of Hamilton and through him to attempt to negotiate a cessation of hostilities. A wealth of conspiracy theories were spawned by his actions. It is generally thought that Hess was acting on his own initiative and without Hitler's blessing. It was rumoured that a few days after his flight, a Junkers Ju 88 landed at RAF Acklington and taxied to a remote corner of the airfield. Here, it was met by some waiting figures. A short time later, it took off without any opposition from the RAF.

June was a relatively uneventful month for 72 Squadron. There were no confrontations with enemy aircraft. Another Spitfire (P8166) was lost in an accident when Sgt Allan Casey ploughed into the boundary hedge on landing.

On 9 July, 72 Squadron left RAF Acklington for the last time during the Second World War and moved south to RAF Gravesend. In the opposite direction came 74 Squadron with their Spitfire VBs. During the month the Squadron undertook formation flying, air firing, camera gun practices and dusk landings.

On 2 August 1941, Plt Off. D. Steven was killed when his Spitfire (P8045) crashed 10 miles to the north-west of RAF Ouston near Wallington Hall. At the time he had been formation flying with five other aircraft at 25,000 feet. Four days later, two 74 Squadron Spitfires succeeded in damaging a Junkers Ju 88. For the remainder of August, operational patrols and numerous practice flights were flown. At the end of the month, a Whitley played the role of a hostile bomber for the Spitfires. A number of co-operation flights with Army units also took place.

During September, Sgt Coxton was killed in a flying accident. There was also a collision between two 74 Squadron Spitfires on one of RAF Acklington's runway, which injured Flt Lt. Scott. Early the following month, 74 Squadron left for North Wales.

Unlike many other Spitfire Squadrons, 167 Squadron was formed relatively late in the war in April 1942 at RAF Scorton. The following month, it was sent north to RAF Acklington to relieve 43 Squadron. Fourteen of its aircraft arrived on 23 May, 1942. At 7 a.m. the next day, Red Section was ordered to scramble and climb to a height of 24,000 feet. After numerous vectors directing it in a southerly direction, Red 2 caught sight of an enemy aircraft bearing a black camouflage scheme flying north-east at an altitude of 15,000 feet. The Spitfire flew over it, identified it as a Junkers Ju 88, and dived towards it in line astern. Red 1 attacked first, firing a two second burst from its cannon and machine guns at a range of around 600 feet. The Junkers took evasive action by descending rapidly with Red 2 on its tail. The Spitfire fired several bursts and a six-foot section of the enemy's wing tip broke off. Red 1 also attacked from the port quarter before passing under its tail, opening fire again using the last of its cannon ammunition. By this point, the enemy bomber had entered a spiral dive through the cloud. Not deterred, the two Spitfires followed close behind, shooting as they descended. At around 7,000 feet, the Junkers levelled out and headed south, although it was still losing height.

Red 2, having used up his ammunition for both his cannons and machine guns, broke off the pursuit and returned to RAF Acklington. The other Spitfire, Red 1, followed the Junkers, which was now flying south for a further 3 to 4 miles before it too gave up the chase. At no stage did the enemy aircraft return fire. The Squadron record book records the following about this incident:

> We were not amused by a certain high-ranking officer who commented, 'It got away. Why didn't they ram him?' He should have given credit to our two boys and acknowledged that the Jerry pilot must have been very experienced.

At the end of May, as its aircraft were about to depart for RAF Scorton, 167 Squadron was informed that its next posting would be in the north of Scotland:

> Hell's Bells, the Squadron is posted to that much dreaded outpost of Fighter Command, called Castletown, as from 1st June, just when it will be getting warmer down here and presumably mid-winter up there. Why on earth were we sent to Acklington for this week? Kites one place, crews and pilots scattered. Kits down here. What a life for the poor harassed Orderly Room staff and how well Cpl. Bunting and his fellows have worked. Somebody higher up just moves one bit of paper on a board, irrespective of where the Squadron is at the moment.

The above sentiments are probably true of many of the Squadrons that had fleeting stays at RAF Acklington during the Second World War. 130 Squadron, like 167 Squadron, was briefly deployed from RAF Scorton to RAF Acklington, although it had a small detachment there previously. Its Spitfire VBs arrived shortly before Christmas 1943 and carried out a squadron formation flypast with nine machines. Its aircraft remained at readiness over the festive period, with training also being undertaken. On Boxing Day, one Spitfire carried out an exercise with the Royal Navy at Newcastle. Good weather on 29 December enabled twelve pilots to take part in low-level cross-country flying. The last entry in the squadron's record book for 1943 complains that, in the preceding year, they had been all over the country, posted overseas and had to make do with poor accommodation: 'With the dawning of 1944 and the great events, each and everyone of us should stand prepared and ready to give of his utmost to finish the Hun off once and for all in no uncertain fashion'—a prophetic statement written in squadron's record book.

On 4 January 1944, 130 Squadron returned to RAF Scorton. 222 Squadron left RAF Catterick for RAF Acklington on 25 February 1944. Here, they operated under 147 Airfield Unit in preparation for the invasion of France. By this time, there was little emphasis on the air defence of northern England as raids by German aircraft were now almost non-existent. All 222 Squadron's Spitfire Vs were airborne on 28 February, a perfect day for flying.

Heavy snow showers interrupted flying at the beginning of March. While at RAF Acklington, 222's Spitfires did not train in aerial combat, but practised attacking targets on the ground. The weather had improved by the 5th, when many of the aircraft were practicing dusk landings and night flying. A Spitfire (BL940) had a minor accident on landing when an inner-tyre tube burst, causing the aircraft to end up on its nose. The following day, twelve pilots took part in an escape and evasion exercise. They were driven to a point some 18 to 20 miles from RAF Acklington and then had to make their own way back; two of the pilots were back at the airfield in under two hours, having stolen an Army truck.

On the morning of the 7th, two Spitfire Vs took off on a routine practice flight. Both pilots performed some elementary aerobatics then one (EP550) crashed near Edlingham, killing its pilot, FS Morris, a South African, as well as injuring a civilian. Morris was buried at Chevington Cemetery. The following day, dusk and night landings were carried out. As Fg Off. McAuliffe was approaching the airfield to land, his engine stuttered and cut out. He managed to nurse his machine down, but given the aircraft's speed and the shortness of runway remaining, McAuliffe had no option but to retract his undercarriage to slow his progress. He skidded to a stop a short distance in front of the hangars. It was later discovered that the Spitfire's engine failed because its fuel tank was empty. It had not been refuelled and the airman responsible was disciplined for his negligence.

Instructions were received by 222 Squadron on 9 March that it was to move to RAF Hornchurch. It departed the following day and, in a few months, would provide protection for convoys and the invasion beaches. Training decreased over the next few months at RAF Acklington as other squadrons headed south for D-Day. In the early part of 1944 the air defence of the sector was maintained by a detachment of Spitfire Vs of 504 Squadron from RAF Digby which arrived in April, as well as some Typhoons from 3 TEU.

On 2 July, ten Hurricanes of 309 Squadron's B-Flight arrived from RAF Drem to take over air defence duties. The detachment of 504 Squadron left two days later. The opportunity was now taken to reconstruct the airfield. By 1943 its inadequacies were becoming apparent. Wg Cdr Reid, 409 Squadron, had made two reports of the excessive wear to aircraft tyres caused by loose stones. He related that, in no less than six cases, if an examination had not been carried out on the aircraft, the tyres would have probably burst on the next sortie. Intensified efforts were made to keep the runways and taxiways clear of stones. This was not easy. Some three years earlier, in an attempt to remedy the boggy patches hindering operations, shale was laid. This contained sharp points which did not agree with aircraft tyres. It was most prevalent around one of the dispersal areas. It was resolved to cover the ground with soil and seed it with grass. Later, in an effort to remedy the situation permanently, it was decided to place steel strips known as Sommerfeld Tracking over the muddy area. There was a further problem with those aircraft pens which had been constructed with sandbags. They were becoming dilapidated and personnel from 350 Squadron carried out some initial restoration work by removing loose sand. The Works Department then were going to replace it with closely packed earth which would be consolidated by grass.

During summer 1943, work was also undertaken to extend the north–south runway from 1,380 yards to 1,490 yards. Most of it was carried out by the Acklington Airfield Construction Flight. The following summer, 5022 Airfield Construction Company, which had its headquarters in Newcastle, laid out three new surfaced runways—the longest nearly 2,000 yards—in the traditional 'A' pattern. The building work continued until late 1944. By then, the two pre-war F-type hangars had a Bellman hangar and sixteen small blister hangars for company. The airfield did not see much use until early 1945. One exception was a squadron of Fleet Air Arm Corsairs, which were briefly based here in December for an Army exercise—one of the few times in RAF Acklington's history that aircraft from the Royal Navy operated from it.

## Foreign Spitfire Squadrons

    350 Squadron (Belgium): July–August 1943, Spitfire VC
    349 Squadron (Belgium): August–October 1943, Spitfire VA, Spitfire LFVB
    316 Squadron (Polish): September 1943–February 1944, Spitfire IX, Spitfire LFVB
    322 Squadron (Dutch): March–August 1944, Spitfire VC, Spitfire XIV

In the latter stages of the Second World War, RAF Acklington hosted several Spitfire squadrons manned by foreign nationalities. The first to arrive was 350 (Belgium)

A 349 Squadron Supermarine Spitfire VB (AA944) that has come to grief in a landing accident at RAF Acklington in late 1943. (*Aldon Ferguson*)

Squadron on 20 July 1943. After Belgium was overrun by the Germans, several of its squadrons fled to France and fought on. When France surrendered, these squadrons were ordered to return to their home country by their government in exile. Some refused and left for Britain instead. Initially, they were incorporated into established RAF squadrons; however, in February 1942, the first unit manned mainly by Belgium nationals was formed. It was 350 Squadron whose motto was 'Of all the Gauls, the Belgiums are the bravest'. It undertook offensive missions across France for a year until it was transferred to 13 Group Fighter Command and moved to RAF Acklington for a break when several new pilots were posted to the squadron.

During an exercise on 6 April 1943, Sub-Lt A. Boussa was to fly to a point some 70 miles off the coast and the other 350 Squadron Spitfires were to try to intercept him. While flying at 1,000 feet and some 65 miles to sea, Boussa caught sight of an aircraft around 6 miles away and decided to investigate. As he closed, he recognised it to be a Dornier Do 217 in grey and brown camouflage. He dived on it and performed a near head-on attack. At about 3,000 feet, he fired a short burst with machine guns only in order to get the correct deflection. This was followed by one long burst with cannons and machine guns from about 2,400 feet until he passed over the enemy aircraft. During this burst, he saw strikes on the sea all around the Dornier, which then turned to starboard and fell into the sea, sinking immediately. Boussa circled over the area and saw a large oil patch, followed a few seconds later by a body floating in the sea.

On 11 May, while carrying out practice interception flying, Fg Off. Le Large's Spitfire VB (BL370) suffered engine failure at 2,000 feet. He selected a suitable field at Laverock Hall Farm near Blyth to attempt a forced landing. The ground was very wet and muddy; after making a perfect touch-down, one of the Spitfire's cannon dug in. The aircraft flipped and was extensively damaged.

In early June, 350 Squadron left for RAF Ouston, where it undertook convoy patrols. During a landing approach, two of its Spitfires collided and crashed on the edge of the airfield, killing both the pilots. The Squadron was later informed that it was to move back to RAF Acklington, although this prospect was met with little enthusiasm: 'An invitation down south would have considerably changed our outlook on life.'

By 20 July, it had settled in at RAF Acklington on what was the eve of Belgium National Day. It was marked by a dinner for all ranks in the airmen's mess. The Squadron CO made a speech in which he predicted that the next feast day would take place on the Continent. On the National Day itself, most of the personnel were given the day off, so there were non-stop celebrations in the bar. The exception was one section which maintained their Spitfire VCs at readiness. On the 23rd, cannon tests and low-flying practice took place. The same day, two aircraft were scrambled to intercept an enemy aircraft reported off the Farne Islands. On investigation, it turned out to be an RAF Mosquito. Three days later, 350 Squadron's Blue Section escorted convoy *Hatch*—consisting of a liner and a destroyer—out of Newcastle. At the end of the month, three sections of fighters provided aerial cover to the northbound convoy *Kingsmith*. While coming into land on the 27th, Sgt F. Verpoorten noticed black smoke pouring out of the exhaust of his Spitfire VB (AR383). At 500 feet, his engine cut out and he glided to 200 feet. Realising he was not going to reach the runway, he raised his undercarriage and crashed in an adjacent field. Sub-Lt Boussa stated in the accident report:

> The pilot has shown great professional abilities when about to crash. In a few seconds he put his undercarriage up, switched off the contact and managed with great skill to avoid huts in front of him and crash into a small corn field.

In early August, the Belgium Squadron's Spitfires continued training as well as maintaining a section at readiness to protect the sector. On the 25th, 350 Squadron left RAF Acklington for the last time, bound for RAF Hutton Cranswick. Its place was taken by another Belgium unit—349 Squadron—which had been formed only a few months earlier.

The weather was cold and dull in September. Many of the personnel suffered from colds and resorted to wearing woollen underwear. Some of the Spitfires were posted to RAF Digby for two weeks while those remaining at RAF Acklington continued training, which included some dusk and night flying. AOC, AVM Hill, inspected 349 squadron on the 2nd. A few days later, eight of its Spitfires practised high altitude flying. There was some jubilation when the initial issue of stationery arrived. It was first requested in June. Up until then, they had to go round begging essentials from other units. A 'Driver' exercise took place on the 15th; this involved two 349 squadron Spitfires protecting a convoy from mock attacks by a 409 squadron Beaufighter flown by Wg Cdr Reid. In the first attack, the Beaufighter (the 'Driver' aircraft) would probably have dropped a bomb on a destroyer before being shot down. In the second attack, the Beaufighter was 'shot down' before it was able to attack the vessels. In the third and final attack, the Spitfires were unable to intercept the Beaufighter before it could 'bomb' the convoy. Later, back at RAF Acklington, Wg Cdr Reid became involved in a heated argument concerning the assessment of the exercise. Towards the end of the month, most of 349 Squadron's Spitfires had left for Cranfield where they were to have new Merlin engines installed. The medical officer, Plt Off. Adam, claimed to have invented a drug which prevented sea sickness so was posted for three days to an air-sea rescue station. He 'came back very shaken having spent some time underwater in one of HM submarines piloted by inexperienced crews.'

The first re-engined Spitfires began returning to RAF Acklington on 27 September 1943. The same day, the Belgians dispensed with English cuisine and cooked themselves a continental dinner including lobster, game and wine. Wg Cdr Reid and the Station Adjutant were invited. Afterwards, speeches were made, 'including one wishing us a long stay at Acklington. This was politely cheered but only mildly appreciated.'

By 3 October, flying had resumed on a small scale with the Merlin-engined Spitfires. There were English lessons for the many of 349 Squadron's ground crew who lacked a knowledge of the language. One of the Spitfires sustained some minor damage due to the failure of the aircraft's pneumatic system causing it to run into a pile of earth near the end of the runway. Having just had their Spitfires upgraded, the pilots were informed that their unit was to be re-equipped with the long range and low-flying

Spitfire LF VB. By the 16th, twenty had been delivered. Later in October, the squadron was instructed to move to RAF Friston. A road party left in two utility Fords on the 21st, but the main party were transported in a special train. Their aircraft left the following day.

With the departure of the Belgians, it was now the turn of 316 Polish Squadron flying Spitfires to provide fighter cover at RAF Acklington. The squadron had been withdrawn from Southern England for a period of recuperation after providing fighter sweeps over Europe. While flying north from RAF Northolt to their new base, one of the Spitfires were crash landed but the pilot was unhurt. By the end of September 1943, the squadron had settled in: 'Rather lazy life compared with that at Northolt.'

From 7 October, the squadron had one section at readiness, one at fifteen minutes, and a third at thirty minutes. Training was also undertaken including air-to-ground firing and, three days later, there were eleven exercises in dog fighting, formation, and low flying. Training continued throughout November and, at the beginning of December, eighteen aircraft flew to RAF Ayr for instruction at 14 Armament Practice Camp. Intensive air-to-air firing and cine-camera practice was the order of the day. On the ground, pilots shot clay pigeons and even trained with revolvers. No sooner had the squadron returned from RAF Ayr than they were temporarily detached to RAF Digby. Twenty aircraft returned to RAF Acklington on 4 January. Two aircraft were scrambled on the 6th and again on the 14th. Otherwise, flying during January consisted of further training. On the 19th, fourteen pilots undertook navigational exercises. Near the end of the month, there was a twenty-aircraft formation as well as low flying.

On 15 February 1944, the squadron left for RAF Woodvale, but this was not quite the end of a foreign presence at the airfield. A detachment of Hawker Hurricanes flown by 309 (Polish) Squadron were present for much of the summer. Matters had gone full circle, as this was the first type flown by a Polish squadron squadron from RAF Acklington in the early years of the war.

Another nationality represented in the RAF by its own squadrons were the Dutch. Like that of the Belgiums the contingent was relatively small. When Germany invaded the Netherlands in May 1940, the country's Air Force fought back with great determination. In the process, it lost nearly 95 per cent of its pilots. Some of those who survived managed to escape to Britain to form the nucleus of two RAF Squadrons—320 (Netherlands) and 321 (Dutch). Much later, in June 1943, a further RAF unit—322 Squadron (Dutch)—was established, whose motto was 'Actions not Words'. It was equipped with Supermarine Spitfires displaying both RAF roundels and the Dutch orange triangle. On 9 March 1944, the aircraft departed from their base in southern England for RAF Acklington, 'not without feeling of regret for it was at Hawkinge that many pilots did their first operational flying. Everybody felt very near to 'things' there, the French Coast being visible very often.'

The pilots found their new quarters to be centrally heated and rather too warm. On a more positive note, the aircrew were pleased to find that they were to be serviced by their old Echelon (No. 3074), which had many Dutch personnel. The pilots were less than impressed with the roads in Northumberland, describing them as little more than pathways. Shortly after arrival, the squadron received their first Spitfire XIV. A lot of time was spent in obtaining the proper equipment to enable high altitude flying and flying was further delayed by the late arrival of the railway wagon containing the pilots' parachutes. By the 14th, the Spitfires were ready to participate in exercises. A-Flight performed a mock attack on a number of ships including three destroyers, five trawlers and a submarine. In the afternoon they provided air cover for a convoy. Sqn Ldr Bailey paid a visit to the Squadron to give some advice to the pilots on flying the Spitfire XIV.

By 17 March, the squadron had received six of their new machines. The Squadron's commander flew one for the first time and was suitably impressed. He told his colleagues that he was struck by the terrific power delivered by the Griffon engine. Even at the extreme altitude, he did not feel cold or experience any ill effects. He went on to remark that, at this altitude, Solway Firth on the opposite side of the country was clearly visible. The next day, a convoy protection exercise was held which involved circling over six ships travelling north for ten minutes. Orders came on the 29th for A-Flight to make a practice move of six aircraft with their ground crews to RAF Boulmer. At 9.16 a.m. the following day the tannoy ordered the pilots of 322 Squadron to be ready to move. All baggage had to be packed and placed outside the billets immediately. The aircraft took off just after 10.00 a. m. and arrived at RAF Boulmer seven minutes later. Two Spitfires maintained a patrol over the airfield while the others landed and were refuelled. The road party consisted of an ambulance, field kitchen and ground crews as well as a moveable flying control; 'everybody enjoyed the exercise very much and on the whole it was pretty successful except for trouble with starting the Griffon engine.'

On the last day of March, 322 Squadron was ordered into tents. This experience did not go down too well as there was a severe frost during the night. While at RAF Acklington, the squadron was part of 147 Airfield HQ, which was intended to be a mobile unit. Three sections of Spitfires took part in exercise 'Window Eric' in the afternoon. A formation of Halifax bombers, flying at altitudes from 13,000 to 20,000 feet to the north of Newcastle in hazy conditions, acted as the hostile force. The 'enemy aircraft' took evasive action as well as dropping considerable quantities of 'window' to confuse the radar:

> The exercise was intended primarily for night fighters but nevertheless the pilots enjoyed the exercise which was something different especially owing to the excellent evasive action taken by the bombers.

On 5 April, a party was held at the new NAAFI, organised by the Dutch Welfare Committee for ground personnel. The next day, a further practice move was undertaken, again with RAF Boulmer being the destination. When the 'convoy' reached the airfield, they were instructed to dig defensive trenches. *En route*, the Spitfires flew at 450 mph at low level across RAF Milfield in full squadron formation: 'The Station HQ and all the precious files would have been riddled by bullets had it been real.'

On arrival at their destination, some of the Dutch pilots befriended the local residents who provided them with tea and cakes, served by the daughter of the house: 'everybody relaxed a little before a nice fire, but alas not for long. Fg Off. Meljers came in to remind us that, however pleasant the surroundings, trenches had to be dug for war never waits.'

Two Spitfires suddenly appeared and performed a 'beat up' of RAF Boulmer just as 322 Squadron were thinking of lunch. Aircraft became bogged down while taxiing on the grass. It took nearly two hours—and considerable effort—to free them according to the squadron log book:

The domestic site [for the airfield] was picturesquely erected along a sandy beach somewhat distant from the airfield. To several Dutch pilots the tents brought back memories of when the war was yet young. Now the war has matured, yet tents like 'Johnny Walker' go on for ever. The Squadron Adjutant drove the 'readiness pilots' to and fro, being careful to avoid the mined area. As the day wore on and we had been told to treat the inhabitants as 'friendly', a halt was made at The Old Fishing Boat Inn where all the members of the village who are in the Forces have their photographs in a large frame. In order to have a look at these stalwart members of the community it was thought that a visit would be diplomatically speaking, advisable, the liquid amenities being of course purely coincidental.

By 10 April, the squadron had received twenty Spitfire XVIs. Fg Off. Burgwal was flying one of them that day at 45,000 feet when he glimpsed an aircraft emitting what appeared to be black smoke flying over the sea at about 28,000 feet. He flew towards it to investigate, but it disappeared before its identity could be established. The pilot thought it may have been a Junkers Ju 88, although one cannot help wondering that it may have been some form of jet if it was emitting trails of smoke.

On the 11th, 322 Squadron suffered a major blow when it lost one of its most experienced pilots. Fg Off. Jacob Van Hamel's Spitfire XIV (NH700) crashed at Tossen Hill near Whitton, Rothbury. At the time, he was involved in a high altitude test and it was believed that the cause may have been oxygen failure. Some days later, a letter was received from rifleman Seccombe who witnessed the accident:

The roar of the engine was as if it was going all out and looking up I saw it enter a cloud and disappear for a second and re-appear again diving upside down at an extremely fast speed. I thought it was going to pull out but instead it dived straight to earth and burst into a large sheet of flame and also caused a very large explosion.

From an entry in the Squadron's record book:

Van Hamel was buried locally at the little cemetery of Chevington where other pilots are buried. Near the grave could be seen the names of pilots belonging to the Fighting French, Norwegian and other countries at present under the Nazi yoke. A gallant lot of young men through the maze of unpredictable events have found their resting place in this part of Northern England along the North Sea. Good-bye Van Hamel, a good friend, a good companion. Many pilots remarked on the loss to the squadron of such a keen and likeable pilot.

On the 19th, the pilots were informed that certain experimental aircraft were flying over Britain and that further data could be seen at the Station Intelligence Office. Unfortunately, there are no further details as to what it revealed. It is possible it relates to jet aircraft that were being flown by both the Allies and the Germans and may relate to the sighting earlier that month. The Squadron was informed that they were to leave for RAF Harford Bridge. The vehicles departed on the 20th, taking three days to reach its destination: 'Some impressive convoys were seen, all roads may or may not lead to Rome, but they certainly seem to lead somewhere.'

No. 322 Squadron Spitfires flew to their new base on the 23rd. They spent much of the summer of 1944 defending southern England from V1 flying bombs.

# 6

# Hawker Typhoon Squadrons

1 Squadron: July 1942–February 1943, Typhoon Ib and Hurricane IIB
198 Squadron: February–March 1943, Typhoon 1b
63 Squadron: June 1943, Mustang I
56 Squadron: February–March 1944, Typhoon 1b
164 Squadron: March 1944, Typhoon Ib
609 Squadron: March–April 1944, Typhoon 1b
555 Squadron: (3 TEU), May–June 1944, Typhoon

For most of the Second World War, the protection of north-east England in the hours of daylight was the responsibility of squadrons of Hurricanes and Spitfires. The exceptions were Gloster Gladiators at the beginning of the conflict and Typhoons and Mustangs towards its end. The Hawker Typhoon became better known for its role as a ground attack aircraft, but it was originally intended as a fighter to replace the Hurricane and Spitfire. The Typhoon was very nearly cancelled because the early aircraft suffered from structural failures, with the tails separating from the fuselage in flight; the cockpits also had a tendency to fill with carbon monoxide.

The black Hawker Hurricanes of 1 Squadron arrived at RAF Acklington on 8 July 1942, along with a Handley Page Harrow carrying some of the ground crews. The French pilot, Andre Jubelin, described his arrival in his book *The Flying Sailor*:

We flew without incident through the sunny afternoon, from the picturesque Kentish countryside over the Yorkshire moors till at last we arrived in Northumberland. Our new aerodrome was an immense meadow, streaked with magnificent runways of asphalt. It lay in a plain surrounded by wooded hills. After doing our aerobatics on arrival, the squadron broke up. Mac and I prepared to land first. I thought the west wind must be blowing pretty hard, judging by the rigidity of the windsock which scarcely flapped at all against its pole.

No. 1 Squadron had its first three Typhoons delivered on 13 July 1942. Andre Jubelin commented:

They made an extraordinary impression on us. Compared with the Hurricanes which I once found so much bigger than Spitfires, the new machines seem monstrous, with their thick wings, the vast orifice of their air intake and the exceptional degree of spacing between their solid legs.

When taking off, he remarked that it felt as if he was inside a rocket. On 1 August, two pilots were ordered to scramble. That night, there was a further scramble. Throughout the month, there were further alerts. Two of the Squadron's Hurricanes were ordered to scramble on the 11th. This was repeated again in the hours of darkness. During the month, the new Typhoons carried out cannon firing tests, formation flying and other training flights. The Hurricanes still flew most of the operational patrols, including at least one with the Havoc Turbinlite.

In August, some of the aircraft began to depart for other squadrons. Four Hurricane IIs left for 486 Squadron at RAF Wittering on the 15th. A further machine took off for disposal on that day, but returned because of bad weather. On its third attempt to land back at RAF Acklington, it crashed. The pilot, Sgt W. Jones, was dragged clear by two aircraftsmen but not before he had suffered serious burns.

Twenty of the twenty-six pilots in 1 Squadron were declared operational for day flying on Typhoon aircraft on 1 September. It would not be long before they would be in action. A few days later, Sgt Pearce, an Australian, made a belly landing near RAF Longtown in Cumbria. A broken con rod had damaged his engine. He landed in a field and skidded through a fence, before the aircraft burst into flames. Pearce escaped with only shock and bruises. There was further excitement for 1 Squadron the next day, the 6th—A-Flight was scrambled but returned to RAF Acklington without sighting any aircraft. Not long after, at 11.16 a.m., B-Flight took to the air and were vectored by the Sector Controller at Ouston, first northwards to the Farne Islands then back towards Blyth. The Typhoons continued to fly south and were instructed to climb to 30,000 feet.

When over the sea off Redcar, they caught sight of two aircraft at the same height, which then banked and turned west. The Typhoon pilots had now identified them as either Junkers Ju 88s or Messerschmitt Me 210s; the latter type had been intended to be the successor to the Me 110, but only a small number were delivered to the Luftwaffe as the type was very difficult to handle. The intruders turned out to be Messerschmitt Me 210s, each flown by a crew of two. The Typhoons gave chase at 240 mph. Plt Off. Des Perrin turned steeply and closed to 750 feet, firing his cannon. He saw pieces coming off the port engine of one of the Messerschmitts. The Typhoon closed in to about 150 feet and fired a further burst from his cannon. The rudder of the enemy aircraft was damaged. The plane caught fire, then turned on its back and dived vertically. Perrin dived down after the aircraft but blacked out. He 'came to' at 3,000 feet and regained control of his Typhoon. The Messerschmitt Me 210 crashed two miles south-west of Redcar at Fell Briggs Farm. Both crew were killed when their parachutes failed to open.

The second Messerschmitt was attacked by Plt Off. Bridges. When it turned to port, he opened fire and it began diving in a south-east direction. His Typhoon closed to about 600 feet and opened fire again. Hits were observed on the top of the Me 210's fuselage. Pieces began flying off and the port engine caught fire. Bridges turned steeply

A Hawker Typhoon (R7919) of 1 Squadron at RAF Acklington in 1942. (*Aldon Ferguson*)

Only a small number of Messerschmitt Me 210s were built for the Luftwaffe, so they were a rare occurrence in British skies. Two examples were shot down by Hawker Tempests of 1 Squadron from RAF Acklington on 5 September 1942. (*ww2 images*)

and he too blacked out with his aircraft going into a spin. He recovered at 4,000 feet, east of Whitby. The Me 210 (2H+HA) came down at near Fylingthorpe, Yorkshire. The German crew (members of 16/KG6) were captured, one of whom landed in the sea after parachuting to safety. The wreckage was examined by Sector Intelligence who concluded that they were Me 210s. The machines were painted dark grey or black and had white crosses on the wings. They were only the fourth and fifth enemy aircraft to have been shot down by the Hawker Typhoon since it entered service with the RAF and the first Messerschmitt 210 to be shot down over Britain.

Four aircraft were scrambled to patrol the base on 10 September, but this time, no enemy aircraft were encountered. Towards the end of the month, a convoy patrol was flown and exercises were conducted with the Army. At that time, 1 Squadron had twenty Typhoons 1b, one Hurricane 1, and one Miles Magister on strength.

In October 1942, Phillip Sayer, Gloster Aircraft's chief test pilot, arrived to carry out tests on a new gun sight. He had the distinction, in May 1941, of being the first British pilot to fly a jet aircraft. On the 21st, a Wednesday afternoon, he took off in a Hawker Typhoon (R7861), accompanied by Typhoon (R7867) of 1 Squadron, flown by Fg Off. Dobie, to carry out gun firing tests at Druridge Range; nothing was heard from either aircraft again. There were rumours at the time that Phillip Sayer was testing a top secret rocket which exploded and blew off his wing. The most likely explanation is that the two Typhoons collided in mid-air although there was good visibility that day. A patch of oil was later discovered some 4 miles out to sea off Amble. Despite a painstaking investigation, the only other evidence that came to light was an eyewitness who thought he saw something crash into the sea off Coquet Island.

On 9 November, Typhoon 1 (R7868), piloted by Plt Off. T. Bridges was struck on the ground by Typhoon (R8630) and damaged beyond repair. There was a further accident on the 21st, when an aircraft flown by Fg Off. Watson made a forced landing. The aircraft caught fire and was burnt out, but its pilot escaped without injury. Training continued for the remainder of the year interspersed with the occasional scramble.

During January, there were further scrambles but the aircraft, when intercepted, turned out to be 'friendly'. Hostile aircraft were reported in the Sector on the 27th. White Section was ordered into the air at 9.25 a.m., followed by Yellow Sector twenty minutes later; no contact was made.

On 9 February, the Hawker Typhoons of 1 Squadron departed RAF Acklington for the last time when they flew south to their new posting at RAF Biggin Hill. The move did not come a moment too soon, as the pilots were in the 'bad books' of the local constabulary. They had been riding their bicycles without lights to The Trap, a public house popular with aircrews and, on a number of occasions, had had been arrested for this offence. In response, the pilots, on leaving the pub, all mounted their bicycles together and knocked down several policemen who tried to stop them; this lead to a complaint from the Sheriff's Office.

No sooner had the Typhoons of 1 Squadron left that their place was taken by those of 198 Squadron. On 13 February 1943, the unit suffered the first of a number of accidents during its short stay at RAF Acklington. Typhoon (R7690) flown by Sgt Wilks made a belly landing on the airfield after trouble with its undercarriage. The aircraft was being flown back from RAF Henlow where modifications had been made on it.

198 Squadron had a further accident on the 16th. While taking off on an operational scramble, Typhoon (DN439) was struck by a cross-wind, causing the aircraft to ground loop, damaging its undercarriage and mainplane. Its pilot, WO W. Mount, was unhurt.

AVM Malcolm Henderson, AOC 13 Fighter Group, paid a visit to 198 Squadron on the 20th. Six days later, the unit suffered a further accident. FS Freitag, flying Typhoon (R7653) had to make a forced landing on the airfield when his engine failed. His aircraft caught fire, but he managed to extricate himself before the fire gained serious hold. He sustained minor injuries and some burns. This was the first flight of this aircraft since it had returned from modification at Henlow.

During mid-March, RAF Acklington and several other airfields were placed on special alert because of enemy activity in the region. On the 11th at 9.47p.m., four enemy aircraft were reported to be in the vicinity of the airfield. Earlier that day, Sgt K. Bowman had taken off on an operational scramble. When some 25 miles out to sea and at 16,000 feet, his Typhoon I (R8935) experienced engine failure. By the skilful handling he managed to nurse the aircraft back to the coast and made a wheels-up landing at Radcliffe, near Amble. On landing, in spite of a cut face and a blow to the head, Bowman unloaded his cannon and stood by his Typhoon until the police arrived. He was later congratulated by the AOC for making a successful forced landing.

During March, numerous training flights were flown, some of which involved air-to-air firing. There was an escape and evasion exercise on the 18th. Twenty-two pilots were taken some five to six miles from RAF Acklington and then dropped off in pairs. No English was to be spoken by them. Local police had been warned and RAF Regiment Patrols were sent out. Two pilots reached the main guardroom after making the last stage of their journey on bicycles left unattended by two RAF Regiment officers engaged in the search. Four others, including the CO, reached the perimeter track before being captured. 198 Squadron left for RAF Manston on the 23rd, with 350 (Belgium) Squadron's Spitfires taking its place.

Another aircraft that started life as a fighter in the RAF but, like the Hawker Typhoon, was later adapted for the ground attack role was the North American Mustang. The type put in a brief appearance at RAF Acklington with a detachment from 63 Squadron. During June, five Mustang Is carried out a week's training in artillery co-operation with the Army. During their stay, the six officers and thirty-five other ranks lived in tents at the south-west edge of the airfield. This was not the first time aircraft based at RAF Acklington had exercised in conjunction with the Army. In May 1941, five Lysanders and two Proctors undertook artillery co-operation training. The following month, Lysanders from 'C' Squadron carried out tactical reconnaissance exercises with the Northumberland Division as well as practicing dive bombing on the Redesdale Artillery Range.

At the end of the war, 19 Squadron (mentioned elsewhere in the book) flew Mustang IVs from RAF Acklington. In 1944, Hawker Typhoons became a common sight in the skies over Northumberland. Their pilots were not guarding its air space from attack by enemy aircraft but sharpening their skills in destroying targets on the ground in preparation of the invasion of France. Permission had been given in late 1943 for squadrons in the 2nd Tactical Air Force to use RAF Acklington and its ranges in the run-up to the invasion of Europe.

On 23 February 1944, 56 Squadron arrived. Not long after, a Typhoon I (JP611) of 1 Squadron now based at RAF Martlesham Heath, made a forced landing near Acklington. Most days were spent firing cannon and rockets on the local ranges. A visit by members of 56 Squadron was made to the officers billets at Warkworth Grange: 'though plain, give great pleasure as they are like a real last war Squadron Mess. Beer and poker holds sway.'

The weather was particular good for flying on 5 March 1944. Many of the residents of Newbiggin turned out to watch the air-to-ground firing at the nearby range. In the evening there was dusk and night flying. Fg Off. David Hill was one of those involved. He took off in Typhoon (MN123) at 8 p.m. and never returned:

> We only assume that he had an engine 'out' and went into the sea or the rather remote and deserted hills. This is a very severe loss to the Squadron. His charming personality and quiet efficiency were a great help to the Squadron and will be sadly missed.

On the 7th, 56's Hawker Typhoons left for RAF Scorton: 'In spite of many snags, mainly due to the physical incontinence of the camp, we have done quite a lot of work and have received all the help possible.'

No sooner had 56 Squadron departed than 164 Squadron arrived with their Typhoon Is for just over a week's stay. Hot on their heels came 609 Squadron, who had spent some time at RAF Acklington in October 1939. In early 1944, the unit had been assigned with 198 Squadron to the 2nd Tactical Air Force. While at RAF Acklington, the pilots practised dive bombing, although around that time it was announced their main armament would be rockets. On 23 March, shortly after the squadron's arrival, a Typhoon (MN140) took off for a practice flight piloted by Fg Off. F. Detal, a Belgium. Not long after, it crashed and burst into flames near North Seaton Hall, Northumberland, killing its pilot. It was thought that the accident was caused by the Typhoon performing a very tight turn which resulted in Detal losing control. Two days later, the Squadron suffered a further accident. A Typhoon (MN179) burst a tyre on landing, causing the aircraft to turn over onto its back. Its pilot sustained minor injuries.

Typhoons from 3 TEU (Tactical Exercise Unit) were briefly based at RAF Acklington to again provide fighter cover. Sixteen aircraft arrived from RAF Honiley on 29 May and were temporarily given the designation 555 Squadron. The unit occupied one of the dispersal sites and part of the Station Head Quarters for office accommodation. On 5 June 1944, shortly after its arrival, the unit suffered a fatal accident. WO J. Gilbert's Typhoon I (R7822) was flying at low altitude when its engine failed. Gilbert carried out an excellent forced landing with his wheels up at Low Newton-by-the-Sea. Unfortunately his aircraft hit a haystack and burst into flames. Gilbert was unable to escape as the cockpit hood was jammed and rescuers could not release him. There was a further death on the 8th, when an aircraftsman of 3 TEU was found dead in his bed. He had expired from natural causes. With the return of the Spitfires of 504 Squadron, the Typhoons of 3 TEU were relieved of their air defence duties and returned south on 13 June. The following year would see numerous examples of the Typhoon again being based at the airfield with 56 OTU for training purposes.

7

# Night Fighter Squadrons
# 1940–1944

600 Royal Auxiliary Air Force Squadron: October 1940–March 1941, Beaufighter
IF (detachment)
141 Squadron: May–August 1941, Defiant I
141 Squadron: January–June 1942, Beaufighter IF
219 Squadron: June–October 1942, Beaufighter IF
25 Squadron: December 1943–February 1944, Mosquito VI and XVII

In the first year of the war, there were no specialised night fighter squadrons at RAF Acklington. The Hurricanes and Spitfires were expected to provide air defence both in daylight and when darkness fell. It was challenge enough for their pilots to fly them at night, let alone hunt down enemy bombers. Successes were few and far between. Towards the end of 1940, the situation began to change. 600 Royal Auxiliary Air Force Squadron, based at RAF Catterick, detached a number of its Blenheims and later Beaufighters to RAF Acklington. They were equipped with a primitive form of airborne radar and had a crew of two. The pilot could concentrate on flying while the second crew member could search for the enemy aircraft. 600 Squadron detachment ceased in April 1941.

In April 1940, 141 Squadron received its first Boulton Paul Defiants. For the following two years, it spent most of its time in Scotland, but during the spring of 1941, a detachment of its aircraft were sent to RAF Acklington. Nine Defiants of 249 Squadron had previously spent a few days in early June 1940 at the airfield for air firing practice. It was a somewhat retrograde step as the Defiant did not carry airborne radar and was single-engined. On 2 May 1941, B-Flight of 141 Squadron arrived with five Defiants and personnel for night flying duties.

It was not long before they were in action. The Luftwaffe launched heavy air raids on Clydeside and Belfast in the morning of the 6th. Around 120 enemy aircraft were operating over 13 Group area. Some twenty-five Hurricanes, twenty Spitfires, and sixteen Defiants—most from airfields in central Scotland—were airborne between midnight and 4.30 a.m. to counter the attacks. The 141 Squadron Defiants at RAF Acklington were also involved.

On the 5th at 11 p.m., Plt Off. Meredith had taken off with air gunner Sgt Mott to patrol over Hartlepool in N3430. They were then ordered northwards to the Farne

Islands. Shortly after midnight, off Cresswell, the pilot sighted an aircraft about 200 feet below and just to port flying north-west. Meredith turned to port and dived to 200 feet below the aircraft, which he recognised as a Heinkel. Mott fired one very short burst from below. There was a blinding flash. The He 111H (5J+KL) turned to starboard and dived, then hit the sea and exploded. Another Heinkel He 111 crash-landed near the village of Westerhope, Northumberland, after being mauled by a Defiant of 141 Squadron based at RAF Ayr.

The next night, there were further heavy raids on the Clydeside area, with Greenock picked out for particular attention. There were 225 enemy aircraft in 13 Group area. Fg Off. Day and air gunner Plt Off. Lanning had taken off at 11.25 p.m. to patrol over Blyth and Seaham. They were then ordered to orbit over Ashington. Some time later, they spotted a small black dot flying west around 1,000 feet below them. The Defiant dived and manoeuvred to attack the enemy bomber—a Heinkel He 111H (A1+CK)—from below. After a few short bursts of fire, its port engine and wing burst into flames. It dived away, almost colliding with the Defiant and disappearing out of sight. A radio message was intercepted indicating that the Heinkel pilot was going to attempt to fly his crippled machine back to France, but he got no further than the grounds of St. George's Hospital, Morpeth, where it made a forced landing. Despite the plane being on fire as it hit the ground, all five crew managed to escape and were taken prisoner. One of the Germans spat on a nurse who had attempted to render first aid to his injuries. The wreckage burned furiously for over forty minutes. Day and Lanning flew their Defiant back to RAF Acklington, where they refuelled and re-armed.

On their second sortie, they saw a Junkers Ju 88 silhouetted against a bank of cloud near Seaham. Lanning opened fire and the bomber turned away. After a second burst, there was still no visible damage to the Junkers. The Defiant then attempted to execute its next attack at very close range. At this vital moment, its guns temporarily jammed and the bomber disappeared into the night. The Defiant crew claimed it as damaged, but the following day, a Junkers Ju 88 that had made a forced landing was found with its crew on Holy Island. It was credited to Day and Lanning, but in Bill Norham's well researched book *Luftwaffe Losses over Northumberland and Durham*, the author is of the opinion that its demise may have been the responsibility of another night fighter.

On 21 May, Plt Off. Benson landed his Defiant at RAF Acklington with the undercarriage up. The damage to the aircraft was considerable but the crew were not injured. Around a month later, Plt Off. Houghton and air gunner Sgt Allan were on a night patrol in their Defiant when it was fired on by anti-aircraft guns south of Blyth; they survived unscathed. At the beginning of August, 141 Squadron withdrew its detachment of Defiants from RAF Acklington. They were replaced by Defiants from 410 Squadron. Their stay was short lived, as by early September, they had moved to RAF Ouston.

No. 141 Squadron returned to RAF Acklington in early 1942; this time, it was not just a detachment, but the whole squadron. Its Defiants had been replaced by Beaufighter IIs. Like the Defiant, it carried a crew of two but any similarity ended there. The Beaufighter was twin-engine and equipped with airborne radar. It was the most heavily armed fighter in the RAF during the war—it had four 20-mm Hispano cannons in the underside of the forward fuselage and six .303 inch Browning machine guns in the wings, two in the port wing and four in the starboard wing.

A-Flight of 141 Squadron moved from RAF Ayr to RAF Acklington on 18 January 1942, followed by B-Flight on the 29th. Until that time, all the ground crews of fighter squadrons—both those out on flights and dispersals and those working in the hangars on major servicing and repairs—were all on the strength of the squadron. But from now on the personnel who carried out the major servicing—usually in the hangars—would not be on the strength of the Squadron but would be members of a servicing echelon. Those who had previously been responsible for the major servicing of 141 Squadron aircraft were now transferred to No. 3059 Servicing Echelon, which would now follow the squadron wherever it went, as with other echelons and their squadrons. There was some resentment over this change as the men affected felt they were no longer part of an operational squadron.

For the first four days of February 1942 there were heavy and sustained falls of snow. Flying was not resumed until the 5th, when the main runway had been cleared. Air firing and night flying tests were carried out over the next few days. Five Beaufighters were ordered into the air on the night of 15th, when a force of forty Luftwaffe bombers dropped mines at the mouth of the Tyne and attacked harbour installations. Fg Off. Benson and radio observer Sgt Brandon took off just after 7 p.m. and were ordered by the Sector Controller to take up a position 8 miles to the east of Blyth. A GCI radar station then took over and vectored the Beaufighter onto an enemy aircraft. After a chase lasting around five minutes, contact with the enemy was lost. The Beaufighter flew back to the vicinity of RAF Acklington where it was directed towards another aircraft which, almost immediately, registered on the Beaufighter's radar. Benson then closed on the target and obtained visual contact at approximately 450 feet. He recognised it as a Dornier 217 and fired one two-second burst from behind. A further two bursts followed and strikes were observed on the fuselage and tail. The Dornier was then at 1,500 feet and disappeared into cloud about 10 miles east of Blyth. According to Fg Off. Benson, the very heavy slipstream made keeping visual contact against the dark background most difficult. He claimed the Dornier as 'damaged' but shortly afterwards it was confirmed destroyed by Ouston Intelligence. Reports had been received from the Royal Observer Corps that an enemy aircraft had crashed in flames into the sea 4 miles east of Blyth, shortly after 8 p.m. There were no more contacts with the enemy that month. Beaufighter (X7568) crashed on the airfield on the 24th, but its two crew members were uninjured. Lewis Brandon later recorded his exploits in the book *Night Flyer*.

The snow returned at the end of the month and the wintery weather continued into early March. Many of the roads around RAF Acklington were blocked by snow drifts up to 9 feet deep. The wind was so fierce that the runways were blown clear of snow. Conditions improved towards the end of March, allowing flying to resume. During the month, 141 Squadron carried out only ten individual operational patrols, all at night. The usual training programme continued with AI radar and GCI exercises, ZZ homings and landings, cine-camera gun exercises, air firing, and night flying tests.

Four Beaufighters were sent on operational patrols on the night of 15 April. That night, there was considerable activity by German aircraft, thirteen of which made landfall between Berwick and Scarborough. One enemy aircraft approached RAF Acklington with its lights on and dropped incendiaries which fell some 3 miles away. Pilot Flt Lt Cosby and radio observer Plt Off. Komaroff claimed to have damaged one of the German aircraft. Two enemy aircraft of KG506 were operating in the area on the night of the 22nd, with one off them off the coast near Blyth. A 141 Squadron Beaufighter on a practice flight was vectored onto the enemy bomber, but no contact was made. Three days later, at around 4 a.m., a Beaufighter (X7588) crashed into a hillside on the moors near Cragside, Rothbury, about 10 miles from RAF Acklington. It had been a fine night for flying and this was the second trip for Pilot Sgt Johnston and his radio observer Sgt Tait that night; they were both killed and the aircraft wrecked. Cloud at that time extended down to about 400 feet and it was thought the Beaufighter was flying just below it when it struck the slope of the 1,000 foot high hill. Plt Off. Goucher took off at 8.30 a.m. to look for the missing aircraft.

> With the arrival of May came the thoughts of summer time, the long light evenings, clear nights and bags of flying. The weather on this day was good, both night and day and during the early hours of 1st May the Luftwaffe appeared around this coastal area.

At 2 a.m., the first of about thirty enemy aircraft approached from the south-east, entering the Group area to the east of Scarborough. They spread out along the Group's front as far north as St. Abb's Head. About twenty German bombers crossed the coast between Tynemouth and Acklington. Five Beaufighters of 141 Squadron were airborne to counter the hostile force. A Beaufighter flown by CO, Wg Cdr Heycock, and Plt Off. Brandon was vectored onto a Dornier 217, which took evasive action by diving away. Heycock managed to keep it in visual contact and dived after it before opening fire at a height of 6,000 feet. The Dornier 217 then disappeared into cloud. After flying south, the Beaufighter's radar made contact with another Dornier 217. Almost immediately the bomber appeared in sight. Heycock then opened fire from behind with strikes being seen on the starboard wing, fuselage and tail. Blue sparks were emitted by the Dornier, after which it entered a steep dive and at one point looked as it was going to crash. It pulled out of the dive and the Beaufighter descended to make a further attack. Further hits were registered on its fuselage and tail. This time the enemy aircraft shot back, scoring some hits on the Beaufighter. The Dornier then vanished into cloud some 25 miles east of Blyth, apparently out of control. No. 141 Squadron claimed it as damaged.

Shortly before midnight on 19 May, three Beaufighters took to the air, as numerous German aircraft had been detected off the east coast. Only a few radar contacts were made. There were no visual sightings. There were several more alerts as the month drew to a close, but the enemy bombers generally remained out of range, attacking targets well to the south. On the 27th, 141 Squadron commenced air-to-ground firing with the Beaufighters at the ranges at Druridge Bay.

There was a raid by about thirty German aircraft on the night of 4-5 June. Five Beaufighters of 141 Squadron were airborne and three of them opened fire on the enemy bombers. WO Hamer and radio observer FS Walsh had taken off on a practice flight shortly before midnight. Hamer was later ordered to 20,000 feet as enemy aircraft were approaching from the east. A contact was obtained but then lost. After receiving another vector, the Beaufighter got a further radar contact. At a range of 1,000 feet, Hamer could make out the shape of a Dornier 217. On closing to 300 feet, he opened fire. The target took evasive action but hits were registered on its engine. The rear gunner of the Dornier returned fire and hit one of the Beaufighter's engines before the enemy plane vanished in the haze. The Beaufighter landed safely back at RAF Acklington.

Wg Cdr G. Heycock took off at 12.35 a.m. on the 5th with radio observer Plt Off. Watts. He was then handed over to Goldsborough Chain Home Low Radar Station. After a long chase, the Beaufighter's radar picked up a contact at its maximum range of 4½ miles. Heycock then identified it as a Dornier 217, closed in to 150 feet and opened fire. The enemy aircraft promptly made a steep turn to port and dived away. Heycock had anticipated this and was able to dive steeper than the Dornier, keeping in visual contact, but it escaped by making another turn and crossing directly above the Beaufighter.

The third contact with the enemy was made by Fg Off. J. Benson and radio observer Plt Off. Brandon. At about 1.30 a.m., they got a contact at 7,500 feet at the maximum range, east of the Tyne. The enemy aircraft was weaving gently. The Beaufighter closed in and identified it as a Dornier 217 by its exhausts. A two-second burst was fired from behind, but no strikes were seen. Benson had to pull up to avoid a collision. Before the Dornier disappeared, the dorsal gunner managed to hit the Beaufighter, causing some minor damage. The skirmish took place 12 miles east of Seaham. The same night there were a number of Turbinlite patrols by Havocs based at RAF Acklington (mentioned elsewhere in the text).

Most of the flights made by 141 Squadron were usually of a more routine nature, but one practice flight on 9 June did not go as intended. Sgt Clee, pilot, with radio observer Sgt Grant and Sgt Marshall, a new radio observer to the squadron, took off shortly before 4 p.m. on a night flying test. Trouble developed with the undercarriage of their Beaufighter (X7574) when it hit a bump on take-off. Grant and Marshall were ordered to bail out and made safe parachute descents without difficulty. The jumps were made when the aircraft was flying straight and level and at an altitude of 6,500 feet. Sgt Clee remained in the Beaufighter and flew it back to RAF Acklington where he made a successful crash landing.

On 21 June, 141 Squadron was ordered south to RAF Tangmere on the south coast. 43 Squadron had departed RAF Acklington to the same airfield earlier in the month. Fourteen Beaufighters left in formation on the 23rd. They landed at their new base in perfect weather: 'The change from the chilly winds of Acklington was enjoyed by all.'

No sooner had 141 Squadron departed, than the Beaufighter IFs of 219 Squadron flew north from RAF Tangmere to take its place. Ever since its formation in 1939, the unit—whose motto was 'From Dusk till Dawn'—had specialised in night fighting.

It had built up a formidable reputation, having destroyed numerous enemy aircraft by the time it arrived at RAF Acklington on 23 June 1942. Some thirty ground crew flew to their new posting in Handley Page Harrows; the rest came by rail. With the summer solstice just passed, there were long hours of daylight in Northern England. The squadron records relate:

> The most outstanding conclusion drawn from the first night on was that as far as night flying went it was 'a piece of cake', the Northern lights enabled visuals to be obtained at a range of 4 or 5 miles, even at 1 a.m. cockpit lights and torches are eliminated.

On 27 June 1942, Sqn Ldr Topham flew one of the new dihedral tailplane Beaufighters and was impressed with the new machine. He was one of the RAF's top night fighter aces and by the end of the war was credited with the destruction of thirteen enemy aircraft, five of which were claimed while he was serving with 219 squadron.

The weather was good on the first day of July. A firing test was carried out; when night fell, five Beaufighters were up, sharpening their GCI skills. The next day, Sqn Ldr Topham tested one of the new Beaufighters that were in the process of being delivered to the Squadron. There was an accident later that day when Sgt Lewis could not get the undercarriage of his aircraft (R2244) to lock properly and crashed on landing. He was unhurt, as was his navigator. Another more serious accident took place in the early hours of the 6th. Plt Off. Carroll and navigator Sgt Hobday had been airborne for just seven minutes in Beaufighter VIF (X7940), when one of its engines burst into flames. The pilot parachuted to safety, but Hobday became entangled in the escape hatch and was unable to exit the doomed aircraft. It hit the ground at 2.57 a.m., 400 yards from Causey Park Hall, just over 4 miles to the north of Morpeth. A lamb and two ewes were killed in the explosion, but the trapped crewman survived the experience with only a broken ankle and burns to his face. The Squadron diary remarked that it was 'an extraordinary lucky escape.'

Six Beaufighters hurtled down RAF Acklington's runway not long after midnight on 7 July. The ICI chemical works and other industrial sites on Teesside were under attack from fifty bombers of Luftflotte 3. Under GCI control, Sqn Ldr J. Topham was directed towards a Dornier 217 at around 12,000 feet near Amble. Once his Beaufighter (X8221) had closed to within 900 feet of the target, Topham made visual contact. The pilot of the Dornier tried to evade his pursuer by performing violent dives and climbs. These tactics were to no avail as Topham narrowed his range to around 700 feet and opened fire, hitting the tail and fuselage of the Dornier. The bomber dived towards the sea followed by the Beaufighter, whose crew eventually lost sight of it. As Sqn Ldr. Topham circled, he caught sight of an explosion several miles away. On closer investigation, a large number of small fires were seen on the sea. It was thought the Dornier he destroyed was U5+BT of 9/KG2. Soldiers of a coastal battery at Amble told RAF Acklington that they had seen tracer fire in the sky to the south. This was followed by a burst of flames that fell towards the sea.

Later the same night, another 219 Squadron Beaufighter, flown by Flt Lt John Willson and directed by Northstead GCI radar station, intercepted a Dornier 217,

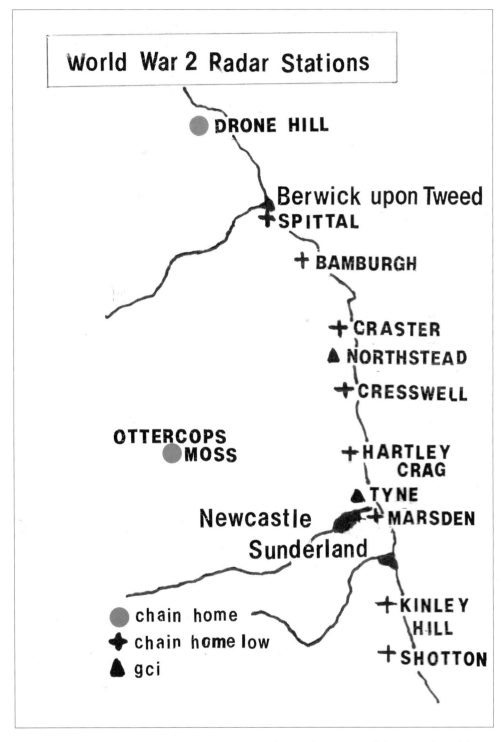

The location of radar stations in north-east England in the latter part of the Second World War. (*Malcolm Fife*)

some 20 miles out to sea off Seaham. When the Dornier had closed to a range of about 4 miles it was detected by the night fighter's radar. The navigator, Plt Off. D. Bunch, guided the Beaufighter closer to the enemy plane, until Willson caught sight of it flying about 1,000 feet above him. The bomber's crew were now aware they were being followed and its gunners opened fire as it performed evasive action in an effort to shake off the Beaufighter. It descended rapidly from 13,000 feet to 4,000 feet, but the Beaufighter was still on its tail. Willson opened fire. The enemy gunners replied, hitting his tail. By this time, the bomber was emitting clouds of black smoke. Some 50 miles east of Whitby, it finally managed to shake off its tormenter by diving down to 300 feet over the sea and then vanishing. It was thought that the crippled aircraft managed to almost reach its base in the Netherlands where it crashed, killing its crew of three.

Despite being mid-summer, the weather over the next few days was bad and there was little flying. By 18 July, there had been some improvement and seven aircraft were airborne on test flights during the day. At night, five crews undertook a GCI exercise. The improvement in conditions did not last; the weather closed in again. On the 25th July, it was noted: 'quiet during the day but night was very eventful ... the Hun was over this sector.'

A return visit was made on the 26th by twenty-two Dornier 217s of KG2, flying from the Netherlands. Their main target was a shipyard on the Tees and the ICI works at Billingham. In response, three Beaufighters were scrambled shortly after midnight with 1 Squadron Hurricanes. Wg Cdr Moon chased one bomber over a considerable distance but it eventually escaped. Sqn Ldr Topham and his observer, Fg Off. Berridge, had more luck, shooting down two Dornier 217s in the space of fifty minutes. The first was destroyed at a height of 10,000 feet. It received numerous hits from machine guns and cannon before turning over twice and bursting into flames. It then plunged towards the sea but disappeared into the murk of the night before Topham could see exactly what happened to it. The second Dornier put up more resistance. As the Beaufighter closed in for the kill, the gunner in the dorsal turret fired back. The hostile aircraft took evasive action but it was not enough to save it. Sqn Ldr Topham opened fire at a range about 600 feet. The Dornier turned to port and plunged towards the sea in flames. When it hit the water, it was seen by the Beaufighter crew to explode.

Fine weather at the start of August enabled night flying practice and tests to be undertaken. An Army co-operation and recognition exercise was also laid on, with two Beaufighters and an Oxford. There was considerable enemy activity on the 8th, with several German bombers flying almost over RAF Acklington. The following night, there were further raids by German bombers but none of them entered the sector patrolled by RAF Acklington's squadrons. On the 11th, five pilots of B-flight carried out air firing practice. FS Watson took off in the afternoon and soon after found that the port elevator of his Beaufighter was not functioning. He instructed his navigator, Sgt Miller, to bail out in case there was an accident on landing. Miller parachuted to safety, conveniently landing on the airfield. Watson decided he could land the Beaufighter using only the trim and touched down without incident.

There was unfortunately a serious accident late at night on the 19th. Plt Off. Carroll was flying Beaufighter VIF (X8219) over the North Sea on a GCI test. When some 40 miles off the coast at 11,000 feet, the aircraft's elevator failed, causing it to go into a steep dive. Despite this, both Carroll and his navigator, Plt Off. H. Kendrick, managed to bail out. Four 219 Squadron Beaufighters took off to search for their colleagues in the dark. Three rescue launches were also sent to search the area where the aircraft had crashed into the sea. The next day, one found Plt Off. Carroll, some four miles north of the wreckage. He was none the worse for the experience. A Douglas Havoc involved in the search had shone its searchlight on him but failed to see him. Aircraft continued searching for Plt Off. H. Kendrick, but could find no trace of the missing airman.

On the night of the 28th, bombs fell on or near Sunderland, Seaham, Alnwick, and Acklington. Several 219 Squadron Beaufighters took off in response. Northstead GCI vectored Flt Lt Horne and his navigator, FS Alcock, on to an enemy bomber at 14,000 feet. The pilot first caught sight of it when it was 2,000 feet in front of him. When the Beaufighter had closed the distance to just over 400 feet, Horne opened fire. The bomber was hit on its inner wing and entered a steep dive. Although the Beaufighter followed, the crippled machine disappeared from view at an altitude of 8,000 feet. Horne claimed a Heinkel He 111 destroyed. This brought 219 Squadron's score of enemy aircraft destroyed to forty-four. In the book *Luftwaffe Losses over Northumberland and Durham* by Bill Norman, the author believes that Flt Lt Horne mistook a Ju 88 for a He 111. The same night, a Junkers Ju 88 was brought down near Seaham. Two of its crew were picked up by a convoy, but the other two were lost. The survivors stated they were attacked by a night fighter around the same time as Flt Lt Horne recorded in his report. The captured Germans said their Junkers had caught fire shortly after being shot at. One of the engines failed and the pilot attempted to fly to the coast, where he intended to make a crash landing. But the fire had by now such a grip that the pilot gave the instruction to abandon the aircraft. The pilot was the last to leave the doomed machine and narrowly escaped plunging into the sea with it.

There was a further raid on the night of 6–7 September 1942, when the Luftwaffe struck targets on the Tees with around fifteen aircraft. 219 Squadron flew a number of patrols and chased a number of the hostile aircraft, but the closest they came was around 5 miles. Several crews were airborne on the night of the 15th; enemy aircraft were detected but they did not enter the Sector. On the 19th, tests were carried out during the day: 'At night the Hun was over earlier than usual and 'A' Flight had some chases.'

Sqn Ldr J. Topham was on a practice flight with Fg Off. H. Berridge when they were vectored towards enemy aircraft approaching Sunderland. He eventually spotted a silhouette against a moonlit cloud some 2,000 feet above him. It was travelling very slowly and Topham had to lower his undercarriage to prevent his Beaufighter overtaking what was by now recognisable as a Dornier 217. The enemy aircraft then executed a number of violent evasive manoeuvres at an altitude of between 9,000–12,000 feet in an attempt to shake off the night fighter. They were unsuccessful, and Topham closed to within 600 feet and opened fire. The bomber began the emit clouds of black smoke and showers of red sparks before bursting into flames. It fell into the sea from about 8,000 feet, near the mouth of the River Tyne. The four man crew of the Dornier (U5+KR) perished in the crash. There was a narrow escape for Sgt Lewis on the 23rd, when his aircraft struck a ventilator on RAF Acklington's gym on take-off. The undercarriage collapsed on landing but Sgt Lewis was unhurt.

No. 219 Squadron's final encounter with the Luftwaffe while based at RAF Acklington took place on the night of 16 October 1942. Crews went to Newcastle for dinghy drill during the day. At night, enemy aircraft bombed Sunderland, starting large fires. At the time, a Beaufighter was airborne on a GCI exercise. The pilot, Fg Off. Farrar, and navigator, Sgt Crozier, decided to fly south to investigate. Soon, they had made radar contact with a hostile aircraft above them. As the Beaufighter closed in, a searchlight illuminated the intended target, a Dornier 217. Farrar opened fire; within seconds, the Dornier was a mass of flames and plunged into the sea near Roker, Sunderland. Some of the burning wreckage floated on the sea before sinking. It was Fg Off. Farrar's first destruction of an enemy machine.

On 19 October, 219 Squadron was informed that it was to move to RAF Scorton: 'Nice, probably get more business there.' The next day, A-Flight took off for their new base. B-Flight departed on the 21st, with the ground crews travelling by rail arriving in the afternoon: 'All agree it is a move for the better although Scorton station is still in an unfinished state and billets not as good as Acklington.'

Towards the end of December 1943, 25 Squadron, equipped with the Mosquito VI, arrived for a brief stay at RAF Acklington. This was not the first visit for this squadron, as two of its Beaufighters had been deployed here in an effort to bolster the night fighter defences at the end of May 1941. In December 1943, two aircraft were placed at readiness and a further two at thirty minutes notice, but this was not the main reason for 25 Squadron's move to RAF Acklington. Shortly after their arrival, the first Mosquito NF.XVIIs were delivered to them. By the end of the month, 25 Squadron had received five examples. This new version of the Mosquito, with its American airborne radar, was so secret that each aircraft carried the suffix 'g' in their serial number; it denoted that it should have an armed guard placed on it at all times when it was on the ground. Strict limitations on the use of this equipment were imposed, including a total ban on its use over enemy-held territory or within range of possible German electronic intelligence sensors. This was why RAF Acklington was selected for the training of 25 Squadron. Wellingtons arrived with the new Mosquitos and were used to familiarise the crews with the advanced airborne radar. Training exercises were flown in conjunction with Northstead GCI. There was no flying on 25 December when 'at midnight a very fine fireworks display was put up from the control tower by certain revellers in celebration of Xmas Day.'

The Wellingtons were flying the next day, continuing their role as flying classrooms. On New Year's Eve, Wg Cdr Wight Boycott was flying a Mosquito when he was asked to search for a Beaufighter from RAF Charterhall that had gone into the sea. Unfortunately, he could find no trace of it. There were strong winds at the beginning of January, but the training continued including air-to-sea firing practice. On the nights of the 4th and 5th, the waxing moon and exceptional visibility made practice interceptions easy. Eight aircraft were airborne. No. 25 Squadron were also gaining the impression that their equipment was infallible. The following night, there was a

A Luftwaffe Dornier Do 217 flying over the Netherlands. Many of the air raids on north-east England were launched from this country. The Do 217 was a more powerful version of the better-known Dornier 17. (*ww2 images*)

An all-black de Havilland Mosquito NF.11 (DD750). Towards the end of the war, Mosquitos replaced the Beaufighter in the night fighter role. (*ww2 images*)

scramble, but the aircraft turned out to be 'friendly'. Six patrols were flown on the nights of the 7th and 8th, but not without incident. A Mosquito flown by FS Forryan with Sgt Bulter came into land, but approached the airfield too high. The aircraft bounced on landing, one of its wingtips caught the ground, and it cart-wheeled. Fortunately, there was no fire, but the machine was badly damaged. Forryan had both legs broken while Bulter was thrown out, sustaining nothing more than cuts and bruises. The Squadron Records comments: 'A shaky do for the crew.'

Although the weather at the beginning at January was ideal for flying, it began to deteriorate by the middle of the month. On some days the airfield was covered by fog and on the 15th flying had to be curtailed when a change in the wind direction covered the airfield in industrial haze from Newcastle; it then hung around for several days. By the 20th, the weather had improved and training resumed. That day, a 25 Squadron Mosquito took a member of the Royal Navy from Northstead GCI for a flight. It turned out to be one that he would not forget in a hurry. When the aircraft became airborne, its undercarriage would not lock up or down. The pilot then made two approaches. The first was so low that the plane bounced on its retracted wheels, bending the propeller tips. On the second attempt, the pilot set the Mosquito down at around 120 mph. It skidded across wet grass for about 900 feet before it came to a rest with its tail twisted off. Nine Mosquitos undertook practice interceptions on the night of the 21st and 22nd. A further aircraft was scrambled and sent to investigate an aircraft that had been orbiting over Flamborough Head for over two hours. It was later thought to be a British bomber, but the radar plot faded before the Mosquito arrived. On the 29th, visuals were made on three Lancasters and two Stirlings on a practice interception exercise by a single Mosquito. All were claimed to have been 'murdered'.

The first fall of snow in the area fell on 4 February 1944. The following day, 25 Squadron left for RAF Coltishall with seventeen Mosquito NF.XVIIs on strength.

# 8

# Canadian and
# U.S. Night Fighter Squadrons

406 Squadron: 5 May 1941–1 February 1942, Blenheim IF and IVF, Beaufighter IIF
410 Squadron (detachment): 6 August 1941–September 1941, Defiant
410 Squadron: 20 October 1942–21 February 1943, Beaufighter IIF, Mosquito II
409 Squadron: February–December 1943, Beaufighter VIF
416 Squadron USAAF: 10 June–4 August 1943
409 Squadron: 23 February–19 December 1943, 5 February–1 March 1944, Mosquito XIII

For much of the war, Canadian squadrons were responsible for providing the night fighter force to defend north-east England. The first Royal Canadian Air Force (RCAF) night fighter unit in Britain was 406 Squadron, formed on 10 May 1941 at RAF Acklington. Its motto was 'We Kill By Night'. A few days later, it received its first Blenheim. By early June, it had eight Blenheim Is and one Blenheim IV on strength. Not long after, the much superior Bristol Beaufighter arrived.

Operational duties commenced on 17 June 1941. As the weather was poor at RAF Acklington, two of its aircraft were deployed to RAF Ouston. On the 25th, a 406 Squadron aircraft was dispatched to carry out a search for some German airmen reported to be in a dinghy in the sea. Shortly before midday two airmen were located. The Blenheim's radio was faulty so it flew to RAF Thornaby to report the position of the airmen. In the afternoon, a 406 Squadron Beaufighter took off to look for a German flying boat which had reportedly been also searching for the men who had landed in the sea. There was no trace of the aircraft. As June drew to a close, the squadron received its first six Bristol Beaufighter IIs which would replace the short-lived Blenheims. In addition, a Beaufighter V—a Beaufighter II with a Boulton Paul gun turret installed immediately behind the pilot—arrived for the squadron. It was intended to be used operationally on dark nights and evaluated for its handling characteristics at low speeds with the guns trained on a target. The same day it arrived, a Beaufighter (R2348) landed with one engine on fire. The pilot Flt Lt Hillock was commended by AOC No. 13 Group for his safe landing.

On 22 July, two of 406 Squadron's aircraft spent an hour endeavouring to intercept an enemy machine but their efforts were to no avail. It had been hoped the squadron

Crews of 406 Squadron, RCAF, being dropped at the dispersal near their Bristol Beaufighters in September 1941. (*ww2 images*)

would have been fully operational by the end of August, but this was delayed because some of the aircraft were still being fitted with exhaust flame dampers to make them less visible at night.

The first fatal accident suffered by 406 Squadron took place on 14 September when Beaufighter IF (R2473) crashed some three miles south-west of the airfield while approaching to land. It dived into the ground at an angle of 45 degrees, killing the crew of two—pilot Fg Off. H. Finlay and wireless operator and air gunner, FS E. Vickers. They were given a full military funeral and buried locally in Chevington Cemetery. The Squadron supplied the escorts, pall bearers, and firing party.

There were heavy air raids on North and South Shields on 30 September, killing eighteen people and badly damaging numerous houses and industrial premises. An enemy aircraft also dropped anti-personnel bombs on RAF Ouston. The raids did not go unopposed; 406 Squadron had seven of its aircraft airborne that night. Beaufighter II (R2388) had to return to base because of radio failure. Sqn Ldr J. Leathart obtained a radar contact on one enemy aircraft but was unable to close to visual range, as he was distracted by anti-aircraft fire from the ground and from naval ships escorting a convoy. An enemy aircraft had a narrow escape when it turned and rapidly dived away before Beaufighter II (R2307) was close enough to attack. Wg Cdr D. Morris had more success in Beaufighter II (R2378). He chased an enemy bomber that was descending and heading back across the North Sea. After making radar contact, he caught sight of a Junkers Ju 88 at 9,000 feet, approximately 3,000 feet in front of him. The Beaufighter closed in and, at a range of 300 feet, opened fire with both cannons and machine guns. Hits were seen on the Junkers fuselage, which responded by shooting back. After a third burst of gunfire from the Beaufighter, the enemy bomber turned slowly to starboard and went into a steep dive, its cockpit ablaze. It then crashed into the sea some 50 miles east of the mouth of the Tyne. It is thought the identity of the Junkers was possibly 4D+MR. A bullet had struck the radiator of the port engine of Morris's aircraft and he returned to RAF Acklington on one engine. Once on the ground a close examination of the Beaufighter revealed that bullets had also struck the starboard engine.

The Germans were not deterred by this loss, returning on 2 October to bomb Tyneside again. The attack was mounted by fifty bombers, of which forty-nine reached north-east England. They included eleven Dornier Do 217s from II/KG2, seventeen Junkers Ju 88s from III/KG30, three Dornier Do 217s from III/KG40, twelve Heinkel He 111s from III/KG40 and three Junkers Ju 88s from KGr 606. There were numerous fatalities in these heavy raids, mainly in and around South Shields. Five of 406 Squadron's Beaufighters did their best to defend Tyneside from the enemy attack on what was a bright moonlight night. At 10 p.m. Flt Lt Hillock and Sgt Bell located a Junkers Ju 88 flying between Sunderland and Newcastle. They had visual contact with the enemy bomber and pursued it northwards up the coast until it was some 15 miles east of Blyth. The Junkers took evasive action by diving from 11,000 feet to 500 feet. The Beaufighter fired three short bursts, hitting the aircraft on the fuselage. Despite coming within 150 feet, the Beaufighter lost contact with its quarry as it merged into the night.

Wg Cdr Morris with Sgt A. Rix as his radar operator had more luck. At 10.50 p.m. they caught sight of a Heinkel He 111 crossing the coast near Lexbury. It made violent manoeuvres in an attempt to shake off the Beaufighter. While over Alnwick, Morris opened fire. The enemy aircraft shot back before diving down from 9,000 to 5,000 feet and heading back towards the coast. The Beaufighter remained on its tail and opened fire again. At 2,500 feet, the Heinkel was still in a dive and at this point Morris lost contact with it. It was later reported that one member of the crew had parachuted from the bomber to escape being burned by the fire in the fuselage and had been captured near 'a small town'. A flash was seen off the coast which was thought to have been caused by the crippled machine crashing into the sea. Although 406 Squadron counted it as a definite 'kill', this may have been wishful thinking. A Heinkel He 111H-6 of III/KG40 is recorded in Luftwaffe Records as landing in a seriously damaged condition at Soesterberg in the Netherlands. It was minus the radio operator Walter Kaiser who had bailed out during the flight.

Wg Cdr Morris returned to RAF Acklington to re–arm, then took off again. At 9.15 p.m., contact was made with a Dornier Do 217 approaching Tynemouth from the east. The Beaufighter closed in on the bomber using its AI radar. When it was within 300 feet, Morris fired a first burst. The Dornier shot back, although its rudder was now damaged and its mechanic seriously wounded. A second burst from the Beaufighter's guns was followed by a terrific explosion. The enemy aircraft disappeared as Morris flew through a cloud of sparks. Four parachutes were observed above the sea some three miles east of Tynemouth. Three of the crew of the Do 217 (U5+GN), including the injured mechanic, were picked up by a trawler. The pilot, Fritz Menzel, was drowned before he could be rescued. For these victories, Wg Cdr Morris was awarded the Distinguished Flying Cross and his radar operator, Sergeant A. Rix, received the Distinguished Flying Medal.

In the early morning of 16 October, around 3.15 a.m., Sgt Schoolbread and Sgt Farquharson made radar contact with some very slow-moving targets. The crew of a second Beaufighter noted:

> [They] obtained visual of a peculiar shape like a very stubby fuselage and broad short wings without visible engines or tail planes. After overshooting owing to the slow speed of this object, they had several radar readings but no visual contacts. It was subsequently presumed that the objects pursued during these patrols were barrage balloons. Eleven had broken away from their moorings around the Tyne, which agreed with the controller's observed blips and the position was such as times and wind would lead one to expect. A wind varying in direction from NNE to EAST in high altitude and gale [ropes] dragging on the water, may explain apparently variations in course as if steered by aircraft.

Three radar contacts were obtained by a Beaufighter in the evening of 21 October. The enemy aircraft employed extreme evasive tactics and vanished.

In early November, several Beaufighters were unserviceable while awaiting spare parts from the manufacturers. In the evening of the 7th, two members of the Canadian Press arrived at RAF Acklington to experience at first hand the operations of 406 Squadron. There had been little enemy activity recently because of the full moon. While a dinner was taking place in the mess, to which the journalists had been invited, a message was delivered stating that enemy aircraft were approaching the coast. Everyone rushed in the direction of the dispersal hut. Two Beaufighters which were at readiness and took off immediately, followed a short time later by a further two. On their return, Plt Off. Harding stated that he had fired his guns at an enemy aircraft and had seen the shells register hits on its fuselage. He claimed one Heinkel He 111 as damaged. Sqn Ldr R. Wills in another Beaufighter found that the throttle arm had stuck at full on and he was unable to throttle back one of the engines. He was forced to land on one engine: 'The press representatives departed the following morning well satisfied.'

At this time, 406 Squadron also had a detachment of aircraft at RAF Scorton. The weather improved on 14 November and practice flying and training resumed. Flt Lt Hillock with Sgt M. Bell took off in Beaufighter II (R2435) in the late afternoon on a routine night flying test. A few moments after the aircraft had taken off, it began to climb violently as though the stabilizer had been wound fully tail heavy. All efforts by the pilot to counteract this failed. From a height of 100 to 150 feet the aircraft was belly-landed in a wood of small trees just beyond the south-west boundary of the airfield. Although the Beaufighter was completely destroyed, neither of its crew were hurt. A Court of Inquiry found that a new tail assembly had been incorrectly installed.

Sgt L. Dumares with W. Staines took off on 25 November in Beaufighter II (R2389) to search for a German meteorological reconnaissance plane that had been regularly appearing over the north-east coast of England. These planes were often referred to as 'weather willies'. The Beaufighter flew a 120 miles out to sea but the enemy aircraft was not seen.

An official Air Ministry photograph of B-Flight, 406 Squadron, RCAF, with one of their Merlin-engined Bristol Beaufighter MK IIFs (T3037). (*Imperial War Museum*)

There was a further visit by the press on 3 December 1941, this time from newspapers located in the north of England. After dinner, the guests watched Beaufighters of 406 Squadron take off for patrol on what was a clear moonlit night. To the disappointment of the journalists, the aircraft returned from their patrols without encountering any enemy aircraft. The visitors were then allowed to interview the pilots. Accounts of the work of 406 Squadron appeared not long after in several newspapers, including the Yorkshire Post and the Sunderland Echo. At 8.15 a.m. on the 8th, a car full of airmen returning to their quarters at the end of night duty overturned on the perimeter track. Aircraftsman Popely of A-Flight was killed while the other occupants escaped with minor injuries. On a more positive note, technicians from the Canadian Broadcasting Corporation arrived later that day to record Christmas messages to be broadcast to friends and relatives at home. In what turned out to be an eventful day, Sgt Schoolbread and Sgt Farquharson were on a practice flight when they detected an unknown beacon flashing in the neighbourhood of Rock Midstead Farm to the north of Alnwick. An investigation on the ground was made by special signals officers Fg Off. E. Tull and Plt Off. W. Wadsworth:

> No mechanical reason for the beacon could be discovered but tales of suspicious actions of a retired Army Colonel and his wife, former residents of Berlin made an interesting story which was forwarded to 13 Group Headquarters for further investigation.

The initial results of the investigation of the 'ghost beacon' were disclosed at the end of December. It was concluded that enemy agents were not involved.

On 8 December, there were heavy air raids on Tyneside. It was speculated that RAF Acklington may also have been a target, as several bombs fell 2 miles to the south of it. Sector ordered six Beaufighters to intercept the German aircraft. Plt Off. H. Underwood, with Sgt Horex, took off at 9.45 p.m. on their first operational flight against the enemy. Radar contact was soon made with a Dornier Do 17 at a range of 9,000 yards. When visual contact was established at 500 feet, the Beaufighter was found to be below the Dornier and therefore silhouetted against cloud. This was later blamed on faulty instruments giving an incorrect altitude. The Dornier crew realised they were about to be attacked, the pilot took evasive action, and the aircraft disappeared into the night.

Sqn Ldr Willis, accompanied by Sgt Wilcox, took off in an unfamiliar Beaufighter (T3038), as their usual aircraft was unserviceable with an oil leak in the starboard engine. They had to return to RAF Acklington as the radio was faulty and messages from the controller could not be understood. This would have made it impossible for them to be directed towards the enemy from the radar on the ground. A third Beaufighter became airborne shortly after 10 p.m. and was vectored north towards the Drem sector. No enemy aircraft were detected during its patrol. Plt Off. D. C. Furse and Plt Off. Downes in another Beaufighter made momentary visual contact with a Junkers Ju 88, but had no chance to open fire. Their equipment also malfunctioned. A fifth 406 Squadron Beaufighter took off at 10.30 p.m. and was ordered to orbit the airfield. They continued to do this until they were forced to land due to the failure of an engine. Their landing resulted in some damage to the aircraft.

Wg Cdr D. Morris was eager not to miss the opportunity of confronting the enemy, but his aircraft was already in the air. Despite the protests of the Engineering Officer, he commandeered a Beaufighter (R2461) which had been designated unserviceable. With G. B. Houghton as his radar operator, he took off at 11.20 p.m. and flew out to sea in a south-easterly direction. At a point about 25 miles north-east of Newcastle, Morris simultaneously got both a radar and visual contact of a Heinkel He 111 passing behind him. The Beaufighter dived and closed in, to be met with fire from the lower rear gunner. The German bomber took evasive action, but Morris succeeded in firing several bursts from his cannon at a range of 300 to 450 feet. With all cannon ammunition exhausted, the attack was pressed home with the Browning machine guns. The Heinkel crew fought back with accurate fire from the upper and lower rear gun positions, then visual contact was lost when the enemy aircraft disappeared into cloud. During the engagement, both aircraft had descended from 9,000 feet to 2,500 feet. At the lower height, the radar in the Beaufighter would not operate effectively, preventing Morris from chasing the enemy any further. A bullet had pierced the Beaufighter's port engine causing it to seize. The starboard engine had also malfunctioned. Rapidly losing height, the Beaufighter crossed the coast at no more than 300 feet and, almost hedge-hopping the rest of the way, made it back to RAF Acklington.

A gift of a bottle of scotch was received from Air Cdre L. Stevens, who had held the post of AOC RCAF Overseas, to mark the victories by 406 Squadron: 'the Celebration took place immediately after the receipt of the bottle.' Sgt Dawe took off for a practice flight at 7.45 p.m. on 20 December. Just under two hours later, both his engines failed at a height of 13,000 feet. Instead of abandoning his machine, he managed to carry out a forced landing on what was a very dark night. Four days later, Sgt Davis and Cpl Morling of the Provost Marshal's Branch, Air Ministry, arrived to investigate the causes of the engine and equipment failures which had resulted in several forced landings in the previous weeks.

All practice flying on the 25th was completed before midday, and the members of 406 Squadron were given the rest of the day off. Christmas Dinner for the airmen took place in several sittings between 11.30 a.m. and 1.30 p.m. The officers' dinner was held in the station mess after the King's Speech at 3.30 p.m.; the party was brought to an abrupt end at 6 p.m. when there was a warning that several enemy aircraft were approaching the east coast. A Beaufighter that had been at readiness took off to intercept, but no German aircraft were seen. There was bad weather on the 29th and it was assumed that the enemy would not put in an appearance, but Sgt Marriot and Sgt Didben were ordered to take off to investigate a possible intruder. It turned out to be a Coastal Command aircraft seeking its way home. Soon after there was another report of an enemy aircraft approaching the coast from the south-east. Several radar contacts were made by Sgt Marriot's Beaufighter, ten miles to the east of Blyth. Marriot was unable to make visual contact with the aircraft. By this time, Wg Cdr Morris and Plt Off. Rix were airborne in another Beaufighter and patrolling the coast. Brief contact was made with an enemy aircraft, but it was too far away to be intercepted.

A further 406 Squadron Beaufighter flown by Plt Off. J. Firth and Sgt Harding was ordered to patrol over Acklington at a height of 10,000 feet. A hostile bomber was detected approaching from the north-east and they were instructed to intercept it. The Beaufighter was vectored to within five miles. It was then handed over to the GCI radar station to direct it accurately to the vicinity of the German aircraft, which then registered on the Beaufighter's radar at a range of 12,000 feet. After closing to around 2,000 feet, Firth could make out the shape of a Junkers Ju 88. Two short bursts from the cannons and machine guns caused the Junkers to burst into flames and begin disintegrating. On its way down from 11,500 feet, it made what looked like a stall turn before diving steeply. The crew of the Beaufighter then caught sight of an explosion through the clouds. A Special Constable in the village of Cresswell later reported that he had seen the Junkers Ju 88 fall into the sea, some 3 miles offshore. It was in flames and in three pieces. The last piece to fall burned for about ten minutes on the surface before disappearing. The Junkers Ju 88 was S4+LH of KGr. 1./506. There was no trace of its crew of four.

New Year 1942 got off to a bad start. A Beaufighter (R2281) took off on a test flight on the 6th, but its port engine failed just as it was leaving the ground. Ice caused the aircraft to skid into a Nissen hut at the end of the runway, completely destroying the aircraft; its crew of two were unhurt. Worse was to come. Plt Off. H. Wooler with Sgt T. Williams took off in Beaufighter (T3037) at 9.15 p.m., but crashed ten minutes later at Storswood Colliery, Widderington, narrowly missing two houses. The aircraft was seen to emerge from a cloud, apparently stall and go into a spin. The bodies of the two airmen were thrown clear of the aircraft when it struck some trees in a small wood, seconds before it hit the ground. Plt Off. Wooler from Jamaica was buried

*Left:* Flt Lt Johnson and Sgt Morris pose for the camera beside a Merlin-engined Bristol Beaufighter II, 406 Squadron, RCAF, September 1941. (*ww2 images*)

*Below:* Flt Lt J. Maclennan, the Intelligence Officer of 406 Squadron, RCAF, hanging aircraft recognition models in his office. (*Imperial War Museum*)

locally in Chevington Cemetery. Six pilot officers of the Squadron acted as honorary pale bearers. The funeral of Sgt T. Williams took place in his home town of Llandeilo, Carmarthenshire.

Plans were now in hand to move 406 Squadron to RAF Ayr and for 141 Squadron to take its place. The first to leave were an officer with seventy-seven NCOs on 15 January. The same day, AVM Edwards, AOC RCAF Overseas, paid a visit to RAF Acklington. A farewell party was held for the officers in the home of Sir Leonard and Lady Milburn, located near the airfield. The first aircraft departed on the 17th, but the weather closed in the next day and delayed further departures. On the 28th, an attempt was made to ferry the remaining aircraft to Ayr. Four took off, three of which had to return to RAF Acklington. Most of the remaining personnel had departed by rail by the end of the month. Several aircraft had to stay behind, as the weather did not improve until early February.

## 410 Squadron

Soon after 410 Squadron was formed in June 1941 at RAF Ayr, its single-engined Boulton Paul Defiants deployed to RAF Drem, 20 miles to the east of Edinburgh. The aircraft was noted for having a four-gun turret situated just behind the pilot. All offensive armament was concentrated in it and there were no forward firing guns. It was envisaged that the Defiant would be able to destroy formations of enemy bombers using just these turret guns. This concept was flawed as it did not envisage that the hostile aircraft would be protected by agile fighter aircraft which could out-manoeuvre the Defiant. As it was vulnerable to attack, the Defiant was soon relegated to the night fighter role. From August 1941, until 410 Squadron moved away from RAF Drem in the summer of 1942, it regularly had detachments at RAF Acklington and RAF Ouston.

Boulton Paul Defiant I night fighter (V1110) of 410 Squadron, RCAF, probably at RAF Drem, January 1942. (*Imperial War Museum*)

On 16 March 1942, one of 410's Defiant Is (V1183) crashed on an air test from RAF Acklington, killing both its crew, Plt Off. I. Constant and Plt Off. W. Lewis. It stalled while performing unauthorised low flying near Dissington Hall, Stamfordham, which at that time housed WAAFs. Another 410 Squadron Defiant crashed near Beacon Hill, Longhorsley, while on patrol from RAF Drem. The pilot was killed, but the air gunner parachuted to safety.

After a short stay at RAF Scorton, on 20 October 1942, 410 Squadron in its entirety deployed to RAF Acklington. By this time, its Defiants had been replaced by the Bristol Beaufighter IIF. The day after its arrival, the squadron carried out high and low evasive exercises. The aircrew were informed that they would shortly receive Mosquitos to replace their Beaufighters: 'loud cheers on all sides.'

On the 24th, there was great excitement with the arrival of a dual-control Mosquito for training. The next day, several crew members did 'circuits and bumps' in the new aircraft. Fg Off. Jack Devlin made his first flight in the Mosquito on the 26th. During the flight, one of the Mosquito's engines decided to expire. Despite the fact that he was not familiar with the type, coupled with a malfunction of the flaps, Jack Devlin managed to return to the airfield and made a perfect landing at 140 mph. The squadron record book records: 'very good show indeed.'

At the end of October, the unit had ten Beaufighter IIs, one Mosquito III, one Oxford and one Magister. During November, training continued during the long hours of winter darkness, although much of it including air firing, beam approaches and single engine landing exercises, was undertaken in daylight hours. A flight of Beaufighters stood by, ready to scramble at a moment's notice. Fg Off. Johnston, with his navigator Sgt Deyer, took off at 5 p.m. on the 8th to intercept what was thought to be a hostile aircraft. They returned within fifty minutes, as the unidentified aircraft turned out to be 'friendly'. A somewhat poignant entry occurs in the Squadron records for 11 November: 'Another Armistice Day comes by. The good news from Africa makes one hope that it will be the last observed under the present conditions.'

Unfortunately, this would not be the case. The following day, a mock attack was carried out on RAF Acklington. All 410 Squadron members were up by 5 a.m. for the exercise which commenced at 6.45 a.m. There was a further mock air raid on the last day of the month which involved an attack by several of the squadron's aircraft. Later that day, actual enemy aircraft were detected heading across the North Sea towards the coast. Three aircraft were scrambled at 8.35 p.m., but no contact was made, as the hostiles turned and headed towards home.

Mosquitos continued to be delivered throughout December. A German weather reconnaissance aircraft was detected flying over the North Sea on a number of occasions and during the month, 410 Squadron made a considerable effort to intercept it. On the 6th, three crews of A-Flight patrolled the skies for the 'weatherman', as it was called but there was no sign of it. Further patrols went out on the 8th, 9th and 11th involving three aircraft but these also proved fruitless. There was another alert on the 16th, but it turned out to be an allied machine. Two days later, B-Flight was scrambled at 10 p.m., but no contact was made 'as the bandits were already heading home.'

Training continued, even on Christmas Eve, with air-to-sea firing at the ranges and beam approach exercises. 'Fg Off. R. Currie reported seeing an elderly man in a red suit making a ZZ approach with reindeers at 4,000 feet at approximately 23.59 hours.' An entry in the Squadron record book relates:

Flying continued even on Christmas Day. Another Christmas, not white other than in the song 'I'm dreaming of a White Christmas'. Morale of the squadron reached a new peak today. Everyone well fed and happy though hoping to be back home next year. Many fine greetings from our Prime Minister, Governor General, Minister for National Defence, Air Vice Marshal Curtis and our Air Officer Commanding were all gratefully received and cordially reciprocated.

A Christmas Dinner was held in the Officers' Mess on Boxing Day: 'A Grand Dinner and Wizard Party.' But it was not all festivities that day. Three crews from A-Flight took off in search of the elusive German weather reconnaissance aircraft.

410 Squadron's strength at the end of 1942 was as follows:

PERSONNEL

|  | Aircrew | Ground Crew | Total |
| --- | --- | --- | --- |
| RCAF Officers | 24 | 6 | 30 |
| RCAF Airmen | 12 | 148 | 160 |
| RAF Officers | 1 | 0 | 1 |
| RAF Airmen | 12 | 58 | 70 |
| U.S. Signal Corps | 0 | 1 | 1 |

AIRCRAFT

| | |
| --- | --- |
| Bristol Beaufighter II | 8 |
| De Havilland Mosquito II | 16 |
| De Havilland Mosquito III | 1 |
| Airspeed Oxford II | 1 |
| Miles Magister | 1 |

The Commander-in-Chief of the RCAF was less than impressed with the Squadron's paperwork for December and dispatched an abrupt letter from his office in London. There were various discrepancies between the operational record book and other forms submitted—for example, according to form 540, three crews attempted to intercept the German weather reconnaissance aircraft. Another form contradicted this, mentioning only one. A further entry recorded that 22 December was a quiet day with only some practice flying carried out. A corresponding entry showed that three aircraft had undertaken a patrol.

In early 1943, the Squadron continued training and converting to the Mosquito NF.11 night fighter. There was a major setback on 23 January when a Mosquito II (HJ919) stalled during a tight turn while low flying. It plunged into the sea about

A memorial to RAF Acklington in Chevington Cemetery. (*Malcolm Fife*)

Chevington Cemetery, which is located a short distance to the south east of the site of the former RAF Acklington, close to Broomhill. It contains the graves of many airmen stationed here who perished in flying accidents as well as seventeen airment who were shot down over Northumberland. (*Malcolm Fife*)

a mile from Seahouses Coast Guard Station. The pilot, FS Garth Mills, and his navigator were both reported as missing. Three days later, 410 Squadron suffered a further accident, although fortunately it was less serious and no one was hurt. While attempting to land, a Mosquito NF.11 (DZ246) overshot and collided with a petrol bowser as well as a shed. During the month, 410 Squadron were also in action against enemy bombers. On the 22nd, eight Dornier Do 217s and seven Junkers Ju 88s from IX Fliegerkorps dropped bombs on a number of towns on the north-east Coast. At 8.30 p.m., three Mosquitos of B-flight were scrambled from RAF Acklington. One of them, flown by FS B. Haight with Sgt Kipling, made contact with a Dornier Do 217 at 9,000 feet. The Mosquito closed in on the enemy bomber and, when only 300 feet from it, opened fire. The port engine was hit and the Dornier entered a spiral dive. The Mosquito followed it on its downward descent, opening fire twice more. At 3,000 feet, Haight lost sight of the enemy aircraft when it disappeared into low cloud. He was credited with its destruction, as at the same time, an enemy bomber was seen by members of the Royal Observer Corps to crash into the sea off Hartlepool.

At the end of February 1943, 410 Squadron departed south to RAF Coleby Grange.

## 409 Squadron

409 Squadron, was the third and last Canadian night fighter squadron to be based at RAF Acklington and replaced 410 Squadron. By the time 409 Squadron deployed to the base, raids by Luftwaffe aircraft were becoming a rare occurrence, so there was little opportunity for the aircrew to test their skills in actual combat. Much of their time was spent on training and practice flights. When 409 Squadron arrived, it had fifteen Bristol Beaufighter VIs, two Airspeed Oxfords and one Miles Magister. An air detachment of 409's Beaufighters moved to RAF Drem on instructions of 13 Group to maintain 'Night State' at that station. One aircraft was to be at readiness, with a second to be available within thirty minutes.

On 24 February, the day after the squadron's arrival at RAF Acklington, one of its Beaufighter VIs (X8109) crashed at RAF Ouston. The pilot had to make a forced landing at this airfield as an engine had caught fire. In order to bring the aircraft to an abrupt halt to facilitate his escape, he retracted the undercarriage immediately he touched down. There was a further accident on 17 March; while taking off, a Beaufighter (X8259) struck some trees on the edge of the airfield. The aircraft received some damage, but was able to land safely.

There were several heavy air raids on Tyneside during March 1943. Beaufighters based at RAF Scorton mounted many of the interception sorties and destroyed a number of enemy bombers. Four scrambles took place from RAF Acklington on the night of 22 March. One Beaufighter made a fleeting contact with a German aircraft: 'the enemy is very wary when he comes over and flies low and jinks violently.' The Squadron log book goes on to state: 'One enemy aircraft crashed in this area and is believed to be the result of a chase. No claim is made.'

Not long after, the squadron had second thoughts and decided to claim it. Two nights later, on 24–25 March, there were a further four scrambles. Fifty-two Luftwaffe bombers had taken off to attack Edinburgh. The raid turned out to be a disaster for the Germans. Only fourteen aircraft managed to reach their target, and a number of others got lost in poor weather and flew into high ground in Scotland and Northern England. A Junkers Ju 88 (3E+HM) of 5./KG6 was encountered by Sqn Ldr G. Elms, who fired a large number of three-second bursts at it. A claim was initially put in for damaging it but it was later confirmed destroyed. The enemy aircraft had crashed 4 miles east of Earlston in the Scottish Borders, killing its crew.

With the reduction in Luftwaffe activity over Britain, some of the aircraft used by Fighter Command were switched to a ground attack role. In mid-April, three Beaufighters of 409 Squadron departed for RAF Middle Wallop to undertake operations against the German forces in Continental Europe. They destroyed several railway locomotives in France while operating from the south of England. Also in mid-April, a letter was received from the CO of RAF Eshott ordering that pilots of 409 Squadron and 309 Squadron should be instructed not to make low-level flights over his airfield or any others in the region which were occupied by Operational Training Units. Around the same time Sgt Hildebrand, flying a Beaufighter (X8209), crashed on landing when the undercarriage collapsed.

On 15 May 1943, four aircraft were scrambled to intercept a raid on the Newcastle area. Two fleeting visual sightings were the only contacts made. A Beaufighter flown by Flt Lt Bower was fired on by anti-aircraft guns despite flashing downward recognition lights and shooting off Very flares—'a shaky do' exclaimed the entry for that day in the squadron records.

Four days later, a Beaufighter (X8209) flown by Sgt Hildebrand crashed on landing when its undercarriage collapsed. The pilot was uninjured. High wind and occasional showers were experienced on the 23rd. Cine-camera gun and CGI exercises were undertaken with Northstead radar station.

Early the next day, German bombers were detected approaching the coast. A formation of thirty-six Junkers Ju 88s of KG6 and thirty-five Dornier Do 217s from KG2 and II./KG40 along with Dornier Do 217s of KG66, acting as pathfinders, had been ordered to attack factories and industrial installations in the vicinity of Sunderland Docks. Sqn Ldr G. Bower with Sgt W. Beynon took off at 2.40 a.m.; when their Beaufighter was at an altitude of 9,000 feet, Bower glimpsed a twin-engined aircraft flying above them, but it disappeared a few seconds later. The GCI controller then vectored them on to another target. A short time later, Beynon made radar contact. When over North Tyneside, Bower could make out the shape of a bomber some 2,000 feet ahead of him. As he got closer, he identified it as a Dornier Do 217. When the Beaufighter had closed to around 750 feet, he opened fire. The second burst of fire from both the cannons and machine guns hit the Dornier's starboard wing. A third burst caused the starboard engine to catch fire. The bomber ceased taking evasive action and entered a gentle dive. At 3,000 feet, it rolled over and then plummeted into the sea. It is thought the identity of the Dornier was U5+HH of 1./ KG2; its crew of four were listed as missing. A further two German bombers were lost in the raid from undetermined causes. This Do 217 had the distinction of being the last German aircraft of the war to be destroyed by an Acklington-based aircraft. The same night, Sgt Hildebrand and Plt Off. Wakeman claimed to have damaged a Junkers Ju 88. Installations around Sunderland Docks sustained serious damage.

On 25 May, three Beaufighters flew over local towns and villages escorted by some Spitfires as part of the 'Wings for Victory' week. At the beginning of June, three Beaufighter VIs of 409 Squadron returned from detachment to RAF Peterhead. The detachment would be resumed later in the year. On 12 June, the port engine of a Beaufighter (X8216) failed on take-off, causing the pilot, FS Allen, to swing his aircraft and crash into a field adjoining the airfield. Both crew members received minor injuries but their aircraft was extensively damaged.

The strength of 409 Squadron at 30 June was twenty-six Beaufighter VIs, one Airspeed Oxford and one Miles Magister. Its personnel consisted of the following:

|                     | RCAF | RAF |
|---------------------|------|-----|
| Officer Pilots      | 17   | 0   |
| Officer Aircrew     | 8    | 6   |
| Officer Ground Crew | 4    | 0   |
| OR Pilots           | 6    | 0   |
| OR Pilots           | 0    | 10  |
| OR Ground Crew      | 200  | 17  |

At 4.30 p.m. on 5 July, there was a serious accident. Tiger Moth (DE509), with Fg Off. B. Kelly and Plt Off. F. Burnard of 65 Squadron, Ayr, was undertaking flights as part of a training scheme with local army units. The aircraft took off without warning across the runway in use. On becoming airborne, it collided with a Beaufighter (X8151) of 409 Squadron, piloted by Plt Off. A. Mc Phail, which had taken off from the main runway. A catastrophic accident was avoided thanks to Mc Phail's flying skills. When a collision was imminent, he executed a climbing turn to starboard, but the Beaufighter had been struck under the port wing, damaging its port elevator and the rudder. Its airspeed indicator stopped functioning and the aircraft became difficult to control. After making four circuits, another Beaufighter was scrambled to assist Mc Phail. It lead him towards the runway and he made a successful landing without the use of his flaps. The Tiger Moth was not so fortunate, being totally wrecked. Fg Off. Kelly and Plt Off. Burnard were taken to the sick quarters where they were placed on open arrest, pending a charge for a flagrant disobedience of airfield and flying regulations being placed against them.

A distraction from the routine duties of the squadron occurred on 8 July 1943, when two officers of the Soviet Military Mission, Major Rudoy and Capt. Diky arrived at the station, accompanied by their Russian speaking liaison officer. The purpose of their visit was to observe Fighter Command's methods of night fighter operations and methods of interception. There was some concern as to how much they should be allowed to see. Permission was granted from the Air Ministry allowing them to visit the GCI radar station at Northsteads, but they were not to be made aware of the most recent developments in airborne radar sets. Wg Cdr Reid of 409 Squadron, who was at that time Acting Commander of RAF Acklington, undertook to explain to the Russians the operation of the equipment used for night fighter interceptions. The delegation stayed until the 10th. The previous day, a Beaufighter II (T3143) piloted by Fg Off. Leask with LAC Pearson as passenger, crashed when landing after a test flight. The starboard undercarriage did not appear to fully lock down. The aircraft touched down at a speed of around 140 mph, running off the end of the runway and through a hedge. It was only at this point that the undercarriage gave way. The aircraft's fuselage was badly damaged, but its crew was unhurt. The cause was attributed to a manufacturing fault which resulted in the failure of the hydraulic system through loss of hydraulic fluid when the flaps were selected as 'down'.

At the beginning of August, Wg Cdr Reid of 409 Squadron made a further report to the Station Commander regarding excessive wear to the Beaufighter's tyres. On examination of the tyres, it was found that six were so badly cut and worn that there was a high probability they would burst on the next landing. The main source of the problem was the shale that was laid on one of the dispersal areas some three years previously in an attempt to overcome the boggy nature of the ground. Measures were undertaken to sweep up loose stones on the runways. It was decided that this area should be cordoned off and seeded with grass.

On the 5th, one aircraft was dispatched on an air-sea rescue mission to search for the crew for a Flying Fortress that had come down in the sea off Berwick-upon-Tweed. There was no trace of it, despite a one-hour search. Two days later, the weather was still poor. A Beaufighter was detailed to intercept a Flying Fortress which had just crossed the Atlantic but had missed its destination of Prestwick and was flying east towards Norway. Unfortunately, it crashed before the Beaufighter could render assistance. The wreckage was found a short time later, but there were no survivors. A break from routine training took place on the 18th, when a Beaufighter undertook a North Sea patrol taking it to within 30 miles of the coast of Norway: 'It was uneventful as Jerry would not play.'

By mid-August, most of 409 Squadron's aircraft had been equipped with Mk VIII AI radar which pleased the crews as it was more accurate and straightforward to use than the earlier versions. Around this time, a Junkers Ju 88 had been making daily weather reconnaissance flights over the North Sea. The Beaufighters of 604 Squadron took off from RAF Scorton in the morning of the 23rd to ambush it. They orbited over the sea for some time until they were informed by radar that it was 6 miles ahead. The Junkers Ju 88's port engine caught fire after being hit by the cannon and machine guns of one of the Beaufighters. With his aircraft now burning furiously and both engines issuing clouds of white smoke, the German pilot attempted to ditch. The crippled Junkers bounced on the water once and then exploded. It sank in ten seconds, leaving only an inflated dinghy on the surface, but with no sign of life. A report was received that two German aircraft were searching for the downed aircraft (D7+FH) and its four man crew. Two 409 Squadron Beaufighters were scrambled from RAF Acklington to intercept them. After patrolling for over seven hours they returned without sight of the German aircraft.

Weather was cloudy with 2,000 feet visibility on the 30th. Word was received that an armada of Danish fishing vessels was sailing east across the North Sea in an attempt to escape the occupying Germans. Some ten aircraft were involved in the search at different times of the day. The boats were eventually sighted in the afternoon, some 240 miles due east of the coast of northern England. There were around twenty-five in number, of all shapes and between 40 and 70 feet in length. Many were under sail. The following day two aircraft were dispatched from RAF Acklington to look for the Danish boats but could not find them.

A further search and rescue mission was undertaken on 3 September. Two aircraft were dispatched to look for a plane that had ditched near the mouth of the Tyne. They found it just before dawn, still floating in the water with the crew nearby. Rescue craft were directed towards them. On the 26th, a Beaufighter was scrambled to look for a Liberator that had flown from North America and had overshot Britain. Sqn Ldr Bower was unable to find it, having to spend most of his time flying through solid cloud. At this time, 409 Squadron also had a detachment at RAF Peterhead.

Training continued in October. On the 14th, a dinghy demonstration was held and related in the squadron records:

A preview by the Squadron Engineer Officer to the somewhat sceptical aircrew that the dinghy would actually pop out and inflate once the immersion switch was wet. The demonstration was called 'Wing Dinghies—their application and mis-application'. Duly at 13.25 hours in best R.C.A.F. tradition, all the aircrews assembled agape before the mighty Beau which stood there in majestic splendour. In his best manner Mick took the centre of the stage, announced that the demonstration was about to begin, signalled to the chief aide and stepped back with the look of a proud father who is showing off his first born son to neighbours. A pan of salt water had been prepared in readiness. The stage was set. The aircrew stepped back apprehensively so that when the cover and the dinghy popped out no-one would be hurt by hurtling bits. All was ready—the Sergeant plunged the immersion switch into the water. Everyone watched the wing. Every eye glued on the dinghy—and nothing happened. Switched the switch around—still nothing happened. Then he began frenziedly splashing around—still nothing happened. Mick began to fidget—still nothing happened. He sent an erk (aircraftsman) into the cockpit to pull the release lever there. A faint hissing ensued, Mick relaxed. The hissing continued and a faint thread of steam came from the panel. Again everybody cowered back under cover and waited—and waited. Finally Mick had the cover pulled off the wing. The dinghy was still rolled tight and the $CO_2$ bottle was manufacturing dry ice as fast as it would go. Mick had the dinghy pulled out onto the ground. Inert it lay there hissing malevolently. Mick struggled with it but it still lay without movement. This proved too much for the crowd. Their release of breath sounded like a clap of thunder and they came out from under their shelters. Ribald comments were heard as the crowd went about their duties. At tea time on passing the hangar there it was a fully inflated dinghy. Not to be beaten Mick had tried another bottle and it worked. Mick stood by beaming happily—but the aircrew still wear a sceptical look when immersion switches are mentioned.

There was a scramble on 20 October, as enemy aircraft were reported to be approaching the sector. Nothing was seen but a lone Halifax. Enemy aircraft were notable by their absence in autumn 1943. Routine training continued on most days. For example, on 7 November there was night flying training, GCI runs, dusk landings, calibration tests and camera gun exercises. Having to maintain detachments at RAF Coleby Grange and RAF Peterhead put a strain on the resources of 409 Squadron. Serviceability of the Beaufighters at RAF Acklington reached a low ebb. Two aircraft were scrambled on 12 November to locate a lost Airspeed Oxford. Despite inclement weather, it was found and escorted to RAF Acklington—'an exceedingly fine effort.'

A few days later on the 15th, the weather was clear but there was a strong wind. 409 Squadron was instructed to keep its Beaufighters on day readiness after completing their night duty. They were less than pleased with this. At 8.45 a.m., the FOC (Flight Operations Centre) reiterated this request. The 409 Squadron officer who took the call thought that this was unreasonable and suggested to FOC 'that if he remove his shanks from the table put aside his tea and take down the blackout curtains he would witness one Anson and two OTU Spitfires performing wondrous capers above his head.'

FOC replied that the order had come from the operational Spitfire squadron who could not taxi their machines in the high winds. The over exasperated 409 Squadron officer 'then offered to have his pilots taxi all Spitfires into the wind at the end of the correct runway, get out, then strap in the Spitfire pilots so all would be ready for a quick getaway.' The Spitfire squadron then agreed to go onto readiness state in place of the Beaufighters!

Drama of different form occurred on 7 December. Fg Off. Sandford's aircraft suffered port engine failure. Once he managed to bring the Beaufighter under control, he broke cloud to find himself over Newcastle among barrage balloons. He managed to avoid them and land safely back at RAF Acklington. On the 17th, 409 Squadron was ordered to move in its entirety to RAF Coleby Grange. Fifteen Beaufighters departed the following day. The ground crew travelled by a special train consisting of three passenger coaches and twelve freight wagons. When it stopped at some stations as it made its way south, some members of the public attempted to board it, believing it was the London express.

This was not the end of the Canadians' association with RAF Acklington. The squadron returned briefly in February 1944 when it re-equipped with the Mosquito NF. XIII. It still had some Beaufighters on strength on 20 April 1944, when three of these aircraft were ordered on a defensive patrol over the Humber as enemy aircraft had been reported in the area. One of the Beaufighters experienced an engine fire when some 40 miles offshore. The pilot, Flt Sgt Sherret, managed to extinguish the flames by feathering the engine and flew back to RAF Acklington on one engine. In early May, 409 Squadron returned south again.

The summer of 1943 saw an American Night Fighter squadron alongside the Canadians at RAF Acklington. 416 Squadron had been formed at Orlando Air Base in Florida at the beginning of that year. It trained on the Douglas P-70 Havoc, a modified A-20 Havoc bomber, which used a US version of the British Mk IV radar. At that time, the P-70 was the only American night fighter available. After completing its initial training by April, the squadron crossed the Atlantic on the RMS *Queen Elizabeth* and landed in Great Britain on 11 May. Here, it received Bristol Beaufighters until an American night fighter became available. It was not unusual for RAF Squadrons to operate US aircraft, but it was far more unusual for USAAF to have British-built machines on charge.

In early June, B-flight 409 Squadron moved to a new dispersal point to make way for 416 USAAF Squadron. Lt Ratz arrived with an advance party on 8 June 1943. This was followed two days later by the main detachment, which arrived by rail from RAF Cranfield. It consisted of twenty officers and around 160 enlisted men. The move was completed the following day, when a further five officers and eighty-six men of other ranks arrived. Training was to start immediately. By the 12th, only four of the squadron's Bristol Beaufighter VIs were at RAF Acklington. A conference was held in the Station Commander's Office with 416 USAAF Squadron's CO, Major Davis, to co-ordinate a training programme. Up to this point, the Americans had settled in without any trouble. Matters took a turn for the worse on 21 June. A 416 USAAF Squadron Beaufighter IF (V8769) crashed at Hermitage Farm, Warkworth, killing its pilot, Lt Leggett. The crash was attributed to engine failure due to fuel shortage.

On 1 July, Lt-Col. Frank Carroll, Inspector General of the 8th Fighter Command, USAAF, arrived by air to carry out an inspection of the squadron; he stayed only a few hours. There was a shortage of accommodation for the American personnel. They were transferred to tents that were thought appropriate for their training, as they would be under canvas for their future deployments. At the weekly meeting of the Station messing committee, 'complaints re food from 416 Squadron USAAF have been surprisingly few and of a minor nature which is gratifying in that few of their personnel have been in the country for long. A friendly and co-operative spirit appears to prevail in this unit.'

At 4.30 p.m. on 15 July, a Beaufighter flown by Second Lieutenant Kelly with Cpl Simpson made a very heavy landing, which caused its port undercarriage to collapse. Neither of the occupants were hurt but the aircraft sustained damage to its fuselage, engine and propeller.

Six days later, a signal was received from HQ 44 instructing that 416 Squadron USAAF was to move to RAF Portreath in Cornwall prior to its deployment to Ras El Ma near Alexandria, Egypt. Fighter Command requested Coastal Command to supply four Bristol Beaufighters with experienced crews to escort the American squadron on its flight to the Middle East. To ensure these aircraft were fit for purpose, they were to arrive at Acklington before the end of the month. Here, they were to undertake long-range endurance flights at an altitude of 8,000 feet. A farewell dinner was organised by 416 Squadron in the Airmen's Dining Hall on 24 July, to which the Station Commander and staff were invited; this was followed by an all ranks dance. Due to the unauthorised arrival of another USAAF Squadron at RAF Portreath, the departure was delayed.

On 1 August, a Beaufighter 11F (V8832) crashed on take-off, coming down in a field adjoining the airfield, ploughing through a hedge and a fence. The pilot escaped without injury, but his radio observer sustained injuries to his spine and was taken to Ashington Hospital. Members of the RAF Regiment guarded the wreckage. The cause of the crash was the failure of a governing device on the starboard airscrew.

The tangled wreckage of a USAAF Bristol Beaufighter of 416 Squadron. The US star on its fuselage is visible on the right side of the photo. (*ww2 images*)

Another view of the wreckage of a USAAF Bristol Beaufighter of 416 Squadron, which came to grief during training at RAF Acklington in 1943. (*ww2 images*)

On 3 August, 416 Squadron USAAF received a message to move immediately. At 1 p.m. the next day, eleven aircraft, led by the four Beaufighters of Coastal Command, took off for RAF Portreath. Shortly after take-off, Beaufighter (KV904), flown by Fg Off. Brewer and radio/observer Fg Off. Lawniski, experienced a fire in one of its engines. It crash landed close to RAF Eshott and caught fire. Its crew were pulled clear from the flames by PC Laudie and Special Constable Hall of the Broomhill Police. They were taken to Ashington Hospital, suffering from burns, lacerations and shock. 416 Squadron USAAF never reached its intended base in Egypt, ending up in Algeria instead. Wg Cdr Graham, the Station Commander, attended a conference at RAF Digby, where the future arrival of more USAAF squadrons was discussed. However, no further USAAF squadrons were destined to use RAF Acklington during the Second World War.

# 9

# The Douglas Havoc Turbinlite

1460 Flight and 539 Squadron: December 1941–January 1943

Perhaps the most unusual aircraft to be deployed at RAF Acklington in the Second World War was the Douglas Havoc Turbinlite. In the early months of the conflict, Britain's defence against night-time raids by enemy bombers was found to be sadly lacking. Airborne radar was bulky and had to be installed in twin-engined aircraft such as the Blenheim. In an attempt to give the fighter aircraft more agility, seventy Douglas Havocs were fitted with AI Mk 1V radar plus a powerful searchlight in the nose powered by heavy batteries. These aircraft were to track down enemy bombers and, when close to their quarry, switch on their searchlight. Accompanying high performance fighters, such as the Hawker Hurricane, would then dispatch the hostile aircraft illuminated by the Havoc. It was one of those ideas that worked well in theory, but was very difficult to put into practice.

Initially, several flights were formed with the Havoc Turbinlite across the country, with a total of ten airfields eventually being home to the type. 1460 Flight began to form at RAF Acklington on 15 December 1941. Sqn Ldr Denholm arrived a few days later to take command of it. Continual poor weather in January 1942 reduced flying to a minimum, but a number of elementary Turbinlite practice flights were made in conjunction with 43 Squadron's Hurricanes. Additional aircrew continued to arrive at the airfield during that month.

Snow and fog limited activities in early February. Flt Lt J. Morton and Plt Off. J. Slater arrived with the Flight's second Turbinlite aircraft from RAF Heston. The first full night Turbinlite practice was carried out on 11 February, with Sqn Ldr Denholm flying the Havoc and Flt Lt May, the satellite aircraft. The exercise was a failure, as the radio of the aircraft acting as the target broke down so that it was impossible to effect a radar interception. The next Turbinlite exercise was held on the night of 25–26 February; it also turned out to be a failure. The choice of a Hurricane as the target aircraft proved unwise because of its far superior performance. The airborne radar of the Havoc also failed. Later in the morning of the 26th, a Havoc Turbinlite took to the air again and successfully illuminated the target aircraft for the first time. In the afternoon, a series of experiments were carried out on the effect of the Turbinlite's

*Above:* A Douglas Havoc Turbinlite of 1458 Flight, Middle Wallop. This type served at ten RAF airfields including RAF Acklington. (*ww2 images*)

*Left:* A close up of the Turbinlite searchlight in the nose of a Douglas Havoc. (*ww2 images*)

electrical fields on the remagnetisation of the aircraft's nose and the consequent effects on its compass. It was determined that some slight and progressive magnetisation was produced. By the end of February, 1460 Flight had two Havoc Turbinlites and a Boston on strength. Due to a shortage of spares, it was possible to fly only two aircraft at any time.

There was a further spell of bad weather at the beginning of March when snow blocked the roads leading to RAF Acklington. There were also strong winds. The first successful Turbinlite exercise took place on the 7th. Flt Lt J. Morton took over command of the Flight from Sqn Ldr Denholm, who took up a new posting at RAF East Fortune. Another new arrival was 'Bruce', an Alsation dog and the mascot of 603 Squadron. The unit was asked to look after him as the squadron was about to be posted overseas. Two further Turbinlite aircraft—AW406 and BJ474—arrived during the month. One of the Flight's other aircraft sustained some damage to its propeller and fuselage when it struck an angle of glide indicator while taxiing out to take off on the 16th. By the end of March, a total of thirty-nine Turbinlite practices had been carried out, of which twenty-one had been successful. However, many were carried out in daylight hours.

A shortage of spares again limited flying. A Havoc (BJ472) burst its port tyre, swung and broke its port undercarriage on landing at the beginning of April. On the 30th, there was a further mishap. Aircraftsman Raeburn was hit on the hand by a propeller whilst removing a chock. His hand was badly cut and two of his fingers damaged. By this time, the Flight had five Havoc Turbinlites on strength. They flew seventy-two practices in April of which fifty-two were considered successful.

Mr C. Johnston, a Douglas aircraft representative, paid a visit to 1460 Flight at the beginning of May 1942. His advice was of great benefit to aircrews and maintenance staff alike. Unfortunately, the Flight suffered its first fatal accident a few days later on the 10th. A Havoc Turbinlite (AW392) was on a practice flight when its port engine failed. Its pilot, Sgt M. Kent, lost control and the aircraft spun into a railway embankment at Mossy Ford, south-west of Alnwick. It burst into flames, killing both its pilot and the observer, Sgt L. Lucas. On the 20th, there were reports of enemy aircraft near the base. Plt Off. Jones was ordered to take off in a Havoc Turbinlite with Flt Lt A. Hutchinson of 43 Squadron flying a Hurricane II (BD954) as the satellite aircraft. Shortly after take-off and before joining up, the Hurricane's undercarriage jammed in the down position, causing the aircraft to stall and crash near Eshott, killing Hutchinson. The first operational mission for 1460 Flight had ended in disaster.

Enemy aircraft were reported over the Tyne on 5 June. Havoc I Turbinlite and a 43 Squadron Hurricane were on a practice interception when they were diverted shortly before 1 a.m. to investigate. Four contacts were obtained under GCI control, but the Havoc did not have sufficient speed to hold them for more than a few moments. Sqn Ldr Morton took off in Hurricane (AW406) with another 43 Squadron Hurricane to relieve them. Contact was made under GCI control on an enemy aircraft approaching Newcastle at 12,000 feet from the east, some 40 miles off the coast. The Havoc then made contact on its own radar at 8,000 feet range and accelerated to its maximum speed. After eight minutes, the range had been reduced to 3,000 feet, all the aircraft being then at 10,000 feet, with the Havoc slightly below the enemy aircraft. The Hurricane was then sent forward to be in position to attack the enemy aircraft when it was illuminated; however, as the Hurricane climbed, it became visible to the target plane against the light northern sky. The enemy aircraft did a steep turn and dropped its bombs to the north of Newcastle. The target—by this time also exceeding the speed of the Havoc Turbinlite by over 100 mph—could have been illuminated but the Hurricane was hopelessly placed for an attack.

A further attempt to confront German bombers was made on the night of 5–6 July. Flt Lt Sumner was ordered to take off but the hostile aircraft had left the sector before he could reach it. The following night, a Havoc Turbinlite was ordered towards a bombing raid, but it was at the extreme south of the sector and the aircraft had vanished before any contact was made. The following day proved eventful in another way—at 4 p.m., a visiting Beaufighter overshot and crashed into a Boston (AX926) picketed at the dispersal; extensive damage was done to the aircraft. During July, 257 Squadron took over the role of supplying the satellite aircraft from 1 Squadron, which was in the process of converting from Hurricanes to Typhoons.

Fifteen members of the aircrew carried out a dinghy practice on the River Coquet on 1 August. On the night of 9–10 August, about ten German aircraft were reported in the area. A Boston Turbinlite was sent out on patrol and after half an hour was vectored onto an enemy raider. In spite of a twenty-minute chase, no contact was obtained. Six days later, on the night of 15–16 August, enemy aircraft were again detected in the sector, but due to the weather conditions, none of 1460 Flight's aircraft took to the air. Around that time, formation practice was carried out with Typhoons acting as the satellite aircraft instead of Hurricanes, but the Typhoon was deemed unsuitable for this role due to the great disparity between its performance and that of the Havoc Turbinlite.

A Boston III Turbinlite (similar to the Havoc Turbinlite) participated in a novel use of this type of machine when it took part in a search for a pilot of a Beaufighter of 219 Squadron which had crashed into the sea. It was hoped that the aircraft would find the pilot's dinghy with its searchlight. The mission was unsuccessful but the pilot was rescued when the sun rose.

On 2 September 1942, 1460 Flight became 539 Squadron. It had the following aircraft on strength—seven Boston Turbinlites, seven Hurricanes, and one Magister. Most of the Hurricanes came from 1 Squadron, which was also at RAF Acklington at that time. Three days later, 1 Squadron borrowed back two of the aircraft when there was enemy activity in the area. By this time, many of the Turbinlite aircraft were developing faults which were attributed to the extra weight carried in the form of the searchlight and its batteries.

On 19 September, 539 Squadron made its first operational flight when a Boston III Turbinlite, accompanied by a single Hurricane, was ordered on patrol. A fleeting radar contact was made with an enemy aircraft which was soon lost when another aircraft passed between the Boston and its target. Two days later, a small party was held to mark the passing of 1460 Flight. Disaster struck shortly after with entry for the Record Book for 4 October recording:

This was a black day for the squadron as two Hurricanes crashed with fatal results. Sgt R. Timewell in Hurricane IIc, BN205, and Flt Sgt B. Williams in Hurricane HN382 took off at approximately 15.25 to do practice aerobatics. Sgt Timewell crashed at Burscugh, Lancs and was killed and Flt Sgt Williams crashed at Gilsland and was reported missing believed killed and later confirmed killed.

Three of the squadron's other aircraft searched over land and sea until the fate of their comrades became known. On the 11th, a Boston Turbinlite and a Hurricane were diverted from an exercise to investigate a report of enemy aircraft. Three radar contacts were made but all were 'friendly'. A further Boston Tubinlite with its Hurricane were ordered into the air to patrol over the airfield. There was a further accident on the 13th. A Boston III (WB401), piloted by Plt Off. Jones and a Hurricane II, flown by Flt Sgt Herbert, were taking off together when a tyre burst on the Boston and the two aircraft collided. The Boston's crew survived unscathed but the Hurricane's pilot sustained some cuts and bruises. Both aircraft were damaged beyond repair.

At the beginning of November, an instruction was received stating that all Turbinlite aircraft with wrinkled skins were to be grounded. This was occurring in the vicinity of the batteries. With many of its aircraft unable to be flown, a number of 539 Squadron's Hurricanes carried out air-to-air firing and formation flying. There was further flying after dark but the weather closed in suddenly and this was brought to an end. A Hurricane II (AM282) was still in the air at the time. When attempting to land, the aircraft stalled and crashed near Red Row, Acklington, killing its pilot, Sgt Pilot Betant. There was good weather on the 21st, with a number of Turbinlite aircraft involved in exercises. When a Hurricane II (BN292) was coming into land, two aircraftsmen walked across the end of the runway. To avoid them, the pilot, Plt Off. Fletcher, pulled up the nose of his aircraft. Owing to his low airspeed, he made a heavy landing and damaged the undercarriage. There was a small party on the 29th, when there was a 'night off' after sixteen consecutive nights of flying. The next night, there was considerable activity when both Boston Turbinlites and the Hurricanes carried out an exercise with ground defences. On his way back to base, Sgt Pilot Allison's Hurricane (BD770) developed engine trouble. Instead of parachuting to safety, he attempted to make a forced landing 2 miles south of Ashington. The aircraft crashed and burst into flames with its pilot receiving burns.

December began with fine, bright weather. The Hurricanes did low flying and the Boston Turbinlites some formation flying. Sqn Ldr Morton flew a Spitfire as a satellite to the Boston Turbinlite. It was concluded that the Spitfire could be used for this role, although the Hurricane remained the first choice. Sgt Butcher made a forced landing in NB603 near Warkworth on the 21st, due to a glycol leak. The following night, no less than four Tubinlites participated in exercises. On Christmas Eve, four Boston Turbinites and four Hurricanes entertained the station with some formation flying. There was snow on the 29th and the engines of the Boston Turbinlites at readiness had to be run every two hours.

The Boston Turbinlites made numerous practice flights on 2 January 1943. Sgt Allison, with Sgt Brown as his navigator, had been airborne for about an hour when their Boston Turbinlite's starboard engine failed. On their way back to RAF Acklington the airspeed indicator, altimeter and rate of climb indicator all stopped working. It was a dark night with no moon and the glide indicator was not working either:

> In spite of all difficulties, Sgt Allison with the assistance of Sgt Brown made a completely successful landing and is considered to have shown a very high standard of skill and judgement under the most difficult conditions. He was recommended for a gong.

On 23 January, there was a formation flight with five Bostons and three Hurricanes. Later that day, the Squadron's CO addressed a gathering of its personnel and stated that 539 Squadron along with other Turbinlite units were to be immediately disbanded. There is a hint of bitterness about this in the last entry of the Squadron's record book:

> So after twelve months of untiring effort first as 1460 Flight and then as 539 Squadron the unit comes to the end of the road. With much activity by the Orderly room staff the personnel are slowly dispersed and the aeroplanes disposed of. During the 12 months some 3,000 hours flying have been done and much valuable experienced gained by the crews who have remained keen throughout. Their keenness sorely tried but always kept to high level by the splendid example set by Sqn Ldr Morton, the CO of the unit. The Squadron did not adopt a motto as its future always seemed uncertain but its epitaph might well read, 'How hard they strove but with little reward'.

The RAF had invested a great deal of time and effort in trying to perfect the interception of enemy aircraft with the Tubinlite, but it proved to be completely ineffective. The Beaufighter with its cannon and machine guns coupled with its advanced airborne radar would prove a far more effective answer to night-time raids than a flying searchlight.

# 10

# Second Line Flying Units 1939–1945

Throughout the Second World War, a number of second line flying units operated from RAF Acklington alongside the front line squadrons. Most of these provided aircraft to act as 'targets' for fighter pilots to sharpen their combat skills. In addition, they were often in the sights of the anti-aircraft guns that defended the River Tyne and the surrounding area. No. 13 Group Target Towing Flight was formed at RAF Acklington on 16 July 1941. It operated four Westland Lysanders II and III with a fifth aircraft in reserve. They would tow a canvas target behind the aircraft on a cable. Live rounds could then be discharged at this airborne target by attacking aircraft. It was not unknown for the towing aircraft of some units to be hit by stray bullets from over-enthusiastic pilots.

On 8 December 1941, No. 13 Group Target Towing Flight was redesignated No. 1490 Target Towing Flight. New aircraft types were enlisted to provide air gunnery practice. They included Hawker Henleys and two Miles Masters, with the latter arriving on 1 March 1942. Not long after, Miles Martinets were also taken on strength. Now known as No. 1490 (Fighter) Gunnery Flight, the unit moved to RAF Ouston on 4 September 1942. In the early months of 1943, it had seven Westland Lysanders, two Miles Masters, one Miles Martinet, and one Hawker Henley.

In June 1943, a new target towing flight was formed at RAF Acklington. It was given the designation of No. 1630 Anti-Aircraft Co-Operation Flight. It got off to an inauspicious start. When Fg Off. Copeland arrived at Acklington on 31 May 1943 to form the towing flight, he found that no aircraft or ground staff had arrived. He then proceeded to RAF Locking to be briefed on towed target operations before returning to RAF Acklington a week later. By 13 June, four Westland Lysanders had been delivered, but as no ground crew had arrived they had to be serviced by the Station Flight. Seventeen ground personnel were transferred from the RAF Regiment No. 6 Anti-Aircraft Practice Camp in the latter part of the month. Target towing operations were still delayed by a shortage of pilots and winch operators.

On 2 July, two Lysanders—(P9111) and (T.1747)—were air tested. A week later, they were flying practice runs over the No. 6 AAPC gunnery range. On the 12th, AOC of 72 Group, Air Cdr Dacre, paid a visit to 1630 Flight. Before he left, he was handed a list of personnel still required to make the unit fully functional. To

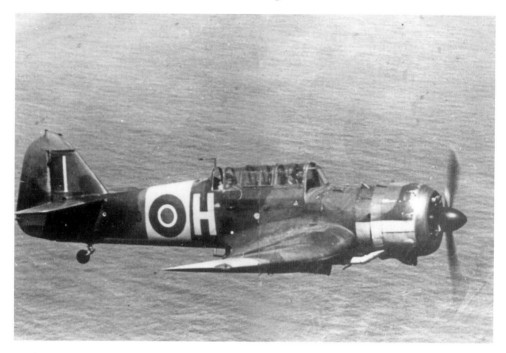

A Miles Martinet flying over the sea. This was the first aircraft to be designed for the RAF to be employed in the role of a target tug. RAF Acklington had a long association with the type which operated from the airfield during the Second World War and into the late 1940s. (*ww2 images*)

add to its problems, 1630 Flight had to move out of Station Flight hangars to the dispersals to make room for the incoming 350 (Belgium) Squadron. In addition, the Station Commander requested that cables and a drogue be fitted to a Miles Martinet belonging to the RAF Acklington Station flight. It was then flown on the 18th, towing targets for air-to-air firing by 416 (American) Squadron. Despite all this, time was still found to fly ATC cadets in one of the Lysanders a few days later.

Targets were also regularly towed over the anti-aircraft gunnery range. One of the aircraft was involved in an embarrassing accident. Whilst coming into land, Lysander (T.11747), piloted by Plt Off. Finbow, flew too low and the target it was towing caught on a blister hangar. This caused the aircraft to 'nose down'. The undercarriage wheels bounced on the perimeter track causing damage to the port leg. The pilot then completed another circuit before attempting to land again. He made an excellent touch down on the undamaged wheel, but on nearing the completion of the landing run, the damaged port-side wheel came into contact with the ground, causing the aircraft to turn over onto its back. Both Finbow and his winch operator survived the experience unhurt. Their Lyslander was not so lucky, being damaged beyond repair and classified as Category F.1—'reduction to spares'.

In the summer, regular flights were flown to provide targets for No. 6 Anti-aircraft Practice Camp. For example, on 13 August: 'eighteen drogues requested—eighteen provided, weather fine but rough, flying very trying at low altitude, also taxiing difficult in Lysanders.'

While most of the flights flown were for target practice of anti-aircraft gunners on the ground, the unit was also requested to supply targets for air-to-air firing by 409 Squadron. A member of 2803 Squadron, RAF Regiment, was taken for a flight to examine the effectiveness of the camouflage of the Bofors gun sites, which were part of RAF Acklington's anti-aircraft defences.

On 3 September 1943, Lyslander (N1210) was delivered as a replacement for the one lost in the accident mentioned above. Further flights were flown to provide air-to-air gunnery practice for 409 Squadron and 316 Squadron. Most of its effort was devoted to providing targets for the anti-aircraft crews. On 20 November, seven sorties were flown supplying a total of twenty targets for them.

On the 1 December 1943, No. 1630 Anti-aircraft Co-operation Flight ceased to exist, being absorbed into 289 Squadron. No. 6 RAF Regiment Anti-Aircraft Practice Camp remained in existence until 20 November 1944, when it too was disbanded. 289 Squadron had a detachment of Vengeance target-towing aircraft at RAF Acklington throughout much of 1945.

No. 3 Aircraft Delivery Flight was formed in April 1941 to deliver fighter aircraft to Squadrons in Nos. 9 and 12 Fighter Groups. During its life, it was based at a number of airfields including RAF Detling and RAF Catterick. It flew aircraft such as Tiger Moths and Oxfords. On 8 November 1943, it moved to RAF Acklington, but its stay there was short-lived, as it was disbanded by the end of that month. No. 4 Aircraft Delivery Flight's residence at RAF Acklington was somewhat longer. It arrived on 25 November 1943 and did not leave until 8 March 1944. It was also responsible for delivering fighter aircraft to operational units. Earlier, on 8 June 1941, when it was based at RAF Grangemouth, one of its Dominie Is (X7333), crashed on take-off from RAF Acklington.

Like most other RAF airfields of any consequence, RAF Acklington had a station flight which had a small number of aircraft used for transport and training purposes. A Miles Martinet (HP147), more usually used for target towing, was dispatched on a communications flight on 7 July 1943. It was flown by a Belgium more used to flying Spitfires. As the pilot was not familiar with its controls, the aircraft failed to take off, went through a hedge and ended in a neighbouring field.

# 11

# Airfield Defences
# 1939–1945

At the outbreak of the Second World War, unlike many other European countries, Britain had few modern fortifications. Other than coastal defences, almost no attempt had been made to construct strongpoints to deter an enemy advancing overland, as a land invasion by a foreign army was thought to be almost unthinkable. However, as Germany overran one country after another in 1940, there was alarm that Britain would be next. A network of defensive lines were hastily prepared across the length and breadth of the country. Although no large-scale forts were built, hundreds of concrete pill boxes began to appear on the coast and at key locations. It was hoped that infantrymen firing from the protection of a pill box could fend off an enemy attack or at least delay the advance. In the months leading up to the war, most RAF airfields possessed few, if any, defences. It had been believed they would be so far behind enemy lines that they would be invulnerable to attack by enemy soldiers. Several pillboxes were hastily constructed early in the War to defend RAF Acklington from a surprise attack.

When Norway was overrun in early 1940 there was serious concern that it would be used as a springboard to attack Scotland and Northern England. It was thought an attack might be launched with hundreds of Junkers Ju 52s dropping paratroops on strategic locations. Consideration was given to the fact that airfields could be subject to poison gas attacks, leading to decontamination centres being built at many RAF airfields, including RAF Acklington.

As war clouds gathered over Europe, on 25 August 1939 soldiers of the Durham Light Infantry arrived at Acklington for guard duty. They were replaced on the 28th by the Royal Northumberland Fusiliers. Shortly after the outbreak of hostilities, the camouflaging of RAF Acklington began. At this stage the measures taken to protect the airfield were far from adequate. The Air Vice Marshal of 13 Group wrote to Fighter Command requesting four Bofors guns, commenting that the camouflage scheme was very effective but stating RAF Acklington was still an obvious target for low-flying aircraft. He pointed out that, although it was at that time a satellite airfield of RAF Usworth, it had three front line squadrons and should be given greater priority. Despite his pleas, he was informed that no Bofors guns would be available for a considerable time. Instead, four Lewis machine guns would be delivered as soon as possible.

In May 1940, work was underway to create permanent emplacements for Hispano guns to provide defence against low-flying aircraft. It was requested that the rifle range be demolished to give a greater field of view for one of the positions. This was denied on the grounds that it was almost always in use. In the event of a major attack, most of the RAF personnel on the station would be issued with rifles to assist with its defence. To prevent RAF airfields from falling into enemy hands and being used by their aircraft, there were plans to plough up grass airfields like RAF Acklington.

In June 1940, Winston Churchill proclaimed:

Every man in RAF uniform ought to be armed with something—a rifle, a tommy gun, a pistol, a pike or mace and everyone, without exception, should do at least one hour's drill and practice every day. Each airman should have his place in the defence scheme. It must be understood by all ranks that they are expected to fight and die in the defence of their airfields. Every building which fits in with the scheme of defence should be prepared so that each has to be conquered one by one by the enemy's parachute or glider troops. In two or three hours, the army will arrive. Every airfield should be a stronghold of fighting airmen and not the abode of uniformed civilians in the prime of life protected by detachments of soldiers.

At the end of July, with the invasion scare at its height, ninety RAF personnel, whose sole duty was ground defence, arrived at RAF Acklington. Early the following month, a mobile anti-tank gun was delivered. Soldiers from the King's Own Scottish Borderers relieved the Northumberland Fusiliers in their role in guarding the airfield. The Inspector of Aerodrome Defences GHQ Home Forces paid a visit to RAF Acklington on 27 August 1941. At that time, 1 Company of the 13th Battalion Highland Light Infantry was responsible for the protection of the airfield. Its strength was four officers and forty-eight other ranks. They were taking the place of the 70th Battalion Royal Northumberland Fusiliers, who were away for one month's training. Six pillboxes for internal defence were under construction: 'These defended localities are very well sited and well-constructed and are very nearly completed. The wiring is nearly complete and particularly well-constructed.'

The pillboxes at RAF Acklington were of unusual design, having built-up walls on top to provide an enclosed light anti-aircraft gun position. The battle headquarters— the nerve centre for defending the airfield from a ground attack—was also nearing completion. There were fourteen machine guns which were able to fire on the landing ground, the most likely place where parachutists would descend. Further defences included six light anti-aircraft posts, four Hispano cannon, and six Bofors guns. In addition, there were five 'Armadillos'—armoured flatbed lorries with machine guns mounted on them. However, the Local Defence Commander confided in the Inspector of Aerodrome Defences that the RAF defence officers were all too old and suggested they should be deployed otherwise.

At 9.12 a.m. on 30 September 1941, an enemy aircraft dropped three 1-kg anti-personnel bombs on RAF Acklington; there was no damage or casualties. Although German bombers were marauding over north-east England almost every day in the early years of the war, direct attacks on RAF Acklington were almost unknown. This may have been partly due to decoy airfield sites, one of which was at Long Houghton. This was a 'K Site'—a day-time dummy airfield complete with decoy Hurricanes. It was in operation by the Spring of 1940, despite considerable opposition from the local residents. A night-time decoy airfield, known as a 'Q site' was created at Widdrington, to the south of RAF Acklington. Few at Acklington knew of its existence, as it was staffed by an independent organisation. On one occasion, it was bombed and thirty sheep were killed. Many people rushed to the site in the morning as meat was rationed at that time.

In January 1942, the RAF Regiment was formed, the sole purpose of which was to defend RAF airfields and installations. Up until that time, protection had generally been provided by the Army. Its first units were little more than platoons or flights in strength and were equipped with a variety of machine guns and Hispano cannons. In time, the RAF Regiment developed two types of units—one for ground defence and the other for light air defence equipped with Bofors guns. But for much of 1942, the Royal Northumberland Fusiliers still stood guard over RAF Acklington. In the summer, a brigadier inspecting the station suggested that the Battle Headquarters be moved. However, the RAF thought there was nothing wrong with the current site. There were also 'six old armoured lorries', presumably Armadillos, two of which were on the airfield itself. A further two were hidden in Broomhill Wood while the remaining examples were to be found in Acklington village.

The first members of the RAF Regiment 2799 Squadron began arriving in early September. On the 7th, soldiers of the Royal Northumberland Fusiliers marched out of Acklington Village. 'Xmas', a large scale exercise, took place on the 13th between 5.15 a.m. and 8.30 a.m. to test the defences of the airfield. Counter-sabotage precautions were taken by 2799 Squadron. Units of the Home Guard attacked parts of the airfield, including the Battle Headquarters. It was defended by two armoured fighting vehicles, two Sten guns, and five rifle men. It was concluded that the attackers could have overrun parts of the airfield but would have sustained very heavy casualties. Also, 'enemy efforts' to draw off mobile protective units before launching their major thrust compromised some of the defences. This feint would have had serious repercussions for the defence of the airfield. Some of the members in the Home Guard participating in the exercise were so keen that even when they were 'killed', they refused to retire from the attack.

In March of the following year, a memorandum was received from Fighter Command indicating that the RAF Regiment would become responsible for the light air defence of the airfield from the 1 July. They would man eight 20-mm Hispano cannon and four Bofors guns when they became available. A further exercise to test RAF Acklington's defences took place on 6 June 1943. The local Home Guard again acted as the hostile force. Simulated gas attacks were included in the attack. It was concluded that the 'enemy' would have suffered heavy casualties—so much so that they would have rendered their attack ineffective. An advance party of 2803 Anti-aircraft Squadron consisting of one officer and eight other ranks arrived from Peterhead on 29 June and took up quarters in Acklington Village. The main party of

2799 Squadron under Sqn Ldr Aldridge left for RAF Linton-on-Ouse. Its departure from RAF Acklington was deeply regretted, as this unit was held in high regard. The main party of 2803 Squadron, consisting of four officers and 143 other ranks, arrived on 3 July. Forty-three of them were transported to RAF Eshott where they were to be responsible for the anti-aircraft defence of this airfield as well.

In the summer of 1943, a new camouflage scheme was applied to RAF Acklington. On 8 July 1943, Flt Lt Wilson arrived to examine its progress. He took a flight over the airfield in a 409 Squadron Oxford, accompanied by the civilian Assistant Camouflage Officer of No 2. Works Area based at Newcastle. The following day, a full-scale gas exercise commenced at 9 a.m. Tear gas and smoke were released on various parts of the station to simulate poison gas. Incidents with practice blister gas were also arranged to provide decontamination training. For almost the duration of the war, training exercises involving mock gas attacks took place at RAF Acklington, an indication of how seriously this threat was taken, even in the closing stages of the conflict. In October it was decided to erect a Bofors gun pit in the north-east corner of the airfield. No. 2803 Squadron requested concrete blocks for the construction of it and a further two at other points on the airfield.

By January 1944, there were few raids by enemy aircraft on Britain. RAF anti-aircraft guns had been removed from all airfields except those housing night fighter squadrons, which included RAF Acklington. The role of the RAF Regiment at that time was under review. At the beginning of 1944, despite the lowering level of threat, it was decided to place armed guards each night on the aircraft based on the airfield. Many contained top secret equipment in the form of the latest versions of airborne radar.

By 1944, the threat of German troops launching an attack on airfields in Britain was a remote possibility. In contrast to his pronouncement in 1940 concerning the defence of RAF airfields, Winston Churchill now commented:

> I do not think we can afford to continue to maintain a special body of troops purely for the defence of aerodromes. The RAF Regiment was established at a time when the invasion of this country was likely and when our life depended upon the security of our fighter aerodromes. Since then it has been reduced but the time has now come to consider whether the greater part of it should not be taken to reinforce field formations of the army. I consider that at least 25,000 men should be transferred. They would be much better employed there than loafing around over-crowded airfields warding off dangers which have ceased to threaten.

During the Second World War, RAF Acklington also played a major role in training RAF personnel to defend other airfields. On 1 January 1943, authority was given to establish No. 6 Anti-aircraft Practice Camp:

> The object of this unit is to train AA Flights of the RAF Regiment in the use of Hispano on various mountings, the Browning on [the] Motley Stork [a gun mount, also spelled 'Stalk'], also, as occasion permits Station Personnel.

The Hispano and Browning were machine guns used to defend potential targets against low-flying aircraft. The formation of No. 6 AAPC did not take place until the following May when Sqn Ldr Gould was appointed to command it. Other members of the RAF Regiment began to arrive from all corners of the country to fill other posts. On 8 May, Gould and Flt Lt B. Johnston picked a site at Hauxley as being a suitable location for the firing range. A few days later, the Station Commander allocated accommodation for the staff and trainees of 6 AAPC. Wg Cdr J. Heffenham, HQ72 Group, visited the unit for the purpose of fixing safety angles at the Hauxley Ranges. A site for the ranges having been selected, the Station Commander of RAF Acklington wrote to the HQ Fighter Command requesting authority for requisitioning an area of land and eleven properties at Hauxley Links, near Amble. A gun emplacement costing £95 (£12,000 in 2016) was also requested.

By the end of May, No. 6 AAPC had four officers and forty-seven other ranks on strength, but training was delayed by the non-arrival of instructors. Three target-towing Lysander Mk IIIs—P9111, T.1504, and R1747—were delivered on 10 June. They did not remain a component of No. 6 AAPC for long, being redesignated No. 1630 Flight and later in the year absorbed into 289 Squadron. The Amble police arranged for civilian billets for eight airmen at Low Hauxley, near the Unit's Range. On the 21st, seven range personnel took up this accommodation. The following day, ninety-four trainees arrived. The number was originally expected to be 120, but some stations found they could not find men to spare. Training commenced on the 23rd. The course included lectures on the Browning machine gun—stripping and assembling, dealing with stoppages and filling the ammunition belt. At Hauxley Range, the trainees were given the opportunity to shoot at a target towed behind a Lysander flying at 500 feet to the front at right angles at a range of 600 feet, and directly towards them as well as overhead. Near the end of June, written warning was given that firing would commence on the Low Hauxley range. Practice with the Browning was delayed as the only pilot in the target towing flight was in hospital. A replacement was eventually found; on the first day of live firing on the 28th, over 30,000 rounds were discharged.

Prior to the first batch of trainees departing the station, CO Wg Cdr Graham addressed them and expressed his appreciation of the great improvements on the camp site since it was taken over by No. 6 AAPC. He stated that before they arrived it was a collection of ramshackle huts in a wet field but repairs to them and the laying of red shale in the surrounding areas had made a great improvement.

In July 1943, the first anti-aircraft squadron basic training course on both the Browning machine guns and Hispano cannon took place. The students were two officers and forty-two other ranks from RAF Regiment 2703 Squadron and two officers and forty-seven other ranks from 2834 Squadron. They had five days practical work and their firing showed average ability. The second course assembled at RAF Acklington on the 28th. Their discipline and keenness were above average. At the beginning of August, Capt. J. Reid of 4th Northumberland Fusiliers visited No. 6. AAPC to request that his soldiers receive training. Several courses were laid on for personnel of this regiment.

With winter not far away, the CO, Sqn Ldr Gould, visited the Engineering Officer, No. 2 Works Area in Newcastle in order to hasten the erection of the proposed new Nissen huts. He was informed that five were available, providing estimates were submitted by the station for them.

By the end of September, the eighth anti-aircraft course had come to an end and its members dispersed back to their airfields. Their discipline was below average and it was recorded that there was too much slackness among senior NCOs. The ninth course arrived on the 29th and comprised of two officers and forty-eight other ranks from RAF Regiment 2799 Squadron and one officer and forty-two other ranks of 2805 Squadron. They were given five days practical work and firing. The discipline of No. 2799 Squadron was average as was its general ability. The other squadron's discipline was very good, as was its administration and general ability. It was the best group of trainees to undertake instruction up to that time.

In October, all No. 6 AAPC personnel were instructed to proceed to the Anti Gas Section to have their equipment inspected. More daunting for them was a visit to a chamber filled with mustard gas which they had to walk through. There was still a shortage of Nissen Huts for training purposes. Three had been requested by the Station Commander but he was told there was still little chance of obtaining them. There were four in Acklington Village, a short distance from the station, which were commandeered by No. 6 AAPC. Sqn Ldr W. Torrence of 22 Group inspected them on 10 December and approved of their use. Later, he was conducted around the camp and paid visits to the Aircraft Recognition Room and the proposed News and Information Room. He voiced his appreciation of all the work that had been done to turn this camp into a presentable one and also spoke of his admiration of its sound organisation.

A dance for the unit's staff was held in the new NAAFI on 13 December. Food and refreshments were provided and the cabaret was comprised of station personnel. Seven days later, a concert was held in the same premises for both the permanent staff and trainees. On Christmas Eve, every person in the unit was issued with a copy of the Camp Souvenir Magazine. This contained a photograph of the officers, airmen and WAAFs of the permanent staff. It had numerous articles written by the CO, Sqn Ldr F. Gould, and other officers: 'many appreciations and thanks have been forthcoming as it will be a happy souvenir in post war days.'

By New Year's Eve, some twenty training courses had been completed by 6 AAPC. The report on the most recent trainees stated: 'Discipline, kit, and administration was average—general ability—a newly formed unit with a lot of "rough corners". Capable officers who will soon make willing men into an efficient unit.' Wg Cdr R. A. Smith, Headquarters, paid a visit early in the New Year. He inspected Nos. 1 and 2 Camp sites and the ranges, and finished off his visit by opening the News and Information Room. At the conclusion of his visit, he thought that discipline was strict and morale high.

On 9 January 1944, the unit took part in a full-scale anti-gas exercise held on the station from 8 a.m. to 12.00 noon. An attack on the airfield even at this late stage of the war was still taken seriously. The defences and the role to be played by the staff of 6 AAPC were examined by Brig. C. Britten.

However, the days of 6 AAPC were numbered. By the end of March, training was suspended. During the lull in training, a weekly programme, which included gun drill, weapon training, map reading, foot drill and kit inspection, was drawn up to occupy the instructors and permanent staff. There would be plenty of time for this in the forthcoming months, as few further trainees arrived at RAF Acklington for gunnery instruction. On 22 April, a battery of the Royal Artillery arrived on attachment. A short course on their Bofors guns was arranged for the staff of 6 AAPC.

They performed well as most had some theory of this gun from earlier lectures. Much of the time was now devoted to less lethal activities. A conference was held on the 14 May at which it was decided to devote a total of seven hours a week to instruction, three hours a week to sport and physical training, and the remainder of the week to activities of a self-help nature. It was proposed that all the huts should be repainted and that ground be covered in a further layer of ash. The unit would also take part in the station garden scheme, involving the growing of vegetables. At the end of May, approximately 100 personnel from the RAF Holding Unit, RAF Acklington, and 6 AAPC took part in a 'Salute the Soldier' parade at Amble.

As the summer wore on, the personnel at Low Hauxley Range spent their time stripping, cleaning, and reassembling Hispano magazines. Back at camp, time was devoted to organised games and the maintenance of the huts. At the end of August, there was a brief resumption of training when the sixth Anti-aircraft Squadron Basic Training Course assembled. This consisted of two officers and forty-nine other ranks from RAF Regiment 2846 Squadron and two officers and forty-eight other ranks from 2770 Squadron. On 1 September, personnel from RAF Acklington attended Hauxley Range for air-towing firing. There was now little need for the training of machine gunners to defend RAF airfields, as by the end of 1944 the Luftwaffe had been decimated. The 6 Anti-aircraft Practice Camp was disbanded on 11 November 1944, never to reform.

Another unit that was based at RAF Acklington towards the end of the war was No. 147 Airfield HQ. Unlike those mentioned previously, its function was not to defend RAF Airfields but to take the war to the enemy. With the invasion of Europe fast approaching, the idea of this unit was to create mobile air arms independent of a fixed geographical location. They would be equipped with large numbers of vehicles which would transport all the necessary tools to service squadrons operating from makeshift airfields near combat zones. As the lines of conflict changed, the Airfield Units could quickly pack up the engineering equipment and supplies and move to a new airstrip. On 14 February, authorisation was given for the formation of 147 Airfield HQ at RAF Acklington. This was to be controlled by 25 Base Wing HQ, also located at Acklington. The flying units were to comprise of 409 (RCAF) squadron (already based there) and 322 (Dutch) squadron, which was due to arrive in the near future. These squadrons are covered in more detail elsewhere in the book.

The existing permanent facilities were to be used for accommodation as winter quarters but were to be forfeited in favour of tents when the weather became warmer. Instructions stated that the permanent executive officers were to have the most comfortable quarters. Airfield executive officers would be next in priority, together with aircrew. Other officers who were not training or who were not capable of carrying out their duties due to lack of equipment would have a low priority. No officers were to be allowed to live off camp. Also, no officers in 147 Airfield were allowed to have a batman; this included the aircrews of 409 Squadron. Officers were also to ensure that all their equipment could easily be carried. It was stated that mobility was most important and that the 'Airfield' was a self-contained unit which could not rely on outside help and would be required to live off its own provisions for up to fourteen days. In extreme conditions, the Airfield may become cut off by the enemy. Its personnel had to be able to use rifles to defend themselves. Transport was divided into echelons: No. 1 Echelon was fast-moving, carrying a maintenance party; No. 2 Echelon consisted of an immediate advanced party to keep aircraft operating in a minimum possible time and was to carry fuel, oil, oxygen, etc.; No. 3 Echelon contained the main party; No. 4 contained heavy equipment; and No. 5 contained the demolition party.

Physically fit personnel were transferred from the staff at RAF Acklington to man the newly formed 147 Airfield. A conference of all Airfield Officers was held on 1 March 1944. Due to a shortage of accommodation, it was decided to transfer 24 Base Wing to Newcastle. Training got underway the next day, with twenty members of the servicing wing sent on the assault course which included trench digging and firearms training.

On 3 March, 409 Squadron Beaufighters took part in an exercise to intercept bombers. They scored twenty-nine destroyed and one damaged. Three days later, the motor driving courses commenced, followed not long after by map reading courses. Beaufighters of 409 Squadron were involved in another exercise on the 14th, in which they claimed ten bombers destroyed. Some personnel of 147 Airfield were put under canvas not long after. The first practice move was undertaken on the 19th with three vehicles—representing recce, advance and main parties—travelling north to RAF Boulmer. By the end of March, all the Servicing Wing were living in tents. A large number of the motor vehicles had been delivered. As well as practical training, the personnel received lectures on a wide range of subjects including anti-gas training, the difficulties of the decontamination of aircraft and firefighting. At the end of the month, there was a skeleton move of a single Spitfire of 322 Squadron with fifty airmen to RAF Boulmer.

The arrival of April saw the aircrew of 409 Squadron moved under canvas. Heavy rain fell all the next day and, much to the dismay of those under canvas, it was discovered their new lodgings were far from waterproof. All the personnel then returned to their previous billets; the tents were dried out and re-waterproofed. A practice convoy move took place involving equipment for 409 squadron. The following day, the 8th, 322 Squadron moved to RAF Boulmer. The main points of the exercise were to see that the aircraft were operational after their deployment and that the domestic needs of the personnel were attended to. This was the first complete move of a squadron involving 147 Airfield and was considered a success.

On the 11th, the repair and inspection section of 409 Squadron was moved to RAF Boulmer. The next day, the first large convoy practice was undertaken. At the same time, in an effort to avoid damp ground, the domestic tented site was moved to higher ground in Acklington Village. Catering marquees were also erected at the new location. It was hoped that shortly after this, 147 Airfield would be capable of operating totally independently of RAF Acklington. A-flight of 409 Squadron moved to RAF Boulmer briefly before returning the following day. Airfield HQ lost one of its two squadrons when 322 Squadron left for RAF Hartford Bridge on the 20th. Five days later, information was received that 147 Airfield HQ and 409 Squadron were to move to RAF Hunsdon early in May. It was then renamed '147 Wing' as part of the 2nd Tactical Air Force, but it did not deploy to Europe until early 1945.

# 12

# Diversion Airfield
# 1939–1945

Since the day it opened, RAF Acklington had a significant role as a diversion airfield and staging post as it was situated approximately halfway between the south of England and the far north of Scotland. Many early single-engined aircraft had a range of only 400–500 miles and would find it a convenient airfield for refuelling before continuing to their final destination. RAF Bomber Command had most of their airfields concentrated in Lincolnshire and Yorkshire. When formations of their aircraft were returning from raids over Germany they sometimes found that the weather had closed their home base. RAF Acklington, being located close to the coast, was an ideal location to divert to as they returned across the North Sea. The list of diversions below is probably incomplete as the information contained in the daily entries of the station's log during the early years of the war is often fairly brief and confined to major incidents. It becomes much more comprehensive for the closing stages of the conflict.

On 21 December 1939, two squadrons of Handley Page Hampdens were ordered to take off at first light from RAF Scampton and RAF Waddington. Their mission was to bomb the German pocket battleship *Deutschland*, which was reportedly off the coast of Norway. Unable to find their target, the twenty-four Hampdens flew back to Britain through sleet and rain showers. Their intended destination was RAF Leuchars, Fife. The squadrons became separated in the bad weather and 44 Squadron made landfall to the south of Dunbar. The Firth of Forth had experienced some of the first air raids of the war and Spitfires were scrambled from RAF Drem on the assumption that the aircraft were hostile. The pilots from 72 Squadron, on seeing the approaching aircraft, reported that they were Handley Page Hampdens. 602 Squadron's Spitfires were less cautious and immediately opened fire on the RAF bombers. In the ensuing chaos two of the Hampdens were shot down, with one of the crew losing his life. On realising their mistake the Spitfires escorted the remaining Hampdens back to RAF Drem.

Meanwhile, the Hampdens of 49 Squadron, after flying at about 1,000 feet over the North Sea, made landfall further south over Holy Island. They narrowly escaped the same fate as the other squadrons when Hurricanes from 43 Squadron dived down to attack them. The bombers fired off Very flares to show they were 'friendly'. A few minutes later, they were preparing to land at RAF Acklington. While in the circuit, Hampden (L4072) requested that it be allowed to land first as it was running short of fuel. On approach to the runway, one of its engines stalled and the bomber lost height. It then struck a flagstaff and a tree in a park at North Broomhill close to the edge of the airfield finally colliding with the Church of Christ Chapel. Both the aircraft and the building were then consumed by fire. The Hampden's pilot, Sgt Marshall, was thrown clear of the conflagration. He was taken to Alnwick Infirmary with a fractured leg. The second pilot/navigator also survived. Less fortunate were Sgt S. Potts and AC1 E. Humphrey, who were trapped in the flaming wreckage, despite the attempts of two members of the public to rescue them. Potts was put to rest in Chevington Cemetery. The navigator who should have been on the Hampden had fallen asleep at RAF Scampton and was seen running after his aircraft as it took off. He was later court martialled. A second Hampden from 49 Squadron ran out of fuel some distance from RAF Acklington and had to make a forced landing in a field north of Belford. In this instance, none of its crew suffered serious injuries.

In the early hours of 7 April 1940, a Hampden (L4054) appeared over St. Mary's Lighthouse. The aircraft had had taken off the previous day for offensive operations in the district of Sylt in north-west Gemany. The pilot was Wilfred Roberts, an Australian, and the navigator was Plt Off. Keith Brooke Taylor, from New Zealand. Also on board were AC1 Denis Sharpe and Sgt Andrew Mc.Nicol. While over Sylt, the crew of another aircraft reported seeing a Hampden, possibly L4054, coming under intensive anti-aircraft fire. When the Hampden appeared over the coast near Newcastle, it repeatedly signalled 'SOS' on a lamp. St. Mary's lighthouse keeper replied to the 'SOS' signal and immediately informed the appropriate authorities. The standard procedure to assist a lost aircraft was to train searchlight beams over a wide area towards the nearest suitable RAF airfield. In this case it was RAF Acklington which lit its flare path. The lighthouse keeper signalled the circling aircraft to proceed there. Although the crew of the Hampden acknowledged this message, the aircraft made no effort to head in that direction. It continued to fly in the vicinity of St. Mary's Lighthouse until one of its engines failed. Three of the crew parachuted into the sea but were drowned. The fourth remained in the Hampden until it crashed around half a mile from St Mary's Lighthouse. There was a huge explosion triggered by the bombs still on board. It was speculated that the aircraft's undercarriage may have been too badly damaged for it to land at RAF Acklington or that with bombs still on board the pilot did not wish to endanger the airfield. A further Hampden, this time from RAF Lindolme, made a successful landing at RAF Acklington on 19 March 1941, after a bombing raid on the port of Kiel.

Another twin-engined bomber in service with Bomber Command at the beginning of the war was the Armstrong Whitworth Whitley. It was popular with its crews, despite being vulnerable to enemy fire. In the evening of 3 September 1941, eighty-five Wellingtons, thirty Hampdens, nineteen Whitleys, four Stirlings and two Manchesters took off from Bomber Command Airfields in England. Their target was the German battle cruisers the *Scharnhorst* and the *Gneisenau* and the light cruiser *Prinz Eugen*, which were at Brest in north-west France. Although some of the bombers had reached the estimated position of the enemy warships, the attack was aborted due to worsening weather conditions. The Whitleys, which had taken off from RAF

Linton-on-Ouse in Yorkshire, were instructed to divert to RAF Acklington, as fog now covered the east coast of England. One of them collided with trees at Turnbull Farm, North Broomhill, about a mile short of the runway. The Whitley Mk V (Z6869) crashed and caught fire, killing four of the five crew—Plt Off. Andrew Law, FS Wallace Trewin, Sgt Robert Ward, and Sgt Charles Steggall. Three of them were buried locally in Chevington Cemetery. Law had experienced two crashes earlier that year, including sixty-four hours adrift in a dinghy in the North Sea. The rear gunner, Plt Off. E. Comber-Higgs, survived.

Only four days had elapsed when a further disaster struck RAF Acklington. A Whitley Mk V (Z6932) of 10 Squadron took off from RAF Leeming on 6 September 1941 on an air test of its instruments. With a deterioration in the weather it was instructed to divert to RAF Acklington. The crew mistook RAF Brunton, a few miles to the north and also close to the coast, for RAF Acklington. The airfield was still under construction at the time but the Whitley made a successful landing. Three soldiers approached the crew and informed them that they had landed at the wrong airfield. They were told that they would locate RAF Acklington if they followed the railway line south. The Whitley began the take-off run. As it was about to become airborne the aircraft struck a steamroller and the nose pitched upwards. The pilot tried to evade a line of high tension cables but was unsuccessful. The Whitley stalled and crashed. The wreckage burst into flames. Soldiers descended to render assistance but the only crew member they could save was the rear gunner, Sgt Whitlock, who had sustained serious back injuries. He was taken to a nearby farmhouse in the back of a van and then to Newcastle General Hospital. Two of the soldiers were later commended for their bravery in rescuing him from the burning aircraft. When Sgt Whitlock had recovered he returned to Brunton to thank the men who had saved his life. The three crew members who were killed were Sgt W. Stuart, RCAF, Plt Off. R. Austin, RNZAF, and Sgt Bryant. The first two were buried in Chevington Cemetery. Sgt Whitlock was killed when the Wellington he was flying in crashed in 1944. In a twist of fate, he was the only crew member to be killed.

In the early hours of 1 October 1941, a Hampden of 408 Squadron crashed after hitting a Wellington of 9 Squadron, which had landed an hour or so earlier. This gives an indication as to how busy RAF Acklington was handling bomber diversions, even in the early stages of the War. Another Whitley—this time from 190 Operational Conversion Unit—was guided into RAF Acklington with Sandia lights and directions from the air traffic controllers on 13 March 1943. It had lost its way on a cross-country flight.

One of the most enigmatic diversions of the war took place four days later. At 3.10 a.m., a message was received from 13 Group that a diversion of three aircraft was to be executed from RAF Tempsford. It was the base of a top secret squadron which dropped agents of the Special Operations Executive (SOE) into enemy occupied territory. The three aircraft touched down at 6.15 a.m., 6.22 a.m., and 6.28 a.m. Instructions were passed to RAF Acklington that none of the crews were to be questioned. Unfortunately, the airfield's official records do not give any further details on the type of aircraft or their mission.

Shortly after midnight on 15 April, the first of fifteen Wellingtons began to arrive, having been diverted from RAF Disforth. At the beginning of May, an Avro Anson of 100 AFRU, RAF Dumfries, made an emergency landing after suffering icing and becoming lost. A few weeks later, a lost Lancaster was pointed in the right direction by fighters on an operational scramble. After orbiting Blyth, it was turned and headed south towards its base.

In the summer of 1940, the RAF received its first four-engined bombers, in the shape of the Short Stirling. With a fuselage length of 87 feet and a wingspan a few inches short of a 100 feet, it was one of the largest aircraft in the RAF's inventory in the Second World War. On the afternoon of 1 December 1943, nineteen Stirlings and twelve Halifaxes flew towards the Danish coast, where they dropped anti-shipping mines. During their return, the Stirlings were diverted to RAF Acklington. The weather along the coast of Northumberland was far from perfect, with fog covering the ground. The first bomber arrived safely at 10 p.m. and was followed by several others. At 10.40 p.m., a Stirling (EH880) of 75 Squadron was approaching the airfield from the north-east when it struck the roof of Cliff House Farm, at North Togston near Amble. Five children sleeping in the top storey perished in the accident. Their parents, who were playing cards with two friends downstairs, managed to flee from their wrecked home. One of the visitors then noticed that a member of the crew was still alive. He freed him from the blazing wreckage and rolled him on the ground to extinguish his flaming clothes. The other six crew members died in the crash. WO G. Kerr, the pilot, was buried in Chevington cemetery. The bodies of the other crew were given a military escort to Acklington Station to be transported to their next of kin. They were Sgt L. Copsy (flight engineer), Sgt D. Wort (navigator), Sgt R. Smith (bomb aimer) FS D. Holt (wireless operator) and G. Lucus (gunner). Sgt K. Hook escaped with second degree burns and outlived the Second World War. The RAF had a presence at the funeral of the five children of the Robertson family. The three older girls had been a familiar sight in and around Amble, helping their father deliver milk from his horse-drawn cart. After the accident the parents left the area.

Early December 1943, RAF Acklington had some unusual visitors in the form of five troop carrying gliders and their towing aircraft. They were *en route* to the gliding school at Inverness, but as daylight was fading, they decided to land and continue their flight the following day. Some twenty-five USAAC officers and eighteen NCOs were given accommodation for the night. Due to the increasing number of large formations of bombers that were now using RAF Acklington as a diversion airfield, a conference was held to discuss how the handling of them could be improved. It was decided that standard procedure should be laid down for both their arrival and departure.

The new year was only three days old when the first major diversion in 1944 occurred. At 6 a.m., information was received concerning a diversion of Bomber Command aircraft. Shortly afterwards, a total of seventeen Lancasters landed. After parking their aircraft, the crews made the necessary telephone reports to their home base. Later that day, all the Lancaster crews went to their aircraft to prepare for take-off, but this was cancelled due to poor weather. They eventually departed the following morning, except for two aircraft that had become unserviceable.

The next major diversion occurred on 29 March, with the arrival of three Stirlings and five Lancasters. This was followed by twelve Lancasters on an operational mission from RAF Waddington being diverted because of poor weather at their home base on 9 June. 8 August was a particularly busy day for RAF Acklington. Three North American Mustangs of 335 Squadron USAAF, landed at 5 p.m. They had been providing protection for Beaufighters attacking a convoy off the coast of southern Norway. A Mustang flown by Maj. Blanding was badly shot up in the process. Despite suffering from a compound fracture of the skull and multiple shrapnel wounds, he 'showed admirable courage and will power and brought his aircraft in with practically a perfect landing.'

Only after Blanding had instructed the other two Mustangs to return to their base at Deebden, he allowed himself to be taken to the station sick quarters. Later the same evening, he was transferred to Newcastle General Hospital. During the afternoon that day, a Flying Fortress from the USAAF airfield at Glatton flew into RAF Acklington. The purpose of its visit was to pick up the crew of another Fortress, which had been rescued from the sea by an air-sea rescue launch from Blyth. The crew from 457 Bomb Group had spent two days in their dinghy before being found. They were on their last operational mission. A Barracuda, Proctor and Stirling also dropped in that day for refuelling.

On 9 September, a USAAF Liberator from Old Buckenham airfield arrived to pick up a further aircraft crew who had been pulled from the sea by the Blyth rescue launch. At 10.02 p.m., a Fairey Barracuda made an emergency landing as it was having trouble with its fuel supply. It continued its journey the following day after being repaired by the station's engineers. On 30 September, the visit by a rare type of RAF aircraft—the Westland Welkin—was witnessed. First flown in November 1942 and designed as a high attitude fighter, it was never used operationally. Only sixty-seven examples were built. Most ended up in storage but two examples were used by the Air Fighting Development Unit at RAF Wittering. One of them (DX289) had to make a forced landing at RAF Acklington because of the failure of its port engine. An internal glycol leak had occurred whilst the aircraft was flying at 40,000 feet. At 20,000 feet, the engine burst into flames. The pilot considered bailing out but by putting the Welkin into a dive he managed to extinguish the flames. He then set course for RAF Acklington. The aircraft appeared over the airfield with smoke pouring from one engine. The pilot was unable to feather its propeller but none the less made a successful landing. It remained until the 29 October, during which time it had an engine change to return it to a serviceable condition.

The Welkin was not the only aircraft to experience engine trouble near RAF Acklington at that time. On 3 October 1944, a Mosquito (DZ645) of 618 squadron, RAF Beccles, landed on one engine. The aircraft was immediately towed to a hangar where it was placed under guard as it had top secret equipment on board. Earlier that day, a Wellington radioed a message that it wished to land as it was flying on one engine. On landing, its undercarriage collapsed halfway along the runway and the aircraft blocked runway twenty-three. It remained there for much of the day until a crane was obtained from RAF Woolsington to remove it. The following day, a single

Halifax that had been on an operational mission, touched down at RAF Acklington. A second aircraft landed at RAF Eshott. On the 10th, an Air Transport Auxiliary pilot made an emergency landing in a Spitfire IX after sodium flares were lit to assist it to find the airfield. Five days later, another Spitfire with undercarriage trouble made it safely down. It was nearly midnight on the 15th when RAF Blakelaw advised that nine Halifaxes returning from a bombing raid were going to be diverted to RAF Acklington. The airfield pointed out to Sector Headquarters that it could handle the aircraft but their departure may be delayed as only one 450 gallon bowser was available for refuelling. In view of this, it was decided to send the Halifaxes to RAF Charterhall instead.

At the beginning of November, high winds rendered inoperable the 'aerial lighthouse', which functioned in a similar manner as to that of a lighthouse for ships. This was the first occasion it had failed for this reason. A Short Stirling, piloted by Fg Off. Davis with a crew of six, made an emergency landing at 2.40 a.m. on 9 November. Its electrical system had failed and it was completely lost. Meals and accommodation were laid on for them. RAF Acklington was notified on the 16th to expect thirty Flying Fortresses in the afternoon but this was later cancelled. Two days later, nine Lancasters landed between 6.28 p.m. and 7.05 p.m. They belonged to 431 squadron from RAF Croft. Halifaxes and Stirlings were also expected and accommodation was prepared for their crews, but they did not materialise.

A more routine visit took place on the 26th, with the arrival of four Oxfords on a cross-country flight from RAF Montrose. At 8.58 p.m., Sector passed a plot of an aircraft that appeared to be lost and flying around in circles. The flying control at RAF Acklington stated they would endeavour to land the aircraft, despite visibility at only 1,200 yards with a cloud base of 500 feet and falling fast. Shortly after 9 p.m., searchlights were used to home the aircraft. A few moments later it called the airfield on the 'guard frequency' (a frequency reserved for emergency communications from aircraft in distress) and was given homing directions. The aircraft was now flying at a height of 1,500 feet. As it approached the airfield, mortar signals were fired. Its pilot then reported that he could see the airfield lighting but was confused by a long line of lights nearby. These turned out to be the street lighting of Broomhill. The local police were informed and turned the lights off. At 9.40 p.m., the pilot reported that the flare path was clearly visible and he would attempt to land. The aircraft touched down safely. It turned out to be a Beaufighter from RAF Northcoates which was returning from an operational mission. The pilot stated he had become completely lost when approaching the coast.

Later the same night, Sector reported a 'heavy aircraft' which required assistance, 10 miles south of Acklington. A cloud searchlight (searchlight beams which were reflected off the undersides of the clouds) and mortar signals were employed to guide the aircraft towards the airfield. The Lancaster landed at RAF Acklington with only fifteen minutes of fuel left.

On 28 November, a distress message was received from a Wellington which was having trouble with its tail plane. It came in very low, but landed safely. After consulting with his base at RAF Kinloss, the pilot took off, but Flying Control observed that the bomb doors were open and attempted to radio him. This met with no success so they informed his home base by telephone requesting them to relay a message to him.

The end of December 1944 saw several aircraft make emergency landings at RAF Acklington. At 5 p.m. on the 18th, a mayday message was received from a Coastal Command Mosquito returning from operations over Southern Norway. It was given the bearings to the airfield, where it landed safely. Some of its instruments were not functioning. The following day, the weather was very bad, with visibility less than 800 yards. An Airspeed Oxford was reported to be in trouble. Flares were fired and, a short time later, it appeared out of the gloom and landed at RAF Acklington. Its pilot belonged to the Air Transport Auxiliary and was flying between RAF Brunton and RAF Northolt.

A distress call was received not long after midnight on 22 December from a Lancaster from RAF Waddington which was returning from a bombing raid. Both of its starboard engines had failed. The pilot located RAF Acklington with the assistance of mortars and rockets fired from the ground. He landed with only twenty minutes of fuel. The Lancaster belonged to 463 squadron of the RAAF (Royal Australian Air Force). At this point, the bombing raids over Germany were reaching a climax with heavy raids on most nights. In the first year of the war such missions occurred relatively infrequently and involved small numbers of twin-engined bombers, unlike the huge formations of four-engined aircraft in the closing stages of the conflict. Two Avro Ansons and three Miles Masters landed later the same day. One of the Masters had a taxiing accident when its propeller hit a petrol bowser. The pilot stated that his aircraft's brakes were faulty.

An echo of the past occurred when one of the few remaining Gladiators sent out an emergency message. It was flying some 70 miles out to sea at a height of only 200 feet in very poor visibility and a cloud base of 600 feet. Flying control sent it bearings and homed it in to RAF Acklington. Ironically, the Gladiator piloted by Flt Lt Braithwaite, belonged to the Meteorological Flight based at RAF Thornaby. It was followed by an Oxford flown by Fg Off. Simmons, who was directed to the airfield by Sector Controllers. He caught sight of RAF Acklington only when mortar flares were fired above the cloud level. The pilot stated he was flying to RAF Drem from RAF Gatwick and had not caught sight of the ground since leaving London. At the same time, a de Havilland Dominie, with a Czechoslovakian Group Captain and Wing Commander, landed. The aircraft was flying from RAF Hendon to RAF Tain in the north of Scotland. It departed the following day when there was some improvement in the weather.

On Christmas Day, information was received that there may be a mass escape attempt by German POWs. Guards were placed on all the aircraft and the all drivers were warned. The guards were not removed until 2 January 1945. On December 26, a Lancaster flown by an Air Transport Auxiliary pilot touched down and stayed two days until the weather improved. On the 27th, there was a bomber diversion of 38 Group consisting of eight Halifaxes of 298 and 644 Squadrons from RAF Tarrant Rushton. Forty-eight crew, including eighteen officers stayed until the following day; 'the crews expressed appreciation of facilities and hospitality extended to them.'

At 10.25 p.m. on the 29th, an Avro Anson landed with wireless trouble. After the crew had supper, they took off shortly after midnight for their destination of RAF West Freugh. A Spitfire from RAF Boulmer made a forced landing on New Year's Day, after it had been involved in a mid-air collision over the sea. As a consequence it had lost part of its propeller. Owing to its excessive landing speed, the Spitfire's undercarriage collapsed and the aircraft formed a temporary obstruction on runway twenty-three; the pilot was unhurt.

There were heavy falls of snow during January 1945. At first RAF Acklington could no longer handle night diversions except for emergencies, as snow obscured the landing lights. In the morning of the 11th, a distress call was received from a Mosquito of the Pathfinder force. It was experiencing trouble with its starboard engine and was given permission to land. During the morning of the 14th, thirteen Avro Ansons of 62 OTU descended on RAF Acklington, as they could not land at their home base, RAF Ouston, because of fog. By the afternoon, the fog had cleared and the Ansons departed. Wg Cdr Roberts of 62 OTU 'rang up to thank all concerned for the reception that the crews received.'

The next day, three Wellingtons arrived. Returning from operations, they could not reach their base at RAF Langham because of poor weather. They were followed by two Mosquitos from RAF Watton on the 16th: 'Both pilots expressing thanks for excellent homings and service.'

During the latter part of the month there were few diversions, as snow fell heavily over Northumberland. A Hawker Tempest flown by a woman pilot of the Air Transport Auxiliary was guided into the airfield with the assistance of flares on 19 January. A week later, RAF Acklington was completely closed with over a foot of snow blanketing the airfield. The number of personnel available was too small to clear this. A 'Snogo' snow clearing machine, which had been lent to RAF Eshott as their requirements took priority, was used on runway twenty-three on the 28th. The efforts to clear the snow were in vain, as there were further falls during the night. By the next day, the 'Snogo' had broken down. By the 31st, the runway was nearly serviceable. Just after 2 p.m., twenty-six USAAF Liberators appeared in the sky above RAF Acklington and began circling overhead. As the runways were still covered with snow and ice, they were directed to land at RAF Eshott.

On 1 February 1945, a Typhoon from RAF Milfield, piloted by Fg Off. Renny, made a forced landing. His engine had started to fail while over the sea and he immediately pointed his aircraft towards RAF Acklington and came straight in. The Typhoon touched down on the short runway, running off the edge and onto the grass. By this time the propeller had almost stopped rotating. The Station diary relates, 'the pilot was extremely lucky to avoid a crash.'

That evening, just after 6 p.m., the airfield lights were turned on and pyrotechnics were fired continuously in an effort to aid a Spitfire missing from RAF Eshott. This was to no avail as it was learned some time later that the aircraft had crashed west of its airfield. A Mosquito, piloted by Flt Lt Topham, made a landing on one engine on the evening of the 7th. On the 10th, a Beaufighter from RAF Winfield was homed and landed with its starboard engine unserviceable. The next emergency landing was on the 18th, when a Douglas Dakota from RAF Wymeswold arrived with engine trouble. It departed later the same day. At 11.22 p.m., two Spitfires from RAF Boulmer were diverted here as their runway was blocked by a crash. Five Wellingtons from RAF Nuneaton, Leicestershire, were diverted to RAF Acklington because of bad weather. Pyrotechnics were lit to assist them locate the airfield.

At 10.20 p.m. on 22 February, operations at Sector Headquarters, Newcastle, contacted RAF Acklington concerning a Wellington in difficulties. It was flying over the sea to the east of the airfield on one engine. All the airfield lights were turned on and the fire tender alerted. Twenty minutes later, the aircraft appeared over the airfield and orbited it. It then descended and touched down on runway twenty-three, but overshot and burst into flames near the airfield boundary. Although the fire tender and ambulance arrived on the scene almost immediately, the pilot and navigator could not be rescued because of the ferocity of the fire. The wireless operator WO F. Goodey managed to drag himself out and was found 50 yards from the burning wreckage. The bodies of the pilot, Fg Off. Rowe, and the navigator, Fg Off. Allen, were recovered later and taken to the Station's mortuary. By 3 a.m., the wreckage had almost completely burnt out. The Wellington (NC692) was from 105 Operational Training Unit, RAF Bramcote, and had been on a training flight. A de Havilland Air Ambulance arrived on the 24th to take WO Goodley to the RAF Hospital at Cosford. Its departure was delayed until late in the evening because of gale-force winds. A Court of Inquiry was held into the accident at RAF Acklington two days later.

A diversion of twenty-six Lancasters from No. 3 Group landed within forty-six minutes at 6 p.m. on 23 February. Twenty-one of the aircraft were from 149 squadron, RAF Methwold, and the remaining five from 514 Squadron, RAF Waterbeach. A servicing crew of twelve men and three petrol bowsers were loaned from RAF Eshott and worked all night to refuel the planes. They departed the following morning, except for three which had developed minor defects.

For the remainder of 1945 and for years after, RAF Acklington continued to act as a diversion airfield for aircraft in distress. Further incidents are related in the following chapters.

# 13

# Airfields in Northumberland in the Second World War

In the months leading up to the declaration of war in September 1939, there was only one other airfield in north-east England other than RAF Acklington—namely, RAF Usworth.

## RAF Usworth

RAF Usworth, some 30 miles south, was immediately to the west of Sunderland. Opened in 1932, it had been designed to accommodate a single squadron of the newly-formed Royal Auxiliary Air Force. In 1937, 103 Squadron arrived and operated beside 607 County of Durham squadron. The regular RAF squadron's stay was short-lived, leaving 607 Squadron with its Gloster Gladiator biplanes to defend one of Britain's most important industrial regions. Work commenced on laying two concrete runways in September 1939; this was not completed until March 1940. During this time, 607 Squadron operated from RAF Acklington, returning the following summer with Hawker Hurricanes. Spitfires also flew patrols from what was now a Sector Airfield in Fighter Command. On 15 August 1940, it was singled out for a major attack by the Luftwaffe but many of the enemy raiders were destroyed before they could inflict damage on the airfield. It was bombed several more times in the year, but again escaped serious damage.

When 607 Squadron departed in January 1941, RAF Usworth was downgraded to a training role. From March 1941, it trained fighter pilots using Hawker Hurricanes. There were also Fairey Battle target tugs and several other types, including Boulton Paul Defiants. Among the pupils who attended 55 OTU was a Czechoslovakian named Augustin Preucil. On 18 September 1941, he stole a Hawker Hurricane I (W9147) and flew it to Belgium where the aircraft was handed over to the Germans. During his time in the RAF, Preucil had been gathering information, which he handed over to the enemy. In 1947, he was arrested and executed in Czechoslovakia.

On 28 April 1942, 55 OTU moved to RAF Annan. During its time at RAF Usworth, there were a large number of training accidents, with some sixteen Hawker Hurricanes being lost in the vicinity of the airfield. The airfield was far from ideal for

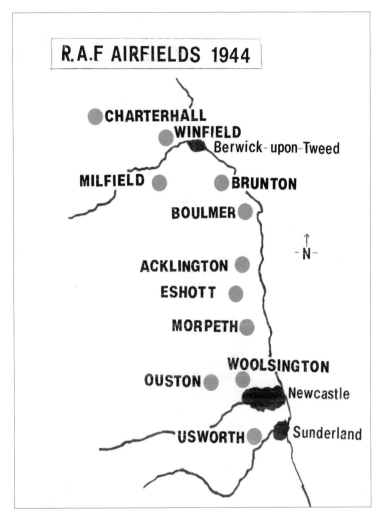

*Right:* The location of RAF airfields in north-east England in 1944. (*Malcolm Fife*)

inexperienced pilots, as the area often suffered from industrial haze and there were numerous tall chimneys as well as barrage balloons in the vicinity. From June 1942, airborne radar operators were trained on Avro Ansons of 62 OTU. When this unit departed around a year later, RAF Usworth spent the final years of the Second World War in relative obscurity, no longer hosting any squadrons or significant training units. In the post-war years, it was used by flying clubs and small civil aircraft, finally closing as an airfield in 1984. Much of it now lies under the Nissan Car Factory. It still retains a link with its past, being home to the North-East Aircraft Museum.

## RAF Ouston

In the summer of 1939, land was requisitioned at Ouston, west of Newcastle, for a purpose-built fighter airfield. Unlike RAF Acklington and RAF Usworth, the site was well inland, probably to make it less vulnerable to an attack from the sea but its relative inaccessibly meant that construction was slow. It eventually opened on 10

March 1941 as a Fighter Sector HQ for 13 Group, replacing Usworth in this role. Communications aircraft of 13 Group had been using a grass strip at Ouston from late 1940. They included a Vega Gull, two Magisters, three Gladiators, a Hornet Moth, a Proctor and a Miles Whitney Straight. Many of them would have been frequent visitors to RAF Acklington, some 22 miles to the north-east, which was a 13 Group Airfield. 317 Squadron was the first operational unit at RAF Ouston, arriving at the end of April 1941. No. 13 Group Anti-aircraft Co-operation Flight sent a detachment from RAF Turnhouse the following month. Throughout the war, target tugs flew from here providing air-to-air firing practice for squadrons based at RAF Acklington and units based at other Northumberland Airfields.

During its first year of existence, the airfield served as a satellite for 55 OTU's Hurricanes at Usworth until it moved to RAF Annan. In the same period, several front line fighter squadrons came and went including 81 Squadron Spitfires, 122 Squadron Spitfires and 232 Squadron Hurricanes. In 1942, 410 Night Fighter Squadron had a detachment of Defiants here. 281 Squadron also flew Defiants from the airfield, but on air-sea rescue missions. Ouston's last operational squadron was 350 Squadron, which spent most of June and July 1943 flying convoy patrols before returning to RAF Acklington. On 21 June 1943, 62 OTU arrived from RAF Usworth which was now too small for its increasing number of Ansons. The unit continued to train radar operators for the night fighter force until it disbanded in June 1945. A further training unit, which specialised in training French pilots on Spitfires, was based at RAF Ouston from July 1945 to March 1946.

At the end of the war, the airfield was allocated to Training Command which flew Harvards from it until 1948. It also became home to 607 (County of Durham) Auxiliary Air Force Squadron, which first flew the Spitfire F Mk 22 and then the Vampire FB 5. During the 1960s, Northumbria University Air Squadron Chipmunks were based here and it also acted as a relief landing ground for 6 FTS Jet Provosts operating from RAF Acklington. The airfield closed in 1974 and became an Army Barracks. The three runways still survive in the early twenty-first century.

## RAF Woolsington

In addition to the RAF airfields of Acklington and Usworth, in the 1930s, there was also a civil airport at Woolsington, near Newcastle. The Newcastle Aero Club had trained pilots for the RAF there since 1936. The grass airfield was requisitioned for military purposes when war broke out, bringing to an end the civilian flying school. 13 Group Fighter Command initially had their flight of communications aircraft based here, before moving them to RAF Ouston. Woolsington then became a satellite of this airfield and was heavily used in the war. Much of it was said to resemble a scrap dump, as 83 MU [Maintenance Unit] was based here. Its main task was to salvage the remains of aircraft that had crashed in northern England and bring them back to Woolsington. Air Sea rescue squadron moved here with Ansons and Walruses from RAF Ouston in June 1943. They departed in the autumn of that year for RAF Drem.

Woolsington remained a grass airfield until 1954, when the first concrete runway was laid. It is now the airport for Newcastle, one of Britain's major regional airports, with both scheduled and holiday flights to many destinations in Europe.

## RAF Eshott

1942 saw a great expansion in the number of airfields in Northumberland, all of which were used for training. This part of the country was ideal for this, as the skies were relatively uncluttered and the threat from enemy air attack was relatively low. Further south, large numbers of bombers were operating both day and night on bombing missions over the Continent. In early 1941, a site at Eshott, some 2 miles south-west of RAF Acklington, was surveyed with the intention of establishing a further fighter station here. Construction began the following year, but its role was changed to that of a training airfield. While it was being built, the site was attacked by German bombers. It had three runways, one of which was 5,700 feet long and therefore suitable for large aircraft. Unlike some other Northumberland airfields, it had essentially only one flying unit—57 OTU, responsible for training fighter pilots throughout the war. This unit arrived in November 1942 and remained at RAF Eshott until it was disbanded in May 1945. Spitfires 'handed down' from front line squadrons were the main type it flew. There were also smaller numbers of Miles Masters, Magisters, and Martinets. The strength of the unit was over a hundred aircraft. Aircraft accidents were a frequent occurrence, numbering on average four or five a month including two fatalities, but this was regarded as acceptable for a training unit of this type.

In March 1943, RAF Boulmer became Eshott's satellite airfield, which alleviated some of the pressure. Towards the end of the war, RAF Eshott was staffed by over 1,500 RAF personnel and a further 440 WAAF. In the early post-war years, the airfield was a relief landing ground for RAF Acklington. Its military service came to an end in 1948 after which it lay abandoned for many years. In the late twentieth century, it was brought back to life as a civil airfield for small private aircraft.

## RAF Boulmer

RAF Boulmer was located on the coast. It started life as a decoy airfield for RAF Acklington, some ten miles to its south. It had three fake runways with mock-up Spitfires and Hurricanes, and at night was illuminated to give the impression of an active airfield. On several occasions, it was bombed and machine-gunned. In 1942, the land was requisitioned to construct an actual airfield, with some urgency to complete it to relieve the pressure on RAF Eshott. The first Spitfire from 57 OTU landed there on 1 March 1943. Basic training was carried out at RAF Eshott and the advanced part of the course was undertaken at RAF Boulmer. Hawker Hurricanes from 59 OTU, located at RAF Milfield, also used it as a satellite airfield in 1943-44. When 57 OTU was disbanded after VE Day (6 June 1945), RAF Boulmer was reduced to a care and maintenance status. In the early 1950s, additional land was acquired to build a large radar station there. In the 1960s, it was used as a relief landing ground for aircraft based at RAF Acklington, mainly 6FTS Jet Provosts. The airfield was abandoned and it has since been returned to farmland, with most of its runways ripped up. The radar station, however, continued in operation; in 2016, it is the only surviving RAF station in Northumberland.

## RAF Morpeth

There was a further training airfield south-west of the town of Morpeth, located 12 miles from RAF Acklington. While most RAF aircraft in Northumberland were single seat types, this airfield was home to the Blackburn Botha, a four seat, twin-engined aircraft intended as a torpedo bomber but demoted to the training role. RAF Morpeth became active in early 1942 when it hosted 4 Air Gunnery School training thousands of air gunners for Bomber and Coastal Command. The unpopular Botha was replaced by the Avro Anson in 1943. Air-to-air firing was carried out over the sea at the Druridge Range. In August alone, some 325,000 rounds of ammunition were expended. The Gunnery School closed in December 1944, after completing sixty-nine courses. In the spring of the following year, 80 OTU was formed at RAF Morpeth for training French pilots to fly Spitfires. Its stay was short-lived as it moved to RAF Ouston in July 1945. Flying ceased after this, and by 1950, many of its buildings had been demolished. In the following decades, trees were planted over much of the site.

## RAF Milfield

The most remote of Northumberland's airfield was RAF Milfield, some 20 miles to the north-west of RAF Acklington. It was situated far inland and rather surprisingly very close to the foot of the Cheviot Hills, five miles north-west of Wooler. The site was surveyed in 1940, when it was intended to build an airfield for the training of bomber crews. Construction began in 1941, by which time the criteria had changed and it was to be a fighter training station. The first unit to be based here was 59 OTU, which arrived in August 1942 with seventy-one Hurricanes and twelve Typhoons, as well as Fairey Battles and Miles Martinets. Training included air-to-air firing, formation flying and advanced navigation. As the threat from enemy fighters decreased, RAF Milfield became increasingly involved in the instruction of ground attack techniques for the forthcoming invasion of Europe. No. 1 Specialised Low Attack Instructors School was established at the airfield with Hurricanes in December 1942. A new ground attack range was constructed with tanks and simulated convoys as targets at Goswick Sands opposite Holy Island. Target towing facilities were also ramped up. The north tow operated between Holy Island and the Farne Islands and the South Tow between Dunstanburgh Castle and the Farne Islands, with the tug aircraft operating parallel to the coast.

No. 59 OTU closed in January 1944, but the Specialised Low Attack Instructors School remained, being absorbed into the newly formed Fighter Leaders School. This was divided into five squadrons—three with Spitfires and two with Typhoons. Its original intention was to give experience in strafing, dive bombing, and rocket firing to pilots of the 2nd Tactical Air Force USAAF using live ammunition. Mustangs and P47 Thunderbolts also descended on RAF Milfield to participate in highly realistic ground attack exercises in the months leading up to D Day. At the end of 1944, 56 OTU was reformed at RAF Milfield with Tempests and Typhoons. The final phase of the course was undertaken at RAF Brunton. At the same time, the Fighter Leaders School left for southern England where it was thought it would be better placed, being nearer the conflict. By this time, the airfield was staffed by over 1,100 RAF personnel plus around 500 WAAFs. The Tempests and Typhoons of 56 OTU continued to fly from RAF Milfield until February 1946, when it was disbanded, having outlived many similar units by nearly a year. Like most other airfields in Northumberland, it closed shortly after the end of the Second World War, but the site retained an aviation connection, being used by the Border Gliding Club. By the end of the twentieth century, most of the airfield's buildings had been demolished and the runways removed.

## RAF Charterhall

In September 1939, the next RAF airfield to the north of RAF Acklington was at RAF Drem, close to the Firth of Forth. Two further airfields were established a short distance across the border in Scotland in the early years of the war. Like most of those in Northumberland, they were built on the First World War landing grounds and used for training purposes. The largest of the two airfields was RAF Charterhall, situated 3 miles north-east of Greenlaw. It opened in May 1942, and housed 54 OTU responsible for training night fighter crews initially with Blenheims and later with Beaufighters. These aircraft often made use of RAF Acklington if bad weather prevented them from landing back at their base. The last unit to use the airfield was 303 Squadron Mustangs on an air-to-ground firing course in March 1946.

## RAF Winfield

RAF Charterhall's satellite airfield was RAF Winfield situated some six miles to the west of Berwick-upon-Tweed. It had a relatively brief existence, closing in May 1945. Both locations have been returned to agriculture, but unlike some other airfields, they have not altogether vanished, as their runways and some buildings still survive.

## RAF Scorton

Also worth a mention is RAF Scorton which was situated in Yorkshire 9 miles south-west of Darlington. For much of the Second World War, night fighter squadrons operated from there protecting the industrial centres of Tees Side and Tyneside. Often, their aircraft were airborne along with those from RAF Acklington when there was enemy activity over north-east England. Little remains of the airfield today, with the land having been quarried for sand and gravel.

# 14
# 1945–59 OTU and the Last Months of the War

59 OTU: February–June 1945, Typhoons, Masters
19 Squadron: May–August 1945, Mustang IV
140 Squadron: 12 July 1945–19 Sept 1945, no aircraft

In the last months of the Second World War, RAF Acklington reverted to its role as a training station. The threat from enemy bombers was fading as fast as the boundaries of the Third Reich were contracting. The RAF had stopped building new airfields in Britain in 1943 and, the following year, began to run down some of its units. While the war in Europe was drawing to a close, it was expected the conflict against Japan could drag on for many more years. It was intended to launch intensive attacks on the mainland, with large numbers of ground attack aircraft. It was probably with this in mind that it was decided to reform 59 OTU at RAF Acklington to instruct fighter-bomber pilots.

No. 59 OTU had been formed to train fighter pilots at Crosby-on-Eden in 1941 and disbanded in February 1944. By that time, it had flown no less than 101,335 hours, during which 1,485 pilots had been trained. At its closure, it had a large fleet of aircraft which included seventy-seven Hawker Hurricanes, eighteen Miles Masters and fifteen Miles Martinets. No. 59 OTU officially reformed on 26 February; however, at that time, it existed only on paper. At the beginning of March, pilots from front line squadrons began to arrive to take up posts as instructors. Grp Capt. P. Hawks was posted to RAF Acklington from Fighter Command Headquarters as Station Commander. At 10.20 a.m. on 4 March, Oxfords and Hurricanes of 288 Squadron arrived from RAF Ouston. Later in the day, a detachment of Vultee A-31 Vengeances of 291 Squadron also deployed to RAF Acklington. They would serve as targets and target tugs for training purposes. No. 6168 Servicing Echelon arrived from Western Europe, where it had been attached to the 2nd Tactical Air Force, only to be disbanded and absorbed into 59 OTU. Its personnel arrived by rail, with their equipment and tools following on ten three-ton vehicles. Next came 6257 Servicing Echelon, which had also been withdrawn from Western Europe. It was also to become part of 59 OTU. More pilots—including two Canadians from 440 Squadron and others from 68 and 181 Squadrons—arrived in the days immediately before 20 March, when the first training course was due to begin.

On 20 March 1944, No. 1 Course commenced with the arrival of twenty-two pilots. All were interviewed by the Station Commander, who was also in charge of the training wing. Each pilot was told that he was to consider himself as a qualified pilot on a conversion course to fly and fight in Hawker Typhoons. It was explained that absolute obedience was expected and that breaches of flying discipline would not be tolerated. The intake for the course consisted of eleven officers and eleven NCO pilots. Nine already had considerable experience as instructors in Canada on Harvards and other elementary types. Around the same time, all personnel of Northstead GCI radar station were confined to camp due to a suspected case of diphtheria. Fortunately this proved to be a false alarm.

The course commenced flying on 23 March. By the evening of the following day, all had successfully made solo flights on the Typhoon. The second phase of the course involved gunnery training. The pilots were also instructed in dive bombing and rocket firing; a number produced exceptional results. At the conclusion of this phase, the pilots were given a brief lesson in night flying in the Miles Master. This was to familiarise them with the layout of the airfield lighting and to demonstrate the type of approach required when flying the Typhoon in the dark. Each pilot then notched up about four hours night flying over the next seven days. This was assisted by the officer in charge standing at the end of the runway giving instructions to the pilots on their circuits and approach. He was able communicate with the aircraft by means of a headphone and microphone linked by a long cable to a VHF set in the airfield control caravan. The participants also had to attend lectures covering navigation, signals, glider towing and operational sorties with rockets and bombs.

In the final stages of the course the pilots were given the opportunity to fire guns and rockets. 59 OTU could not obtain the facilities they initially requested and had to make do with the Milfield Range located at Holy Island. Improvisation was the order of the day. Concrete blocks on the beach were painted yellow to act as targets for rocket firing and the workshops at RAF Acklington constructed a floating target. Not long after it had been moored in position, the official target arrived. A white circle 200 feet wide was also marked out on the beach for dive bombing practice. By using the two floors in the range hut with a radio set on each, it was possible to run a dive bombing and rocket firing programme concurrently. The course concluded with formation flying. Take-offs were carried out in pairs followed by squadron landings—flying line astern then breaking and landing in rapid succession. A wing of thirty-two aircraft, led by the instructors, filled the sky at the end of the training.

On 10 April, eight officers and seven service NCOs arrived for Course No. 2. Within three days, they had all soloed on the Typhoon. This was to be 59 OTU's last course. A signal was received at the end of April stating that the expected intake of new pilots for the third course had been cancelled. Despite this, the number of Typhoons on strength had increased to forty-three from twenty-three just a month earlier. A further signal was received on 24 May defining the future role for RAF Acklington. When 59 OTU was disbanded, it would become a forward airfield in the Newcastle sector with one day and one night fighter squadron. RAF Eshott, RAF Ouston, and RAF Boulmer would be reduced to 'care and maintenance', but remain as satellite airfields for RAF

Acklington. By the end of that month, 59 OTU aircraft began to depart when fourteen Typhoons and three Miles Masters flew out to 56 OTU at RAF Milfield.

On 6 June, 59 OTU was officially disbanded without ceremony. All its pupils and many of its instructors had already left. During its short existence at RAF Acklington it suffered two accidents to its aircraft. The most serious occurred on 26 March, a few days after flying had commenced. Flt Lt W. Leray was undertaking a height climbing exercise when his aircraft suffered engine failure, later attributed to a mechanical fault. He managed to make a forced landing on Goswick Sands near Holy Island. The Typhoon Ib (JP851), caught fire with the wreckage being covered by the sea when the tide came in. The pilot fared somewhat better, suffering from shock and some bruises to his legs and chin. The medical officer at RAF Brunton, the nearest airfield, attended to him. A less serious incident took place on 18 May. WO J. Spencer's Typhoon 1b (MN944) experienced engine failure and made a forced landing in a field 1.5 miles to the north of Warkworth.

Throughout 1945, RAF Acklington continued its role as a place of refuge for aircraft in distress. Late at night on 2 March, four Spitfires from RAF Boulmer landed there as there had been a crash on the runway of their own airfield. One of the diverted Spitfires taxied into RAF Acklington's petrol dump and damaged its wing tip and propeller. Two days later, a Warwick from RAF Thornaby was homed on GCI radar and put down on the airfield. Later that evening, a further Warwick was diverted to Acklington. On the 17th, a Typhoon from the OTU at RAF Milfield managed to land, without its flaps functioning, on its third attempt. Its pilot was on his first solo in the type and the chief flying instructor radioed instructions to help the distressed aircraft land safely. He again provided assistance to a Wellington from 62 OTU that could not lock its wheels or get its flaps down. It was brought into land successfully. At 10 p.m. on the 29th, an aircraft was heard orbiting over the airfield. Radio contact was established and not long after a Lancaster from RAF Wigsley touched down. It took off three hours later, as it was on a cross-country exercise and had landed at Acklington by mistake.

On 8 April, personnel from the station went to the help of a Percival Proctor, which had made a forced landing near Bedlington. Later the same month, an Airspeed Oxford running short of fuel was homed on the airfield and landed without a problem. Shortly before 7 p.m. on 3 May, flying control heard a distress call to RAF Coltishall from an aircraft using the call sign 'Presta Yellow 4'. When there was no reply, it called 'any airfield on the East Coast'. The controllers at RAF Acklington answered. The pilot informed them that he was running short of fuel. Using the airfield's VHF homing, assisted by fixer stations in Newcastle, it was determined that the aircraft was some 110 miles east-south-east of the airfield. A bearing was given, but after 15 minutes the pilot informed the controllers that he only had 2-3 minutes of fuel left and that he intended to abandon his aircraft, a North American Mustang. RAF Acklington instructed him to keep transmitting so they could obtain a fix of his position. The last message heard was 'Presta Yellow 4 bailing out now'. The wheels were set in motion for an air-sea rescue operation. The high speed launch was dispatched from Blyth to the last known position of the Mustang. A Warwick ASR aircraft searched the area and reported that they had located a dinghy. At 8.45 p.m. the launch reached the dinghy and picked up the pilot. In just over two hours he was back on dry land. The entry in the diary for RAF Acklington for that incident ends with the comment: 'This can be counted as a very successful rescue.'

Early in the morning of 26 June, the beacon crew at RAF Acklington reported an aircraft circling overhead and firing red flares. All the runway lights were turned on and the aircraft landed safely. It was a Fairey Firefly from RNAS Drem which was very short of fuel and had become lost. During the following month, there were several more unscheduled visitors. Five Wellingtons *en route* from RAF Lossiemouth to RAF Kirkbride diverted to RAF Acklington owing to poor weather on 5 July. Eleven days later, a Mosquito piloted by a Group Captain sent out a distress call, stating that the aircraft was flying at 10,000 feet and was icing up. He was successfully guided to RAF Acklington and landed without further incident. The next day, twelve Tiger Moths from RAF Leuchars and a further eleven from RAF Montrose landed for refuelling and then took off for Carlisle. In the late morning of the 26th, an Anson appeared over the airfield and began circling and firing red flares. The aircraft had suffered an engine failure but landed safely.

For most of 1945, 288 Squadron had a detachment of aircraft which provided targets for other units. A Vultee Vengeance flown by Fg Off. Matthews *en route* from the squadron's main base at RAF Hutton Cranswick on 30 July was unable to lower its undercarriage. The pilot managed to execute a successful belly landing beside the main runway. The RAF received some 1,300 Vengeances, many of which were assigned for close support operations against the Japanese. The Vengeance often performed dive bombing attacks against jungle targets which were otherwise difficult to strike. Those in Britain mainly served in the more mundane role of target tugs in no less than ten squadrons.

Not long after midnight on 1 August, six Fairey Fireflies from RNAS Drem landed at RAF Acklington, as their own base was covered in sea mist. An hour later, two Beaufighters from RAF East Fortune were also diverted there for the same reason. Twelve Mustangs of 64 Squadron from RAF Horsham St. Faith landed here for refuelling on the 23rd whilst on exercise and were airborne again by the early afternoon. Four days later, a Mosquito from RAF Charterhall, flown by Plt Off. Hardy, undershot while landing. It caught one of its undercarriage legs in the boundary fence. The aircraft continued flying and put down on one wheel 50 yards from the edge of the main runway. Hardy was unhurt.

Up until the end of 1944, RAF Acklington usually housed at least one fighter squadron to protect the airspace of north-east England. This changed at the beginning of 1945, when it was transformed into a training base. The air defence of the region was not altogether neglected as a detachment of three Mosquitos from 125 Squadron, instructed to carry out coastal patrols, arrived at the end of April. They returned to their home base the following month with the cessation of hostilities.

On 8 May, VE Day, the formal surrender of Germany to the Allies was announced over the tannoy at RAF Acklington by the commanding officer Wg Cdr Petrie. All armed aircraft on the airfield had their guns unloaded. At 11 a.m., there was a special

Thanksgiving Service in the station chapel. Festivities included a large number of outdoor sports and an all-ranks dance in the evening. The use of RAF Acklington as a reception centre for repatriated prisons of war was considered, but appears to have proceeded no further. At the end of May, RAF Acklington was again home to a fighter squadron. Based at RAF Peterhead for long range escort duties with Coastal Command, 19 Squadron equipped with the North American Mustang IV, was instructed to move to the Northumberland airfield. Eighteen of their aircraft flew to RAF Acklington on the 23rd, where they 'arrived in time for tea. First impressions were very favourable. In spite of the previous night's work a large part of the squadron managed to try out the new bar.'

The following day was spent moving into the dispersals. The flying training programme scheduled for the next few days was delayed, as the wrong crystals had been supplied for the radio transmitter sets in the planes. The pilots had a look at the air firing range on the 29th, and in the afternoon paid a visit to Fighter Command Sector operations:

Most of the squadron went and surveyed a lot of bored people in the ops. room with the W.A.A.F.s knitting in different corners of it and then a very fine tea was laid on in an equally fine mess. After that as the ops. room was inadvertently almost in Newcastle, the boys went to try their luck there. It was considered very inferior to Aberdeen.

As May drew to a close, some formation flying and target practice on drogues were carried out. At that time the only other flying units at RAF Acklington were the detachments of 288 and 289 Squadrons with a small number of Vengeance target tugs.

June commenced with a close formation flypast of 19 Squadron's Mustangs over the Group HQ at Nottingham. They also flew over a number of airfields on their route in Squadron formation. It was intended to repeat this on the 5th, but poor weather precluded this. Instead, air-to-ground firing practice was carried out: 'In the evening the pilots took on the ground crews at snooker in the airmen's mess and were beaten 4–1 the result was put down to the beer consumed by the pilots.'

A further sign that the war was rapidly drawing to a close came in the form of an order that all the guns on the Mustangs were to be removed except for those in armament practice camps. Also, little flying was now done at weekends. The squadron record book's entry for Sunday 10 June: 'A quiet day, most people devoting the morning to sleep and the evening to a few quiet beers.'

Weather was poor on the morning of the 12th. By the afternoon, it had improved slightly, but the sky remained very cloudy. Both A- and B-flights took off to carry out practice interceptions. The former completed the exercise without incident. Two Mustangs of B-Flight, the first flown by Flt Lt Clayton, followed by the second flown by Flt Lt A. Young, entered cloud at around 4,000 feet. When the leader broke through the cloud base he found he was alone—there was no sign of Young's Mustang IV (KH867). Throughout the afternoon and long into the evening, his colleagues, flying usually in pairs, searched in vain. It was later reported that the crew of a Norwegian ship had witnessed a plane dive into the sea and explode. It was thought that Young may have broken through the cloud at 500 feet and had no time to pull out of the dive.

Practice flying continued over the next few days but was hindered by the shortage of aircraft. On Sunday 17 June, 'a large party of pilots cycled over to Warkworth, where they had a lazy afternoon and evening and had a small sortie on the river.'

The following morning, a number of Mustangs took off for cross-country flying. On Wednesday 20 June, the weather was again bad with low cloud. Despite this, Flt Lt Shirreff took off with two other Mustangs to gain more information on the meteorological conditions. As they flew north, conditions deteriorated further and Shirreff instructed the other two aircraft to return to RAF Acklington. Whilst doing so, the formation entered a bank of mist and the leader called for individual climbs and then to re-join above the cloud. When they cleared the cloud, one of the aircraft was missing. Flt Lt Robert Williams had continued flying at low level and his Mustang IV (KH664) had hit a railway embankment near Berwick-upon-Tweed, killing him. Despite this loss, the squadron played a football match against SHQ in the evening. A further formation flypast was made over RAF Hucknall, near Nottingham, on the 25th. Air-to-ground firing took place over the following days. On the 29th, an exercise with HMS *Glasgow* was undertaken. Six of 19 Squadron's Mustangs carried out mock attacks on the ship to provide its anti-aircraft gunners with practice: 'It was a most enjoyable exercise and a novel experience being allowed to beat up one of HMS ships without being fired on.'

A few of the new pilots took to the air on the last day of the month:

> In the afternoon there was a fairly large sortie to Warkworth beach where the braver members played cricket in bathing trunks. However the weather was not very ripe for sunbathing and proceedings were cut short by rain and the party adjourned to the mess where they spent the rest of the evening trying to keep quiet in the bar.

At the beginning of July, the Mustangs had their spinners painted blue and white—the old squadron's colours. In what was becoming a regular occurrence, there was a further flypast over 12 Fighter Groups Headquarters at Hucknall, this time involving five squadrons. RAF Acklington contributed nine Mustangs on what was described as an appalling hot day. Five Mitchells arrived on the 9th, bringing with them 140 Squadron aircrew returning from the Netherlands. During the next few days, further personnel arrived with their servicing echelon. While at RAF Acklington, the squadron was non-operational and did not have any aircraft. It was disbanded later that year. In the morning of the 12th, flying was restricted by visibility limited to only 200 yards. In the afternoon there was a series of lectures on air gunnery. The rest of the day was taken up with a cricket match between the ground crew and pilots with the former winning; the squadron record book mentions:

> In the evening there was an ENSA show which was attended by most of the squadron in sheer desperation to find something different to do. At the end of the performance, most of us were confirmed in our former beliefs that it is safer to stick to the normal routine and not go looking for something different to do.

The following day, the weather improved and there was formation flying in the morning followed by local flying. In the afternoon there was a practice interception which involved a scramble of four Mustangs. They were ordered to climb to an altitude of 25,000 feet and then fly up and down for nearly half an hour:

> In the evening the Sergeants Mess had a big dance which from all accounts the uproar could be heard from some way off, went with a pretty good swing. The accounts aren't any two lucid as no one seems to remember very much about it.

In the middle of July, the serviceability of 19 Squadron's aircraft was high, with a considerable amount of local flying carried out. On the 24th, the first night flying for a long time was undertaken. There was a good moon and the last aircraft did not land until 4 a.m. A few days later, cloud prevented the practice interception of several Mosquitos. 288 Squadron still had a detachment at RAF Acklington in the summer 1945. One of their Vengeances, flown by Fg Off. Matthews, was unable to lower its undercarriage at the end of a flight from RAF Hutton Cranswick, the unit's main base. The pilot managed to make a successful belly landing adjacent to the main runway.

August began with long days of sunshine. On the afternoon of the 2nd, a sea fog engulfed the airfield and several aircraft had difficulty landing. By the August Bank Holiday, the weather had changed and it was raining heavily. The squadron's spirit was further dampened when they heard they were to move to RAF Molesworth. They did not have a very high opinion of this airfield. A farewell party was held on the 10th, 'which went with a swing and a great success.'

Three days later, 19 Squadron's Mustangs roared down RAF Acklington's runway. They were bound for RAF Bradwell Bay for a gunnery course before proceeding to their new base. The following day, eighteen Mosquitos of 219 Squadron flew in from Twente in the Netherlands. On 15 August, it was all over. The Second World War had come to an end. Unlike VE day, there was no special announcement over the station tannoy of VJ day, as most of the station personnel had already heard the news on the radio. In the afternoon, there was a football match between the Officers' Mess and the Sergeants Mess. A dance was held in the evening and the following day, there was an impromptu concert in the station cinema. With many personnel posted on leave, there was little flying during the remainder of August. There was one incident. A Mosquito from RAF Charterhall caught the port leg of the undercarriage on the airfield boundary fence. The aircraft continued flying and landed on one wheel, 150 feet from the edge of the runway. The pilot was unhurt.

# 15

# Post-war Fighter Airfield 1945–1946

219 Squadron: August 1945–April 1946, Mosquito NF.30
263 Squadron: September 1945–April 1946, Meteor F.3
288 Squadron: August 1945–May 1946, Vengeance IV (detachment only)

At the end of the Second World War, there were over 500 RAF airfields in the British Isles. With the cessation of hostilities, many were rapidly run down and closed, but RAF Acklington avoided this fate and was to retain its role as a forward base for fighter aircraft to protect north-east England. 219 Squadron, equipped with the Mosquito NF.30, capable of intercepting aircraft up to an altitude of 39,000 feet, was to provide the night fighter capability. Day-time fighter cover was to be undertaken by the Meteors of 263 Squadron, the first jet aircraft to be permanently based at RAF Acklington.

The early part of September was taken up with formation flying, as 219 Squadron's aircraft were to give a flypast at the forthcoming 'Battle of Britain' Open Day. On 11 September, Mosquito NF.30 (NT.270) suffered a failure of its port engine immediately after take-off. The valve collets in a cylinder became displaced and this led to a valve spring breaking. The aircraft made a circuit on one engine and, approaching too fast without flaps, made a belly landing. It then burst into flames and was reduced to ashes. Its crew—Flt Lt E. L. Jones and FS J. Prince—suffered severe burns to their hands and faces They had arrived from 54 Operational Training Unit only six days earlier; this was their first flight as members of 219 Squadron.

To commemorate the anniversary of the Battle of Britain, a parade was held attended by all members of 140 and 219 Squadrons, Squadron Headquarters and the WAAF personnel. It formed up on the perimeter track between first and second hangars. Prayers were said by Padre Sqn Ldr Day, then Wg Cdr Berry addressed the parade:

> He reminded everyone of the events during the Battle of Britain, of the Squadrons that had taken part and helped win the vital Battle. Then the CO went to speak of the present and the future and to show us that though the Battle of Britain had been won and the War in Europe and Asia had now ended, we were still involved in a very grim struggle and it was up to each and everyone to give unstintingly of their best

so that we might achieve a successful peace. The parade then marched past Wg Cdr Berry who took the salute at the main flagstaff.

On 17 September, numerous night flights were undertaken. The following day, bad weather grounded all aircraft. The next day was not much better, so the aircrew made do with 'a fine game of rugger'. A group exercise was carried out on the 25th—219 Squadron and 125 Squadron from RAF Church Fenton undertook a mock bombing raid on Peterborough. The Squadron's records relate: 'It was most successful as we were not intercepted until leaving the target.'

At the end of the month, a formation fly past was staged over Newcastle and the surrounding districts for Thanksgiving Week. Around the same time, the last Belgian member of 219 Squadron departed for his homeland. The Meteors of 263 Squadron arrived on the 21st: 'The squadron dispersal on the north side of the airfield proved well set out, clean and comfortable.'

Sqn Ldr A. Gaze flew to Prestwick on the 27th, where he gave an aerobatic display to mark the Air Transport Auxiliary's departure from the airfield. 263's aircraft also took part in the Thanksgiving celebrations. Twelve Gloster Meteors flew over Newcastle, Whitley Bay, Morpeth and Sunderland on the 29th.

At the beginning of October, the Meteors were scrambled as part of an exercise held by 12 Group. Their mission was to intercept a number of Avro Lancasters flying at 15,000 feet. The Meteors 'attacked' some 15 miles south of Durham. The bombers' escort of Mustangs offered up little opposition. A less successful exercise was held on the 16th. At 9.15 a.m., nine Meteors took off for RAF Church Fenton, where they were refuelled. In the afternoon, all the aircraft were scrambled but one returned to base within a few minutes. Ground control did not keep in constant touch with the aircraft and the squadron failed to make contact with the enemy. The pilots caught sight of a few escort Mustangs but no interceptions were attempted.

There was yet another exercise at the end of the month detailed in the squadron's record book:

At 13.30 hours Wg Cdr W. E. Schrader DFC and Bar, briefed pilots taking part in the Squadron dispersal—a full dress rehearsal briefing took place reminding all of the hectic operations not so long ago. His aircraft took off at 14.40 hours. The ground crews standing on bays had a 'grandstand' view of the Meteors taking off in formations of three. For the purpose of todays operation a 'State of War' existed between England and 'Scotia' owing to a dispute over the boundary. Meteors acting as Fighter Bombers were to attack targets, in fact an English 'Pearl Harbour'. The Squadron flew, climbing to 9,000 feet to Farne Islands then turned to port to attack Turnhouse and Milfield at zero feet. The Scots were caught napping—some fighters were seen but no attack made. The Meteors flew in and away and hedge hopped back to base. A general 'natter' followed in dispersal and all agreed a successful operation. Weather proved fair with fair visibility.

Eleven aircraft of 126 Squadron and twelve aircraft of 65 Squadron from RAF Hethel used RAF Acklington as an advanced base for operation during this exercise. Although the days of large numbers of four-engined bombers returning from raids on Germany and diverting to RAF Acklington were now a thing of the past, three Lancasters had to land there 10 October. Their original destination was RAF Thornaby but it was closed because of bad weather. Fifteen Spitfires of 122 Squadron flying from RAF Hawkinge to RAF Wick called on the 19th for refuelling.

Less fortunate were five Ansons which also arrived for refuelling on 1 November. They were marooned for five days because of adverse weather conditions. The day after they had departed a Halifax (PM460) flown by Fg Off. Blake made an emergency landing. It was *en route* from RAF Edzell in Scotland to RAF Brawdy in South Wales when its radio, radar and two compasses failed. This was not the only problem—the pilot was flying on three engines with the fourth on the verge of failing. Flying Control at RAF Acklington heard the distress calls and turned on the airfield lights immediately. The Halifax flew straight in. Its crew were very relieved to have made a safe landing and stated that they were completely lost with little fuel left. They thanked the personnel at RAF Acklington for their assistance.

On 29 November, a Vengeance of 288 Squadron, flown by WO Lockyer, suffered engine failure immediately after take-off. Lockyer managed to land safely with flames coming from the exhaust. There was a detachment of a small number of Vengeances of 288 Squadron for target towing duties at RAF Acklington up until June 1946. During November, six Mosquitos and an Oxford of 219 Squadron left for two weeks detachment at B 158 Lubeck airfield in the British occupied sector of Germany. They returned on 1 December but had to land at RAF Charterhall because of adverse weather conditions. The crews that remained at home carried out a group formation exercise with 264 Squadron from RAF Church Fenton and 307 Polish Squadron from Horsham St. Faith. 219 Squadron's Mosquitos were again to perform as bombers and attack Hatfield. In an attempt to deceive the defences the aircraft flew all the way to Brussels in Belgium and then headed back to England to perform the raid. This ruse did not work and, despite the efforts of their Mustang escorts, 219 Squadron's Mosquitos received a severe mauling by the Meteors assigned to protect Hatfield.

In November 1945, a number of the Meteors were grounded for modifications. Gloster employees fitted dive brakes and 100-gallon ventral tanks on two of the aircraft. Flying was further restricted because of a shortage of ground crews. During December, flying training continued by both day and night. On most days, the Meteors of 263 Squadron carried out practice flights which included low flying, aerobatics and cross-country runs. The squadron's Airspeed Oxford was flown on 18 December on a photographic mission with several Mosquitos.

Since the summer of 1945 more than a hundred members had been demobbed or posted. Flt Lt Mullenders was posted to the Belgium Air Force Training School:

We were very sorry to lose our old friend. He was a captain in the Belgium Air Force prior to the outbreak of the war, he fought the Germans in obsolete biplanes, was later decorated for his work in the underground movement after Belgium ceased to resist. With the Gestapo on his trail, he left Belgium, fled to Spain and joined the RAF Reading 616 Squadron in early 1943.

On 3 December 1945, twelve Spitfire IXBs of 130 Squadron and fourteen Spitfire IXs of 165 Squadron, all from RAF Manston, descended on RAF Acklington. They were *en route* to RAF Charterhall, but were diverted at five minutes notice for refuelling. On take-off, one Spitfire of 130 Squadron damaged its tail wheel. A Liberator from RAF Disforth found refuge at RAF Acklington on the 14th, when it was the only airfield open in the north of England. The following day, two Avro Yorks arrived. By the next day, the weather had improved enough to allow one of the Yorks and the Liberator to return to their bases. The other York became unserviceable and remained at RAF Acklington until the 28th.

Christmas activities included a party in the NAAFI for the children of the station personnel. They were entertained by a series of films in the cinema followed by tea. Then Father Christmas came down the 'chimney' (which had been built round the door) and distributed presents to the children. These gifts had been made by the airmen and WAAFs in their spare time. On Christmas morning, a soccer match was played between the sergeants and the airmen. Then the sergeants visited the Officers' Mess before both the officers and senior NCOs proceeded to the Airmen's Mess where the airmen and airwomen were served with a traditional Christmas dinner. During the afternoon, there was a free cinema show and at night there was an all-ranks dance in the Acklington Club. To celebrate New Year's Eve, there was a fancy dress ball in the Officers' Mess.

Flying resumed on 1 January 1946; however, it did not get off to a good start. The undercarriage of a Meteor flown by Flt Lt Walton collapsed, causing a belly landing. The pilot was unhurt. A Warwick from RAF Kinloss landed short of fuel on the 17th. Three days later the airfield had to be closed due to ice patches on the runways. On

A Gloster Meteor of 263 Squadron after a landing accident on 24 March 1946. Accidents with early jets were a common occurrence. (*ww2 images*)

the 21st, two Tiger Moths piloted by Fleet Air Arm pilots had to land in a field to the south, as ice and snow covered the runways. The Meteors of 263 Squadron had been due to depart for RAF Charterhall, just across the border in Scotland, on the 21 January but this was postponed because of the ice on RAF Acklington's runways. A thaw on the 24th made the move possible. The deployment to this airfield consisted of nine Meteors and an Oxford. Five of their Meteors were left at RAF Acklington. While at RAF Charterhall, the course was interrupted by several spells of bad weather.

Unlike many contemporary airfields, RAF Charterhall was retained by Fighter Command as No. 3 Armament Practice Station within No. 12 Group. It began operating in this role—to provide weapons practice for operational fighter squadrons—from 1 November 1945. On a typical course, the APS instructors gave lectures on all subjects, including the assembly and dismantling of .303 inch and .50 inch Browning machine guns, and 20-mm Hispano cannon and their belt-fed mechanisms. Talks were also given on pyrotechnics, bombs, bomb carriers and rocket projectiles. The pilots were shown instructional films on dive bombing and the theory of the gyro gun sight. The live firing of weapons was carried out at the air-to-ground range at St. Abbs. In addition, there were two bombing ranges, both near Holy Island, one at Fenham Flats and the other at Goswick Sands. Aircraft towed targets out over the North Sea for air-to-air gunnery practice. Despite an acute shortage of photographic staff, all films taken during these sorties were shown to the pilots and analysed.

No. 3 Armament Practice Station had a number of its own aircraft which acted as targets or towed drogues. They included six Miles Masters II, sixteen Miles Martinets, two Tempest Vs, and two Spitfire IXs. RAF Milfield no longer had any resident aircraft and in early 1946 it became a satellite airfield of RAF Charterhall. The pilots of 263 Squadron were part of No. 4 Course in which 91 Squadron, equipped with the Spitfire XXI, also participated.

Throughout most of February, 219 Squadron continued to carry out practice flights from RAF Acklington both during the day and night. At the end of the month, seven of its Mosquitos again flew across the North Sea to Lubeck, Germany, for a two week stay. Their departure had been delayed by poor weather on the Continent. It was not much better in England. A Halifax diverted to RAF Acklington on the 14th, as it could not land at RAF Thornaby. The pilot had been flying around for some time with neither his compasses nor radio functioning before he touched down. Six days later, a Sea Otter landed in a 40 mph gale. It was unable to turn off the runway so it taxied to its edge and was tied down to wait a lull in the wind.

On 1 March a formation of nine Meteors led by Sqn Ldr Brandt landed back from RAF Charterhall having completed the course there. Nine days later, 219 Squadron's Mosquitos arrived back from Lubeck. On the 25th, 219 Squadron was off on its travels again. Eleven aircraft took off for RAF Spilsby for a four week attachment to the No. 2 Armament Practice Station. AVM J. Baker, AOC 12 Group, arrived by Anson on the 22nd to interview candidates for permanent commissions. The following day he paid a short visit to 263 Squadron and made a short flight in one of their Meteors. In an announcement by 12 Group's command that took many airmen by surprise, it was ordered that No. 3 Armament Practice Station be closed down with immediate effect on 29 March 1946. RAF Charterhall would be placed on a care and maintenance basis and become a satellite airfield of RAF Acklington along with RAF Milfield. To take its place, RAF Acklington would cease to be a front line fighter station and would now become No. 2 Armament Practice Station.

There was another surprise for RAF Acklington personnel, when they received a report from the Coast Guard that a Halifax had landed on the disused airfield at Boulmer. At the time, a Flying Control Officer was visiting the site and he spoke to the pilot, who stated that he was on a ferry flight from Edzell to Yorkshire. Unable to locate RAF Acklington in rapidly deteriorating weather and with the aircraft's radio transmitter not working, he 'was so thankful to find Boulmer and put down there.' The Halifax remained there for several days and was guarded by the Army personnel who were occupying the airfield at that time.

April was marked by the depletion of RAF Acklington's Fighter Squadrons. The first to leave was 263 Squadron, which departed for RAF Wittering on 2 April 1946. 219 Squadron's Mosquitos arrived back from the Armament Practice Camp at RAF Spilsby on 17 April, before the squadron began moving at the end of the month. The final twelve aircraft departed on 1 May for RAF Wittering. The squadron was disbanded not long after its departure. The weather in April was not good for flying. It delayed the departure of 219 Squadron for several days. 41 Squadron's Spitfires had great difficulty in landing for refuelling on the 15th. The visibility was down to 1,500 yards and a great number of flares had to be fired off from the runway controller's caravan to guide the pilots. RAF Acklington was informed on 24 April that Prime Minister Clement Attlee was to make a visit by air in three days' time.

Later that afternoon, his Avro York arrived at the airfield to plan out the taxiing and parking arrangements. It also brought a Eureka beacon with a crew of two to operate it. This additional navigational device would be needed. At 9.43 a.m. on 27 April, the York took off from RAF Northolt with the Prime Minister on board, arriving overhead RAF Acklington at 11 a.m. The weather could not have been worse. The cloud base was only 300 feet and the visibility around 2,000 yards. The York homed in on the Eureka beacon, but failed to break cloud at an altitude of 250 feet. Its pilot then put the aircraft into a climb to 3,500 feet. At this height there was little cloud. The pilot flew around for thirty minutes hoping that the weather below would improve. At 11.55 a.m., he made another attempt to land. He first flew out to sea to lose altitude. Five minutes later, the aircraft was in the circuit 100 feet above the ground preparing to touch down. Just then a rain squall engulfed the airfield and the pilot had to abort the landing. After another low circuit, during which the AFC shot off forty yellow Very cartridges, the York got in safely. The Prime Minister Clement Attlee was met by Wg Cdr R. W. Stewart, the Station Commander, and the Lord Mayor of Newcastle, J. A. Clydesdale. Later in the day the York left without the Prime Minister.

# 16
# Armament Practice Station
# 1946–1956

## 1946

During May 1946, No. 2 Armament Practice Station moved to RAF Acklington from RAF Spilsby and would remain there for the ten years. There was great activity on the Druridge Ranges readying them in anticipation for their use by Fighter Command Squadrons. The Armament Practice Station also operated a substantial fleet of its own aircraft, including target tugs and dual control trainers for gunnery instruction. Many of the machines were somewhat 'long in the tooth' and had been handed down from other units. It was not long before one of them was involved in an accident.

On 1 May, a de Havilland Mosquito (TA492) took off on a return flight to RAF Spilsby at 5 p.m.:

> [It] was observed to be flying very low and smoke was seen to be pouring from the port engine. The aircraft then disappeared behind the trees and soon after flying control were informed that the Mosquito had crashed near Chevington. An ambulance and crash tender were dispatched. They found that the pilot Flt Lt. Frost was injured but not seriously and the passenger Fg Off. Clubley was suffering from slight bruises.

As well as being a training station RAF Acklington was still frequently used as a diversionary airfield by aircraft in distress as well as for other purposes. On the 2nd, an Avro Anson landed with a stretcher case on board. An ambulance was in attendance to transport the patient. The following day, a Warwick, flying from RAF Eval to RAF Brackla, developed an oil leak and made an emergency landing. The crew were collected by a Lancaster. A Dominie from RAF Halton gave ATC cadets air experience flights on the 18th. Even at the height of the Second World War, the RAF still found the resources to give flights to air cadets in the Station's flight's Oxfords and sometimes even in aircraft from front line squadrons.

Also during May, it was declared that RAF Milfield, a satellite airfield of RAF Acklington, would be closed. In early June, preparations were made for the arrival of the first two squadrons—Nos 1 and 130. There was an outbreak of scabies on the

Station which was checked by the disposing of all the blankets and the issuing of new ones. On a more positive note, officers and personnel from RAF Acklington took part in a parade and march past in Newcastle on 8 June as part of 'Victory Day', the first anniversary of the end of the Second World War: 'These had been strenuously trained during the preceding week and put up an extremely good show on the actual day.'

Aircraft from RAF Acklington carried out a formation flypast over the City. One formation consisted of Mosquitos and Spitfires and the other of Miles Martinets. Members of the local press were flown over the parade in Newcastle by one of the Station's Oxfords. Later the same day, a Dominie of Morton Air Services landed at RAF Acklington with photographs of the 'Victory Day' celebrations in London. They were rushed to the Evening Chronicle, so they could met the press deadline.

The Station's Annual Sports Day was also held in June. It was favoured by perfect weather and attracted a record number of entries. Miniature silver cups and medals were presented to winning contestants by Mrs R. W. Stewart, the CO's wife. Tea was served in marquees during the afternoon. In the evening, there was a cocktail party in the Officers' Mess.

On 17 June, thirteen Meteor F.3s of 1 Squadron and fourteen Spitfire IXBs of 130 Squadron descended on RAF Acklington. During their stay they experienced a number of minor accidents. A Spitfire burst a tyre and swung off the runway as did a Meteor F 3, damaging three sodium flares. On 11 July, a Dominie flying ATC Cadets burst a tyre on landing but no injuries were sustained. Later that month, the Station received a phone call from a member of the public stating that a Harvard had forced landed between Alnwick and Wooler. The local police conducted a search but could not find the aircraft. At that time, RAF Ouston operated Harvards but none of them were reported as missing.

On the 25th, there was another report of a crashed aircraft. Unfortunately, this time it was not a false alarm. Morpeth police had been notified by a group of hill walkers that they had discovered the remains of a crashed aircraft on the west summit of Cheviot at Cairn Hill. An ambulance was dispatched to the police station at Wooler. Here, it was confirmed that the aircraft was a Warwick (HG136) of 280 Squadron, which had been reported missing two days earlier. A Lancaster and two Lincolns had overflown RAF Acklington early on the morning of the 24th while searching for it. The rescue party from RAF Acklington set out on foot towards the crash site but the first attempt to reach it was unsuccessful because of a dense mist. When it cleared and they reached the remains of the Warwick, all three of its crew members were found to be dead: 'After much strenuous work over rough and hilly ground the bodies were recovered from an elevation of 2,600 feet, where the accident occurred and brought back to the Station.'

On 29th July, the remains of Flt Lt Herbert Cody, the pilot, and Flt Lt Wyett were escorted to Acklington Railway Station and placed on a southbound train. The third crew member, Flt Lt Chad, was buried in Chevington Cemetery with appropriate honours. The Warwick they had been flying was *en route* to RAF Leuchars where it was to be scrapped.

The next two units that arrived for training were 85 Squadron (ten Mosquitos) on 7 August followed by 54 Squadron (nine Tempests). The latter departed at the end of the month while 85 Squadron returned to their home base in early September. During the summer months, a local farmer was employed to cut the grass on the airfield. He had been instructed on airfield procedure for his safety and that of the aircraft. The Armament Officer complained that the resulting hay was being stored in one of the hangars within the danger area of the explosives hut. It was promptly removed.

There was some excitement on 12 September 1946 when all personnel were warned to keep an outlook for two prisoners of war who had escaped in an aircraft, but were later advised it had been recovered. At that time, there were many German captives still awaiting their return home. Over the next two days, gale-force winds blew across the airfield, causing an accident to a taxiing Spitfire flown by a Fleet Air Arm pilot. Three Meteor F.3s of 74 Squadron and one from 266 Squadron flew in on the 19th. The weather was still bad at the time and the further five aircraft from both squadrons did not arrive until the 23rd for their course with 2 APS.

During the month of October, there was an outbreak of tonsillitis coupled with numerous cases of colds and influenza. This was attributed to dampness in many of the airmen's billets, which in many cases were Nissen huts. A further problem for the Station at that time was that users of the public road near the end of one of the runways were ignoring the Aldis signals from the Air Traffic Control caravan instructing them not to proceed when aircraft were taking off or landing. Some days,

A group photograph of the aircrew of 85 Squadron in front of a Mosquito at RAF Acklington in 1946. (*RAF Museum*)

there were nearly a hundred aircraft movements. On 28 November, there was an unidentified aircraft flying over the airfield. Due to low cloud, it could be heard but not seen. A mortar was fired to warn it away. This did the trick as it then disappeared. Towards the end of December, bad weather delayed the departure of 41 Squadron and 56 Squadron at the end of their training course. RAF Acklington was closed for flying from 21 December until the end of the year.

## 1947

91 Squadron was the first to arrive in the New Year for training. Their Meteor F.3s arrived on 6 January, followed by 257 Squadron's on the 12th. Inclement weather during the remainder of the month restricted flying. There were heavy snow falls on some days and snow ploughs had to be used to clear the runways. The freezing conditions persisted for a further two months in what was one of the most extreme winters to be endured by Britain in the 20th Century.

On 10 February, RAF Acklington was requested to drop food supplies to the villagers of Allanheads, some 30 miles south-west of Newcastle. This was not possible at the time due to the prevailing conditions. The following day, an Oxford took off and headed towards the village, but it was unable to reach it because of the weather. Heavy snow falls made it impossible for a supply drop to be made on subsequent days. Despite those frequent snow falls, RAF Acklington managed to remain open most of the time. On the 15th, 91 Squadron departed as '92 Squadron', having been renumbered during its stay at the Station. The same day, an Oxford swung on take-off and landed in deep snow. The aircraft was undamaged. Five days later, gale force winds blew the snow into drifts onto the runways, but they were soon in service again. Throughout the night and well into the morning of the 26th, there were heavy falls of snow accompanied by gale-force winds of up to 65 mph. Snow drifts from 10 to 20 feet engulfed the airfield and by this time much of the overworked snow clearing machinery had become unserviceable. The airfield was now closed. Emergency snow clearance parties were sent to assist stranded railway trains at Acklington LNER Station. By 3 p.m. the following day one runway had been re-opened. Some of the machinery had been repaired and worked throughout the 28th to make the airfield fully operational.

By 2 March, two runways were back in use. Two days later, conditions had improved enough so that fourteen local sorties could be flown. On the 5th, RAF Acklington was advised to stand by as a diversion airfield for an Oxford from RAF Hullavington that had been involved in a search for adverse icing conditions. Later that day, weather again began to deteriorate. There were further snow showers in the afternoon, rendering the perimeter track almost impassable. All the snow ploughs were again unserviceable, but flying was still just possible. By 6 a.m. the following day, a further 2 inches of snow had fallen; however, despite this, Acklington's aircraft were still able to perform eighteen sorties. For the duration of the emergency, a portable flare path was laid each evening to cope with possible diversions as many of the permanent runway lights were obscured by snow. From 9 to 11 March, extensive work was carried out on snow clearing with particular attention to the taxiways. On the 12th, a 141 Squadron Mosquito NF.36 (RK986) swung off the runway while taking off in a 15 knot crosswind. Its undercarriage collapsed with the machine coming to rest some 50 yards from the runway. The Mosquito was a write-off, but both crew members were uninjured.

The following day, the airfield was again covered in a deep layer of snow. By 16 March, the main runway was again clear, thanks to the efforts of the snow plough drivers who worked every evening until midnight. No flying was possible until the 20th, by which time winter had begun to loosen its grip over the land. As the snow melted, the Station experienced flooding in the vicinity of the airmen's cookhouse. By the 25th, the last remnants of snow and ice had been cleared from the runways. With little flying during this month, the opportunity was taken to redecorate the Control Tower. This task was taken over by the airmen, as the Clerk of Works had said he would arrange for it to be done at some vague time in the future.

On 1 April, 29 Squadron and 1 Squadron, both flying Meteors, departed at the end of their much interrupted course. There was very little activity at the ranges throughout the month. A Tiger Moth, flown by a Mrs Walker, arrived from Balado Bridge, Fife, on the 25th. The pilot had been refused permission to land because of gale force winds, but Mrs Walker ignored this and managed to touch down with extreme difficulty, damaging the Tiger Moth in the process. Tennis, badminton, and squash were all played at the Station during the month. The gymnasium was open three days a week, although attendance was rather small; this was attributed to it being a long walk from the billets.

May, in contrast to April, was a very active month for 2 APS. It flew 188 sorties, notching up 195 flying hours. Most were related to 23, 141, and 264 Squadrons, which trained here during the month. There was one serious accident on the 8th involving a De Havilland Mosquito of 141 Squadron. As had happened previously, the aircraft swung on take-off and careered off the runway. It went on to demolish the little-used station gym. Both the pilot and navigator survived the experience without an injury. Their aircraft was a complete write-off. Despite the loss of one of their aircraft, 141 Squadron flew 169 sorties amounting to 163 flying hours during their stay at RAF Acklington.

At that time, 2 APS operated a variety of aircraft to tow targets and provide gunnery practice for the visiting Fighter Command Squadrons—Mosquitos, Miles Master 2, Miles Martinet Mk I, and Spitfires. Oxfords were used as transports. There were sixty-nine officers, 655 other ranks and, rather surprisingly, eight German prisoners of war at the station.

By June 1947, the Germans had gone. The month was only two days old when a Mosquito NF.36 (RK972) of 141 Squadron had a mishap. After touching down, the propeller struck the ground and the aircraft swung off the runway. As it ran across the grass, its port undercarriage leg collapsed. Fortunately, the Mosquito did not catch fire and the crew were unhurt. 141 Squadron departed for their home base a few day later. Fire broke out on the rubbish dump shortly after 9 p.m. on the 12th. The smoke endangered aircraft landing and taking off, but was soon extinguished by the fire crew using a 1945 Monitor Crash Fire Tender.

On 17 June, 25, 29, and 85 Squadrons arrived from RAF West Malling for air firing practice. All of them were equipped with the De Havilland Mosquito NF.36. Most of the airborne targets used for live firing were just banners towed behind an aircraft. RAF Acklington also had a fleet of 'winged targets', which were a somewhat more realistic form of prey. They were actually small gliders towed behind an aircraft tug. In the summer of 1947, a new version of the winged target with a wingspan of 32 feet—somewhat larger than those already in use—was received by the APS. The AOC of 12 Group arrived at RAF Acklington on the 14th to witness a demonstration of the new targets the following day. They turned out to be something of a disappointment. One broke its tow line over the sea and another one on take-off. A very strong cross wind severely handicapped the proceedings. A few days later, 25, 29, and 85 Squadrons carried out a live firing exercise on a 32-foot winged target which was later successfully landed back on the station. Later that day, another 32-foot glider target was being towed behind the tug aircraft when the cable snapped shortly after take-off. The winged target crashed in Broomhill but there were no injuries.

A more serious accident occurred to an APS aircraft on 25 July. The brakes of Mosquito FB.6 (TA490) failed on landing in a crosswind. The aircraft ran off the runway and its undercarriage collapsed. Both crew were unhurt. Another 2 APS aircraft was involved in an accident on 5 September. This time it was a Spitfire XVI, which bounced heavily on landing, causing its port undercarriage to collapse. A replacement was delivered a few days later from 9 MU Cosford. During that month, Acklington harked back to its role as a Second World War airfield, with Spitfires of 63 Squadron temporarily based there.

It was all change on 6 October, when the first De Havilland Vampire attachment to APS arrived. This consisted of no less than three squadrons—54, 72, and 247—from 11 Group, RAF Odiham. Two days of ground training then commenced. A fatal accident occurred on the 16th when a Vampire F1 (TG301) of 247 Squadron stalled and dived into the sea after performing an air-to-ground attack on targets in Druridge Bay. As it was low water, the air-sea rescue launch was unable to get to the scene of the crash, so the wreckage had to be dragged ashore. The pilot, John Jack, aged twenty-three, was buried in Chevington cemetery. The weather closed in at the end of October, which limited flying training. It greatly improved the following month and was taken up by gunnery training of the three Vampire squadrons. On 3 November, a 32-foot winged target was successfully towed off and was fired at by four Vampires. Two days later, a further two gliders were launched. One of them was lost over the range when a 20-mm round broke its cable. The other was smashed on landing. More seriously, a Vampire of 54 Squadron suffered from brake failure on landing on 12 November. It ran off the end of the runway and through a hedge before it came to rest. The pilot was unhurt, but the aircraft was damaged beyond repair.

A new gymnasium, which had been created from a former rifle range, was opened in the autumn to replace the one demolished by the Mosquito earlier in the year. A Sports Day was held on 7 June. Throughout the summer months, the Station's personnel played in cricket matches, although players were confined to net practice on the base. Golf was played at Almouth Village Golf Club and there was swimming in the sea. In the autumn, football proved popular but there was not much enthusiasm shown for rugby. Dances and the Station cinema were the main sources of entertainment. There were also education classes which taught academic subjects such as mathematics, physics, French, history, etc. There was also instruction in shorthand, typing and woodwork. The Station also had a small library with around 400 books.

The three De Havilland Vampire Squadrons departed at the end of November. However, 1947 ended on a low key, as they were the last to use the ranges that year. The instructors and staff pilots made good use of the break by practising their own air firing and instrument flying.

# 1948

The aircraft of 25, 29, and 85 Squadrons, all flying Mosquito NF.36s, arrived on the morning of 5 January for a two month stay. The following day, they carried out camera exercises and despite the not too favourable weather, continued with this for the next three weeks. Live firing was due to start on the 26th, but conditions were so poor that it had to be cancelled. In February, it was much better. Three towed targets were successfully launched during that month. Only one was recovered to the airfield. Of the other two, one was shot down into the sea by the Mosquitos and the other had to be cut adrift over the sea due to an engine failure of the towing aircraft. The one that landed back at RAF Acklington had numerous cannon holes in it.

A comprehensive programme of sports was played by the Station personnel, even though it was winter. There was cross-country running, football and rugby. Hockey matches had to be abandoned as there were so few players of this game left at the station. Boxing was held in the gymnasium but there was not much support for this. Entertainments in February included the first 'live show' held on the Station for a considerable time. It was very successful with over 300 people being present at the performance. The station dance was also well attended. Efforts to start a dramatic club and unit concert party met with little enthusiasm.

On 8 March, De Havilland Hornet Is of 64 Squadron arrived on attachment from RAF Linton-on-Ouse. No. 65 Squadron followed later in the month. The Hornet in some respects resembled the Mosquito and had been designed as a long range fighter for use in an island hopping campaign against the Japanese in the South Pacific. The war ended before any reached this theatre. The RAF received almost 200 examples of the Hornet, which remained in service until it was eventually replaced by the Meteor. Capable of 475 mph at 21,000 feet, the Hornet was the fastest piston-engined fighter to be flown operationally by the RAF.

More Hornets arrived in May in the form of 19 Squadron from RAF Church Fenton. Miles Martinets were attached to RAF Thorney Island and RAF Tangmere in June for target practice by Royal Auxiliary Air Force Squadrons. Back at RAF Acklington, two of the unit's aircraft were involved in accidents—a Martinet (NR299) and a Mosquito

FB 6 (TA555). In the former, the pilot forgot to lock down the undercarriage and as a consequence it collapsed when the aircraft touched down. The following day, the 15th, the starboard undercarriage cross tube of the Mosquito failed and the landing leg collapsed on contact with the ground. In both cases the pilots escaped unhurt.

Wg Cdr A. C. Carver took over as commander of the Station from Wg Cdr R. Smith, who was posted as sick to No. 1 PHU. Meteor IVs of 266 Squadron arrived on 5 July. Seven days later, one of the aircraft had a brake failure on landing and ended up in gulley at the end of runway twenty-three. The pilot was unhurt. Night flying was carried out on the 22nd in order to test a target drogue which had been illuminated as an experiment. Due to a full moon, the trial did not prove particularly successful. The next day, the first Mark II 32-foot towed target was launched. Cine shots were taken of it for Fighter Command. After flying exceedingly well, it damaged its nose on landing. While off duty, a large number of the Station personnel spent their leisure time playing golf at the Foxton Hall club. There was also a Carnival Dance held in the Acklington Club that proved very popular.

The weather was poor in August, which limited flying by 266 Squadron before their departure. Flooding occurred in the local area and none of the radio telephone communications would operate for three days because of a fault at the GPO. Berwickshire was particularly badly hit, with the region being inundated by one-third of its annual rainfall in a space of six days. It was described as the greatest natural disaster in the history of the Borders. On the 25th, an Avro Lancastrian of RAF Transport Command arrived with food parcels for the victims of the flood. They were a gift from the Dominions. After being unloaded from the aircraft, they were conveyed to the town of Duns for distribution. The APS suffered a further accident to one of its aircraft—this time a Spitfire (TE342). It suffered brake failure on landing, causing it to ground loop. A Martinet also suffered engine failure on a cross-country flight. Its pilot made a successful emergency landing at RAF Leeming.

There were no squadrons attached to RAF Acklington in September. The target-towing pilots took the opportunity to practice cross-county flights, forced landings and formation flying. Tragedy struck when a Martinet (EM639) crashed, killing its pilot, Clarence Harker. The aircraft was about 600 yards from the end of the runway on its final approach when a puff of white smoke was seen from the engine and a loud bang was heard. The Martinet made a sharp turn to starboard and dived to the ground. It was thought that the loss of control of the aircraft may have been due to a stall or a failure of one of the flaps. The engine was underpowered when the accident occurred. There was yet another accident to one of RAF Acklington's aircraft when a Mosquito VI (TA597) lost power in both engines. It belly-landed near Craster and caught fire, totally consuming the aircraft. The pilot and his passenger escaped with only minor burns.

During November, 23, 141, and 264 Squadrons completed their training course, but not before one of their aircraft was involved in a crash. A Mosquito NF.36 (RK978) of 264 Squadron made a controlled descent through cloud in very poor visibility. It touched down too far along the runway and overshot, ending up in a ditch. Owing to bad weather, the arrival of 54 and 73 Squadrons of the Vampire Wing from RAF

Odiham was postponed from late November to early December. There was not much improvement in the weather in the last few weeks of the year. A Hastings was stranded at RAF Acklington from 22 November until 3 December. Weather improved somewhat on that day allowing it to depart and the two squadrons of Vampires fly in. It soon deteriorated again. Two days later, a formation of Auxiliary Squadron Spitfires, *en route* from RAF Thornaby to RAF Turnhouse, sought refuge there. An Anson, bound for RNAS Abbotsinch, arrived a short time later.

On 7 December, two Wellingtons touched down shortly before midnight, as they were unable to reach their destination. All airfield lighting was illuminated in the late evening of the 13th for a Mosquito missing from RAF Leeming. The elements could not prevent the arrival of a Dakota from RAF Upper Heyford transporting thirty airmen on a Christmas Grant at a charge of two shillings a head for the RAF Benevolent Fund. In the weeks leading up to Christmas, there was a minor crime wave on the Station. Entry by way of a window was made to the NAAFI and two wallets were stolen. A few days later, £8 (£160 in 2016) was stolen from the Red Shield Club. The thief again made his entry through a window. A concert party arrived at RAF Acklington to give a performance to all ranks. Several handbags and some items of clothing were stolen from the ladies cloakroom. All the property with the exception of £2 was quickly recovered by a well organised search. In the early hours of the morning of the 18th, two airmen were arrested by the civil police and charged with the above offences.

A Christmas party was given for the children of service personnel on the 22nd. Father Christmas was played by Cpl Adams. He arrived in a Miles Martinet, then led the children into the Acklington Club. Here, they enjoyed a film show consisting of four cartoons and were then entertained by a conjuror. Tea was provided in the Airmen's Dining Hall and Father Christmas distributed the presents from the Christmas tree. All sections of the Station contributed generously to the funds of the party and the tree was contributed by the Duke of Northumberland. A USAF Boeing B 29 was diverted to Acklington late in the evening of the 30th, as its intended destination, RAF Waddington, was experiencing foul weather. This aircraft was probably among the largest types ever to land at RAF Acklington. The following day, a snow alert was broadcast over the tannoy. Snow fell in the evening but had disappeared by New Year's Day.

## 1949

The year began with the arrival of 1, 56, and 222 Squadrons, all flying Meteors, on 3 January for a month's stay. Their training syllabus was not completed owing to bad weather on eight of the seventeen flying days and because of trouble experienced in the attachment of the banner or drogue targets. A number of them disintegrated in flight, reducing the number of effective sorties even further. Several of the aircraft also became unserviceable. A Mosquito III of the APS was undergoing single engine checks by Sqn Ldr Hunt of the Examining Flight, EFS, when it had to make an emergency landing on the disused airfield at Eshott, as the undercarriage had failed to retract. The same aircraft was involved in another incident when it was again being test flown on a single engine. The live engine failed but the pilot managed to perform a successful emergency landing back at RAF Acklington. A third incident occurred to a Miles Martinet on the 20th. Owing to a shortage of fuel and poor visibility at RAF Acklington, its pilot made an emergency landing at the disused airfield at Brunton. The aircraft had to be brought back to the base by road.

On 25 January, a Harvard T2 (KF.666), being flown from RAF Dyce, Aberdeen, to RAF Honiley near Coventry, made a refuelling stop at RAF Acklington. The pilot then took off in weather conditions below the agreed minimum for the flight. He also failed to provide himself with a watch for navigation as well as a serviceable microphone for radio communication. Two and a half hours into his flight, the pilot became lost and the Harvard began to run short of fuel. Eventually, the pilot was instructed by Air Traffic Control at RAF Dishforth to abandon the aircraft. He successfully parachuted to safety: 'This is a classic example of poor preparation and a cavalier attitude to flying discipline and good airmanship.'

At the end of January, RAF Acklington ceased to be a 'Master Airfield' which meant that its air traffic control facilities were not manned outside normal working hours. A further three Meteor Squadrons—66, 92, and 63—arrived at the beginning of February for a month's stay. A large number of their aircraft took part in a flypast over Edinburgh and Glasgow to promote an RAF recruiting campaign. Flying training was only possible on 9.5 days of their attachment. A total of 268 effective air-to-air sorties (against an intended 406) and 168 effective air-to-ground sorties (174 intended) were carried out. Non-effective sorties were caused by:

| | |
|---|---|
| Drogues shot away | 46 |
| Stoppages | 49 |
| Trouble with Miles Martinets | 30 |
| Meteor unserviceable | 10 |
| Bad weather | 7 |
| Faulty harmonisation | 4 |
| Ricochet | 1 |

A Meteor of 63 Squadron was hit by a ricochet while on air-to-ground firing, but no serious damage was sustained. On 2 February, an APS Martinet made a forced landing at the disused airfield at Brunton. Another Martinet was dispatched to pick up the pilot and a guard posted on the abandoned aircraft.

The RAF Odiam Wing, comprising of 54, 72, and 247 Squadrons flying Vampire F.3s, arrived on 1 March. The towed gliders were used for the first time as a regular feature of the air firing syllabus. In all, forty-four glider sorties were flown of which thirty-one were successful. At the beginning of the month, there was a report from the Coast Guard that a parachute had been seen descending into the sea off Holy

Island. A lifeboat was launched and two aircraft from RAF Acklington took part in the search. Nothing was found and the aircraft were recalled after two hours. At that time, there were no search and rescue helicopters in service with the RAF and such missions were still undertaken by fixed wing aircraft. At South Range, Druridge Bay, VHF experiments using adapted aircraft equipment were undertaken to improve the recording of the hits by aircraft at gunnery practice. It was intended to replace the ten-foot hessian-covered wooden frame with a more accurate form of strike recorder. The results would then be communicated back to the pilot. A compulsory education scheme also came into operation in March; eighty-eight airmen in their first year attended once a week and 104 in their second year once a fortnight.

In April, RAF Acklington hosted the Mosquito night fighters of 25, 29, and 85 Squadrons. This type of aircraft seemed particularly accident prone on visits to this airfield. There were a further two incidents on the 22nd. A Mosquito (RL205) swung on landing in a crosswind and the port undercarriage collapsed. The pilot was unhurt and the damaged aircraft was cleared from the airfield within six hours. Later the same day, Mosquito (VT.118) hit a hedge shortly before touching down but it came to rest safely. The Mosquitos returned to their base at RAF West Malling on the 22nd. Three days later, the Hornet Wing arrived from RAF Linton-on-Ouse and Church Fenton. One of the aircraft succeeded in making contact with the hedge in the undershot area. Visual checks were made on the undercarriage as it flew over the airfield; on its second attempt, it landed safely. There was a more serious incident involving a Hornet (PX353) of 65 Squadron, when both engines failed on take-off. The pilot retracted his undercarriage and landed on the end of the runway with the minimum of damage. This time, the runway was cleared in 2.5 hours.

On 2 May, RAF Acklington received a report from the police at Whitley Bay that two aircraft had been seen to collide and crash into the sea. Air-sea rescue launches from Amble and Blyth were dispatched and two Hornets returning from exercise were diverted to search the area. Nothing was seen, but the search was continued until all aircraft had been accounted for. 18 Group gave the order to abandon the search after 1¼ hours. The Hornet Wing—comprising 19, 41, 64, and 65 Squadrons—returned to their home bases on the 19th, having flown 679 sorties during their stay. Of these, 390 were air-to-air firing at drogues and fifty-nine air-to-air attacking towed gliders. Some nineteen gliders were completely destroyed, ten were 'probables', three were damaged and seven escaped without a scratch. There were also 230 flights involving attacking targets on the ground. A few days after the Hornets departed, the Mosquitos of the Coltishall Night Fighter Wing took their place. They stayed until mid-June. At the end of the month, a Martinet carried out a wheels-up forced landing on the disused airfield at Boulmer, after its engine had failed on a towing exercise. Neither crew member was injured; the aircraft was repairable.

No fewer than four squadrons were deployed to RAF Acklington in July 1949. They were 56 and 63 Squadrons from RAF Thorney Island and 74 and 245 Squadrons from RAF Horsham St. Faith. All flew the Gloster Meteor F.4. While carrying out gunnery training, a Meteor of 56 Squadron was hit by a ricochet. Slight damage was sustained to the port motor nose fairing but no blame was attached to the pilot. A Dakota from RAF North Luffenham made an emergency landing on one engine on the 7th. On the 25th, a Meteor of 245 Squadron, flown by Flt Lt Meyer, developed a technical defect in the lower cannons when the safety flap was set to 'fire'. Some of the discharged rounds hit civilian property in Red Row village, but fortunately there were no injuries.

The following month, there were two accidents involving APS aircraft. A Martinet (JN543), piloted by P. I. Jones, crashed on landing as Jones had forgotten to lock the undercarriage. Emergency crews managed the clear the wrecked aircraft within 30 minutes. It had obstructed both runways in use at the time. A second Martinet collided with a stationary vehicle on the perimeter track. Both the above accidents were the subject of a Board of Inquiry. A further Martinet (MS891) made an emergency landing at the disused airfield at Boulmer on 3 August. It was later repaired and flown back to RAF Acklington. The Martinet was the first RAF type to be designed as a target tug. Its design was based on the Miles Master trainer, which it superseded on the production lines at Woodley. Either a wind-driven or a motorised winch was fitted, carrying six flag and sleeve drogue targets. The RAF received the first of over 1,700 Martinets in 1942. Prior to that, the RAF adapted aircraft such as the Lysander to perform target towing duties.

During that month, 43, 222, 257, and 263 Squadrons, all equipped with Meteor F.4s, were undergoing firing practice at the Station. There were also fifteen members of the Royal Danish Air Force undergoing technical training on the Meteor. To add to the toll of accidents, a Meteor F.4 (VT227) being flown by an inexperienced pilot, undershot while landing on runway 23. The aircraft's undercarriage was torn off and it eventually ended up on its belly at the intersection of the two runways. A second Meteor (VT.137) of 257 Squadron was involved in a further accident on the 30th. It suffered brake failure on landing because a cable sheered at a nipple connection. To avoid overshooting into a quarry, the pilot swung the aircraft off the runway but it ran into a 25-foot deep gulley and was severely damaged. After this incident, the gulley was sometimes referred to as 'Meteor Valley'. Three squadrons arrived on 3 October: 25, 29, and 85 Squadrons, with their Mosquitos from RAF West Malling. Later in the month, their place was taken by the Meteors of 1, 43, 66, and 92 Squadrons. Another arrival was a single Tempest V flown by Flt Lt Reed for glider towing trials as a possible replacement for the ageing Martinets.

The Hornet Wing—composed of 19, 41, 64, and 65 Squadrons—from RAF Church Fenton and RAF Linton-on-Ouse began another attachment on 14 November. For the first six days, the weather was unfit for air firing and the squadron pilots undertook the ground training syllabus. On the 28th, a decision was taken by Fighter Command to extend the Hornet Squadron's stay to 15 December in lieu of the Horsham Wing, who were in quarantine due to an outbreak of polio. During November, a Vampire (TG380) undershot while coming into land and struck a hedge, losing the port undercarriage leg. The pilot was reprimanded by the Station Commander. One wonders why the hedge—the nemesis of so many landing aircraft—was not brought to book as well.

## 1950

On 8 March, the first Tempest Vs arrived to replace the Martinets in the target towing flight. During that month, a Martinet (NR662), suffered an engine failure while in the circuit on approach to the airfield. The pilot made a wheels-up landing on the grass at the side of the runway. No injuries were suffered. The Gunnery Flight's Meteor IVs were grounded at that time because of a shortage of spares. A scrounging trip to RAF West Raynham obtained parts for the Vampire, which was able to take to the air again. Two new Mosquito IVs were also delivered to the Gunnery Flight. 25, 29, and 85 Squadrons, which had been on attachment since the end of February, departed on the 14th with their Mosquito NF.36s.

During April, a Mosquito FB 6 (RS528), operating from RAF Leeming, crashed into the sea while using the Druridge Ranges. The aircraft failed to pull out of a spin after a steep turn. J. Briers, the pilot, and Flt Lt Cheeseman of 23 Squadron, were both killed. In a less serious accident, an APS Tempest, flown by Flt Lt Thompson, suffered minor damage when he accidently fired the Very pistol in the storage compartment. In the early part of the month, there were three Squadrons of Hornets—19, 41, and 65—at RAF Acklington from RAF Church Fenton and RAF Linton-on-Ouse. They were followed by the Vampires of 54, 72, and 247 Squadrons.

On 4 May, the Duke of Gloucester arrived in a Vickers Viking of the King's Flight. He departed the following day. Adverse weather conditions at that time were blamed for an increase in the numbers of the personnel reporting sick. A large contingent of members of the Royal Observer Corps visited on 4 June. On arrival, they were addressed by the Station Commander, after which they visited a static display of several aircraft. In the afternoon, a flying display was laid on for them. Members of the Royal Observer Corps were also given the opportunity of short flights in a Hastings of RAF Transport Command. The following day, a pilot of a Martinet made a distress call, as pieces were breaking off his aircraft. He nursed his aircraft back to RAF Acklington and landed safely. It was only a few days before yet another Martinet was in trouble. This time, the pilot reported that his engine had failed while flying over the ranges. He managed to get back to the airfield and touch down on a cross-wind runway. At the end of the month yet another Martinet made an emergency landing, as the pilot believed that the engine was on fire. Fortunately by this time, the days of the Martinet with the APS were numbered. Five Tempests were delivered the same month to replace them. A Meteor of 222 Squadron, which was on detachment at RAF Acklington at the time, crashed on landing on 20 June.

July did not go by without further accidents to APS Martinets. One was damaged on take-off when it struck a seagull. At the end of the month, Flt Lt Walker was practising single engine landings in a Mosquito T.3 (HJ983), when it began to swing just before touchdown because of a strong crosswind. The pilot could not fully compensate for this and on landing he retracted the undercarriage to bring his aircraft to a halt. 74 and 257 Squadrons were on attachment during the month. A pilot of one of their Meteor VIIs informed air traffic control on the 17th that all the aircraft's controls were jammed and that the crew were going to bail out. The controls came free just

An aerial view of RAF Acklington, looking north-west, summer 1952. (*The National Archives*)

An oblique aerial view of RAF Acklington in the 1950s. (*RAF Museum*)

Four years on, 85 Squadron have returned to RAF Acklington with their De Havilland Mosquitos for training. This group photograph was taken in early 1950. (*Aldon Ferguson*)

RAF Acklington fire station in the early 1950s. (*The National Archives*)

as the cockpit hood was jettisoned and the aircraft landed safely. There was also an unusual visitor in the form of a civil Vampire. The pilot was *en route* from Harwarden to Hatfield, but had become lost and made an emergency landing at Acklington.

The Station had a rare month free of flying accidents in August, but it was not altogether free of incident. On the 20th, a mayday call was received. The Flying Controller was not on duty at the time, as it was a weekend. Later, news was received that an aircraft, a Spitfire F.22 (PK393) of 607 Squadron had made a forced landing near Boulmer. Acklington, being the nearest RAF airfield, provided personnel to guard the crash site. Gloster Meteor F.8s of 43 and 245 Squadrons were in residence for training at that time. Their ground crews had been transported to RAF Acklington in Dakotas. They departed on 1 September and for several weeks there was a break in units arriving for firing practice.

The time was put to good use with the APS aircraft being overhauled and repaired. On one day, the airfield got a report that an aircraft had come down in the sea. Its pilot was said to have been seen swimming away from the wreckage. A rescue was organised and search aircraft were dispatched from RAF Acklington to scour the area. Nothing was found and it was later discovered that the downed aircraft was, in fact, one of the Station's towed target gliders that had been released over the sea.

During the early part of October, RAF Acklington was classed as a major airfield during exercise 'Emperor'. None of its aircraft took part in the exercise, but a small number were on stand-by for air-sea rescue. Training resumed on the 23rd, with the arrival of 66 and 263 Squadron's Meteor F.4s. The Martinets were the centre of further drama when the engine of one cut out and it had to make an emergency landing. The following day, on the 13th, another radioed it was in difficulty, but it managed to reach the airfield safely. These incidents paled into insignificance compared to what happened at the end of the month. A fishing vessel that had entered the Acklington ranges was accidently shot up during air-to-air firing. Fortunately, no-one on board was injured.

The weather began to deteriorate in November. On the 22nd, two squadrons were due to arrive—one from RAF Linton-on-Ouse and another from RAF Leuchars. They attempted to fly to RAF Acklington, but most of their aircraft were forced to return to their bases because of the poor conditions. Only three aircraft of 92 Squadron managed to reach the airfield on that day. The rest arrived the following day. A few days earlier, a Meteor had been diverted from RAF Middleton St. George and reached RAF Acklington with only five minutes of fuel. There were two accidents during that month. A Martinet (MS891) burst a tyre on take-off and crashed on the runway. Both pilot and target operator were uninjured. The second involved a glider target being towed by a Tempest which refused to be released from its towing cable as the aircraft came into land. The glider destroyed forty yards of fencing as well as marshalling boards before it came to rest.

The bad weather first experienced in November became gradually worse in December. Snow early in the month closed the airfield for a couple of days. 92 Squadron's training programme was disrupted and they elected to leave for their home base of Linton-on-Ouse. No. 222 Squadron decided to remain at Acklington and complete their course. There was one accident in the month when a Harvard from RAF Feltwell crashed on landing. Its pilot survived unscathed.

# 1951

On 22 January, Wg Cdr T. Kean AFC, who had recently attended the No. 1 Course at The Flying College, RAF Manby, assumed command of RAF Acklington. His predecessor, Vice Wg Cdr R. M. B. Duke-Woolley DSO DFC, was transferred to the Staff College at Andover. Earlier the same month, a conference had been held at RAF Acklington to discuss the possibility of moving the APS to RAF Leuchars or operating it from the disused airfield at Eshott during the summer months, while the ORPs (Operation Readiness Platforms) were constructed in the airfield. 1 Squadron was based at RAF Acklington for most of the month for training with its Meteor F.8s.

The weather in February was poor when 74 and 245 Squadrons were at Acklington. On the 16th, a Meteor of the latter squadron, flown by Plt Off. Geoffrey Adams, got lost in poor visibility when its compass failed. Despite being given homing bearings, the aircraft ran out of fuel before it could reach the airfield. Adams attempted to make a forced landing near Whittingham, Northumberland, but the aircraft struck some trees and somersaulted in a field on Thistleton Farm, near Callaly. Farm workers, who witnessed the crash, stated that the aircraft was one of two that circled overhead. It began to descend and turned upside down before hitting the ground. The pilot's body was thrown clear of the wreckage. A guard was placed on the crash site for seven days during which time all the important items were removed. Another 245 Squadron Meteor was struck by a ricochet during air-to-ground firing, but there was little damage to the aircraft.

Commander Thomas, District inspector of Fisheries, North Shields, visited the Station Commander to discuss a complaint on behalf of the Northumberland Sea Fisheries Committee. This concerned the fishing vessel *Vesper* (BK 70) which was alleged by the owner to have been struck by a cannon shell on 25 October 1950. The Station also received new plans to be implemented in the event of a threat of war. Originally, 43 and 608 Squadrons were to be deployed to RAF Acklington but this was now changed to 602 and 603 Royal Auxiliary Air Force Squadrons.

At this time, trials were undertaken with American flag targets. There was a shortage of glider targets, as those allocated for RAF Acklington were diverted to another station. At the beginning of February, forty-seven were available but this had fallen to twenty-three at the end of the month. Sixteen target gliders were assembled while forty were destroyed in target practice and accidents.

In March, the tail plane of a Meteor F.8 (WA929) of 56 Squadron was damaged by a winged target being towed off the airfield. The Meteor was crossing the runway at the time. The Waterbeach Wing—56 and 63 Squadrons—returned to their base on the 27th. Shortly after, the Leuchars Wing of 43 and 222 Squadrons arrived, but stayed for only ten days instead of the usual month because of a shortage of winged targets.

Towards the end of April, Mr Bancroft, Director of Brooklands Aviation, arrived by air to examine the serviceable spares removed from scrapped gliders. A large number of parts were collected and dispatched to the company's factory for incorporation into future glider targets. On the 5th, a Martinet (HP176) of the towing squadron crash-landed in a wood while a short distance to the west of the airfield. Both occupants received superficial injuries but the aircraft was written off. The crash was

The APS operated a small number of Bolton Paul Balliol T2s. VR602 is pictured here in summer 1951. (*J. Johnston via R. L.*)

An APS Hawker Tempest TT5 (SN274) pictured in 1951. Originally designed as a fighter, this type spent its last days in the RAF as a target tug. (*MAP aircraft photos*)

attributed to a faulty fuel gauge. On the 27th, the port gun panel blew off a Meteor (VT.112) belonging to 616 Squadron while the aircraft was in flight. The canopy and the port side of the fuselage were damaged. This accident was blamed on the negligence on the part of the ground crew responsible for the pre-flight inspection. The end of the month saw the arrival of Vickers Valetta of Transport Command with ground crew for 602 and 616 Royal Auxiliary Air Force Squadrons. The former came with seven Vampires and the latter ten Meteor IVs. Adverse weather conditions restricted training by these two squadrons during their stay.

There was little improvement for 605 and 614 Royal Auxiliary Air Force Squadrons' deployment which commenced on 21 May. Flt Lt Chappell of 614 Squadron, who was flying a Vampire (VF.336) became lost in poor visibility on the first day. Running short of fuel, he made a forced wheels-up landing on the beach at the South Range. Shortly afterwards, the Vampire was covered by the rising tide. A working party from the Aircraft Servicing Flight recovered it before the tide went down, with several men going into the sea fully clothed in the salvage process. Flt Lt Chappell fared somewhat better, surviving the experience without injury. On the 30th, a technical failure in the flap system of a Vampire piloted by Flt Lt Morgan of 614 Squadron caused the controls to lock. He managed to land back at RAF Acklington without using the flaps. The previous day, an APS Tempest tipped onto its nose when taxiing to dispersal.

605 and 614 squadrons returned to RAF Honiley and RAF Llandow respectively on 2 June. Two days later, 608 and 613 Royal Auxiliary Squadrons arrived. Better weather enabled firing to commence immediately. The former squadron had nine Vampires along with sixteen pilots and eighty-two ground personnel. The latter had ten Vampires, sixteen pilots, and eighty-eight ground personnel.

On the 15th, the Secretary of State for Air, Arthur Henderson MP, accompanied by Air Cdr F. Crerar, Inspector of the Royal Auxiliary Air Force and Mr Taylor, MP for Newcastle, arrived by air. They were met by AVM Atcherley and the Station Commander. The main purpose of the visit was to watch air firing training of the Royal Air Force Squadrons. Numerous members of the local press covered the event. They saw two Auxiliary pilots attack targets on the ground as well as towed targets. On completion of the flying, there was an opportunity to examine a heavily damaged glider target. The visit was concluded with the Secretary of State for Air giving a speech to the Station personnel and members of 608 and 613 Royal Auxiliary Air Force Squadrons.

He would have been less impressed with some of the other activities at RAF Acklington that month: registered packets had been stolen from the Station post office by a postal clerk; a local hotel was also broken into, with property stolen by three airmen; and there were further thefts of money and cigarettes from the billets.

Several of the APS aircraft did not fare too well either. On 5th June, a Martinet had to make an emergency landing due to an engine malfunction. The following day, a Tempest TT 5 (GN807) suffered an engine failure while flying near Carlisle. The pilot, Sgt C. Wilson, attempted to reach RAF Kirkbride but was unable to do so. As he attempted a forced landing at Lowe Heskett, his aircraft struck a tree and disintegrated into many pieces. Wilson walked away from the wreckage with only a cut to his head. A further Marinet lost its port wheel on take-off on the 20th. The pilot belly-landed next to the main runway. Five days later, yet another Martinet was in trouble—this time having to make an emergency landing.

In mid-June, further RAF Auxiliary Squadrons arrived at Acklington. 609 Squadron's Meteor IVs were followed by 600 and 615 Squadrons at the end of the month. They returned to their base at RAF Biggin Hill on 11 July. Their place was taken by 601 and 604 Squadrons from RAF North Weald, each with ten Vampire F.3s. On 20th July, a Vampire of the latter squadron crashed on landing due to the collapse of its nose wheel. The pilot, Fg Off. Dore was uninjured. At the end of July, 350 members of the Royal Observer Corps visited the Station. A programme of events was laid on for them, including a flying display. Some 270 of the group took the opportunity to experience a flight in a Valletta from RAF Manby.

On 1 August, it was decided by the Air Staff at Fighter Command that it was not necessary to move the target-towing flight from RAF Acklington to the disused Eshott airfield while the ORPs were built. The reasons put forward for this were:

1. Drogues and flag targets would be used by the Towing Flight instead of gliders throughout the whole period of reconstruction. Thus the risk of injuring workmen by gliders and the need for a suitable landing area for gliders no longer existed.
2. While the inner halves of the platforms are being built the Vampires attached to Acklington could use the short runways.
3. The increased accident risk from using the subsidiary runway during this period was acceptable.

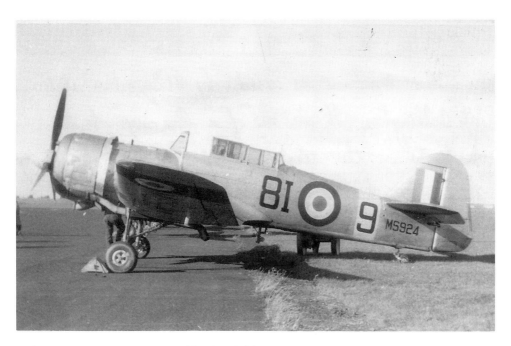

Miles Martinet (MS924) operated by APS Acklington as a target tug. (*R. Rayner via R. L.*)

The staff at RAF Acklington were less than pleased with this decision and had not even been consulted about it: 'The problem still exists of landing and taking off Tempests in strong cross winds when restricted to the short runways only—this may result in a reduction of effort.'

Their request to have an 'unclimbable' fence to protect the bulk fuel installation was also turned down by Fighter Command. The Commander in Chief asked for it to be re-submitted because the installation could be damaged by children.

There was no let-up in the number of squadrons using RAF Acklington for training. At the beginning of August, 601 and 604 Squadrons' Vampire F.3s returned to RAF North Weald. As soon as they had left, 501 and 504 Squadrons—the former with Vampire FB 5s and the latter with Meteor F.4s—flew in. During their stay, 501 squadron achieved the highest average score against a glider target of any squadron attached. On the 18th, sixteen members of the 17th Parachute Battalion Durham Light Infantry TA carried out parachute jumping from a balloon which had arrived from RAF Cardington. Fg Off. G. Collins of the Parachute School, RAF Abingdon, visited the Station to give instructions to the parachutists. To complete the month's movements, no less than three squadrons arrived on the 20th. They were 500 Squadron (nine Meteor F.4s and three Meteor F.3s), 610 Squadron (eight Meteors F.4s, one Meteor T7, and a Harvard), and finally, 611 Squadron (six Meteor F.4s and a single Meteor T7).

At this time, discussions were held concerning the use of GCI (Ground Controlled Interception) and CHL (Chain Home Low) radar stations, so that the APS could fly more air-to-air firing sorties in conditions of bad visibility and low cloud. At the end of August, a CHEL (Chain Home Extra Low) station was situated at Longhoughton and was used to plot aircraft on air-to-air firing during adverse weather conditions on the Druridge Bay air firing range. By the end of the year, Northstead radar station was also manned on a regular basis so that training exercises could be carried out above the clouds. Its personnel were administered by RAF Acklington.

On 3 September, 502 squadron arrived for training with nine Vampire F.5s, accompanied by 603 squadron which brought seven Vampire F.5s, one Meteor T.7 and a Harvard. During their stay, adverse weather limited the number of training sorties that could be flown. The undercarriage of a Vampire of 502 collapsed on landing. Later in the month, their place was taken by further Royal Auxiliary Air Force Squadrons—607 Squadron with nine Vampire F.5s, two Meteor T.7s and two Harvard T.2s and 612 Squadron with eight Vampire T.5s, one Meteor T.7 and two Harvards. Disaster struck the latter squadron on 17 September when a Meteor T.7 (WF842) entered a spin from which it did not recover and crashed at Newham Farm at Belsay. Plt Off. Douglas Robertson and Plt Off. Roderick McKay were killed. 602 Squadron from Renfrew Airport was based at RAF Acklington during the weekend of the 29th and 30th, along with 607 Squadron to take part exercise 'Pinnacle'. They returned the following weekend to participate in the final stage of it.

Twelve Vampire F.5s of 72 Squadron arrived for armament practice on 15 October. Personnel spent the latter part of the month preparing for the AOC's Inspection. AVM R. Atcherly AOC, 12 Group, arrived by car on the 29th, accompanied by three Group

Captains. A further twenty staff officers from Group Headquarters were flown to the airfield in a Dakota. The forty-man guard of honour which greeted their arrival was inspected by the Air Vice Marshal. The recently formed Station band, consisting of four pipers and three drummers, provided the music for the parade of sixteen officers, five WOs, sixteen Senior NCOs, and 499 other ranks.

A conference was held shortly after. The Station was presented with its charter listing its tasks and responsibilities. Each one was analysed and discussed until agreement was reached. Wg Cdr T. Kean, the Station Commander, put forward various problems which he hoped would be investigated by the visiting staff officers. They included the requirement for a gymnasium and sports pavilion. There was also discussion about the need for a decision to be taken on the construction of a second main runway to be built alongside the current one. There was also a request to widen the access road to the new T2 hangar, which had commenced construction in the spring of 1951. It was agreed that the technical part of the camp was inadequate for its purpose. At the end of the conference, AVM Atcherly presented the Station with its Unit Badge, signed and approved by King George VI in July 1951. In his speech, the AOC stressed the importance of RAF Acklington's role to Fighter Command and commended all ranks for their hard work during the summer months in training Auxiliary Air Force Squadrons in air firing. He interpreted the motto on the Station badge as 'We always strive for perfection' and urged all to do so.

At the beginning of November, a communication was received from Fighter Command requiring the Station to provide 332 airmen, two Squadron Leaders and other officers to man emergency labour units in the event of industrial unrest. They were to assist civil Ministries as part of 'Operation Homeland'. Their services were never called upon. Another conference took place on the 27th and 28th to decide whether the 32-foot towed glider targets produced by Brooklands were of the same standard as those manufactured by Lines already in use. It was concluded that the 32-foot target was not as strong as the 25-foot target. Some of 25-foot targets had been modified at RAF Acklington so they could be towed at speeds in excess of 200 knots. It was concluded that future modifications should instead be undertaken at the company's works.

Further trials with the Brooklands-built glider were undertaken in early December. It was decided to use a metal skin instead of fabric. In the years to come, the 32-foot winged target would become a frequent sight in the Northumberland skies. On the 5th, a Vampire of 54 Squadron made a heavy landing and sustained damage to its airframe. Two days later, a Wellington Mk X from RAF Lindholme diverted to RAF Acklington as one of its engines had failed. The attachment of 54 and 247 squadrons ended on the 17th, when they departed south to their base at RAF Odiham. Except for essential services, the Station closed down on Friday 21 December until 1 January 1952. Most of the personnel took advantage of the break. Only 100 or so airmen sat down for Christmas dinner served by the Station Commander, officers, and NCOs. Although work had commenced on the ORPs many months earlier, they were still far from finished by the end of the year; this was attributed to the antiquated equipment used for excavating and scraping.

A damaged winged target after a firing exercise in February, 1953. It was attacked by six aircraft from the RAF Linton-on-Ouse wing. (*The National Archives*)

Wing Comander R. Barton, Station Commander (*centre*), examining a winged target glider. (*The National Archives*)

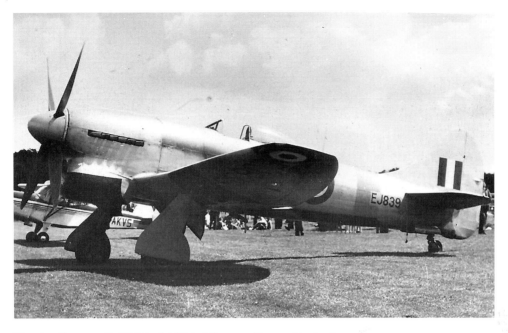

Hawker Tempest 5, EJ839 of APS Acklington. (*Roger Lindsay*)

## 1952

The first days of the New Year saw heavy falls of snow across Northumberland. It was five inches deep on the runways on 2 January. Despite the adverse conditions, twelve Meteors of 64 Squadron and thirteen from 65 Squadron arrived from RAF Duxford on the 6th. The month saw the inauguration of radar-controlled firing for operational squadrons attached to RAF Acklington. All air-to-air firing was controlled by GCI controllers who positioned the target aircraft. Firing was done at heights up to 14,000 feet, followed by a controlled descent back to base. During January, twelve winged targets were consumed, leaving 162 in stock.

The radar trials continued throughout February and, although four day's flying was lost due to snow and bad weather, the use of radar reduced the disruption by weather for air firing by sixty per cent. A full report on the evaluation of radar to assist the training of pilots in air-to-air firing was submitted to Fighter Command Headquarters. Further tests with winged targets manufactured by Brooklands were carried out on the 11th and 12th. They were assembled at RAF Acklington by personnel from the factory. These gliders, in which several modifications and refinements were incorporated, all reached speeds of 260 knots successfully and one reached a speed of 285 knots before one side of the tail plane fell off. At that time, 19 Squadron and 41 Squadrons, each with thirteen Meteor F.8s and one T7, arrived for training. On the 18th, an aircraft of 41 Squadron landed with a fire in its port engine.

In early March, a Fairy Firefly from RNAS Donibristle force landed at the disused Winfield Airfield near Berwick-upon-Tweed. A fuel bowser and refuelling party were dispatched from RAF Acklington. At the end of the month, a Meteor F.8 of 92

Squadron, which had arrived a few days earlier for training with 66 Squadron, struck a blister hangar during ground running.

In April, a Balliol T2 and a Tempest V, both of the APS, collided whilst taxiing. During the month, a glider modified for high-speed towing flight was towed to destruction by a Meteor VIII. The glider became progressively more 'left wing low' as the speed increased and finally broke away at 265 knots and 27,000 feet. Representatives from Rolls Royce, De Havilland, and Gloster Aircraft companies made frequent visits to the Station during that month. Those from Napier and Boulton Paul remained in residence. Throughout the existence of the APS, delegates from many of Britain's contemporary aircraft companies maintained a presence at RAF Acklington to assist and advise on the operation of their machines. At the end of April, Vampires of 23 and 25 Squadron arrived. During their stay, the main runway 05/23 was badly burnt at each end by their jet efflux. They used one of the shorter runways to park because of construction work and after its use the tarmac was described as being almost fluid in places.

The Air Ministry's Grp Capt. McDonald and several other officials visited RAF Acklington on 22 May to discuss possible improvements to the airfield. The Station Commander requested that the ASP (Armament Servicing Platform) should be large enough on which to park eight target tug Tempests plus up to twelve squadron aircraft involved in the firing practice. He also drew the attention of the visitors to the complete unsuitability of the existing hard standings. These were too small, too close to the perimeter track, too few in number, and in a bad state of repair. Consideration had been given to making the tarmac runway into the ASP but this would have been costly to construct. The runway was also required for gliding and target towing in spring and autumn owing to the north-westerly winds at that time of year. The Station Commander, Wg Cdr T. Kean, had most of his proposals turned down. With a sense of frustration he remarked in the Station Diary: 'I don't think this Station will ever be built on a permanent basis!'

In the spring, the Bishop of Newcastle opened a new Roman Catholic Chapel on the Station. An RAF chaplain and a congregation of some seventy airmen and their families attended. A visit of a different nature was that of five US Fairchild C82 Packets, which operated from RAF Acklington between 26 April and 18 May 1952. They were taking part in a training exercise in conjunction with the Parachute Regiment who were to 'launch an assault' on American Air Force bases in England.

June saw RAF Acklington host 257 and 263 Squadrons in the early part of the month and towards the end, 1 and 151 Squadrons. All of them were equipped with Meteor F.8s, except for 151 Squadron which operated the Vampire NF.10. There were no accidents to any of their aircraft, but on the 16th, an APS Balliol suffered engine failure and had to make a forced landing. Wg Cdr T. W. Kean, the Station Commander, was becoming increasingly exasperated with the shortage of personnel, coupled with the slow pace of the construction work. He wrote the following in the diary for June:

> The major development during the month has been the posting away of the few key trade N.C.O.s which we had on strength at a time when unserviceability of both Towing and Gunnery Flight was at its worst. The Operation Conversion Units have

been given sole priority of manning. Acklington together with Squadrons are to lose men. As I see it Acklington should be manned to do its full task if necessary at the expense of disbanding a squadron so as to ensure all squadrons get maximum shooting training while here. Works contractors progress slowly but show a lamentable sign of none being finally cleared up. Contractors seem to be allowed to dispose of their men and equipment before the jobs are cleaned up—ditches and channels, roads and edges of perimeter tracks all are left unlevelled, ungraded and littered with the debris and spoil heaps. I have taken this up with the resident engineer. The one A.S.P. is progressing well—no sign of the other being completed. The O.R.P.'s concreting is finished but lighting pits and fittings are still unfinished. The new hangar has shown little or no progress for the past two months.

A Vampire T.11 dual trainer was allotted to the APS for a month's gunnery trial during June. A total of twenty-one sorties were carried out, until one gun sight became unserviceable. The Vampire was flown back to the makers for repair and modification. 151 Squadron and 1 Squadron completed their attachment in early July. Meteor F.8s of 74 and 275 Squadrons took their place. The former was commanded by Maj. G. Milholland of the USAF. The great number of training sorties flown during that month put a great deal of pressure on the APS. At the end of the attachments it was frequently down to one serviceable aircraft. Three of its Hawker Tempests were involved in emergency landings on 10 July. One had a fuel pump seizure, another

The Airfield's flying control centre in the early 1950s (*The National Archives*)

a partially blocked oil filter and the third, hydraulic failure. The following day, a Valetta made an emergency landing as one of its two engines had failed. Maj. Ramsey, Commander of the local Home Guard, paid a visit on the 24th to discuss the Home Guard's contribution to the defence of the Station. He was asked to provide protection in the defence of the signals outstations, transmitter, receiver and HF/DF stations. Maj. Wigram of the 8th Anti-aircraft Brigade advised where light anti-aircraft guns should be placed to protect vulnerable points.

The first Gloster Meteor NF.11s to be attached to RAF Acklington were flown by 264 Squadron, which was on the Station between 7 and 22 August. The Station held an open day for members of the Royal Observer Corps on the 17th (a Sunday) with over 600 members attending. The programme included a flying display, an exhibition of technical equipment, a static aircraft display and air experience flights. Some 560 Royal Observer Corps personnel were given flights in Anson, Dakota, Hastings and Varsity aircraft. Meteors of 43 Squadron performed an aerobatic display.

After frequent delays, the construction work on the airfield was now beginning to make some progress. The new T2 hangar ('No. 4 hangar') was completed and occupied by the APS Wing. The builders left behind a lot of debris which had to be cleared up. The northern ASP was now about 85 per cent complete and the southern ASP was being excavated and drained. The bulk fuel installation had been finished, but work was still required on the surrounding roads. By the following month, work was again proceeding at a snail's pace. The Station Commander related that:

> No O.R.P.s or A.S.P.s are ready yet—Lighting and filling cracks with bitumen still to be done. 2nd A.S.P. will be ready by Xmas if another man could help them! The existing man will probably take a year longer to finish it alone!! I still think it is much too small and that the grass portion between the hangar approach and the A.S.P. makes it a most unsatisfactory A.S.P.—the most stupid one in the Air Force but unfortunately beggars can't be choosers and it seems to have been a Hobsons choice of either this or nothing.

With the departure of 141 Squadron for RAF Coltishall on 16 September, there was a gap of five weeks without visiting squadrons. This break in training was used to convert the target towing flight from Tempests to Meteor 8s. A Tempest (NV711) suffered damage to its propeller tips as a result of an attempted landing with the undercarriage retracted. The pilot received a severe reprimand from the Station Commander for this mistake. The serviceability of the APS aircraft fleet was hampered by a lack of engine fitters. There was also an acute shortage of transport drivers and cooks on the Station. By the end of September, only four Meteor F.8s had been received for target tug duties. With targets now being towed by jet aircraft with higher speeds, the propeller-driven Balliol aircraft used for gunnery training by the APS were partially replaced by two Vampire jets.

At this time, Northstead Radar Station became a section of the Acklington establishment providing radar control of air firing over the ranges. It had previously only be used on a trial basis for this purpose. The Air Ministry carried out a review of RAF Acklington during September. Wg Cdr T. Kean stressed his concerns to the

Ministry representatives about the shortage of personnel. He also said that, ideally, the APS should have the following aircraft on strength—four Vampire T.11s, two Meteor 8s, one Meteor 7, one Oxford, and seventeen Meteors. The members of the Air Ministry disagreed, and stated it should be—three Vampire T.11s, one Meteor T7, one Meteor 4, one Vampire 5, one Oxford, and fifteen Meteors.

RAF Acklington acted as a refuelling and diversion airfield during exercise 'Ardent', which was held in September and October. The Church Fenton Wing of sixteen Meteors arrived on 28 September for refuelling. Only fifty minutes were allowed for turning them around, but the aircraft required twice as much fuel as forecast. During phase one of the exercise, twelve sorties were carried out by aircraft of 29, 151, and 264 Squadrons during the night of 4–5 October. On the 4th, during the day, eight aircraft of 616 Squadron, seven aircraft of 92 Squadron and four aircraft of 19 Squadron operated from Acklington during the day. On the afternoon of the 9th, 151 Squadron arrived with eight Vampire NF.10s and a Meteor T7 for phase two of the exercise. It were followed by 264 squadron.

Further Meteors arrived to replace the remaining Tempest target tugs. They were late in arriving and many of the modifications were below standard. Numerous problems were encountered when towing the gliders behind a jet rather than the much slower propeller-driven aircraft used previously. Some refused to leave the ground, others refused to let go of towing cable on reaching the ranges. A number of experimental sorties were carried out with the glider targets. The intention was to test the strike recorder and to discover the greatest height at which gliders could be seen by the GCI radar station when towed no more than 12 miles offshore. The 12 mile restriction was set by the limit of coverage of the sea surface by the CHEL station and by the range of the cannon shells.

Training recommenced at RAF Acklington on the 20 October with the arrival of 43 and 222 Squadron's Meteor F.8s. Two days later, there was a fatal accident. Meteor F.8 (VZ461) of 43 Squadron, piloted by Plt Off. M. Prior, crashed into the sea while climbing in cloud preparatory to an air firing exercise. A Court of Inquiry was held and the cause of the accident was attributed to the failure of the artificial horizon instrument. It was not the only investigation held in October. There were two further Courts of Inquiry—one concerning a cannon shell striking the rocks near the Longstone Lighthouse and another into a ship being struck by a cannon shell.

November was the first month in which Vampire trainers were used for dual air firing and Meteors for towing for a Fighter Command squadron. On the 12th, 43 Squadron and 222 Squadron completed their attachment and returned home, after flying some 666 sorties. Meteor NF.11s of 29 and 85 Squadrons from RAF Tangmere and RAF Coltishall arrived for training on the 17th. A few days later, a Meteor from the latter squadron struck a flag target during air firing, sustaining minor damage.

At this time, RAF Acklington became a night diversion airfield for 228 Operational Conversion Unit at RAF Leeming. On four nights a week, a flare path was laid and air traffic control facilities maintained from 5 p.m. until night flying ceased at RAF Leeming. Shortly before the Station closed down for Christmas, a night defence exercise was staged. The airfield was 'attacked' by a force of some sixty RAF Regiment personnel from RAF Ouston: 'Everyone was very enthusiastic and entered well into the spirit of it.'

December 1952 was the last month of Wg Cdr T. Kean's command at RAF Acklington. His final entry in the Station Diary was somewhat downbeat:

> The general state of the airfield is still far from inspiring. The Crowley Russell & Co. contractors continue to make the place into a dump and have now been one year and three months trying to make two O.R.P.S (operational readiness platforms) and two A.S.P.s. (aircraft service platforms). Completion of the 2nd A.S.P. is now 70 per cent completed re concreting but not lighting. There is still no agreement or approval given to the construction of a connecting link between the tarmac, hangars and the A.S.P.—a most crazy and ludicrous situation. The year ends with still no approval being given to the building of a new station education block—a most essential and urgent requirement. Married quarters are just approaching completion—all twenty of the new officer's married quarters are now occupied and seventy-two of airmen's. Re-lining of the airmen's single brick huts with composition boarding has now commenced. This will greatly improve these damp and cold huts.
>
> I hand over command of the Station to Wg Cdr R. A. Barton OBE DFC in January 1953. During my tour of duty I have witnessed the change from the Mosquito to the Balliol and then the Vampire trainer for dual air firing, from the Martinet and Tempest to the Meteor VIII for towing, from the drogue at 120–140 knots to the flag and glider targets at 200 and 240 knots respectively, from visual towing and shooting at 3,000 feet to radar controlled shooting at 20,000 feet—25,000 feet; from two squadrons of fifteen pilots to two squadrons of twenty–twenty-five pilots per day fighter squadron, each averaging thirteen effective shoots each with scores much the same as previously despite the flag target and the much higher altitude. I feel that pilots are now getting much more realistic and more useful training.
>
> Morale in general is high and discipline is good. The policy of increasing the punishment every time an outside charge is preferred against an airman for improper dress or behaviour has paid dividends. I used to get three or four a month—now one in six months. I was proud of their turn out and steadiness in ranks and drill on the annual A.O.C.s parade—I still am—and I appreciate and respect the support they have given me.

# 1953

On 6 January, 54 and 247 Squadrons arrived from RAF Odiham. The former had twelve Meteor F.8s, one Meteor T7 and an Oxford, with nineteen pilots and seventy-eight ground personnel. The latter flew twelve Meteor F.8s and one Meteor T7, with eighteen pilots and seventy-seven ground personnel. The APS flew 497 sorties for a total of 395 hours during the month. One of its Meteor F.7s (WF819) struck a bird in flight, causing slight damage to the nose fairing. On the 15th, a Meteor F.8 of 43 Squadron was damaged when its engine caught fire during landing. The month terminated with a strong gale which caused damage to the hangars, buildings, and equipment. The aircraft escaped unscathed as all were inside at the time.

An APS Gloster Meteor F.8 (VZ522) photographed at RAF Odiham in 1953.
(*MAP aviation photos*)

A De Havilland Vampire T.11 (XE871). The APS had several examples of this type of aircraft, some of which had dual gun sights for gunnery training. (*MAP aviation photos*)

There were six minor accidents during February. Four were caused by Meteor aircraft landing on snow and ice covered runways during a sudden thaw. A further Meteor suffered damage when forced to touch down on a snow covered runway with a towing cable which had failed to release. The result in each of these five cases was minor damage to flaps. A sixth Meteor undershot the runway due to a faulty air speed indicator, damaging its undercarriage. Wintery weather disrupted flying on several days. Five Gloster Meteors had to be diverted to RAF Ouston on the 12th due to a heavy snowstorm. Seven days later, a Valleta carrying the Secretary of State for Air had to be diverted to RAF Acklington as it could not land at RAF Silloth on the west coast.

The following month, a Hastings changed its destination and headed for the airfield. A goose-neck flare path was laid but the aircraft could not land due to low cloud. It made for Prestwick instead. At that time, 56 and 63 Squadrons from RAF Waterbeach, equipped with Meteor F.8s, were attached to the APS. On 12 March, one of them (WK658) sustained damage to its tail surfaces when the pilot's canopy disintegrated. Later that month, an airman was struck by a winged target on the runway while it was taking off. All the gliders were now towed by Gloster Meteors. The remaining three APS Tempest tugs left RAF Acklington for the last time in March.

April proved to be a particularly accident prone month. The most serious involved a Meteor F.8 (VZ501) flown by twenty-year-old Plt Off. Gordon Livingstone of 72 Squadron. The aircraft took off on the 17th for air-to-air firing at a target banner. Livingstone lost sight of the leading aircraft in thick cloud at 7,000 feet. He was then given a number of courses to steer but none of them were followed. Sometime later, he reported that he was still in cloud at an altitude of only 100 feet. After a short unintelligible transmission, nothing more was heard. An oil slick was found at approximately the position of the last plot, about 2 miles off Coquet Island. It was assumed that the Meteor had crashed into the sea. The same day, another 72 Squadron Meteor F.8 (WK677) made a landing on the grass as its port undercarriage wheel would not lower. There was substantial damage to the aircraft. A few days earlier, a Meteor (WA840) of the target towing flight lost its canopy while in flight. The aircraft landed safely. The pilot of another Meteor (WK753) of the target towing flight had to abandon his take-off because the oxygen bottle of the dinghy fouled the control column. On the 15th, a Meteor of 12 Group also had to abort the take-off because smoke began to fill the cockpit. Five days later, a bullet ricocheted off the sea and struck and inflicted serious damage to Meteor F.8 (WH350) of 19 Squadron.

RCAF 410 Squadron, with twelve North American F.86E Sabres, arrived at the end of April, accompanied by eight Vampire NF10s of 25 Squadron. Five days after the start of their attachment, a Meteor 8 target tug was struck by a bullet from a Sabre during air-to-air firing practice. The rear of the cockpit canopy was pierced and the armour plating badly dented. This was not the only incident that day. Another Sabre (19194), of 410 Squadron, skidded off the runway on landing, damaging its nose wheel and denting the nose section. Two days earlier on the 28th, a Meteor 8 (WK754), of the target towing flight, overshot on landing, damaging its front wheel. There was a further incident that day, when a Meteor 8 from the same unit undershot the runway and hit a barbed-wire fence. Its port engine, nacelle and flap were damaged.

On 30 May, 141 Squadron from RAF Coltishall and 264 Squadron from RAF Linton-on-Ouse completed their attachment, which had begun on the 18th. A total of 437 sorties were flown. During June, a number of pilots with 228 OCU from RAF Leeming undertook training at RAF Acklington. The Station's annual sports day was held in the early part of the month: 'there was keen competition, both among our own wings and visiting teams. The meeting provided many thrills and a number of records broken.' On 21 June, a flying display was held for the Royal Observer Corps.

Meteors were again involved in several minor accidents. Meteor F.8 (WK694) collided with a bird in flight which made a large indentation in the starboard mainplane. On 24 June, there were two mishaps. Flt Sgt Mason, flying a Meteor F.8 of the Target Towing Flight, was hit by his own towing cable after losing the attached banner. The elevators of the aircraft were severely bent. In the second, a Meteor F.8 (WK649) flown by Plt Off. Thorman, attached from 228 OCU, collided with the towing cable of a target tug aircraft during an air-to-air firing sortie. The Meteor suffered a large dent to its starboard mainplane.

The following month, on 13 July, another Meteor F.8 (WK752), also from 228 OCU, struck a banner target and suffered serious damage. It managed to land back at RAF Acklington safely. An usual incident occurred a week later to a Vampire T.11 piloted by Flt Lt R. Webster. The throttle jammed at 8,500 rpm on take-off. After flying for 20 minutes to reduce fuel, Webster landed safely by cutting the engine on touch-down. A Gloster Meteor of No. 11 Group Communications Flight suffered minor damage when its undercarriage collapsed on touch-down. Five Chipmunks *en route* to Turnhouse landed at RAF Acklington short of fuel during the month. On the 23rd, an RAF Regiment attachment trained the Station personnel in rifle firing at the Alnwick Range. During the last week of their stay, they built an assault course at Druridge Bay.

On 7 August, 257 and 263 Squadrons Meteor F.8s departed. The next deployment to the APS was not until the very end of the month when Meteor F.8s and NF.11s of 41 and 85 Squadrons flew in. In the intervening period there was much activity. The APS provided a squadron of eight Meteor F.8s for Exercise 'Momentum'. This was the first time the APS aircraft had been deployed as a defensive fighter unit. 151 and 264 Squadrons each had four Meteor NF.11s at Acklington for this exercise.

RAF Ouston had De Havilland Venom FB1s of 14 Squadron deployed at RAF Acklington. One of its aircraft (WE367) was on patrol at 40,000 feet on 15 August under the control of the Air Defence Sector Controller when its engine failed. The pilot attempted to relight the engine without success. As he continued to lose altitude, he caught sight of the disused Boulmer airfield and decided to make a forced landing there. At the last minute he realised that the runway had obstructions on it so he made a wheels up landing on the adjacent grass. The pilot suffered no serious injuries and was brought to RAF Acklington by helicopter.

Exercise 'Gloworm' was held at RAF Acklington on 29 September, but unlike 'Momentum', it was a passive defence exercise. There were a number of simulated emergencies which included unexploded bombs, nerve gas attack and even an atomic bomb dropped on a local town, followed by fires and radioactivity. At this time, 1

Squadron (Meteor F.8s) and 29 Squadron (Meteor NF.11s) were in residence. An aircraft of the latter squadron (WM257) collided with a banner target which had been shot away from its towing cable.

In early October, much of southern England was in the clutches of bad weather. On the 2nd, eleven Canberras were diverted from RAF Binbrook, as were five Lincolns from RAF Wittering. The following day, a further five Lincolns were diverted from RAF Upwood.

Throughout the year, the personnel on the Station had the opportunity to further their education. In October, there were 246 attendances at classes arranged for the RAF Education Test, seventy-nine for the General Certificate of Education, and 117 for Citizenship and Current Affairs course. In addition, education classes were held at Blyth and Boulmer. Two lectures were given for Officers Annual Administration Training. A further four lectures were given by lecturers provided by Durham University. There were eighty attendances for woodwork and thirteen for art classes.

Nos 222 and 245 Squadrons took up residence at RAF Acklington on 19 October, each with about a dozen Meteor F.8s. At the beginning of the following month, a Meteor F.8. (WK886), flown by Sqn Ldr Douglas Ford, crashed into the sea 18 miles off Coquet Island. A search by the Blyth air-sea rescue launch found only an oil slick. The aircraft had been involved in an air-to-air firing exercise when part of the target broke away from the tug aircraft. It was thought that Ford's aircraft struck the drogue spreader bar, damaging the windscreen and hood, rendering him unconscious. The aircraft was seen to behave in an erratic manner before plunging into the sea.

There were several more accidents in November, fortunately none as serious as the death of Sqn Ldr Ford. On the 13th, a Vampire T.11 (WE619) of the APS gunnery flight lost its port wheel fairing and brake air pressure line while in flight. After landing, it ran off the end of the runway but escaped with minor damage. Three days later, the starboard engine of an Oxford II of Fighter Command failed shortly after take-off. It made a successful emergency landing. Two days later, a Meteor F.8 (WH453) was struck by the wing of a glider target which had become detached during an air-to-air firing exercise. Despite the fact that the nose cowling, fin, and rudder were damaged and the windscreen and cowling shattered, Fg Off. Robson was not hurt and managed to land the Meteor back at the airfield.

The General Engineering Flight at that time was suffering from a serious shortage of skilled personnel and had only half the required number of general fitters and mechanics. Throughout the 1950s, Ansons were frequent visitors to RAF Acklington, transporting airmen and vital equipment between Fighter Command airfields. On 4 December, an Anson (VS507) was attempting to land in darkness at RAF Newton at the end of its journey from RAF Acklington. It stalled when attempting an overshoot and crashed on the runway. Six of its seven occupants perished in the accident. The next day, back at RAF Acklington, there was a less serious accident when a Meteor F.8 (WK753) was struck in the ventral tank by a cannon shell whilst towing. A further APS Meteor F.8 (WK649) was seriously damaged on the 21st when it burst a tyre on landing and swung off the runway. The aircraft then collided with a private car and contractor's machinery.

RAF Acklington's pipe band. (*The National Archives*)

Servicing the Goblin engine in a Vampire T.11 at RAF Acklington. (*The National Archives*)

In December, APS aircraft flew 326 sorties, comprised of the following:

| Aircraft Type | Sorties | Flying Hours |
| --- | --- | --- |
| Meteor T7 | 9 | 6.30 |
| Meteor F.8 | 260 | 231.0 |
| Vampire T.11 | 55 | 38.25 |
| Balliol | 1 | 0.40 |
| Oxford | 1 | 0.25 |

Also based at RAF Acklington between 1946 and 1956 was the Fighter Armaments Trial Unit (FATU); it generally used aircraft borrowed from the APS.

Nos 43 and 74 Squadrons (Meteor F.8s) were the last attached squadrons of the year. They had departed by 19 December after completing 763 sorties. After this date, a number of aircraft diversions were handled. On the 20th, four Meteor NF.11s were diverted from RAF Leeming. Four Canberras landed the following day as they could not reach RAF Hemswell. The next day, two Lincolns were diverted from RAF Wittering. At a parade held on Wednesday, 30 December, Grp Capt. J. W. Farmer DFC took command of RAF Acklington from Wg Cdr R. A. Barton OBE DFC.

APS Gloster Meteor F.8 (WK932) in front of one of RAF Acklington's hangers, 1954. (*Eric Taylor via R. L.*)

# 1954

At the beginning of the year, the last Balliol T2 (VR606) was withdrawn from service with the APS. Lack of spare parts had also grounded two of its Vampires. A camouflage scheme was applied to the first of the Meteors, using sea-green paint which had to be scrounged from RAF Duxford. Up until then, the aircraft of the APS sported an attractive natural metal finish.

Nos 64 and 65 Squadrons, each with twelve Meteor F.8s, touched down at RAF Acklington on 4 January for a month's training. During their stay, two of their aircraft were involved in accidents. The first, on 12 January, involved an aircraft of 65 Squadron. A Meteor F.8 (WF660) undershot runway twenty-three by approximately 200 yards. Its nose wheel collapsed and the aircraft skidded along the runway, suffering severe damage. Two days later, Fg Off. J. M. McMinn was flying his first air-to-air firing sortie when his Meteor F.8 (VZ532) struck the towed banner target and damaged his aircraft's nose. The aircraft landed back on the airfield without further problems. There was a spate of aircraft diversions to RAF Acklington on 20 January when the north of England was in the grip of wintery weather. Nine Meteor NF.11s, a Valetta, three Varsities, and a Lincoln all sought refuge there.

There were further diversions throughout the following month. They included a Sea Fury on the 2 February, a Neptune on the 9th, and five Varsities on the 19th. Many of the Station's personnel at that time were sick with influenza and a hut had to be used as an annexe to the sick quarters to cope with the additional admissions. On the 4th, two RCAF squadrons—439 Squadron with twelve F.86E Sabres and 441 Squadron with eleven Sabres—arrived from RAF North Luffenham for three week's gunnery practice. Despite the very bad weather, they managed to complete 510 sorties. A Meteor F.8 (VZ506), which was towing a flag target for the Sabres, was struck in the port wing by a 0.5 inch shell causing damage to the spar. The aircraft managed to return to RAF Acklington without any further trouble.

At the end of February, the total number of personnel at the Station was as follows:

| | Officers | Aircrew | W.Os | F.S. | Sgt | Cpls | A.C.s | Total |
|---|---|---|---|---|---|---|---|---|
| Acklington | 48 | 20 | 4 | 20 | 39 | 78 | 536 | 745 |
| 1108 MCU Blyth (Air sea rescue launch) | 2 | 0 | 0 | 2 | 1 | 5 | 27 | 37 |
| RAF Boulmer | 10 | 0 | 0 | 1 | 5 | 20 | 85 | 121 |
| Attached | 0 | 0 | 0 | 0 | 0 | 4 | 14 | 18 |
| Totals | 60 | 20 | 4 | 25 | 45 | 107 | 662 | 921 |

A Meteor NF.11 (WM155) of 151 Squadron from RAF Leuchars collided with a flag target, damaging the leading edge of its wing. The pilot, Sgt Davidson, succeeded in returning to base without difficulty. This squadron was accompanied for the training course by 29 Squadron. On the ground there were 327 attendances at classes for the RAF Education Test in March. In addition, others attended General Certificate Education courses on English, French, and Citizenship and Current Affairs.

Over 882 sorties were flown by the Meteor F.8s of 257 and 263 Squadrons, in residence in April. A 20-mm cannon shell fired by an aircraft of the former squadron struck the starboard engine nacelle of a target-towing Meteor (WK788) of the APS. Although the aircraft returned safely to RAF Acklington, the incident was the subject of a Court of Inquiry. At the end of the month, an Iceland Airways Douglas DC-4 airliner (TF-ISE) flew into the ranges for a duration of seven minutes.

There was a narrow escape the following month, when a Meteor on the ground accidently fired one 20-mm round into the paint and dope store. During May, a further RCAF unit, 410 Squadron, completed its deployment and returned to RAF North Luffenham. On the 10th, the Duke of Edinburgh, in an Airspeed Oxford, landed *en route* to RAF Edzell to refuel. The Duke, with his instructor and navigator, found time to have lunch with the Commanding Officer in the Officers' Mess. 264 Squadron, with no fewer than eighteen Meteor NF.11s, arrived later in the month for weapons training. No gliders were available for target practice since a number of them had fallen into the surrounding countryside after being released from their

Replacing the 20-mm cannon in an APS Meteor F.8 after servicing. (*The National Archives*)

tug aircraft. After a court of Inquiry assembled at RAF Acklington, it was decided to temporarily suspend target practice with towed glider targets. Pilots were given an additional four flag shots as part of their course.

In July, repairs commenced on the runways. The APS provided a squadron of twelve Meteor F.8s and fifteen pilots for Operation 'Dividend'. They flew from RAF Dyce, Aberdeen, between the 12th and 27th. As work continued on the runways throughout August and September, the APS provided two teams, each with four Meteor F.8s and a single Vampire, to tour Fighter Command Stations for air-to-air firing and gunnery instruction.

On 13 September, a Meteor F.8 back-tracked at speed and ran off the runway ending up in a field. All aircraft airborne at that time had to be diverted to RAF Ouston. The following month, two further Meteors suffered similar fates. On 29 October, twenty-one officers and 450 airmen from RAF Acklington lined the route in Newcastle and Wallsend for the visit of The Queen and the Duke of Edinburgh.

After a break of four months, training resumed at RAF Acklington with the arrival of two Squadrons from the RAF Waterbeach Wing. 56 Squadron came with eleven Meteor F.8s, two Vampire T.11s and eight Supermarine Swifts. The latter was a new type to the RAF, having been delivered just a few months earlier, and the first British swept wing fighter to enter service. It was destined to remain one of the more obscure aircraft to serve in RAF Fighter Command as numerous problems were encountered with the machine. It was operated as a fighter by 56 Squadron, which received fourteen Swifts, all of which had been withdrawn by 1955. Other examples were used in photographic reconnaissance.

No. 63 Squadron accompanied 56 Squadron to RAF Acklington. On 18 November an APS Meteor F.8 (WF855) was towing a banner target for Fg Off. B. Williams of 63 Squadron in Meteor F.8 (WE938). During an attack, Williams misjudged his distance from the banner and, in attempting to pull away, he collided with the target, causing major damage to his own aircraft and minor damage to the target tug. Both aircraft managed to make it back to RAF Acklington without further incident. A Swift II (WK240) ran off the perimeter track on the 27th—one of its undercarriage legs collapsed and the aircraft came to rest on its port wing. At the end of the month, there was a Station defence exercise, 'Fox-Trek'. A mock attack was made by 'saboteurs' provided by the Army. Several were captured and interrogated by airmen defending the base.

Camouflaging of the APS aircraft fleet had been completed by late autumn. On 10 December, the Swifts of 56 Squadron flew back to RAF Waterbeach, followed by 63 Squadron the next day. It was not before a Meteor F.8 (WA999) made a successful wheels-up landing on the grass when the starboard undercarriage leg failed to lower on returning from an air gunnery exercise. Further repair work commenced on the runways in the middle of December, with the airfield remaining in limited operation.

Early morning line-up of APS Meteor 8 target towing aircraft. (*The National Archives*)

An APS Acklington Gloster Meteor F.8 (VZ494). (*MAP aviation photos*)

De Havilland Vampire T.11 (XE934) operated by APS Acklington. (*MAP aviation photos*)

# 1955

The first deployment of the year was sixteen Meteor F.8s of 111 squadron from RAF North Weald and twelve Meteor NF.11s plus one Meteor T7 of 141 Squadron from RAF Coltishall. Ice and snow on the runways disrupted flying on a number of days. On 26 January, the airfield received eight Canberras which had been diverted from RAF Binbrook. Bad weather also disrupted the training of the next two squadrons to deploy. Only twenty-five effective flights were flown by 74 and 245 Squadron's Meteor F.8s during their first two weeks here.

Six inches of snow fell on 12 February. A Hastings, engaged in hay-dropping flights to stranded livestock on the Cheviot Hills, stayed overnight at the end of the month. Hay drops continued well into March. A less welcome object to fall from the sky was a target glider which broke up as the aircraft towing it left the airfield. The wreckage fell on Amble but fortunately there was no damage or injuries to members of the public. There was also a complaint from a civilian aircraft, the pilot of which stated he was 'beaten up' by two Meteors. He had actually flown through the north range at 14,500 feet and had narrowly missed being shot down. It was not the only civil aircraft to infringe this restricted area. On 6 February, a Scandinavian Airline Systems DC-6 (SE-RDT) flew into the ranges very close to where Meteors were live firing. There was a further infringement on 30 March, by a Vickers Viking operated by the British airline Hunting-Clan *en route* from Woolsington to Stavanger, Norway. The air traffic controller at the Scottish centre was informed and stated that action would be taken against its pilot.

On 21 March, the RAF Linton-on-Ouse Wing flew in with eighteen Sabre F.4s of 66 Squadron and sixteen Sabres of 92 Squadron. There was an exercise on the final three days of the month involving these two squadrons and APS Meteors. They flew air defence sorties intercepting a Convair B-36, a six-engined leviathan of the US Air Force. The flights and claims were as follows:

|  | Flights | Claims |
|---|---|---|
| **Tuesday 29 March** | | |
| APS | 4 | 2 aircraft probably destroyed |
| 66 Squadron | 4 | 1 aircraft probably destroyed |
| 92 Squadron | 4 | nil |
| **Wednesday 30 March** | | |
| APS | 8 | 1 damaged, 3 probably destroyed |
| 66 Squadron | 2 | 1 probably destroyed |
| 92 Squadron | 2 | 1 probably destroyed |
| **Thursday 31 March** | | |
| APS | 9 | 4 damaged, 3 probably destroyed |
| 66 Squadron | 2 | 1 damaged |
| 92 Squadron | 2 | nil |

Two major changes to the servicing of APS aircraft were instituted in spring 1955. The Flying Wing strength was increased and a warrant officer put in charge of first-line servicing, with the object of increasing serviceability by expediting recovery. If defects could be repaired within two days, this work was to be carried out completely within the first-line servicing. More complex repairs were to be sent to ASF. The second change was the institution of a system of 'crewing' in the Flying Wing. A crew of one airframe and one engine tradesmen was allotted to each aircraft to carry out first-line servicing and to assist on all second-line servicing.

During April, APS aircraft made a total of 533 flights. The breakdown was:

| Aircraft | Flights | Flying Hours |
|---|---|---|
| Meteor T7 | 45 | 33 |
| Meteor F.8 (day) | 372 | 341 |
| Meteor F.8 (night) | 10 | 4 |
| Vampire T.11 | 79 | 58 |
| Oxford | 10 | 14 |
| Anson | 17 | 19 |

Inspecting the belt feed mechanism for ammunition in a Meteor F.8, prior to a firing practice. (*The National Archives*)

Although there were no accidents to any APS aircraft during April, the pilot of one of 92 Squadron's Sabres (XD710) had to abandon a take-off. His aircraft ended up on the grass next to the runway and was seriously damaged.

Towards the end of May, 23 Squadron arrived with twelve Venom NF.11s and three Vampire T.11s, accompanied by 34 Squadron's fourteen Meteors. One of the Meteors was involved in a minor accident a few days later when the cockpit hood flew off during take-off and struck the tail. The pilot successfully brought his aircraft to a stop.

RAF Acklington received a call on 27 May that a Valetta with a failed port engine was going to divert and make an emergency landing. Ambulance and crash vehicles were put on standby, but the aircraft overshot due to a 20-knot crosswind and flew south to RAF Disforth. A more unusual distress message was picked up three days later—this time from the ship HMS *Northumbria* reporting that it was taking on water. It had a hole in its starboard side, the engine room was flooded and its engines had stopped. The Royal Navy was contacted and dispatched a tug to its assist. HMS *Northumbria* then requested that the following message be relaid to the Flag Officer Scotland: 'Am in tow *Cyprian Prince* proceeding south, speed 6 knots. Hole in starboard side engine room flooded. Request dry dock be arranged. No casualties.'

The Station sports day took place in late May. The weather was fine but cold, which was probably responsible for the relatively small number of spectators.

Between 1 and 14 June, Dakotas of British European Airways and Valettas of Transport Command landed at RAF Acklington whilst carrying out Operation 'Stagecoach'. During the second half of the month, extensive repairs were carried out to the runway and night landings were prohibited.

The Guard of Honour for the arrival of the AOC, No. 81 Group, Air Cdre H. Hogan DFC for his annual inspection. (*The National Archives*)

The Guard of Honour for the arrival of the AOC, No. 81 Group, Air Cdre H. Hogan DFC, for his annual inspection. (*The National Archives*)

From early July, RAF Acklington was designated a master diversion airfield. The AOC Air Cdr H. Hogan inspected the entire Station between 23 and 24 July. He was impressed with what he found. The following signal was received from 81 Group not long after his departure:

> The turnout and bearing of all ranks for my inspection was outstandingly good and I was extremely well satisfied with the standard of drill displayed both by the Guard of Honour and personnel on parade. There was ample evidence that a great deal of effort had gone into preparing the station for the occasion and the attention given to detail was apparent throughout the inspection. I was well impressed by the flying both in the flypast and in the individual aerobatic show. I congratulate your officers and all ranks for reaching such a high standard. Well done.

In mid-July, 29 Squadron departed and 64 and 65 Squadrons' Meteor F.8s arrived a few days later. On 5 August, a Meteor of the former squadron was involved in a serious accident. When Fg Off. T. Withington touched down at the conclusion of an air-to-air gunnery exercise and applied the brakes, the starboard brake failed. He was unable to use the port brake to slow down because it would have caused the Meteor to swing dangerously to port. The aircraft ran off the end of the runway into the gulley known as 'Meteor Valley', sustaining serious damage. The pilot fared somewhat better, surviving the experience without serious injury. The following week, an elderly lady phone the Station alleging she heard a message from a Canberra aircraft informing RAF Acklington that it had engine trouble. According to her, the aircraft was instructed to join the circuit. The caller then put down the phone and informed the local newspaper of this. Inquiries by the Station found no Canberra in the vicinity of the airfield at that time. A Vickers Viking (VW146) could have been in serious trouble. It flew into the range area on the 31st and was reported to the air traffic control centre at Watnall.

No. 152 Squadron departed for RAF Duxford with its Meteor NF14s on 8 September and the following day, 46 Squadron returned to RAF Odiham. No. 610 and 611 Auxiliary Air Force Squadrons arrived from RAF Hooton Park with their Meteor F.8s on the 22nd. From the 23rd to the 26th, the Station took part in Exercise 'Beware'. During phase one, 610 and 611 Squadrons maintained four pairs of aircraft in an operational state during daylight hours. No. 610 Squadron flew nine pairs of Meteors and made seven sightings of 'enemy aircraft', but did not claim any destroyed or damaged. No. 611 Squadron flew fifteen pairs of Meteors, made fourteen sightings and claimed six Canberras shot down. The APS Squadron's six pairs made thirteen sightings on a total of eighteen aircraft, claiming five probably destroyed and one damaged.

Phase two of the exercise took place between 27 and 29 September. Nos 610 and 611 Squadrons maintained two pairs of aircraft in an operational state while the APS Squadron had no less than six pairs ready. The APS flew thirteen pairs making seventeen sightings on a total of seventeen aircraft. Of these, three were claimed as probably destroyed and a further two damaged. No. 610 Squadron made seven sightings on a total of eight aircraft and claimed three probably destroyed. No. 611 Squadron flew seven pairs, made six sightings of a total of six aircraft and claimed two Canberras probably shot down and a further two damaged.

Phase three was the concluding part of the exercise and took place on 1 and 2 October. APS made six sightings on a total of thirty-four aircraft and claimed four Canberras probably destroyed with a further one damaged. Twelve sightings were made by 610 Squadron on a total of twenty-one aircraft. No. 610 claimed one Meteor and two Sabres as probably destroyed. No. 611 Squadron flew eight pairs and two fours. Twelve sightings were made on a total of fourteen aircraft and four Canberras, two Vampires and one Neptune were claimed as shot down and a further three Canberras as damaged.

During November, 72 Squadron and 153 Squadron completed their attachment and returned to RAF Church Fenton and RAF West Malling respectively. Their place was taken by twelve Meteor F.8s of 63 Squadron and twelve Meteor NF.14s of 264 Squadron. On the 1st, Fg Off. B. Burns of 72 Squadron, flying a Meteor F.8, made an attack on a winged target. Whilst firing at the glider it disintegrated and parts struck the Meteor. The aircraft sustained only minor damage and landed safely.

At the end of the year, the APS had the following aircraft on strength:

Meteor F.8s—WK754, WK694, WK747, WH363, WK985, VZ530, WF646, WF683, WH279, VZ443, VZ494, WH317, WK652, WE855, VZ443, VZ494, WK985, and WE855

Vampire T.11s—WZ615 and WZ619

Avro Anson (PH782) and a small number of Meteor T7s

A two seat training Gloster Meteor T7 (WF819) operated by the APS in 1955. (*Raymond Turner via R. L.*)

APS target-towing Meteors. (*The National Archives*)

Avro Anson (PH782) operated by APS Acklington for transport purposes in 1956. It is the process of being refuelled. (*MAP aviation photos*)

## 1956

This would be the final year of RAF Acklington's role as Fighter Command's armaments practice station. On 10 February, 245 Sqn Ldr N. Bowen was carrying out a radar-controlled gun test under Boulmer GCI in a Meteor F.8. When he prepared to land, he found that the aircraft's speed brakes, flap and undercarriage levers all moved freely. After continuous pumping, the three green undercarriage lights eventually appeared and shortly after the Meteor touched down. A complete electrical failure had been experienced. When the aircraft was examined, a small hole was found in the top surface of the starboard wing near the fuselage. A panel was removed and a spent 20-mm shell and part of its driving band were found inside. The main hydraulic lines and electrical conduit was fractured. An investigation was undertaken which ascertained that the incident was more than likely caused by a ricochet from a round from the same aircraft. As February drew to a close, a Venom NF.2 suffered from brake failure and ran into the overshoot area at the end of the runway. No damage was sustained to the aircraft.

On 8 and 9 March, 219 Squadron and 245 Squadron completed their attachment and returned to RAF Driffield and RAF Stradishall respectively. A few days later, 65 Squadron arrived with fourteen Meteor 8s and 64 Squadron with twelve Meteor 8s. Fg Off. B. Nice, flying a Meteor 8 (WL116) on an air-to-air firing live practice, flew into the flag target spreader, damaging the port engine nacelle, the intake nosing and part of the wing. Both 64 and 65 Squadrons completed their detachment on the 27th and returned to RAF Duxford.

In April, there were several minor landing accidents experienced by 141 Squadron's Venom NF.3s during training. The most serious took place on the 26th, when a Venom NF.3 (WX859) was landing after an air firing sortie. After a normal touchdown, the port tyre burst. The aircraft became uncontrollable at a speed of approximately 15 knots and slewed off the runway. The port tyre, tube, and wheel hub were damaged.

Although the closure of the Armament Practice Camp was imminent, it was as busy as ever in May. No. 125 Squadron arrived with eleven Venom NF.3s and one Vampire T.11, along with eighteen pilots. They were accompanied by 152 Squadron with fourteen Meteor NF.11s, twenty-three pilots and ten navigators. During its attachment, 125 Squadron flew 226 flights for a total of 128 hours and 152 Squadron flew 304 flights for a total of 173 hours. On the 14th, 33 and 89 Squadrons arrived to commence the APS attachment. No. 33 Squadron brought ten Venom NF.2s, ten pilots and thirteen navigators. No. 89 Squadron arrived with twelve Venom NF.3s, one Vampire T.11, twenty-two pilots and twenty navigators. On the 26th, Fg Off. A. Smith of 89 Squadron was flying a Venom NF.3 (WX914) on an air firing sortie at 18,000 feet. Descending to Acklington with the firing exercise completed, he was travelling at 500 knots at 2,000 feet when the starboard side of the canopy shattered and flew off. Smith reduced speed and landed safely back at the airfield.

The last two squadrons to train at Acklington were 151 Squadron, with sixteen Venom NF.3s, two Meteor F.8s, and one Vampire T.11; and 222 Squadron, with sixteen Hunter F.4s, two Meteor F.8s, one Meteor F.7, and one Vampire T.11.

The main gate for RAF Acklington in mid-1950s. (*The National Archives*)

Unusually, neither unit returned to its base at RAF Leuchars on completion of the training. Instead, they were declared operational and remained at RAF Acklington during its transfer to Fighter Command.

A Venom NF.3 (WX794) was involved in an accident on 19 June. Its nose wheel failed on landing, causing the aircraft to swing off the runway onto the grass. Neither of its crew was hurt. A visit of a different sort took place with the arrival by air of the Queen Mother on 3 July for a brief stay at Alnwick Castle. On arrival, she was met by the Commanding Officer, Grp Capt. Boult, and the Duke of Northumberland. RAF personnel and their families were given the opportunity to watch the event.

# 17

# Cold War Fighter Airfield 1956–1960

29 Squadron: January 1957–July 1958, Meteor NF.11 (Javelin FAW 6 from November 1957)
66 Squadron: February 1957–September 1960, Hunter F.6

On 27 July 1956, RAF Acklington once again became a fully operational Fighter Command Airfield. 151 Squadron (Venom NF.3s) and 222 Squadron (Hunter F.4s) having completed the last armament training course, remained until early August, now in an operational capacity. On 20 August, a 43 Squadron Hunter (XF.302) on a training sortie from RAF Leuchars, made an emergency landing in adverse weather conditions with cloud down to 400 feet. It had experienced complete hydraulic failure after the shearing of a pipe.

There were no squadrons based at RAF Acklington in September, but sixteen Meteor F.8s were deployed there for a few days to participate in Exercise 'Stronghold'. On 14 November, the port undercarriage leg of an Anson (PH782) collapsed, causing the aircraft to swing off the runway and end up on the grass. Its pilot was unhurt. There was little flying at RAF Acklington at that time as many of the Meteors once used by the now defunct Armament Practice Station had been disposed of. Towards the end of the year, a conference was held to discuss the rebuilding of the station now that it was to be a permanent operational Fighter Command Airfield.

At that time, the airfield main runway, built in the Second World War, was 05/23. It was 5,800 feet long, with the tarmac re-surfaced in 1954. Four years later, it was resurfaced with asphalt. The second runway was 01/19, also built in the Second World War, was 4,550 feet long. The third runway, tarmac and 3,625 feet long, had been withdrawn from use in the late 1940s. The two pre-war F-type hangers were re-roofed in late 1941. There was also a Bellman Hanger plus a T2 Type hanger which had been brought from another airfield and re–erected between March 1951 and August 1952.

The Cold War was brought to the doorstep of RAF Acklington on 8 December. A Vikers Viking airliner (G-AMNK) of Hunting-Clan Airways landed from Dusseldorf, West Germany, carrying twenty-eight Hungarian refugees. They were mining technicians and students on their way to a National Coal Board hostel in County

The Station Commander, Grp Capt. N de W. Boult DFC, welcomes the OC 29 Squadron, Wg Cdr J. A. C. Aiken, on arrival to RAF Acklington, 1957. (*The National Archives*)

A Gloster Meteor NF.XI night fighter of 29 Squadron touching down at RAF Acklington in 1957. (*The National Archives*)

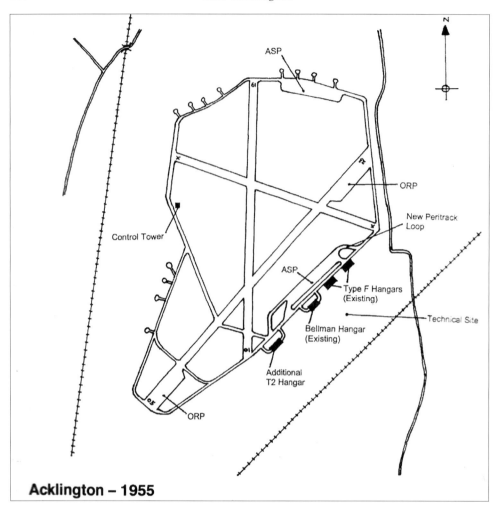

Plan of RAF Acklington airfield in 1955. (*Airfield Research Group/Peter Howarth*)

Hawker Hunter F.6 (XJ687) of 66 Squadron at RAF Acklington in 1958. (*Roger Lindsay*)

Durham. Over 200,000 Hungarians fled their country when the rebellion against Soviet oppression was crushed by the Red Army.

In January, 29 Squadron arrived to take up night fighter duties with sixteen Meteor NF.11s and one Meteor F.7. The following month, 66 Squadron flew in with thirteen Hunter F.6s, three Meteors, and one Vampire T.11. This move completed the establishment of the Acklington Wing. No. 66 Squadron was to provide fighter cover during daylight hours. In addition to these two squadrons, RAF Acklington Station's flight still had a number of aircraft including Ansons, a Chipmunk, and Vampires. A handful of the target-towing Meteors also had a further lease of life. The ranges continued to be used by the two based squadrons plus occasional visiting units. On arrival, 29 Squadron personnel were less than impressed with the facilities. Among the shortcomings listed in the unit's record book were shortage of hard standings and hangar space, poor hangar lighting and a shortage of accommodation for married personnel. Flying was also curtailed, owing to the need to economise on fuel. An average of twelve hours per pilot per month was allowed, which was about half of what was deemed necessary to maintain standards. Being a night fighter squadron, most flying would be undertaken when it was dark. When air-to-air firing exercises were performed, it was found that the targets were either too high or too fast for the Meteor NF.11s.

The crew of Meteor (WD725), Flt Lt C. Cody and his navigator Fg Off. B. Jones, had a narrow escape on 1 April when the aircraft overshot the end of the runway during a formation take-off. The Meteor jumped over a deep ravine and burst into flames when it struck the opposite bank. Cody was knocked unconscious and pulled clear of the wreckage by his navigator and two other pilots. He was taken to hospital with back injuries. The cause of the accident was thought to have been engine failure.

The Squadron was also experiencing problems with the serviceability of its Meteor NF.11s, placing an increasing burden on the ground crews. The shortcomings of the aircraft became apparent in May during Exercise 'Vigilant', when the Sector was reluctant to use the antiquated Meteor NF.11. Their crews spent long periods on the ground watching Hunters being repeatedly turned around and scrambled. When they did take to the air they often could not catch the 'bombers' which had a superior performance. Later that month, the Squadron visited the air-sea rescue unit at Blyth. A number of the crews were hoisted from a dinghy by a helicopter: 'With remarkable ungratefulness Fg Off. Sleigh managed during one hoist to jettison his rescuer into the sea. An action which greatly amused all present with the exception of one.'

By the summer, the restrictions on flying were lifted and the serviceability of the aircraft improved with the arrival of three Meteors from RAF Leeming. Flt Lt Cody was discharged from hospital and returned to duty.

In August, five of 29 Squadron Meteors were condemned as unfit to fly by a visiting inspection team. Within days, replacement aircraft were delivered. Around the same time, Flt Lt J. Brown and Flt Lt M. Harvey had a narrow escape when their Meteor F.7 (WL422) went out of control at 23,000 feet. The crew attempted to bail out, but the canopy would not jettison. Brown managed to regain control of his aircraft at 4,000 feet at which stage the canopy decided to detach itself. The Meteor F.7 landed safely back at RAF Acklington.

Exercise 'Strikeback' was held in September. No. 29 Squadron claimed a number of Valiants and Canberras 'destroyed'. A further fifteen radar contacts were made but subsequently lost due to the poor performance of the Meteor NF.11. Its days were now numbered, as ground equipment for its replacement, the Gloster Javelin, began arriving in the autumn. The first aircraft arrived at the end of October, the last month of operational flying for the Meteor NF.11. No. 29 Squadron had been the first squadron to operate the type in 1951 and would also become the last. It had been intended that it would be the first to be equipped with the Javelin, but other units were given priority and 29 Squadron had to wait two years before the first Javelin arrived.

By the middle of November, three Javelins had been delivered, by which time about half the Squadron's Meteors had departed. A mobile Javelin conversion unit and a radar equipped Valetta to assist with training the pilots on the type had been delivered: 'It was a most heartening sight on 25th November, 1957, when the first Javelin with three red "X" on the tail [29 squadron markings] taxied out and took off.'

Poor weather in December 1957 and January 1958 curtailed flying. February was little better, with snow and ice combining with strong cross winds. Many of the Javelins were unserviceable, being prone to develop obscure hydraulic and electrical faults. Standing out in the open for much of the time did not help matters. Three Meteor NF.12s were added to 29 Squadron for training purposes. There was a great improvement in the weather

Aircrew of 29 Squadron with AOC 13 Group, AVM Earl CBE, on the occasion of the airfield's annual inspection, 19 May 1958. A Gloster Javelin (XA835) forms the backdrop to the photograph. (*The National Archives*)

Radar mechanics working on a Mk 22 AI radar in the nose of a Gloster Javelin, 1958.
(*The National Archives*)

in April, but many of the Javelins remained grounded as there was a lack of know-how among the ground personnel in servicing its radar. One aircraft suffered a brake failure on landing. The nose wheel struck a concrete block and the aircraft came to rest on its nose.

Despite these handicaps, half the squadron had become operational by May. At the end of the month, eight Javelins were scrambled in poor weather as an exercise. On 1 June, 29 Squadron was again declared operational after a break of six months. This was closely followed by further exercises. Valiants, Victors, Vulcans, and Canberras were intercepted at heights up to 47,000 feet and air-to-air firing was undertaken for the first time with the Javelin. Although RAF Acklington was no longer an armaments practice station, its ranges remained in use. There was a further landing accident when a Javelin burst a tyre on landing. The aircraft came to rest off the runway and sustained only minor damage.

The Javelin was the largest aircraft to be based at RAF Acklington. The airfield proved too small for it and in July 1958, 29 Squadron departed for RAF Leuchars. Fourteen of its sixteen Javelins left together. The Squadron Commander summed up their stay at RAF Acklington in the following words:

It was mixed feelings that No. 29 Squadron departed from Acklington. Despite inadequate hangarage and poor facilities it was a happy and informal station which

Gloster Javelin (XH701) after suffering a burst tyre and skidding off the runway, 25 June 1958. (*The National Archives*)

will hold pleasant memories to all of us. Our tame slag heap at the end of the runway was well recognised by all and its loss on the approach will be missed by all.

The second squadron to form the Acklington Wing was 66 Squadron, whose stay at the airfield was somewhat longer than that of 29 Squadron. Thirteen of its Hunters arrived in formation over the airfield on 14 February 1957. Almost immediately, they embarked on air-to-air firing practice, but were restricted by the availability of just one target-tug aircraft. At the end of the month, a party of schoolchildren from Amble visited the station.

The Suez Crisis was less than a year old. Due to the turbulent state of affairs, 66 Squadron's Hunters were deployed to RAF Nicosia on Cyprus. Their aircraft were maintained at ten minutes readiness from sunrise to sunset, ready to investigate any unidentified aircraft approaching the island. They did not return until early July. The Beverley transporting the ground crew home had to divert to RAF Abingdon with a problem with one of its engines. For the remainder of the month, most of the effort went towards preparing for the AOC's inspection. A number of the pilots contracted a mysterious type of influenza and one had chicken pox.

In August, 66 Squadron took part in Operation 'Fawn Delta', in which seven Hunters flew direct to West Germany and returned a few days later. Another aircraft carried out an aerobatic display over Stobbs Camp near Hawick for the benefit

Formation flypast of Hawker Hunter F.6s of 66 Squadron, 1957. (*The National Archives*)

Sqn Ldr A. Osborne, CO of 66 Squadron, climbing into the cockpit of a Hawker Hunter, 1957. (*The National Archives*)

of members of the Combined Cadet Force during their annual training. Exercise 'Strikeback' took place the following month. Carrier groups operating in the Atlantic and North Sea mounted attacks against targets in Scotland and northern England. 66 Squadron was required to maintain six aircraft on a state of readiness from dawn to dusk each day. Interceptions were made on over 80 per cent of the sorties flown.

No. 66 Squadron participated in several more exercises in the autumn. Seven aircraft flew to RAF Tangmere on the south coast at the beginning of November. From here, they flew over France, acting as targets for NATO air defence. Later, on 29 November, eight Hunters deployed to RAF Aldergrove for Exercise 'Iron Bar'. They returned three days later, after flying fourteen sorties to intercept Boeing B-47s, which simulated attacks on Northern Island. At this time, RAF Acklington still had a sizeable number of aircraft in its Station Flight, some of which were used as target tugs. They included an Anson, two Vampires T.11s, two Meteor F.8s, three Meteor FF.7s, and a Chipmunk.

Friday 13 December 1957 turned out to be unlucky for the Squadron. Flt Lt Christopher Bryce took off in a Hunter (XG202) shortly after midday. A few minutes into his flight, he suspected his airspeed indicator was not working properly. He was instructed to format with a Meteor flying in the area which confirmed his instrument was out by some 100 knots. While the two aircraft were flying back to RAF Acklington, the Hunter's engine cut out while turning over Stannington. Bryce thought he may have been able to make it as far as the airfield but then decided he should eject. He parachuted into the grounds of King Edward VI Grammar School at Morpeth. His aircraft came down in a field in one piece and careered across the Hebron-to-Longhirst road and travelled the length of a further field before coming to rest against the garden wall of Butterwell Farmhouse. The engine failure was attributed to a fault in the fuel system. On the 18th, the Royal Observer Corps from Durham contacted RAF Acklington to report that a special constable had seen a long flat glowing object in the sky near the Consett area, 5 miles west of Pontop Pike. It hovered before flying away to the west. The information was relayed to Air Traffic Control at Prestwick.

The lack of spares reduced the number of flyable aircraft in 66 Squadron to around eight at any one time. Bad weather in January 1958 further restricted flying. All Station personnel assisted in clearing snow off the runways on 22 and 23 January. The squadron suffered a further setback on 14 February when Fg Off. B. Schooling took off in Hunter F.6 (XG236) on a high-level sortie to practice instrument flying and flew down the coast to Middlesbrough. Here he turned inland towards Kielder. While flying at 40,000 feet, he carried out a mock attack on a pair of Hunters, also from 66 Squadron. Diving down into cloud, the Hunter hit the side of a hill north of Wainhope near Kielder. The accident was attributed to pilot error, although it was believed there was a fault in the elevator of the aircraft. When it struck high ground, the aircraft was in the process of pulling out of its dive.

At the end of February, the Squadron Leader of 66 Squadron was relieved of his command. With the serviceability of the aircraft now improved, the following month saw the first air-to-air firing practice since November 1957. On 14 May, the squadron

RAF Acklington's Station Flight Avro Anson, 1958. Ansons were used extensively by the RAF as a light transport aircraft in the 1950s and 1960s. They would frequently fly over Newcastle on their way north to RAF Acklington. (*R. Rayner via R. L.*)

was given forty-eight hours' notice to depart to RAF Akrotiri in Cyprus. Unrest in Lebanon was given as the reason for this move. It was scheduled to return in July, but was delayed due to a flare-up of trouble. The Hunters were then put on standby for action in Jordan.

Although there were no based squadrons at the airfield when 66 Squadron was overseas, flying continued as the station flight still operated a number of aircraft. In July, two Beverleys landed after dropping paratroopers in the area. A civil Tiger Moth (G-ANFL) made an unannounced emergency landing. The Hunters of 66 Squadron returned on 10 September. One aircraft (XF.519) could not lower its starboard undercarriage and landed on its port and nose wheels and starboard fuel tank. A few days later, the Hunters participated in the Battle of Britain air display held on the Station and, on 21 September, three aircraft flew over parades in Newcastle and Morpeth. The following month, in Exercise 'Sunbeam', the Squadron intercepted seventy-two bombers and seven fighters. In November, members of the Civil Defence from Morpeth paid a visit. Later that month, two Hunters swung off the main runway on landing, closing it for two hours.

*Above:* Members of 66 Squadron pose for their photograph in front of a Hawker Hunter in autumn 1958. (*Aldon Ferguson*)

*Below:* A 66 Squadron Meteor F.8 (WH275) at RAF Acklington in September 1958. (*Roger Lindsay*)

*Below:* CO, 29 Squadron, Wg Cdr J. A. C. Aiken and Squadron Navigator/Radar Leader, Flt Lt J. Curtiss, in front of their Gloster Meteor NF.11. (*The National Archives*)

## 1959

There was a continual battle against the weather throughout January, with the airfield in the grip of ice and snow. The following month, 66 Squadron made a number of practice dives on the airfield in preparation for the Army fire power demonstration at Warsop Range in March. 1, 56, and 74 Squadrons also undertook firing practice at the ranges in February. The Hunter T7 dual trainer collided with a bird and was badly damaged, a serious loss for 66 Squadron which made great use of it for weapons training. Two Beveleys of RAF Transport Command arrived on 11 April for an exercise with the Parachute Regiment. The following month, 200 paratroops were dropped over the Otterburn Ranges by transport aircraft operating from the airfield.

The Hunters of 66 Squadron made a further foreign excursion—this time to Denmark—where they intercepted 'enemy' bombers, mainly in the form of Canberras. Shortly after their return, a large contingent from the press and TV visited the station to see 66 Squadron's new mascot—a rattlesnake. Towards the end of April, 54 Squadron arrived for armament training with ten Hunters and four Meteors. Around the same time, Princes Margaret, who had been visiting the north of England, departed RAF Acklington for London in a Heron of the Queen's Flight. 74 Squadron made use of the firing ranges in May, followed by 19 Squadron. Later in the year, 54 and 65 Squadrons also made use of these facilities, although by this time there were only one or two Meteor target tugs at the Station.

On 25 June, ten Hunters of 66 Squadron took part in an exercise with Boulmer Radar Station which was marred by radio communication difficulties. Interceptions were carried out on Victors, Vulcans and Canberras. Much of July was also devoted to fighter interceptions for the annual Exercise 'Mandate' held at the end of the month. 66 Squadron's Hunters were called on for two 'Repulse 2' raids in which twenty-one bombers

A 66 Squadron Hawker Hunter F.6 at RAF Acklington. (*Aldon Ferguson*)

were 'destroyed' by them, but great deal of their time was spent on the ground with long periods of inactivity. Although 66 Squadron was a day fighter squadron, an increasing emphasis was placed on its ground attack capabilities. Large numbers of air-to-ground firing was carried out in August, which was a new experience for many of the pilots.

Towards the end of October, the Squadron made another foray to the Mediterranean. This time it spent a week at El Adem airfield in Libya, which at that time was used by the RAF for training. Bad weather in early December at Acklington restricted flying. When it improved, a number of flights were made in connection with an Army Co-operation exercise at Druridge Bay. Further sorties were made to the Otterburn Ranges.

## 1960

At the beginning of the year, 66 Squadron was ordered to return to RAF Akrotiri, Cyprus. In preparation for this, forty-seven practice airstrikes were flown. Ten Hunter F.6s, one Hunter T7, one Meteor T7, and one Meteor T8 departed on 12 January, returning on 7 March. The following month, it was announced that 66 Squadron was to be disbanded. Its newly appointed Commanding Officer remarked in the record book:

> The news of the disbandment of the squadron was a bitter blow to all, particularly after the magnificent record achieved during the last 18 months under my predecessor. It is unfortunate that efficiency and moral cannot be measured in pounds, shillings and pence otherwise the financial planners may have found it less expensive in the long run to keep 66 Squadron in existence.

However, the squadron still had a few more months of life. From 5 April, the Hunters took part in low-level navigation exercises, with and without air-to-ground strikes as well as high-low-high airstrikes. Long range air strikes on targets in the Outer Hebrides were also undertaken. No. 66 Squadron was absent from RAF Acklington for most of June, as its Hunters were participating in Exercise 'Halyard' and were based at RAF Stradishall. Four of its aircraft also participated in the flypast over Buckingham Palace for the Queen's birthday. The following month, a number of its aircraft flew to Riga in Norway for a brief stay.

In August, numerous training flights were flown, including bomber interceptions. During September, numerous rehearsals took place for the RAF Battle of Britain Air Display, although poor weather on the day of the event curtailed flying. A Sea Venom with an engine which was vibrating made an emergency landing at Acklington on 24 September. At 6.15 p.m. around two weeks earlier, Air Traffic Control logged a luminous object emitting a steady white light heading in an easterly direction. No. 66 Squadron became non-operational on 1 October: 'a very sad day at Acklington.'

When 66 Squadron finally disbanded in December, RAF Acklington's career as a fighter airfield was at an end. No operational squadrons would be based at the airfield again, except for a detachment of Search and Rescue helicopters. For a while, the future of RAF Acklington was in doubt, but it was given a new role as a training station.

# 18

# 1957–1975 Search and Rescue Helicopters

For many of the residents of Northumberland, RAF Acklington will best be remembered for its bright-yellow rescue helicopters which were frequently seen flying along its coast. In the early days of the Second World War, little thought had been given to rescuing pilots that came down in the sea. Often their colleagues would search for a missing aircraft in their Spitfires and Hurricanes. The RAF eventually formed specialised search and rescue squadrons using slow-flying Ansons and the amphibious Walrus, which could land in the sea to pick up aircrew. Helicopters did not become available until the end of the Second World War.

Even with the introduction of specialist air-sea rescue squadrons, aircraft from RAF Acklington would often still participate in the search for missing aircrew. In the years after the Second World War and into the early 1950s, helicopters had a very low priority within the RAF. Numerous accidents with early jets such as the Meteor and Vampire—many of which went down over the sea—were the catalyst for the RAF establishing a network of search and rescue helicopters along the east coast utilising the newly introduced Westland Sycamore, adapted for this role

No. 275 Squadron was formed in 1953. Its first rescue was of a Venom pilot who was picked up from the disused airfield at Boulmer and taken to RAF Acklington in August 1953. At that time, there was no detachment of rescue helicopters at RAF Acklington. The north of England was covered by Sycamores based at RAF Thornaby near Stockton on Tees.

Although the prime role of the RAF search and rescue helicopters was that of rescuing downed aircrew, they were increasingly called upon to assist civilians in trouble. RAF Acklington became a permanent base for the yellow rescue helicopters when A-Flight of 275 Squadron—consisting of four crews manning two Sycamores—moved here from RAF Thornaby on 2 October 1957. During December, fifty-six non-operational flights were flown. They included stretcher lifting demonstrations for the Civil Defence Organisation, as well as eight practice supply drops at Coquet Island Lighthouse. At this time, 275 Squadron had a total of fifteen helicopters based at several airfields along the East Coast. In February 1958, a Sycamore was scrambled to Alnmouth to pick up the crew of a Royal Navy Sikorsky S.51 that had made a forced landing. A demonstration was also flown for the hospital staff at Ashington.

A search and rescue Westland Sycamore HR14 (XJ916) of 275 Squadron. (*Roger Lindsay*)

The next month, a helicopter was dispatched to a Balliol aircraft which had made a forced landing at Tedburn, Northumberland. It picked up the crew of two, one of whom was slightly injured.

A Sycamore of 275 Squadron detachment at RAF Acklington attended yet a further air crash on 1 April 1958. An Anson reported that it was running short of fuel in the Ouston area. The Sycamore arrived within a few minutes of the subsequent crash but, rather surprisingly, the Anson's crew signalled that they did not require any assistance. Later the same month, 275 Squadron went to the assistance of a Hunter that had crashed near Middlesbrough. Again their services were not needed, as the pilot had parachuted to safety and police were already on the scene. In the dawn hours of 27 April, Sycamores participated in an escape and evasion exercise. Their role was to pick up escaped POWs at a pre-arranged rendezvous point. Of the twenty-seven starters, fifteen escaped capture and nine of these were winched into the helicopter, at times within yards of the 'enemy force'. In July, a casualty evacuation flight was performed to the Otterburn Ranges. An army officer had been injured when an artillery gun exploded during firing practice.

In April 1959, the 275 Squadron's A-Flight made several appearances on both the BBC and ITV. Landing sites at local hospitals were also inspected at that time. The sports field next to Sunderland Accident and Orthopaedic Hospital was deemed suitable, but that at Durham Hospital, which was found to be covered by flowering shrubs, was unusable. The Sycamores were grounded in May while the rotor pylons were examined. The time was spent preparing equipment for the Westland Whirlwinds which were due to be delivered in the near future. In June, one operational sortie was flown. There were reports of a yellow dinghy adrift. On investigation, it was found to be a range marker buoy lying on its side. In July, two unsuccessful sorties were flown.

The first was to assist in the search for a canoe. The second was for a youth who had been swept out to sea. Two new hospital landing sites were tried out at Tynemouth and Gateshead.

By this time, three Whirlwinds (XJ409, XJ430, and XD183) had replaced the much smaller Sycamores. They were busy in August with six scrambles. A call was received to say that there were two men adrift on a raft in Druridge Bay and a helicopter was requested. Upon investigation, the object turned out to be a plank with a small tree at either end—another false alarm. On 17 August, a call was received that a girl was adrift out at sea on an inflatable raft. The Berwick lifeboat was also involved. The rescue helicopter was informed that the girl had been picked up by a private boat and transferred to the lifeboat which had a doctor in attendance. The next day, a call was received from Blyth coastguard to proceed to the Seaton Sluice area where a boat had overturned and an occupant had been seen clinging to it. A search was carried out with negative result—the occupant had managed to wade ashore. The final sortie of the month was flown on 25 August in search of a boat that had turned over off Dunstanburgh Castle. There was no sign of it as the occupants had swum ashore along and the boat had beached. During the month, the Whirlwinds were also placed at readiness as a Royal Flight was flying across the region and on another occasion during the visit of the Prime Minister of Ghana.

In October, a Whirlwind was requested to fly to Silloth to participate in a search for an English Electric Lightning P1 (prototype) that had crashed into the Irish Sea. Ground crew and a refuelling truck set off by road from RAF Acklington to support the rescue helicopter. The search was called off when the pilot of the missing Lightning paddled ashore in his dinghy. Later that month, A-Flight, 228 Squadron, was instructed to carry out a casualty evacuation flight the following day. It was found that the fan belt for the main rotor gearbox cooling drive was unserviceable. The ground crew searched high and low for a spare but could not find one. They then phoned several motor garages, who could not help, until one of produced an identical belt. It came from a popular make of vacuum cleaner. The ground crew worked all night and the Whirlwind was ready for its mission the following morning. Subsequently, it had to fly through very bad weather, altering its course several times, to reach Lancaster.

On 24 November, a call was received to assist two children stranded on a sandbank in the Solway Firth. The 'children' turned out to be duck hunters who were perfectly safe. During that month, 228 Squadron took over the search and rescue duties at RAF Acklington from 275 Squadron. In December, a Whirlwind was used to ferry drugs from Town Moor, Newcastle, back to RAF Acklington. They were then placed on a Meteor and flown to Aberdeen where they were required for a seriously ill patient.

In February 1960, many of the roads in Northumberland were blocked by snow. An expectant mother was flown from Berwick to a hospital in Newcastle by a Whirlwind, a mission which received extensive press coverage. The following month, an 86 year-old woman, Miss Phyllis Thompson, who was suffering from double pneumonia, was airlifted from her isolated farmhouse and flown to Morpeth Hospital. She later remarked that she enjoyed the flight and would like a helicopter for her shopping trips. The Whirlwinds flew medicines to the fishing fleet sheltering off the Farne

Islands, their only operational mission in April. One of the seamen was a diabetic. At the same time, the Outer Farne Lighthouse keeper was picked up and taken ashore as his wife was seriously ill.

On 21 May, two Javelins (XA823 and XA835) collided at 40,000 feet. XA823 crashed into the North Sea, fifty miles off the Durham Coast, while XA835 came down near Hartlepool. A Whirlwind was ordered to proceed to RAF Middleton St. George to pre-position for a rescue operation. While *en route*, it received a message that a parachute had been seen in a field near Castle Eden. It altered course and picked up the crew of Javelin XA835, ferrying them to RAF Middleton St. George. After refuelling, it set off for two dinghies sighted off Flamborough Head. It picked up one of the crew of the second Javelin, his colleague having been rescued by another helicopter.

During July, a casualty evacuation flight was undertaken for an airman injured at RAF Acklington, who was taken to the Royal Victoria Hospital, Newcastle. No. 228 Squadron's A-Flight flew three rescue missions in August. A man was reported in difficulties in the sea off Seaton Sluice. A long search could not find him; he was later discovered drowned. Also on the same day, boys were reported in distress at Budle Bay near Bamburgh. By the time the Whirlwind arrived, one had been rescued. The helicopter crew discovered the other boy at the bottom of a gulley in the bay. He was winched onto the Whirlwind and artificial respiration was administered but he could not be revived. A rescue mission of a different sort took place in September. A US Navy Grumman Tracker flying over the North Sea had suffered the failure of one of its two engines and requested assistance from RAF Acklington. A Whirlwind was scrambled to intercept it when it crossed the coast and guide it to the airfield.

In January 1961, a 228 Squadron Whirlwind had the distinction of flying the Foreign Secretary, Lord Home, from his residence at Coldstream to RAF Middleton St. George. The following month, a search was made for a missing USAF aircraft in the Carlisle area. A dinghy was found, but there was no trace of the pilot. During spring 1961, the rescue helicopters were the only aircraft based at RAF Acklington since 66 Squadron had disbanded at the end of the previous year. 6 FTS was due to arrive in July. In this month, three rescue missions were performed. They included one to assist the occupants of a dinghy which had overturned off Croquet Island. When the helicopter arrived, it was found that the dinghy had been righted and was underway. On one occasion, a Whirlwind flew to assist bathers who were reported to be in difficulty at Saltburn. They were later identified as beach balls.

Crew members of a Whirlwind (XL113) found themselves having to be rescued on 5 August. They were carrying out a winching practice at Cullercoats Bay when their engine failed:

The pseudo survivors in the dinghy must have been surprised when instead of being winched up into helicopter XL113 they hauled it down into the sea! It says a lot for the presence of mind and training of the Helicopter Flight's crew that they were able to extricate themselves from a dangerous and difficult predicament with nothing worse than a ducking apiece.

*Above:* Aircrew from 228 Search and Rescue line up in front of their Westland Whirlwind for inspection in 1961.
(*The National Archives*)

*Left:* An inspection of A-Flight, 228 Search and Rescue Squadron, in 1961. A Westland Whirlwind helicopter in the background.
(*The National Archives*)

They were picked up by the crew of the Tynemouth lifeboat. Another Whirlwind had been dispatched from RAF Acklington and was overhead within twenty-four minutes after the accident had occurred. A replacement for the downed Whirlwind was received a few days later. Later that month, a Whirlwind was requested to look for a boy drifting out to sea on a mattress at Seaton Sluice. No trace could be found of the boy or the mattress, which was assumed to have sprung a leak and sunk. On 24 August, there was a similar incident at Seahouses but, in this case, a rescue had been effected before the helicopter arrived. A Whirlwind was dispatched on 17 October to ferry a doctor and police to Crosby near Carlisle to standby for an overdue Dakota. The crew located the wreckage of the aircraft shortly after their arrival. Unfortunately there were no survivors.

In March 1962, both Whirlwinds were involved in airlifting six paratroops who had suffered an assortment of broken limbs after making a drop onto the Otterburn Range. They were flown to Newcastle Royal Victoria Infirmary. Three scrambles were undertaken in May, all for aircraft crashes. Two of them were for Jet Provosts based at RAF Acklington. In the first, the pilot was killed but in the second, the crew of two ejected successfully and were picked up by the Whirlwind. The third flight was on 18 May to search for the crew of a Javelin (XH755) from RAF Middleton St George, which had crashed in the sea of Tynemouth. The pilot was located and winched on board the Whirlwind but there was no trace of the navigator. There was a further call-out for an aircraft that had crashed into the sea off West Hartlepool in June. This time, the report turned out to be false. A search was also made for two boys who had disappeared in the sea off Blyth on 18 June.

A further sortie was made at 4.20 a.m. on 14 August to a mid-air collision involving two 6FTS Provosts at RAF Ouston. The pilot of one of the aircraft was reported as missing. The Whirlwind crew located his body in a wood not far from the scene of the accident. The other operational flight that month was made to a capsized dinghy in Beadnell Bay. Its occupants had been taken on board a fishing boat shortly before the helicopter arrived. In September, a Whirlwind made a flight to the Solway Firth on the opposite side of the country in response to a report that two youths were clinging to an upturned canoe. One youth was rescued by a fishing boat and the body of the second was recovered by the helicopter the following morning.

On 11 November, a Whirlwind flew to West Hartlepool to pick up a doctor who was then transported 3 miles offshore to a listing freighter. A heavy sea was running at the time and the wind speed was 40 knots. The captain, who was suffering from kidney problems, was transferred to hospital. There was more drama involving a ship on the 18th. At dusk, a coaster was drifting towards the rocks at Blyth. Its crew had been taken off by two lifeboats and a fishing boat. The helicopter airlifted them off these vessels and took them ashore. The following day, the Whirlwind returned their crew to their ship. At the end of the year, 228 Squadron began converting to the new Whirlwind 10.

During January 1963, the rescue helicopters were extremely busy. Thirty-three operational missions were flown, of which twenty-nine were supply drops to isolated farms cut off by heavy falls of snow. The ground crew worked overnight to ensure the

Whirlwinds were ready to fly the following day. A further two missions were made to the crash site of a Canberra near Keswick. Snow and ice retained its grip over the countryside into February. A further fifty-three sorties were made, carrying essential supplies to remote farms. In addition, there were eight casualty evacuation flights, many performed in appalling weather conditions, which airlifted a total of eleven patients. On 6 February, there was a call-out for a serious ill person. Both helicopters were grounded in the hangar because of very high winds. The problem was overcome by using a coach and a 5-ton lorry to act as a windbreak while the Whirlwind took off. The sortie was entirely successful.

On 18 April, a Jet Provost from RAF Acklington crashed 9 miles south-west of the airfield. The crew of two were picked up by a Whirlwind and returned to Station Sick Quarters. The second helicopter assisted in locating the wreckage and collecting the parachutes. The following day, the crew of the Jet Provost were flown to the RAF Hospital at Nocton Hall. In August, an injured boy was picked up and taken to Morpeth Hospital after he had fallen over a cliff at Seaton Sluice. A Whirlwind also rescued the two occupants of a capsized dinghy at Newton-by-the-Sea. The next month, Mr Owen, MP for Morpeth, was provided with an airborne tour of his constituency. In October, a photographic survey of Hadrian's Wall was flown on behalf of the University of Newcastle. Most months, the helicopters flew only one or two operational flights, but a large number of training flights and other tasks were undertaken.

During early 1964, hardly any rescue flights were flown by 228 Squadron. All this changed in May when a USAF Voodoo on a training flight suddenly exploded over the Scottish Highlands near Fort William. It took ten days to locate the wreckage. Among the aircraft involved in the search were no fewer than eight USAF HC-54 Skymasters and eight C-47 Dakotas, as well as the helicopters of 228 Squadron, which were involved in the recovery of the wreckage. At the time, much of the operation was clouded in secrecy and there were many rumours, including one that the Voodoo was carrying nuclear weapons. The Whirlwinds flew a total of thirty-four sorties between 7 and 18 May, involving three crews.

In July, an injured seaman was airlifted from a fishing vessel some 66 miles out to sea and flown to West Hartlepool Hospital. The following month, 228 Squadron was disbanded and reformed as 202 Squadron. Eight sorties were flown, which included searches for missing swimmers and a capsized yacht. In September, life-saving drugs were flown from Newcastle to Loch Leven Hospital, Alexandria, and a soldier with a broken neck was evacuated from the Otterburn Ranges to hospital in Newcastle. At the end of the month, two pilots who had ejected from their Jet Provost near Jedburgh were picked up and flown back to RAF Acklington. A more unusual task for 202 Squadron in November 1964 was a fishery protection patrol between Bamburgh and Amble.

Early in 1965, a Whirlwind was involved in the casualty evacuation of an injured footballer. He was first taken to the Station Sick Quarters and later to the RAF Hospital at Nocton Hall in Lincolnshire. There were several operational sorties in May involving aircraft in distress. The Whirlwinds took off on a couple of occasions when there were emergencies with the locally based Jet Provosts in the circuit. Fortunately their services were not needed. Assistance was also rendered to a USAF pilot whose F-100 Super Sabre came down 2 miles to the west of Middleton St. George. He was picked up, slightly bruised, and conveyed to Royal Victoria Hospital Newcastle for treatment. In April, a helicopter was placed on airborne standby for an aircraft with a shattered canopy.

June 1965 was a busy month for 202 Squadron, with a total of twelve operational missions being flown. Six involved the search for a Hawker Hunter missing off St Abbs Head. The lighthouse keeper on Coquet Island was flown to hospital with a badly slipped disc. A Whirlwind also took off to assist the occupants of a capsized motor boat, but a rescue craft from Seahouses reached them first. In another mission, a helicopter was requested to take an injured climber to hospital, but he died before it arrived. A Jet Provost T.3 crashed on approach to RAF Acklington on 29 July. Both pilots parachuted to safety and were picked up by a Whirlwind. One was taken to the Station Sick Quarters. The following month, a helicopter was sent to assist a pilot from RAF Acklington who made a forced landing in his Jet Provost at Carlisle Airport. Other tasks undertaken in August included lifting a sailor suffering from appendicitis from his trawler and flying him to hospital. A Whirlwind also went to the assistance of swimmers in difficulties off Seaburn. The crew recovered two bodies which they brought ashore. In September, an unsuccessful search was made for a sailor who had fallen off his ship. Exercises were also carried out with the Amble and Tynemouth lifeboats.

Only one rescue mission was flown in October, but it was unusual and received extensive coverage in the press. It involved the rescue of a schoolboy from a cliff at night in total darkness. Winter arrived early that year and snow blocked the roads to RAF Ouston in November. The Whirlwinds from RAF Acklington flew food as well as a doctor to the airfield. The following month, food was dropped to farm animals stranded by snow drifts.

Towards the end of January 1966, another exploit of 202 Squadron received national press coverage, when two small boys trapped on rocks by the incoming tide at South Shields were rescued. Later that year, on 25 June, a search was made for five children in danger. Two children were found by the Whirlwind crew, one of whom was dead and the other died in the helicopter during the short flight across the River Tweed. Of the other three children, two were recovered alive by the police but the third was dead on arrival at hospital. A few days later, two sorties were made to search for a Buccaneer and its crew which had crashed into Luce Bay near Stanraer. July was also a busy month for the rescue helicopters. A Whirlwind flew to a position 75 miles east of the Tyne to a trawler to pick up a seaman with severe abdominal pains. The man was taken to Tynemouth Hospital, whence he was discharged after a twenty minute stay and a dose of aperient. Six days later, on 31 July, a 202 Squadron helicopter rendezvoused with the German research vessel *Gauss* some 77 miles off the River Tyne. A seriously ill scientist was winched up on a stretcher and flown to the Infirmary at Newcastle. There was an unfortunate postscript to this mission, as he died the following day.

In September, an unsuccessful search was made for a man who had fallen off the MV *Leda*. A similar mission was undertaken in November when an officer went overboard from the submarine *Truncheon* as it was leaving the Tyne. Although both helicopters took part in the search, there was no sign of the officer. Two days earlier, a man had also fallen off a fishing boat entering Amble Harbour but again the helicopter searched in vain.

During March 1967, two operational missions were flown. The first took place on the 4th, when Air Traffic Control called out a Whirlwind to investigate an aircraft crash reported on the hills near Rothbury. At the time, a Jet Provost was out of radio contact. When the helicopter arrived on the scene, the wreckage turned out to be that of a Second World War aircraft. Meanwhile, the 'missing' Jet Provost returned to RAF Acklington, landing safely at the end of a thirty-minute sortie. While carrying out a routine sortie on the 14th, the crew of a 202 Squadron Whirlwind caught sight of a small rubber dinghy off the coast near Amble. It was in the process of being blown out to sea. The Whirlwind rescued the two youths on board who were playing truant from their school in Newcastle. On landing back at RAF Acklington, the youths were driven home by the local constabulary.

The following month, Whirlwind XK990 experienced severe vibration and made an emergency landing. The second Whirlwind flew to its assistance but its services were not needed as the crew were unhurt. Throughout the summer, the two rescue Whirlwinds were called upon on numerous occasions. In July, there was a report of an injured seaman on a trawler some 15 miles east of Beadnell. The Whirlwind was scrambled and, unusually on this occasion, was escorted by a Jet Provost. The trawler was located and the seaman, who had serious injuries including a broken leg and crushed chest, was winched on board the Whirlwind on a stretcher and flown to Ashington Hospital. This was the era of the 'Cold War', when vessels from behind the Iron Curtain could sometimes be found lurking off the coast. On 8 July, a helicopter was sent to investigate unidentified ships. Four days later, a Whirlwind rescued a girl who had fallen off the cliffs at Whitley Bay. She was lifted to the top of the cliffs where an ambulance was in attendance.

Saturday 15 July saw 202 Squadron involved in one of the more dramatic accidents during its stay at RAF Acklington. The Edinburgh to Leeds express train derailed near the end of the runway where the main line passed close to the airfield. Ambulances and rescuers had difficulty in reaching the accident because of rough, rain sodden ground. The Whirlwind ferried rescuers to the scene as well as airlifting twenty injured persons to the waiting ambulances. Towards the end of July, a 202 Squadron Whirlwind was requested to go to West Hartlepool where a small child had been seen in the water off the pier. After a twenty-minute search, Sgt Rolberts sighted a body. He was winched down and picked up a four-year-old girl. Despite attempts at resuscitation in the cabin, including oxygen and mouth-to-mouth resuscitation, the girl could not be revived.

As with most years, August proved to be one of the busiest months for rescues. Most involved holidaymakers on the Northumberland beaches being swept out to sea. Among them was a small girl reported to be in the sea near Holy Island. The helicopter crew flew over the area for over an hour without success. On the 17th, a helicopter was scrambled to rescue a man on a raft off the coast at Beadnell Bay. The crew located the raft and winched its utterly exhausted occupant on board. At the end of the month, a Whirlwind was alerted while carrying air cadets on a flying experience sortie. A sailing dinghy had capsized near Cresswell. The helicopter located it and winched a man, a woman and a small child on board. They were then flown to the Sick Quarters at RAF Acklington. The Whirlwind then returned to Cresswell and aided the police in finding three children who belonged to the rescued woman. A Whirlwind was also scrambled by Acklington Air Traffic control to escort a Varsity in difficulties. It landed safely at the airfield with the helicopter in formation.

In September, a Whirlwind took to the air as an RAF Lightning, which was short of fuel, had to make an emergency landing at RAF Acklington. A sailor on a Dutch trawler suffering from perforated stomach ulcers and in need of an immediate operation was flown to hospital. A search and rescue mission was flown on the 30th for three canoes which were reported to be drifting out to sea off Scremerson Beach. In the first few minutes, three survivors were picked up and landed on the beach. Despite an extensive search, one of the canoes with two of its occupants could not be found.

October also proved to be a busy month for 202 Squadron. On the 1st, a further search was made for the occupants of the missing canoe, but again with a negative result. There was a further search four days later at the request of the missing persons' relatives but it again proved fruitless. On the 8th, a further two canoeists were reported to be missing of Holy Island. One was found to be dead when picked up by the helicopter. The other occupant had managed to swim ashore. At the end of the month a search was made for a fully-clothed man reported in the sea off Hartlepool, but nothing was found. Whirlwind XK990 suffered a further engine failure and this time made a crash landing in the vicinity of Acklington airfield. This time the helicopter was damaged beyond repair. One of the three crew members was seriously injured and was flown to Ashington Hospital in the other Whirlwind.

In November, two operational sorties were flown, one of which involved the rescue of two men whose boat had been washed ashore and wrecked at the foot of cliffs to the north of Berwick. Although in most months only a handful of rescue missions were performed, a large number of other flights were made by the two Whirlwinds at RAF Acklington. During this month, they included a practice deck winching with the Blyth Lifeboat, the filming of Lynemouth Colliery and rescue demonstration flights for schoolchildren and air cadets.

At the beginning of 1968, bales of hay were flown from Tweedshaws Farm, Dumfries, to a site some 2 miles away, where around 1,000 sheep were stranded in the snow. A motorist injured in a car crash was flown from Whitehaven to Newcastle. In April a student from 6 FTS, RAF Acklington, was evacuated from the survival exercise area on the Otterburn Ranges. A Whirlwind, together with 18 Squadron's Wessex helicopters and Jet Provosts from 6 FTS, took part in a flypast over Newcastle to mark the fiftieth Anniversary of the Royal Air Force. In May, a patient suffering from acute renal failure was flown from West Cumberland Hospital, Whitehaven, to Newcastle General Hospital. In June, two operational flights were undertaken; one involved a Whirlwind landing at the foot of the cliffs at Cullernose Point to rescue a fallen climber.

August 1968 proved to be a particularly busy month. The extra work load was attributable to the holiday season with more amateur sailors and swimmers in distress than usual. Among the rescue flights undertaken were the search for an aircraft that had ditched off Hartlepool. This was later believed to be a false alarm. There was a report of an overturned dinghy in Druridge Bay but nothing was found. A helicopter was also sent to assist two men in the sea at Seaton Sluice. By the time the Whirlwind arrived they had been picked up by the lifeboat. On the 24th, a helicopter was scrambled to search for an aircraft reported as being on fire and crashing in the Haydon Bridge, Haltwhistle area. Nothing was found. It was later learned that a farmer had fired off a marine distress flare; this had given rise to the alert.

Whirlwind XD165 experienced engine failure on 16 October and successfully carried out a forced landing in the River Coquet at Rothbury. The machine was later recovered by personnel from 60 MU. Also in October, a search was flown for a woman in a cabin cruiser missing in the Solway Firth. She was found walking ashore from her grounded craft and was picked up and flown to safety. No. 202 Squadron Whirlwinds flew several operational missions in the last days of the year. A lighthouse keeper was evacuated from Coquet Island suffering from bronchitis and lung congestion. Two Boy Scouts missing on the snow-covered Cheviot Hills were found and flown to safety. On 31 December, a Whirlwind transported food supplies from Wooler to the nearby village of Uswayford cut off by snow drifts.

In 1969, it was announced that RAF Acklington did not have a future and was to close. Questions were raised in Parliament about the future of the air-sea rescue helicopters based there—such was the importance accorded them by the local politicians and the residents of Northumberland. Although RAF Acklington lost most of its aircraft and personnel during 1969, the search and rescue flight lingered on a corner of the former airfield for another six years. No. 202 Squadron finally departed in 1975 and headed, with its two Whirlwinds, to its newly constructed base at RAF Boulmer. No. 202 Squadron rescue helicopters remained there for forty years and for much of that time had the distinction of being the only RAF aircraft in Northumberland. In 2015, to the dismay of many, the helicopter base was closed. The RAF had relinquished its search and rescue role to the private sector. Northumberland now had to rely on machines based elsewhere in Britain.

# 19

# 6 Flying Training School
# 1961–1968

Acklington reverted to a training airfield with the arrival of 6 FTS from RAF Ternhill in July 1961. The move was completed by 4 August, by which time nearly thirty Provost T.1s had taken up residence. The T.1 had been adopted as the RAF's standard basic trainer in 1953. Its manoeuvrability was quite exceptional for a basic trainer, with the rate of roll being better than 90 degrees per second. Student and instructor were seated side-by-side and adjustable amber screens were used for simulated blind-flying instruction. However, by the time the T.1 arrived at RAF Acklington, it was becoming obsolete. No. 6 FTS was the last still operating the type; it was made up of three squadrons and a Headquarters Flight.

Jet Provosts began replacing the propeller-driven Provosts almost as soon as 6 FTS had arrived at Acklington. The first training flight with a Jet Provost T3 was made on 24 July, but there were only two on strength at that time. The Station Commander, F. Jensen, remarked in the station records for July:

> ... morale remains high ... the activities of the Jet Provost in the circuit, albeit only two as yet, also had a salutary effect ... Although the FTS will be able to resume training on 14th August, as planned, many of the Works services required to bring it to full efficiency remain to be done and some will not be finished for a long time yet. It still will be a very protracted business, to get the whole station to a standard acceptable to me and my staff, even though in the meantime we hope and expect to meet the FTS task 100 per cent.

All three runways were used for pilot training and RAF Ouston was used as a relief landing ground. Airwork Services was responsible for carrying out contract work on the Provost T.1. The old wartime airfields at Brunton, Milfield and Morpeth were used for simulating landing approaches. Unlike in the past when RAF Acklington had been used for training purposes, the aircraft now based there were not involved in weapons training and the Druridge firing ranges were now redundant. Some 25 tons of expended 20-mm projectiles had been recovered from them by the end of July 1962. Normally, such a large amount of ordnance would have been required to be dumped at sea, which was a costly process. In this case, over 99 per cent was ball ammunition, which was inert. It was decided to dispose of the projectiles by dropping them into a disused mine shaft at North Togston, which was 480 feet deep and partially filled with water.

At the beginning of September, twenty-one students from the RAF together with four Malayan, one Jordanian, and one Lebanese student arrived for training on the Provost T.1. A further twenty-four RAF students arrived a couple of weeks later. On 14 September, 'a successful Airman's Dance was held in the N.A.A.F.I. Over 100 young ladies were invited to the station from local towns and villages and everybody had a most enjoyable time.' This was followed a few days later when a cocktail party in the Officers' Mess was attended by officers from neighbouring RAF stations and local dignitaries.

On a less positive note, there were two accidents to 6FTS aircraft in September. The first occurred on the 18th when Provost T.1 (WV623) swung off the runway and struck a gooseneck flare. This was followed by Provost T.1 (WV564) on the 25th, which made a heavy landing, bursting a tyre.

During October, students participated in an Outdoor Exercise 'Black Knowe'. The Station Commander was less than impressed with their performance stating that 'it revealed a disappointing lack of fitness and determination on the part of many of the students and not all who dropped out were foreign student from warmer climes.'

On Saturday 4 November, a Guy Fawkes bonfire was attended by children and adults from the married quarters as well as other station personnel. 6 FTS held its first formal ball at RAF Acklington on the 24th. Many distinguished guests attended, including the Chief Constable and the Mayoress of Moreth. The event was deemed a great success.

Progress was made on the hangar used by the Scheduled Servicing Section, when the doors were refitted. For over a month the airmen working in it were exposed to the Northumberland weather with both ends of the building being completely open. Tragedy struck the Technical Wing on the last day of the month when two airmen— SAC Frankland and SAC Malloch—were killed in a road accident while returning to Acklington. The former was buried in the local cemetery at Chevington. As the year drew to an end, the weather deteriorated with heavy snow falls. Temperatures fell as low as -9C and on 29 December there was 4 inches of snow. Matters were made worse with a shortage of Jet Provost aircraft. 159 Course, which had been transferred from RAF Ternhill with 6 FTS, managed to complete its training of five Malaysian Air Force pilots at the beginning of the month. There were five separate training courses underway at that time which are listed below:

| Flight Course | Hours Flown | | Pupils | Remarks |
|---|---|---|---|---|
| | Dual | Solo | | |
| 159 | 1.15 | 1.25 | 4 | Course completed 8/12/61 |
| 160 | 100.10 | 46.35 | 18 | |
| 161 | 145.15 | 66.45 | 24 | |
| 162 | 73.05 | 23.10 | 20 | |
| 163 | 133.50 | 0.15 | 24 | Comm. Dec. 1961. Second Jet Provost course. |

Airmen from RAF Acklington participate in the St. George's Day parade at Morpeth, 1961. (*The National Archives*)

Air Cadet's gliders at RAF Acklington in 1961. (*The National Archives*)

On 7 December, the Station was visited by a number of newspaper reporters and a film crew from Tyne Tees Television to cover the transition from the piston-engined Provost to the Jet Provost. All the reporters were given the opportunity to fly in the Jet Provosts, but not before they received a thorough briefing on the survival equipment and the ejector seat. None of them became airsick when they were airborne, although one of the journalists was said to have looked unwell when he stepped out the aircraft.

Two debates were organised by the personnel at Acklington during December. The first motion discussed was 'This house believes that modern advertising has reached the ultimate stage of foolishness and futility'; the television addicts were said to have spoken well on this topic. The second was 'This house believes that the freedom of the individual is lost in modern society'. No. 6 FTS's first year at Acklington was concluded with a number of Christmas celebrations. On the 19th, a dance was held in the Airmen's Club featuring the Mel Armstrong Band and went on until 1 a.m. The following day, a Christmas draw was held in the Officers' Mess. On the 20th, a children's party was held and Father Christmas arrived by helicopter. Not only was the party attended by children of the Station personnel, but children from neighbouring institutions were invited to attend.

At the beginning of 1962, four officers were posted to RAF Ouston to establish a flying training squadron there. It would come under the control of the CO at Acklington, but its administration would be the responsibility of the CO at RAF Ouston. As new Jet Provosts were delivered to 6 FTS, most of the flying by the Provost T.1s was transferred to RAF Ouston. A change was also made to the approaches for landing at RAF Acklington. These were moved over from the sea to an inland position in order to avoid the possible risk of a dunking in the North Sea: 'the temperature of which at this time of the year is low enough to freeze the proverbials off a brass monkey.'

On 10 January 1962, the Station Commander and Station Adjutant visited Headquarters of No. 23 Group for the AOC's conference. As a result of this flying visit, the Station Commander became the first member of the staff of 6 FTS to carry out night flying practice in a Jet Provost:

> He expressed great satisfaction with the instrument lighting and the visibility from the cockpit when making a night approach. The Adjutant would have agreed with this but the luggage piled up between him and the windscreen prevented him from making an accurate assessment.

Training was hampered in February by extremely high winds, which particularly hampered solo flying in the piston-engined Provosts. It was not only the aircraft that were vulnerable to the elements—on one occasion the roof of No. 1 hangar began to break up. On 5 February, an exercise took place to test the defences of RAF Acklington. The Royal Northumberland Fusiliers mounted an attack on the airfield in the evening. Pupils of 6 FTS were organised into security patrols and they successfully prevented the intruders from reaching the operational part of the airfield. Most of the attackers were captured, but a few avoided detention and were able to 'decorate' the

Station Commander's residence with a gaudy poster. There was further excitement on the following day. The pilot of a Lightning flying near RAF Acklington reported that a missile had struck his port wing. A Jet Provost was scrambled and flew alongside the Lightning but could see no sign of damage. On the 13th, the pilot of a Provost T.1 radioed that he had fumes in his cockpit. The aircraft landed safely and the engine was cut at the end of the runway.

At this time, there was an increasing conflict of interest between the Piston Provost and Jet Provost pilots over which runway should be used for training purposes. In addition, concern was expressed about the state of runway 01/19 which was deteriorating, causing increased tyre temperatures.

With an improvement in the weather in April, No. 161 training course was able to be completed a month ahead of schedule. Students in this course took part in a survival trek in the Lake District at Easter. Eight Provost T.1s were transferred to RAF Ouston where No. 164 course was to be completed. The reason for this was that construction work was taking place on extending the ASP and only limited parking space was available for the aircraft. However, it helped resolve the problem of Provosts and Jet Provosts operating together. A further twenty-seven pupils arrived on the 25th to commence No. 165 course. Flying training was disrupted the following day when an Anson (VM409) infringed the Acklington circuit. A Jet Provost was sent to pursue it and obtain the aircraft's identity. Vickers Varsities (twin-engined crew trainers) were also causing concern by flying close to the airfield. An effort was made to track down all stations operating this type of aircraft and warn them not to do this in future.

During April 1962, RAF Acklington was officially affiliated to the town of Morpeth. The BBC also recorded two programmes entitled 'School for Pilots'. The first episode, 'Piston Pilot', was broadcast on North Region Children's Hour on the 19th. 6 FTS was also brought to the attention of the public by its newly formed aerobatic team, 'The Cocks of the North'. It flew three Jet Provosts and participated at numerous airshows and events until 1965 when it disbanded.

As summer approached and the weather improved, the pace of flying training picked up. Until then, the only Jet Provost to be involved in a serious accident was XN599 which swung off the runway on 27 March and was damaged beyond repair. The wreck suffered the indignity of ending up in the Acklington fire section where firemen practised their skills on it. On 8 May, 6 FTS suffered a major setback with its first fatal crash. Flt Lt Wyman was practicing solo aerobatics in Jet Provost T3 (XM422) when his machine crashed at Acklington. The Station Commander remarked that: 'Flight Lieutenant Wyman's loss was a bitter blow to the station. He was not only a first class instructor but also, with his wife, much esteemed by all who knew them.'

A day after the crash, 'mayday—mayday—mayday—Foxtrot 33—aircraft on fire' rung out on the Air Traffic Controller's radio. The pilot of the aircraft concerned—a Jet Provost T3 (XN604)—then stated he was heading towards the emergency landing ground at Eshott. The crew, Flt Lt W. Eggleton and Acting Plt Off. M. Hyland, decided to abandon the aircraft and ejected. Both survived the experience without sustaining any injuries. The Jet Provost came down at Felton. The wreckage was sent to Croydon for investigation. It was concluded that the fire warning alarm was spurious and there was no danger to the aircraft. This fault in the Jet Provost resulted in several pilots abandoning their machines prematurely.

During 1962, 6 FTS suffered a further serious accident involving a Jet Provost. Sudanese student Officer Cadet Hag Ali was carrying out 'touch and goes' at RAF Ouston on 17 October in XN601 when he found he could not retract the undercarriage. He then made the mistake of using the emergency gear lowering lever in an attempt to retract it. The Jet Provost reacted by stalling at low level and one wing tip clipped a small power pole at the side of a narrow lane. The aircraft then cartwheeled a couple of times across the ground causing the ejector seat to be thrown up off its rails without firing. The drogue gun then operated, releasing the pilot from his seat, at which point his parachute began to open pulling him clear of the aircraft. He was then dragged a hundred yards or so across the rough field. When rescuers reached the crash scene, Hag Ali was found alive between the inverted fuselage and a wing. After spending a few days in hospital, he was well enough to be released. Grp Capt. F. Jensen, Acklington CO commented in the Station records:

> We are grateful that Hag Ali did not fare worse in the crash—all the evidence is that he was extraordinarily fortunate, favoured by a sequence of highly improbable circumstances. It falls to few to be extricated by one's parachute as the aircraft is ploughing its way on its side along the ground, barely a second before the aircraft disintegrates.

Accidents were not confined to the Jet Provost fleet. In the early morning of 14 August, a disastrous mid-air collision took place between Provosts T.1s XF.684 and XF903 in the circuit at RAF Ouston, killing both student pilots, Plt Off. Hyde and Plt Off. Thomas. The accident took place in the early hours of the morning when they had been practicing night flying. Initially, one body could not be found. It was later recovered from a wood near the scene of the collision.

The last 'passing out' parade of Provost trained pilots was held around two months later on 12 October at RAF Ouston. By the end of the year, most of the aircraft had departed to RAF Shawbury for scrapping.

The first Jet Provost T.4 was delivered to 6 FTS in June 1962: 'All the pilots are very enthusiastic about this new aircraft as in performance it is vastly superior to the Jet Provost Mk 3.'

Student pilots were to receive their initial training on the Mk 3 before graduating to the Mk 4. The following month, a considerable amount of night flying was undertaken. On 5 July, the Duchess of Gloucester and the Duchess of Northumberland visited the station. This was followed six days later by the annual sports day. Outdoor activities were well catered for at RAF Acklington, which had its own mountaineering, sailing and canoeing clubs. More unusually, horse riding proved popular and stables could be found on the Station with several horses: 'some students are making good progress which if maintained will do credit to No. 6 FTS Cavalry Regiment.'

In contrast to this, a Go-Kart Club was formed at the end of 1962 with six karts. A track was marked out on a large tarmac dispersal on the western side of the airfield, well away from the main camp.

Jet Provost T4 (XP662) of 6 FTS in bare metal finish with day-glo patches – the standard colour scheme for RAF training aircraft in the 1950s and early 1960s. (*Roger Lindsay*)

Weather remained good for flying throughout October and the backlog in training was made good. A team from the Central Flying School at Little Rissington arrived at the beginning of the month and tested the flying standards of seven instructors and thirty-five pupils by day, nine instructors by night, and three instructors by day and night. These numbers represented 76 per cent of the instructors and 100 per cent of the students available for testing. The Central Flying School instructors were satisfied with the result.

The strength of RAF Acklington on 31 October 1962 was:

| | |
|---|---|
| Staff Officers | 80 |
| Pupils | 69 |
| Warrant Officers | 17 |
| Senior NCOs | 83 |
| Corporals | 103 |
| Airmen | 315 |
| | |
| Total | 667 |

Weather remained good for flying until the end of the year. On 6 and 7 December, students took part in Exercise 'Kon Tiki'. They were set to task of crossing the ice-covered River Coquet at Warkworth, using rafts constructed on the river bank. Seven of the eight teams managed this without getting wet. Christmas festivities included a children's Christmas party to which the children of the local orphanages were invited. Father Christmas arrived by helicopter and distributed presents to the children.

The New Year brought with it a deterioration in the weather. Snow, ice and strong winds limited flying, so advantage was taken of the adverse weather for survival training. Some student pilots spent nights out in the snow in shelters constructed from survival equipment. Conditions for February were not much better. The CO, F. Jensen, summed it up:

> A very trying month for all concerned, each day bringing some weather factor or another to frustrate us in the flying task—ice, snow, fog, mist, contrary winds or even just lack of diversion airfields. Morale remained good, though in these circumstances increasingly becomes a problem to be reckoned with.

Pressure was about to be further increased on RAF Acklington, as plans were in hand to reduce the number of flying training schools from four to three. To compensate for this, the Station would have to increase its output of students by one-third. On 5 March, a visit was paid by a party of officers and Air Ministry officials to discuss with the Station Commander plans for rebuilding the station. At this time, many of the buildings were still wooden huts dating back to the late 1930s. Later that month, No. 165 course student pilots completed their training. A ceremony was held on the ASP parade ground where the students were awarded their flying badges. The reviewing officer for the parade was the Duke of Northumberland. In the evening, the course members entertained their guests in the Officers' Mess. On the 29th, No. 169 course was formed and the new arrivals were welcomed by the Station Commander.

Over the next few weeks, the weather proved favourable for flying. The newly formed Gliding Club had its first launch on Sunday 31 March 1963. On 18 April, 6 FTS lost a further Jet Provost. Flt Lt Shadbolt and APO Gladwin ejected from their T.4 (XP635) two miles east of Netherwitton at Whitton Shields. Both landed safely. They were picked up by a 228 Squadron rescue helicopter from RAF Acklington, which ferried them back to the Station. The cause of the crash was again thought to be a spurious fire warning indication as a Board of Inquiry carried out an extensive investigation of the wreckage but could not find any trace of a fire.

By the summer, construction of the new airmen's married quarters was well underway but this had an adverse effect on the recreational activities as the sports field could not be used due to the work. There was an increased interest in golf as a consequence, with full use being made of the Station's Foxton Hall membership. Flying Training Command Athletics Championships were held at RAF Cranwell between 9 and 12 June, with the Acklington team being placed fourth in the overall senior station competition.

Good weather in July 1963 enabled the target of 1,268 flying hours to be exceeded by 345 hours. The following month, attention was directed towards the passing out parade for Courses 167 and 168. Five practice parades were held in addition to a dress rehearsal with a band on 28 August. The courses also organised a well-attended passing out parade in the evening. Students on courses 169 and 170 took part in a combat survival exercise on the Otterburn Army Range. This included a 15-mile cross-country night march and a 5-mile 'border penetration', the only equipment being parachutes and survival packs. Unseasonable good weather conditions in December allowed for the set number of flying hours to be exceeded by a considerable margin. The long hours of darkness enable numerous night sorties. The maximum temperature at RAF Acklington during the month was 10.4 C and the minimum was -6.8 C, with total precipitation of 0.92 inches. No. 172 course arrived to commence training. It consisted of sixteen RAF officers plus six officers from Kuwait.

In April 1964, the members of No. 172 course were sent on a combat survival exercise with members of No. 171 course. A less demanding activity was a visit to Morpeth Town Hall later the same month. There, the students heard a lecture on the town's history and were entertained by the Mayor and Mayoress. Flying training was seriously curtailed in May for a variety of reasons, which included public holidays, AOC's inspection, parade rehearsals, and a passing-out parade. The instructional task of 1,297 hours was not completed, with the deficit being 341 hours. No fewer than nine rehearsals were held for No. 170 course passing-out parade, which took place on 14 May. A substantial number of flying hours were also devoted to practicing formation flypasts of Jet Provosts. A major Army Exercise, code-named 'Spring Cocktail' was held in the Otterburn area in late May. The gunners of No. 440 Light Air Defence Regiment required practice at aiming at aircraft simulating rocket and cannon attacks. This was provided by six Jet Provost T.4s from RAF Acklington. They planned to carry out the mock attack with two aircraft operating as a pair with the remainder flying as a section of four in low-level battle formation.

June involved the school in an intensive flying programme, mainly due to the imminent passing out of two senior courses. The courses were handicapped by the students having to travel to RAF Ouston for flying because of work being carried out to improve the runway lighting at RAF Acklington. Training was disrupted further by unpredictable weather for night flying. On the recreation side, the newly formed station Drama Group presented its first production of *An Inspector Calls* in the Station cinema on 16 and 17 June. Final examinations were held on the 29th and 30th for students on Courses 171 and 172. The Iraqi and Kuwaiti students were given an oral examination instead of a written one. The following ranks were on strength at RAF Acklington at this time:

| | |
|---|---|
| Staff Officers | 88 |
| Student Officers | |
| RAF | 71 |
| Iraqi | 11 |
| Kuwaiti | 5 |
| Lebanese | 2 |
| Warrant Officers | 22 |
| Senior NCOs | 92 |
| Corporals and Airmen | 397 |
| | |
| Total | 688 |

In July, Acklington's 'Good Show Trophy' was awarded to FS K. Gill for outstanding work in the Airmen's Mess. On a more ominous note, the Station received updates for its War Readiness Orders. Instructional flying in August was hampered by poor weather and a shortage of aircraft. Serviceability averaged eighteen, as opposed to twenty-two in July and twenty in June. Flying Training Command's newly appointed AOC-in-C, Air Marshal P. Dunn, made his first visit to RAF Acklington on 20 August. Here, he was met by a guard of honour after which he was shown round the base by the Station Commander. In contrast to this formal visit was that by a party of deprived children holidaying at Amble who were taken around the airfield five days later. They were shown all parts of the station and had lunch and tea in the Airmen's mess. The children all stated this excursion was the highlight of their holiday.

The rebuilding of the Station was gaining momentum. Nearly sixty of the 101 airmen's married quarters were completed by the end of August. The contract for the officers' quarters was let in May 1964, with January 1965 set as the date for the first buildings to be handed over.

A further Jet Provost of 6 FTS was lost in an accident on 30 September. Flt Lt D. J. Philips, with his pupil APO John Brown, took off from RAF Acklington at 2 p.m. in Jet Provost T4 (XR664). They flew north along the coast on a navigation exercise. Visibility was good with some scattered clouds. On reaching Eyemouth, the aircraft headed inland to follow the River Teviot. A bird suddenly reared up and was digested by the port engine intake. The crew experienced an initial vibration. Philips then

Jet Provost T4 (XR667) of 6 FTS in the new Training Command colour scheme. (*R. Ashworth*)

twice attempted, unsuccessfully, to relight the engine. The crew decided there was no alternative other than to abandon the doomed aircraft, which had been flying at around 250 feet. The Martin Baker Mk 4 ejector seats were triggered and the pilot and his pupil parachuted to safety, landing on the banks of the River Teviot, close to Crailing, north-east of Jedburgh. Brown landed on a barbed wire fence. The first person to come to his rescue was a girl riding a white horse, the daughter of the local land owner. Not long after, two farm workers arrived in a Landrover and took both the crew members to a nearby farm house. Their stay was brief as a Westland Whirlwind of 202 Squadron based at RAF Acklington arrived on the scene not long after and took them back to the Station. Brown spent several weeks with his ankle in plaster before he could continue his flying training.

Princess Alexandra flew into RAF Acklington on 19 October. She was greeted by the Station Commander, together with the Duke of Northumberland and the Chief Constable of the County, before carrying out official engagements on the 20th. An engagement of a different nature was the deployment of one of the Station's aircraft on an anti-insurgency exercise with the Roxburghshire police, appropriately called 'Spycatcher'. In the early hours of the 25th, Exercise 'Mickey Finn' was staged to test the Station's ability to meet war readiness requirements at short notice. During November, a security check was carried out, but no major breaches of it were detected. All attempts at unauthorised entry were successfully intercepted. December's weather was unkind for flying. Training was further disrupted by a shortage of aircraft, a number of which were undergoing modification. During the month, sixty-nine aircrew and eighty-five ground crew reported sick. A total of six had to be admitted to hospital. This number was by no means exceptional for this time of year.

At the beginning of the New Year, the weather improved and the pace of flying picked up. On 29 January 1965, AVM R. C. Ayling visited RAF Acklington to present 'wings' and trophies to students of No. 173 Course. The weather in February was the best since July, with almost a total absence of rain. Over 1,173 hours of flying was achieved with some of it at night. 12 March saw a Tramp's Ball held in the officers' mess. Grp Capt. J. Forsythe wrote the final entry of Station diary for March 1965:

> The station and all aspects of its activities continues to be a constant source of interest to the county. Barely a week passes without parties of students, police, schoolchildren or scouts, etc., being given a conducted tour of the station. From publicity in the local press and comments made to me and my staff, the Royal Air Force is held in considerable esteem in the north-east of England.

On 2 April, the Officers' Mess was made available to the Mayor of Morpeth for a cocktail to raise funds for the new swimming pool in the town. A large number of officers attended. Other recreational activities held during the month included the screening of the film *Tom Jones* in the Officers' Mess—the last in the film season until the autumn. A graduation ball took place on 22 April to celebrate the graduation of students on No. 174 course of 6 FTS.

The station strength at this time was:

| | |
|---|---|
| Officers, Staff | 94 |
| Students | |
| RAF | 82 |
| Foreign | 2 |
| Warrant Officers | 27 |
| Senior NCOs | 108 |
| Corporals and airmen | 377 |
| Civilians | 129 |
| | |
| Total | 819 |

By May, all Airmen's Married Quarters and about 40 per cent of the Officers' Married Quarters had been completed as part of the reconstruction program. The station commander opened the new NAAFI All Ranks Club, the event being reported in the local newspapers. Bad weather in July, with the sun being absent from the sky for much of the month, caused a backlog in flying training. In an effort to resolve this, much flying was undertaken in the evenings but this did not prevent the completion of Nos. 175 and 176 (UAS) courses. AVM H. G. Wheeler, Senior Air Staff Officer, Headquarters RAF Germany, visited the Station on 16 July to review the passing out parade. During the same month, RAF Acklington's 'Good Show' Trophy was awarded to Master Signaller J. Holland, an instructor in the Ground School. The citation read as follows:

> Master Signaller Holland is the Signals Ground Instructor for the Ground School of the Flying Wing. He tackles his instructional duties with diligence and enthusiasm and has been instrumental in improving the examination results shown for the past three courses to graduates from this unit, i.e. 78½ per cent, 81½ per cent, and 84 per cent. His enthusiasm for his duties extends beyond the normal call of duty in that he has personally devised and constructed training aids for his section. He has also been active as a youth leader and has given freely of his own time to assisting the Youth Club. His efforts are recognised by the award of the Good Show Trophy for the six months ending 30 June 1965.

As the month drew to a close, Jet Provost T3 (XN603) crashed at Eshott, not far from RAF Acklington. Its two crew—Flt Lt J. Walker and PO S. J. Roncoroni—ejected successfully. Again, the cause was attributed to a false fire warning inside the cockpit. Another Jet Provost made a forced landing at Carlisle Airport in July. Later in the year, a further Jet Provost was involved in a mishap. It involved XN602, which made an emergency landing at the disused airfield at Boulmer after its engine failed. When it touched down, it struck a wire fence that had been erected across the old runway. The engine failure was later discovered to have been caused by a sick bag that had been thrown out of the aircraft by a student at the end of the previous flight. It was sucked into the engine as it had not been shut down at the time. The aircraft was sent to 27MU Shawbury for repair but never flew again.

On 15 September, Col. Kydri, Chief of the Air Staff of the Royal Jordanian Air Force, paid a visit to 6FTS. In the same month, Tyne Tees Television recorded an edition of the programme 'North-east Glamour Trail' in the Station cinema. Wg Cdr and Mrs Swart acted as judges on behalf of RAF Acklington. With the arrival of autumn, the weather deteriorated. The airfield experienced its first radiation fog in thirteen years during October. The maximum temperature was 20 C and the minimum temperatures was 1 C with 1.3 inches of rainfall. On 15 November, there was the first snow fall of winter which was heavy enough for machinery to be required to remove it from the runways. It was the last month that Grp Capt. J. Forsythe was in command of the Station and he lamented the fact that he was handing it over with a large backlog in flying training. A farewell cocktail party was held in the Officers' Mess. Film evenings were also held on 7 and 21 November featuring 'The Bridge on the River Kwai' and 'The Pink Panther'.

The next month, there were screenings of 'The Great Escape' and 'Zulu'. Three children's Christmas parties were held on 19 December in the Officers' and Sergeants' Messes, as well as the Hotspur Club. They were attended by the children of the Station's personnel plus a coachload of deprived children from Morpeth. There were further falls of snow around that time which limited flying training.

On 3 January 1966, all Jet Provost airframe spares came under computer control from the Supply Control Centre, RAF Hendon. This was the first batch of equipment in the RAF to be computer controlled. No. 177 Course graduated on 7 January. Flying badges and awards were presented by AVM M. Lyne, AOC No. 23 Group. Later in the month, a Shackleton of 120 Squadron visited RAF Acklington. Its crew gave a presentation to students and some got the opportunity to fly in the Shackleton. Snow and ice again played havoc with the flying training schedule. Locally manufactured hand squeegees were used for the first time in February to assist in snow clearance operations. They were used in areas inaccessible to the runway de-icer machine and were most effective as they produced a very clear surface which did not glaze over during frosty nights. The squeegees were three feet wide and made from ash strip.

A significant event was the commencement of the building of the new Gaydon Hangar. This 320-foot building and its annexes would house the Technical Wing facilities of the Station. It was part of a £3½ million new building programme. It was also intended to replace all the wooden hutted accommodation by mid-1969. During May, social events on the Station included a tombola evening and dance in the Sergeants Mess, a student's dining-in night in the Officers' Mess, and the annual Spring Ball in the Officers' Mess.

In July, the Station Commander received an update to his War Readiness Orders. In the sixties, with the Cold War at its height, there was always the possibility that events would take a turn for the worse and it would quickly become a hot war involving the exchange of nuclear warheads. If a conflict were to break out, RAF Acklington had a role to play in it. It aircraft, pilots, ground crews, administrative staff and logistics units were to provide support to the Scottish Civil Defence Zone Squadrons of the Home Defence Force. On receipt of the appropriate code word, twenty-five Jet Provosts were to be deployed as follows:

Five Jet Provosts, Scottish Region West Zone, Perth Airport
Ten Jet Provosts, Scottish Region North Zone, Dyce Airport, Aberdeen
Ten Jet Provosts, Scottish Region East Zone, Dyce Airport, Aberdeen

Ground crews were to assemble in the hangars to await transport to the above locations in trucks and other vehicles. In addition, Acklington was also to provide support to RAF Coastal Command—a number of its personnel would be flown to RAF Macrihanish on the Mull of Kintyre. A further fifty, including one officer and an NCO, were to be taken to 14MU Carlisle to provide additional security for this large installation. A Landrover with three airmen and an NCO was to deploy to the NATO Radar Site at Brizlee Wood, Northumberland for a similar role. RAF Turnhouse, Edinburgh, would be the base of Nos 14 and 15 Courier and Postal Flights, to which RAF Acklington was to contribute thirteen of its personnel. Finally, some of the higher ranking officers would take up 'global war' appointments in the Scottish Civil Defence Headquarters and other regions in England.

RAF Acklington was to remain open on a twenty-four-hour basis to receive scheduled aircraft. Some of the remaining personnel would form No. 15 Emergency Labour Squadron. A- and B-Flights would live and mess at the airfield but those in the other flights would be based at RAF Ouston. The Stations buildings were to be prepared to give them protection against heat, blast and fallout. Security of key points was to be increased. Weapons were to be issued to the remaining personnel with ammunition in storage at RAF Ouston to be brought back to RAF Acklington. Two Landrovers were to be used by the Radiological Monitoring Flight and two three-tonners by the Decontamination Flight. The War Readiness Orders reassuringly stated that:

> In a general war, it is unlikely that this station will be subject to a direct nuclear attack. However, maximum protection must be afforded to personnel in the event of a local nuclear attack and against nuclear fallout in the immediate post attack phase. The use of conventional and chemical weapons are unlikely but cannot be discounted. There is a continuous threat of sabotage to our operational capability.

In the post-attack and recovery phases, RAF Acklington's role was to ensure that maximum lifesaving and survival operations were implemented. It was to support any continuing air operations, including staging facilities for transport and communications aircraft. It was also to allocate personnel in support of Civil Authorities as directed by Sub-Regional Headquarters. Fortunately, these plans would never need to be implemented.

On a more upbeat note, the RAF Formation Aerobatic Team gave a polished performance to the Station personnel on 1 July 1966. The annual sports day was held a few days later. The event was closed by the traditional 'Chariot Race', which was won by the Flying Wing.

Weather was poor in August, which again disrupted flying training. Heavy rainfall during the weekend of 13–14 August caused extensive flooding of the Station and some of the Airmen's Married Quarters were inundated by 2 feet of water. Although the Battle of Britain Air Display was cancelled, personnel from RAF Acklington took part in the Commemorative Service held in St. Nicholas Cathedral, Newcastle. The Royal Air Force Ceremonial Ensign and Royal Air Force Association Standards were paraded during the Service, which was attended by a congregation of 700, including many school children. Following the church service, the parade contingents, including a 100 student pilots and a guard of honour from RAF Acklington, marched through the streets of Newcastle to the Eldon Square War Memorial.

In the autumn, an additional four Jet Provosts were delivered to 6 FTS. No. 180 Course students graduated at the beginning of December, while Course No. 183 started training. On 13 December, members of No. 182 Course provided entertainment for a group of visiting old-age pensioners.

On 1 January 1967, the electrical and instrument servicing bays were transferred to RAF Leeming, where a three-month centralised servicing trial had started. Weather was poor in January. The maximum temperature was 6.1C and the minimum temperature -3.6C with 1.7 inches precipitation. Two 6 FTS aircraft had the misfortune to be involved in accidents during the month. On the 11th, Jet Provost T.3 (XM474) sustained some damage when it overran runway thirty. The following day, Jet Provost T.4 (XR660) made a nose-high landing and also sustained damage. Both machines were repairable. Fortunately, there was no such mishap for an aircraft of the Queen's Flight which arrived to collect Princes Margaret on the 17th at the end of her visit to Northumberland.

RAF Acklington was represented by the CO, Grp Capt. D. H. Sutton at the opening ceremony of Newcastle Airport, attended by the Prime Minister Harold Wilson on 17 February. A few days later, Northumberland experienced the first snow storm of the winter. Two inches covered the airfield, which was continuously cleared during the night by the Sicard Clearance Sweeper.

The poor weather continued into March. In an attempt to maintain training levels, the Engineering Wing had the difficult task of keeping a sufficient number of the intensely utilised aircraft serviceable. But during the month it managed to exceed the set serviceability level of 60 per cent by 13 per cent. Their finest hour was on 8 March, when 160 hours were flown and, at the end of the day, forty out of forty-four aircraft were operational. Around the same time, the film '633 Squadron' was being shown in the Officers' Mess, Sergeant's Mess and the Hotspur Club.

AVM M. Lyne, AOC No. 23 Group, carried out the annual inspection of the Station on 19 April. Despite winds gusting to 60 mph, the parade was carried out in the open as planned. Unfortunately, the aerobatic display had to be cancelled. Nevertheless, the Air Vice Marshal was pleased at the high standard of drill in spite of the very blustery conditions. Social events at RAF Acklington included members of Northumberland County Constabulary being invited to a games evening in the Officers' Mess: 'The visitors, as is customary, were the victors.' The film 'The Amorous Adventures of Moll Flanders' was screened at the Station in April.

On 1 May, Jet Provost T.3 (XM420) experienced a technical failure of its undercarriage lowering system necessitating a premeditated wheels-up landing on the runway. The pilot and student pilot were airlifted to the Station Sick Quarters by one of RAF Acklington's Westland Whirlwinds. They were not detained there long, as neither had sustained an injury. The aircraft faired less well as it had to be sent away to a Maintenance Unit for repair. In preparation for the Golden Jubilee Celebrations of 6 FTS, one Jet Provost was sprayed with the new acrylic paint scheme which was to become standard on all Flying Training aircraft. Since the 1950s, most RAF training aircraft had supported a bare metal finish with orange 'dayglo' patches.

No. 6 FTS set a new record for a Jet Provost training school in the month of June with 2,446 hours being flown. Also, a new record of 210 hours and forty-five minutes for a single day was established on the 19th. At the graduation of No. 182 Course on the 14th, the fiftieth anniversary of 6 FTS was celebrated. It had its origins as an Army FTS which was formed in 1917. ACM Sir John Davis, AOC-in-C, Flying Training Command, and many other prominent guests attended the event. Heavy rain throughout the day severely curtailed the programme. The graduation Parade was held in a hangar and the flying display had to be cancelled. Indoors, there was a display of aircraft, models and equipment associated with the history of 6 FTS. The celebrations came to an end with balls in the Officers and Sergeants Messes.

No. 185 Course commenced on 25 July and included six Royal Malaysian Air Force officers and one Saudi Arabian officer cadet. With the approach of autumn, the Station workshops undertook a major modification of the runway de-icing equipment in an effort to make it more effective. Only a month after 6 FTS celebrated its fiftieth anniversary, the Station Commander announced that, as a result of a recent Defence White Paper, there was to be a change in the role of RAF Acklington. With the reduction in front-line squadrons, there was no longer the same demand for pilot training and 6 FTS was to be run down and closed. A squadron of Westland Wessex helicopters was to be transferred from West Germany to take its place.

The writing was on the wall for RAF Acklington. The Station Commander, Grp Capt. D. H. Sutton, did not appear to be over enthusiastic about these changes. He made the following comment in the Station diary:

> In view of the excellent record of No. 6 FTS at Acklington as a school in Flying Training Command, its planned rundown and disbandment to make way for an expanding helicopter force is viewed with mixed feelings. Nevertheless the Station has now laid plans to ensure that 6 FTS remains efficient and of high morale until its disbandment. Every effort is being made to reduce to a minimum the personnel turbulence caused by the change in the Station's role.

During the summer, a single Jet Provost performed at a number of air displays, including the USAF open day at Wethersfield and RNAS Culdrose. The last day of the aerobatic season was 30 September. Flt Lt Houghton rounded it off in style by performing for the RAF at Prestwick Air Show and later at Dyce for Aberdeen University Air Squadron Open Day.

*Above:* Graduation parade of 182 course, 6 Flying Training School, 1967. (*The National Archives*)

*Right:* A pilot is awarded his wings at 182 course graduation ceremony, 6 Flying Training School, 1967. (*The National Archives*)

A shortage of bricklayers set back the rebuilding schedule by about six weeks. The large Gaydon hangar and complex of engineering buildings were handed over to the RAF on 30 November 1967. The HQ Engineering Wing, HQ Flying Wing and the Station Commander and his personnel staff were all relocated to the new Gaydon hangar offices.

At the beginning of November, RAF Acklington had twenty-four Jet Provost T3s and twenty-one Jet Provost T4s on strength. With the impending closure of 6 FTS, five aircraft departed during the course of the month. During December, 1,055 hours were flown, of which 853 were instructional flying. Three Jet Provosts mounted a flypast for a passing out parade of recruits at RAF Swinderby. On 4 December, AOC Group, AVM M. Lyne, made his farewell visit to the Station before leaving to take up a new appointment. After inspecting the Guard of Honour, he made a tour of the Station which included the new Gaydon Hangar. The highlight of the day was a visit to a 'survival camp' which had been erected by the Station Survival Officer.

The remainder of the month saw numerous social events held on the Station, including the Christmas Draw and Dances on 15 December in the Officers' Mess. This was followed by children's Christmas parties over the next two days. On 20 December, there was a grand Christmas Party and Dance in the Hotspur Club. The next day, the traditional Christmas Dinner was served to the airmen in the Airmen's Mess by the Officers, Warrant Officers and senior NCOs of the Station. On Christmas day itself, the traditional lunch-time drinks were served to the Warrant Officers and Senior NCOs who were guests in the Officers' Mess. The Officers were then hosted by the Warrant Officers and Senior NCOs in the Sergeants Mess.

An advanced party from 18 Squadron took over No. 4 hangar in mid-December. It had been vacated by the Engineering Wing moving into the Gaydon Hangar. No. 2 hangar was also prepared for use by this unit in the new year. Despite the new role for RAF Acklington, Wg Cdr H. Harrison, the Station Commander wrote pessimistically in the last entry in the Station's diary for 1967: 'The Defence economies following devaluation have again cast doubt on the future of the Station.'

The personnel on strength at RAF Acklington as at 31 December 1967 were as follows:

|  | Station | 18 Squadron | 202 Squadron | Totals |
|---|---|---|---|---|
| Officers |  |  |  |  |
| Staff | 85 | 3 | 12 | 100 |
| Students | 66 | - | - | 66 |
| Foreign Students | 5 | - | - | 5 |
|  |  |  |  |  |
| WO and Master Aircrew Ranks | 18 | 2 | 2 | 22 |
| FS, Chief Tech and Sgt Ranks | 107 | 5 | 9 | 121 |
| Corporals and below | 367 | 14 | 16 | 397 |
|  |  |  |  |  |
| Civilians | 154 | - | - | 154 |
|  |  |  |  |  |
| Totals | 802 | 24 | 39 | 865 |

# 20
# Air Displays
# 1945–1967

For many members of the public in Northumberland, RAF Acklington was associated with its annual air display. This event dated back to 1945, when this airfield along with many other RAF stations were thrown open to the public to commemorate the fifth anniversary of the Battle of Britain. In the words of the Station diary:

> This was certainly a memorable day for the Station, for in common with other RAF Stations, RAF Acklington was open to the public during the afternoon during the previous 24 hours, various types of aircraft had been flown up so that in addition to the Mosquitos of 219 Squadron, there were on view a Spitfire, Typhoon, Mustang, PR Mosquito, Lancaster, Halifax and Horsa glider, Wellington; which attracted large crowds who queued patiently to see inside the various types whose crews were on duty to explain and point out how everything worked. Almost all sections were open; the parachute section and Link trainer proved to be particularly popular, during the afternoon, parachute packing was demonstrated and a parachute was also released. 219 Squadron carried out routine flying and an interesting experiment was tried whereby the R/T communication was broadcast through the tannoy, before landing 219 squadron carried out a very impressive formation flight over the airfield. The N.A.A.F.I. Mobile Wagon provided refreshments, the Automobile Association sent a patrol man who marshalled the very considerable number of cars and extra police on point duty directed the many visitors, many of whom travelled on the three special trains from Newcastle. To conclude the day there was a special all ranks dance in the Acklington Club, in which relatives and friends of station personnel joined.

The only part of the Station that remained 'secret' was its radar station. There was a tragic postscript to this event—the following day, a Spitfire IX (SM278), on its way back to RAF Manston, crashed on the North York Moors near Osmotherley, killing its pilot Flt Lt Catterns; the aircraft had been flying at high speed and at a low altitude in poor visibility.

There was no display in 1946, but a Battle of Britain Air Display was held on 20 September 1947. Mosquito NF.38 (VT587) of 2 APS took off to carry out a practice display on the Wednesday prior to the event. While carrying out a slow roll with one

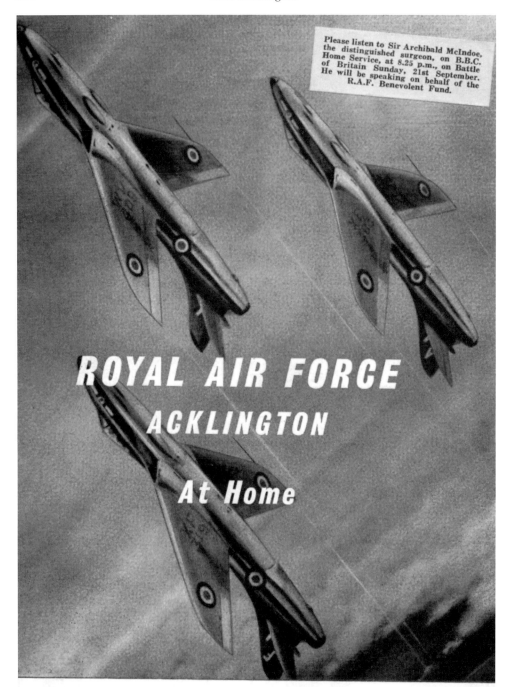

Please listen to Sir Archibald McIndoe, the distinguished surgeon, on B.B.C. Home Service, at 8.25 p.m., on Battle of Britain Sunday, 21st September. He will be speaking on behalf of the R.A.F. Benevolent Fund.

**ROYAL AIR FORCE**

*ACKLINGTON*

*At Home*

**SATURDAY, 20th SEPTEMBER, 1958**

12 noon to 6 p.m.

SOUVENIR PROGRAMME - Two Shillings

The cover of the Battle of Britain Air Display programme for 1958. (*Aldon Ferguson*)

engine feathered, the aircraft stalled and crashed in a field adjacent to the Station. Both the pilot, Flt Lt D. Byrne, and his passenger, Fg Off. C. Johnston MB (a doctor) were killed. Eric Nicholson was examined by Johnston for his demob medical earlier that day. The doctor had told him it would not be long before he achieved his ambition to fly in a Mosquito.

On the day of the actual air display, the weather was poor but had improved somewhat by the afternoon. This allowed a modified flying programme to take place, minus most of the intended visiting aircraft. No. 63 Squadron Spitfire XVIs were based at RAF Acklington at that time for armament training. Two Lancasters, which had been grounded since the previous Thursday by bad weather, took off and returned to their base in the latter part of the day. One Dakota and a Lincoln arrived during the afternoon with the latter staying overnight.

The following year, the Station 'At Home' had an estimated attendance of 6,000. In addition to aircraft, it also involved units of the 83rd Heavy Anti-aircraft Brigade and 670 Light Anti-aircraft Regiment Royal Artillery. The flying display included formation flying by Miles Martinets, a mock combat between a Spitfire and a Mosquito, as well as an attack on a set-piece target on the airfield. A Spitfire gave an aerobatic display, as did a Meteor from 263 Squadron, RAF Horsham St. Faith. Aircraft in the static display included a Lincoln from 44 Squadron, RAF Wyton, a Tempest from 226 OCU Bentwaters, and a Hornet from 65 Squadron, RAF Linton-on-Ouse.

The Battle of Britain 'At Home' day for 1949 took place on Saturday 17 September. The attendance was some 7,500 people, along with 400 bicycles and the same number of cars and motorcycles.

RAF Acklington was one of 72 airfields open to the public on 16 September 1950 to mark the 10th anniversary of the Battle of Britain. Bad weather restricted flying on the day. Much of the programme was flown despite the conditions, although the visiting public were unable to see the Meteor aerobatic team, as the deterioration in the weather precluded any further demonstrations. The souvenir programme listed performances by the following aircraft in the flying display:

1. 2.00–2.10 p.m. Hawker Tempest V (aerobatics)
2. 2.10–2.20 p.m. De Havilland Tiger Moth (crazy flying and balloon chasing)
3. 2.20–2.30 p.m. De Havilland Vampire (aerobatics)
4. 2.30–2.45 p.m. Hawker Sea Fury (aerobatics and deck landings)
5. 2.45–2.50 p.m. De Havilland Hornet (aerobatics and asymmetric flying)
6. 3 p.m. Gloster Meteor aerobatic team arrives from RAF Church Fenton
7. 3.00–3.15 p.m. De Havilland Hornet (formation arrives from RAF Ouston)
8. 3.15–3.30 p.m. attack on airfield defended by anti-aircraft guns.
9. 3.30–4 p.m. Air Race:
   a. Gloster Meteor VII
   b. Gloster Meteor IV
   c. De Havilland Vampire
   d. De Havilland Hornet

   e. De Havilland Mosquito

   f. Hawker Sea Fury

   g. Hawker Tempest

   h. Supermarine Seafire

10. 4.00–4.10 p.m. Gloster Meteor (aerobatics)

11. 4.10–4.25 p.m. Gloster Meteor (formation aerobatic team)

12. 4.25–4.40 p.m. Attack on defended position

13. 4.40–4.50 p.m. Fire fighting demonstration

On the ground, the attractions included bomb trolley rides for children, rifle range tests of skill, electronic fortune telling, a skittle alley, and exhibitions of engines.

ACM Sir James Robb was one of several distinguished persons to attend the 1951 Air Show, which had an attendance of 12,000. The following year, the figure dropped to 7,000. This was attributed to the curtailment of previous displays because of poor weather, but on this occasion there was a full flying display. RAF Ouston hosted the Battle of Britain Air Show in 1953 and 1954 because of re-construction work being carried out at Acklington. The event returned to RAF Acklington in 1955, taking place on Saturday 17 September. The weather was reasonably good, although it was cool and extremely windy. This did not deter the public as around 20,000 people attended. The programme of events was as follows:

2.29 p.m. Pyrotechnic Display.

2.30 p.m. Formation flying by De Havilland Vampires from RAF Ouston, one aircraft performing aerobatics.

A Gloster Meteor F.8 (WA760) operated by APS Acklington. It was only towards the end of Acklington's existence that its aircraft were camouflaged. Prior to this, most of its machines supported a natural metal finish. (*MAP aviation photos*)

2.37 p.m. Avro Shackleton flypast, RAF

2.45 p.m. Vickers Valiant flypast, RAF

2.52 p.m. English Electric Canberra formation flypast, RAF

2.54 p.m. Demonstration by two De Havilland Vampires of an attack on a towed glider.

2.56 p.m. Demonstration by two De Havilland Vampires of an attack on a banner target.

3.02 p.m. Lockheed Neptune flypast

3.04 p.m. Gloster Meteor aerobatics, RAF

3.10 p.m. Height and Speed Judging Competition

3.14 p.m. Formation flypast of North American F.86 Sabres.

3.15 p.m. Demonstration of RATO by two Fairey Fireflies, Royal Navy

3.18 p.m. Percival Prentice aerobatics

3.28 p.m. Hawker Seahawk aerobatics, Royal Navy.

3.36 p.m. Demonstration of Rescue Technique and Handling by helicopter

4.01 p.m. Formation flypast by North American B45 Tornadoes, USAF

4.02 p.m. Formation flying by Gloster Meteors and de Havilland Vampires

4.03 p.m. Hawker Hunter aerobatics.

4.13 p.m. North American F.86 Sabre aerobatics.

4.20 p.m. Formation flying by Fairey Fireflies, Royal Navy

4.30 p.m. Target on airfield attacked by de Havilland Vampires

4.45 p.m. Aircraft from the static park to take off.

In 1956, there was again no air display at RAF Acklington as it was involved in the major Exercise, 'Stronghold'. 131 Squadron temporarily deployed sixteen Meteors from RAF Leconfield for a week. RAF Ouston was again the alternative venue for the air display. At that time, 607 Squadron was based there with Vampires. Hunters of 222 Squadron, which were on detachment to RAF Acklington, flew the short distance to RAF Ouston to participate in the display.

By the following year, Northumberland's air display had returned to its traditional venue. It was opened by the Lord Mayor of Newcastle, Alderman J. Telford, who arrived by helicopter. The weather was good but very cold. Some 27,000 people attended.

There were thirty-five RAF airfields open to the public in 1958, including RAF Acklington. The programme for the 20 September 1958 'At Home' day listed the following participants in the flying display:

1. Arrival of helicopter to open show

2. De Havilland Comet of Transport Command., five minute display

3. Gloster Javelin of 29 Squadron, five minute display

4. Formation of three Vickers Varsities

5. Flypast of Handley Page Hastings of Transport Command

6. Display of aerobatics by Boulton Paul Balliol

7. Display by a helicopter

8. A Shackleton of Coastal Command flies past

9. Demonstration of two Chipmunks of Flying Training Command

10. The first of the V-bombers—a Vickers Valiant of Bomber Command, five minute display

11. Glider aerobatics

12. Three Douglas B66s of USAF fly past

13. Hawker Hunter aerobatics

14. de Havilland Vampire aerobatics

15. The last of the V-bombers. The Avro Vulcan gives a five minute display

16. The helicopter stages an air-sea rescue

17. A demonstration by the Vickers Valiant

18. The English Electric Canberra shows its paces

19. The helicopter 'finds the lady'

20. All aircraft take off for the final fly past.

The 1959 Battle of Britain air display attracted a record crowd of over 30,000 people. It enjoyed fine weather. The highlight of the static display was a Vickers Valiant. The next year, the attendance numbers were well down because heavy rain curtailed the flying display. By 1962, the number of RAF Stations holding a Battle of Britain 'Open Day' had dwindled to just sixteen, although RAF Acklington remained one of them. The planned schedule for the 15 September 1962 'At Home' day was as follows:

A De Havilland Vampire T.11 (XH329) in 1958. At that time, the type was operated by RAF Acklington Station Flight. (*MAP aviation photos*)

1. ATC Band Display
2. Police Dog Demonstration
3. Westland Whirlwind helicopter towing ensign flag
4. Hawker Hunter Aerobatic Team (RAF Chivenor)
5. English Electric Lightning (RAF Middleton St George)
6. Dinghy plus survivor in position for dry winching demonstration
7. Solo Jet Provost take off, RAF
8. Jet Provost aerobatic formation team take off
9. Westland Whirlwind take off, RAF
10. Dry winching demonstration and landing
11. Jet Provost formation team aerobatics, RAF
12. Jet Provost formation team lands, RAF
13. Supermarine Spitfire (RAF Horsham St. Faith)
14. Solo Jet Provost aerobatics (RAF Acklington)
15. Hawker Siddeley Argosy demonstration, RAF
16. Solo Jet Provost aerobatics continued, RAF
17. Solo Jet Provost lands, RAF
18. Fly-past—4 North American F100 Super Sabres, USAF
19. 2 McDonnell F101 Voodoo, USAF
20. Glider aerobatics
21. Glider recovery.
22. Supermarine Scimitars take off, Royal Navy
23. Flypast:
    One Boeing KB-50 aerial tanker, USAF
    One North American F100 Super Sabre
    One Douglas B-66 Destroyer
    One McDonnell F101 Voodoo
24. De Havilland Comet, RAF
25. Supermarine Scimitars aerobatics, Royal Navy
26. Solo de Havilland Chipmunk flypast (RAF Ouston)
27. Supermarine Scimitars land
28. Avro Shackleton, RAF
29. De Havilland Chipmunk aerobatics
30. Bristol Britannia, RAF
31. Avro Lincoln, RAF
32. English Electric Canberra P.R., RAF
33. Jet Provost formation team, 'Aeros', take off for RAF Leuchars
34. de Havilland Chipmunk flypast, RAF
35. Vickers Varsity formation (RAF Manby)
36. Solo de Havilland Vampire takes off (RAF Swinderby)
37. Solo de Havilland Vampire aerobatics
38. Solo de Havilland Vampire lands
39. Hunting Percival Provost formation (RAF Ouston)
40. Two Turbulents take off (civil)

41. Westland Whirlwind takes off, RAF
42. Westland Whirlwind performs 'waltz' and landing
43. Turbulent demonstration and landing
44. Hunting Percival Provost solo aerobatics, RAF
45. English Electric Canberra T.4 formation (RAF Bassingbourn)
46. Vickers Valiant, RAF
47. Height and speed judging competition—Provost.
48. de Havilland Mosquito
49. Height and speed judging competition
50. Avro Vulcan, RAF
51. Handley Page Victor, RAF
52. Supermarine Scimitar formation take off, Royal Navy
53. Gloster Javelin formation (RAF Middleton St. George)
54. Parachute jump
55. Jet Provost 'Balbo' formation take off
56. Jet Provost aerobatic team lands (after aerobatics depending on fuel)
57. Avro Shackleton departs for RAF Kinloss
58. Army/RAF set piece 'battle'
59. Jet Provosts and piston Provosts formation fly past, RAF
60. Jet Provost formation lands

As can be seen by the above list, there was a very extensive flying display, which at the time was considered one of the best ever held at the Station. Private flying trips were provided by the Tyne Tees Flying Club. An estimated 25,000 people attended, along with the Duke of Northumberland, the Sheriff of the County and many other dignitaries.

The Station's annual 'Open Day', held on 19 September 1964, was blessed with near perfect weather. It attracted a record crowd of around 60,000. The rehearsals for the air display were recorded by Tyne Tees Television the previous day and were broadcast in a forty-five-minute programme later that same day. It probably did not have many viewers as it was scheduled for 11.30 p.m. Members of the Northumberland Constabulary were entertained in the Officers' Mess on Tuesday 29 September—a gesture of appreciation for the efficient way they had handled the traffic and crowds on the Open Day.

The following year, the weather was not so kind. The night before the air display, there was a torrential downpour that flooded many of the car parks and forced emergency parking arrangements to be made at the last minute. On the day of the Air Show, 18 September, a record crowd attended despite many visitors being turned away during the latter part of the afternoon due to parking difficulties. Throughout the afternoon a strong wind blew, but the flying programme went ahead with only a few minor changes. The event was attended by AM Sir Patrick Dunn with AM R. Thompson and AVM M. Lyne.

The 1966 'Battle of Britain' air display was cancelled in August due to an outbreak of Foot and Mouth disease in Northumberland. The Station's personnel were determined that the RAF Benevolent Fund should not suffer from the loss of revenue. Donations were made from the Officers and Sergeants messes along with the Airmen's Club. A Station Fete was held later in the year, at which the Red Arrows aerobatic team flew a display.

RAF Acklington's last 'Battle of Britain' air display was held on 16 September 1967. Although the Station remained open for another year, 6 FTS was by then in the process of being run down and many of the personnel had been deployed elsewhere. The final air display was marred by lowering cloud and very poor visibility. Originally it had been intended to have a flypast by sixteen of RAF Acklington's Jet Provosts which would then perform a mock attack on a fort. This was restricted to two aircraft because of the poor weather. Without extensive use of radar by the air traffic controllers, no display would have been possible. Despite all this, a record amount of money was raised for RAF charities. The net profit from the sale of souvenir booklets, refreshments, car parking fees, etc., came to over £4,000. Approximately 35,000 people attended in 5,000 cars, 110 coaches, and 200 motor cycles. American-style toll booths were set up at the entrance to the airfield to collect parking fees from the vehicles. This initiative by the students proved most effective in boosting the revenue. With the end of this popular annual event, air displays became a rarity in north-east England in the final decades of the twentieth century.

# 21

# Run Down and Closure

6 FTS: January–June 1968
18 Squadron: January 1968–August 1969, Westland Wessex

The Westland Wessex HC2s of 18 Squadron arrived from RAF Gutersloh, Germany, on Friday 5 January 1968. Initially, 18 Squadron had fourteen Westland Wessex on strength but the number increased to twenty-two over the next few months. There were also rumours that these would be joined by Scottish Aviation Twin Pioneers, most of which were at that time in the Middle East. Initially, the helicopters operated with 6 FTS, which was not due to close until the middle of the year. On 1 April 1968 there was a parade to mark the 50th anniversary of the RAF. The highlight was a mass flypast over Morpeth and Newcastle of twelve Wessex helicopters of 18 squadron, twelve Jet Provosts from 6 FTS and two Whirlwinds from 202 Squadron. In the evening, a dinner was held in the Officers' Mess which was attended by the Lord Mayor of Newcastle and many other local dignitaries. The Duke of Northumberland proposed a toast to the Royal Air Force. By the end of the month, flying training on Jet Provosts had almost come to an end.

One student was suspended for an incident that took place at the end of March. On a solo night sortie in a Jet Provost T4 (XR663), he became disorientated in cloud and lost control of the aircraft. During the subsequent spiral dive and recovery, the aircraft fatigue meter registered over 7 g. It was so badly damaged that it could not be repaired at RAF Acklington.

In May, twenty-six officers of the RAF and five officers of the Royal Malaysian Air Force graduated from 185 Course. This brought to an end flying training at RAF Acklington. To mark this and the disbandment of No. 6 FTS, a parade was held on 30 May in No. 3 Hangar. The remaining Jet Provosts had one final task to perform—to form the 'R' in the Royal Cipher 'E II R' during the Royal Review Flypast commemorating the RAF's fiftieth anniversary at Abingdon airfield, located to the south of Oxford. On 4 June, thirteen Jet Provosts flew to RAF Gaydon to practise and mount the flypast on 14 and 15 June.

Air Support Command took over control of RAF Acklington from Training Command the following month. The last Jet Provost departed on 12 July 1968,

Westland Wessex HC2, 18 Squadron at RAF Acklington in January 1969. (*Roger Lindsay*)

leaving only 18 Squadron's Wessex and the search and rescue attachment of two Whirlwinds. Great interest in the airfield's new role was shown by local organisations and members of the public. They were not aware that 18 Squadron had been informed that they would be on the move again in the following year and that the airfield's future was now in doubt.

Although 18 Squadron's stay at RAF Acklington was brief, their helicopters undertook a wide variety of tasks while there. During August, three Wessex carried 220 troops in a mock battle before the public at an Army display at Stensall. Another two aircraft were detached to Blaich, Scotland, where they flew under-slung loads and equipment for the Engineering Regiment. In September and October, much of 18 Squadron participated in exercises in Western Germany. Back at RAF Acklington, many of the airmen moved from their billets into three recently completed barrack blocks. A Wessex assisted Durham Constabulary in a search for an escaped convict in November. The next month, two aircraft were based at RAF Lossiemouth and carried bomb disposal teams daily to the Cape Wrath Ranges in Northern Scotland.

Three days into 1969, the Station Commander made the following announcement to service and civilian personnel:

The Ministry of Defence has now announced that 18 Squadron will move to RAF Odiham about August this year and as no subsequent Royal Air Force use can be found for RAF Acklington, it will close as a Royal Air Force Station soon afterwards. On present plans all the civilians at Acklington will become redundant in their present posts when 18 Squadron moves. Consideration is, however, being given as to whether a further possible service use can be found for the Station and the Ministry of Defence will let us know when a decision on this has been reached.

As late as May, RAF Strike Command were considering the feasibility of using Acklington as an administrative base for Boulmer as well as housing the RAF Ouston University Air Squadron. At one stage, basing Andover transport aircraft there had also been considered. All these ideas in the end came to nothing. During March, four Wessex transferred fodder for groups of sheep stranded in snow on the Cheviot Hills. In May, two Wessex were tasked with transporting twenty-four politicians and other VIPs from Edinburgh to Kinloch Rannoch in the Highlands to meet the Duke of Edinburgh. Also that month, the helicopters took part in Exercise 'Sparrowhawk' conducted from RNAS Arbroath. It involved helicopters from a number of squadrons flying at very low level with Hawker Hunters operated by the Royal Navy attempting to intercept them. An entry in 18 Squadron's record book noted: 'the flying was possibly the most operational the helicopter force has ever done under peacetime conditions.'

On 30 July 1969, 18 Squadron departed RAF Acklington for the last time. Eight Wessex flew in formation over Morpeth and Newcastle as a farewell to Northumberland. They then headed south to their new home at RAF Odiham. Here, they were greeted with a barrel of beer by 72 Squadron which had been at RAF Acklington in the early days of the Second World War. After the departure of 18 Squadron, RAF Acklington was rapidly run down and closed. A small corner was retained for housing the two search and rescue Whirlwinds which were to remain here until 1975. The rest of the site was put on the market. There was serious concern about the loss of jobs in what was already an area of high unemployment. Northumberland County Council produced a sales brochure for the former RAF airfield. It opened with the words:

> A Unique Opportunity—The opportunity to develop land at Acklington, Northumberland, exists because of rationalisation of Government defence commitments. The complex comprises 600 acres in all, which includes a hard runway with 180 acres developed with housing, a wide range of other buildings, many of which are new and which are ideally suitable for a large scale research unit, industrial project or recreational development with which aircraft landing and maintenance facilities would be available. The complex is self-contained and all buildings and housing lie within a radius of one mile.

Among the assets listed were a new brick, steel, and concrete hangar with two floors of offices, workshops and storage. There were a further two steel hangars and a single brick and steel example. In addition there was a further large storage and maintenance building along with three accommodation blocks. Adjacent to Acklington village were fifty-six detached and semi-detached houses. There were a further 203 flanking the main complex. Rather surprisingly, despite numerous attempts to modernise the Station, over seventy of the original wooden huts still survived. Finally, there were three runways—5,850 feet, 4,700 feet, and 3,800 feet respectively.

The County Council contacted a number of companies, including Hawker Siddeley Aviation, to see if they would be interested in acquiring the airfield. Their attempts met with little enthusiasm. In the end, the buildings were sold to the Home Office. Two prisons were established on the site, with Acklington Prison opening in 1972. Next to it, Castington Prison was constructed, opening eleven years later for male juveniles. These two institutions had the distinction of being the most northerly prisons in England. A few of the airfield buildings, including the large Gaydon hangar, were incorporated into them. It now serves as the jail's engineering workshop making car parts. The two prisons were merged in 2011 to form Northumberland Prison. Much of the remaining open ground became an opencast coal mine, thus achieving what the Luftwaffe would have loved to have achieved. The runways were ripped up in 1974. By the end of the twentieth century, most traces of RAF Acklington had been completely obliterated by the extraction of coal. The scars in the ground have now been filled in and the land restored and returned to agriculture. A small number of pillboxes constructed to defend to airfield still survive in 2016, but little else. It was if there had never been an airfield here—and one with such an eventful history as well.

# Appendix

## Station Commanders

Wg Cdr J. J. Paine—1.4.1938
Wg Cdr J. S. L. Adams—27.10.39
Wg Cdr B. B. Caswell—20.5.1940
Wg Cdr H. J. Pringle AFC—17.8.1940
Wg Cdr O. G. Morris—31.7.1941
Wg Cdr D. O. Finlay—15.8.1941
Wg Cdr V.S. Bowling—9.12.1941
Wg Cdr C. O. Lott DSO, DFC—21.3.1941
Wg Cdr E. Graham—8.5.1942
Wg Cdr B. Barthold—3.1.1944
Sqn Ldr J. Willis—6.3.1944
Sqn Ldr S. H. Caunt—29.1944
Sqn Ldr E. T. Mitchell—26.8.1944
Wg Cdr G. W. Petre DFC, DFC—6.6.1945
Wg Cdr R. Berry DSO, DFC—18.7.1945
Wg Cdr R. W. Stewart CBE, AFC—1.8.1946
Wg Cdr A. C. P. Carver—1.6.1948
Wg Cdr R. M. B. Duke Wooley DSO, DFC—19.11.1948
Wg Cdr T. W. Kean, AFC—22.1.1951
Wg Cdr R. A. Barton OBE, DFC—6.1.1953
Grp Capt. J. N. W. Farmer DFC—30.12.1953
Grp Capt. N de W. Boult DFC, AFC—5.3.1956
Wg Cdr P. D. B. Stevens—20.4.1958
Wg Cdr R. R. Mitchell MBE DFC—25.8.1958
Sqn Ldr M. T. Bartlett—27.3.1961
Wg Cdr B. A. Colvin—5.6.1961
Grp Capt. F. W. M. Jenson OBE, DFC, AFC—24.7.1961
Grp Capt. J. R. Forsythe DFC—14.6.1963
Grp Capt. P. H. Sutton—10.12.1965
Wg Cdr H. Harrison AFC—23.2.1968
Wg Cdr P. R. Harding—8.11.1968

# Based Flying Units

1 April 1938, No. 7 Armament Training Camp (in 25 Group), redesignated No. 7 Armament Training Station—Fairey Seal.

15 November 1938, No. 2 Air Observation School (AOS) formed from No. 7 ATS—Overstrand, Fairey Seal.

3 September 1939, No. 2 AOS departed to RAF Warmwell to become No. 10 AOS.

1 October 1939, 152 Squadron reformed at RAF Acklington—Gladiator II.

7 October 1939, 609 Squadron arrived from RAF Catterick—Spitfire I.

9 October 1939, 607 Squadron arrived from RAF Usworth—Gladiator I, II.

17 October 1939, 609 Squadron departed to RAF Drem.

27 October 1939, 111 Squadron arrived from RAF Hornchurch—Hurricane.

14 November 1939, 607 Squadron departed for Melville, France.

18 November 1939, 43 Squadron arrived from RAF Tangmere—Hurricane I.

7 December 1939, 111 Squadron departed to RAF Drem.

10 December 1939, 46 Squadron arrived from RAF Digby—Hurricane I.

January 1940, 152 Squadron converted to Spitfire I.

17 January 1940, 46 Squadron departed to RAF Digby.

26 February 1940, 43 Squadron departed to RAF Wick.

2 March 1940, 72 Squadron arrived from RAF Church Fenton—Spitfire I.

1 June 1940, 72 Squadron departed to RAF Gravesend.

6 June 1940, 72 Squadron returned from RAF Gravesend—Spitfire I.

12 July 1940, 152 Squadron departed for RAF Warmwell.

13 July 1940, 79 Squadron arrived from RAF Sealand—Hurricane I.

27 August 1940, 79 Squadron departed to RAF Biggin Hill.

28 August 1940, 32 Squadron arrived from RAF Biggin Hill—Hurricane I.

31 August 1940, 72 Squadron departed to RAF Biggin Hill.

610 Squadron arrived from RAF Biggin Hill—Spitfire I.

14 December 1940, 258 Squadron arrived from RAF Drem—Hurricane I.

15 December 1940, 32 Squadron departed to RAF Middle Wallop.

19 December 1940, 72 Squadron arrived from RAF Leuchars—Spitfire

610 Squadron departed to RAF Westhamnett.

21 January 1941, 315 Squadron formed at RAF Acklington—Hurricane I.

1 February 1941, 258 Squadron departed to RAF Jurby.

22 February 1941, 317 Squadron (Polish) formed—Hurricane I.

13 March 1941, 315 Squadron departed to RAF Speke.

29 April 1941, 317 Squadron departed to RAF Ouston.

1 May 1941, 141 Squadron detachment arrived from RAF Ayr—Defiant I.

5 May 1951, 406 Squadron (RCAF) formed—Blenheim 1F.

6 May 1941, 410 Squadron detachment arrived from RAF Ayr. Third RCAF night fighter squadron—Defiant I.

8 July 1941, 72 Squadron departed to RAF Gravesend—Spitfire VB and VC.

9 July 1941, 74 Squadron arrived from RAF Gravesend—Spitfire II.

August 1941, No. 13 Group Target Towing Flight formed—Lysander.

7 August 1941, 141 Squadron detachment departed to RAF Ayr.

3 October 1941, 74 Squadron departed to RAF Llanbedr.

8 December 1941, No. 1490 Flight (Target Towing) formed from No. 13 Group Target Towing Flight –Lysander, Hawker Henley.

15 December 1941, No. 1460 Flight (Turbinlite) formed—Havoc, Boston.

29 January 1942, 141 Squadron arrived from RAF Ayr—Defiant I.

1 February 1942, 406 Squadron departed to RAF Ayr—Beaufighter IIF.

May 1942, No. 1490 Flight redesignated No. 1490 (Fighter) Gunnery Flight.

23 May 1942, 167 Squadron arrived from RAF Scorton—Spitfire VC.

June, 1942, 410 Squadron detachment ends.

1 June 1942, 167 Squadron departed to RAF Castlemains.

23 June 1942, 141 Squadron departed to RAF Tangmere.

219 Squadron arrived from RAF Tangmere—Beaufighter I.

8 July 1942, 1 Squadron arrived from RAF Tangmere—Typhoon IB.

2 September 1942, 539 Squadron formed from 1460 Flight.

4 September 1942, No. 1490 Flight moved to RAF Ouston.

21 September 1942, 219 Squadron departed to RAF Scorton.

20 October 1942, 410 Squadron arrived from RAF Scorton Beaufighter II.

21 January 1943, 539 Squadron disbanded.

9 February 1943, 1 Squadron departed to RAF Biggin Hill.

198 Squadron arrived from RAF Ouston—Typhoon IA, IB.

21 February 1943, 410 Squadron departed to RAF Coleby Grange—Mosquito II.

23 February 1943, 409 Squadron RCAF, moved from RAF Coleby Grange— Beaufighter VIF.

23 March 1943, 350 Squadron arrived from RAF Fairlop—Spitfire VB.

24 March 1943, 198 Squadron departed for RAF Manston.

1 June 1943, No. 6 Anti-aircraft Practice Camp formed in 72 Group—Lysander.

8 June 1943, 350 Squadron departed to RAF Ouston.

21 June 1943, 63 Squadron detachment from RAF MacMerry—Mustang I.

28 June 1943, 63 Squadron detachment departed to RAF Turnhouse.

20 July 1943, 350 Squadron departed to RAF Ouston.

25 August 1943, 349 Squadron arrived from RAF Digby—Spitfire VB.

350 Squadron departed for RAF Digby.

22 September 1943, 316 Squadron arrived from RAF Northolt—Spitfire VB.

22 October 1943, 349 Squadron departed to RAF Friston.

8 November 1943, No. 3 Aircraft Delivery Flight arrived from RAF Catterick.

22 November 1943, No. 3 Aircraft Delivery Flight disbanded.

25 November 1943, No. 4 Aircraft Delivery Flight arrived from RAF Odiham.

1 December 1943, No. 1630 Flight absorbed into 289 Squadron.

10 December 1943, 278 Squadron detachment arrived from RAF Woolsington—Anson.

19 December 1943, 278 Squadron detachment departed to RAF Hutton Cranswick.

25 Squadron arrived from RAF Church Fenton—Mosquito VI.

409 Squadron departed to RAF Coleby Grange.

21 December 1943, 130 Squadron arrived from RAF Scorton—Spitfire VB.

4 January 1944, 130 Squadron departed to RAF Scorton.

5 February 1944, 25 Squadron departed to RAF Coltishall.

409 Squadron arrived from RAF Coleby Grange—Beaufighter VIF.

15 February 1944, 316 Squadron departed to RAF Woodvale.

16 February 1944, No. 147 Airfield Headquarters formed in 24 Wing (No. 12 Group)—Auster I.

23 February 1944, 56 Squadron arrived from RAF Scorton—Typhoon IB.

25 February 1944, 222 Squadron arrived from RAF Catterick—Spitfire IX.

March 1944, 504 Squadron detachment arrived from RAF Digby—Spitfire VC.

7 March 1944, 56 Squadron departed to RAF Scorton.

8 March 1944, 164 Squadron arrived from RAF Twinwood Farm—Typhoon IB.

No. 4 Aircraft Delivery Flight departed to RAF Clifton.

10 March 1944, 222 Squadron departed to RAF Hornchurch.

322 Squadron arrived from RAF Hawkinge—Spitfire VB.

15 March 1944, 266 Squadron arrived from RAF Harrowbeer—Typhoon IB.

15 March 1944, No. 24 Defence Wing moved to RAF Blakelaw, Newcastle-upon-Tyne.

16 March 1944, 164 Squadron departed to RAF Thorney Island.

21 March 1944, 609 Squadron arrived from RAF Tangmere—Typhoon 1B.

1 April 1944, 609 Squadron departed to RAF Thormey Island.

23 April 1944, 322 Squadron departed to RAF Hartford Bridge.

266 Squadron departed to RAF Tangmere.

11 May 1944, No. 147 Airfield Headquarters moved to RAF Zeals.

29 May 1944, No. 3 Tactical Exercise Unit C Squadron from RAF Honiley, returned 13 June 1944, (designated 555 Squadron).

June 1944, Airfield Closed For Reconstruction.

20 November 1944, 288 Squadron detachment from RAF Church Fenton— Beaufighter, Vengeance.

1945 North-eastern Sector Headquarters formed at RAF Blakelaw, Newcastle, flying from RAF Acklington.

2 February 1945, Airfield Re-opened.

26 February 1945, 59 Operational Training Reformed—Typhoon.

7 May 1945, 289 Squadron arrived from RAF Turnhouse—Spitfire and Vengeance.

18 May 1945, 289 Squadron departed to RAF Eshott.

23 May 1945, 19 Squadron arrived from RAF Peterhead—Mustang.

6 June 1945, 59 Operation Training Unit disbanded.

12 July 1945, 140 Squadron arrived for disbandment—no aircraft.

13 August 1945, 19 Squadron departed to RAF Bradwell Bay.

14 August 1945, 219 Squadron arrived from B. 106, Twente, Netherlands—Mosquito.

19 August 1945, 140 Squadron departed to RAF Fersfield for disbanding.

29 August 1945, 263 Squadron formed. First jet squadron at RAF Acklington— Meteor F.3.

2 April 1946, 263 Squadron departed to RAF Church Fenton.

10 April 1946, North-eastern Sector Headquarters disbanded.

1 May 1946, Armament Practice Station formed (ex 2 APS, RAF Spilsby).

219 Squadron departed to RAF Wittering.

15 June 1946, 288 Squadron disbanded.

23 July 1946, 130 Squadron departed to RAF Odiham.

November 1946, Fighter Armament Trials Unit formed (ex 2 APS, RAF Spilsby).

25 February 1952, Armament Practice Station (APS) became part of 81 Group—Mosquito, Martinet, Tempest, Meteor T7, F.8, Vampire, Balliol.

July 1956, Fighter Armament Trials Unit disbanded.

27 July 1956, Armament Practice Station disbanded.

October 1957, 275 Squadron (various Flights) moved in to cover search and rescue role—Sycamore.

14 January 1957, 29 Squadron arrived from RAF Tangmere—Meteor NF.11.

14 February 1957, 66 Squadron arrived from RAF Linton-on-Ouse—Hunter F.6.

22 July 1958, 29 Squadron departed for RAF Leuchars—Javelin.

1 September 1959, 275 Squadron detachment renumbered 228 Squadron—Whirlwinds.

30 September 1960, 66 Squadron disbanded.

24 July 1961, No. 6 FTS arrived from RAF Ternhill to convert to Jet Provost—Provost T.1.

28 August 1964, 228 Squadron detachment redesignated 202 Squadron—Whirlwinds.

December 1966, No. 6  FTS redesignated No. 6 (Advanced) FTS.

5 January 1968, 18 Squadron arrived from RAF Gutersloh, Germany—Wessex HC2.

30 June 1968, No. 6 (Advanced) FTS disbanded.

4 August 1969, 18 Squadron departed to RAF Odiham.

1975, 202 Squadron (B-Flight detachment) departed for RAF Boulmer.

Airfield closed and put under Care and Maintenance.

(Compiled by Richard Flagg, Airfield Research Group)

## Air Displays

The headquarters building at RAF Acklington in the mid-fifties. (*The National Archives*)

# Battle of Britain Display, 1957

Static Display:

XJ687 Hunter F.6, 66 Squadron, RAF Acklington
WH275 Meteor F.8, 66 Squadron, RAF Acklington
XH688 Javelin FAW5, 151 Squadron, RAF Turnhouse
SX938 Lincoln B2, RAF Flying College, Manby
WJ492 Valetta C1, RAF Flying College, Manby
XJ916 Sycamore HR14, Detached from RAF Thornaby
XF.838 Provost T.1, RAFC Cranwell
WL691 Varsity T.1, 116 Squadron, RAF Watton
WZ583 Vampire T.11, RAF Acklington Station Flight
XE869 Vampire T.11, RAF Acklington Station Flight
WF819 Meteor T7, RAF Acklington Station Flight
WD742 Meteor NF.11, 29 Squadron, RAF Acklington
WH699 Canberra B2, RAF Flying College, Manby
WH960 Canberra B6, 12 Squadron, RAF Binbrook
PH648 Anson C12, RAF Acklington Station Flight
WG185 Balliol T2, 288 Squadron, Middle Wallop

The Flying Display included formation flying by both 29 and 66 Squadrons. Of the other participants, several operated from the airfield while others landed to refuel after their show:

WJ781, WJ972, WJ792 Canberra B6s, 139 Squadron, RAF Binbrook
XK663 Comet C2, CSE, RAF Watton
XD817 Valiant B1, 148 Squadron, RAF Marham
XA904 Vulcan B1, RAF Waddington Wing
WB583 Shackleton MR1, MOTU, RAF Kinloss
WM985, WN112, WV794, XE397 Sea Hawk FB3s, 736 Squadron, RNAS Lossiemouth
XD679 Jet Provost T.1, HQ, RAF Hullavington
WL478, WF829 Meteor T7s Aerobatic team, 4 FTS, RAF Worksop
WK741, WF662 Meteor F.8s Aerobatic team, 4 FTS, RAF Worksop
WK628, WZ849, WD218 Chipmunk T.10s Durham UAS, Usworth
Four unidentified B-45Cs, 47th Bomb Wing, RAF Sculthorpe
Five unidentified F-84Fs, 81 TFW, RAF Bentwaters

Based Aircraft on Airfield:

The following Hunter F.6s of 66 Squadron—XG253, XG237, XG252, XE618, XG202, XF519, XG233, XG153, XG236, XG265, XG266, XG255, XG154, and XK139.

The cover for RAF Acklington's 1957 air display programme. (*The National Archives*)

A line up of Gloster Meteor NF.XIs shortly after 29 Squadron's arrival at RAF Acklington in early 1957. (*The National Archives*)

The following Meteor NF.11s of 29 Squadron—WD786, WM187, WD768, WD749, WD710, WD703, WD617, WM236, WD599, WD625, WM157, WM155, WM224, WD715, WD762, and WM178.
WA909 Meteor F.8, RAF Acklington Station Flight
WK573 Chipmunk T.10, RAF Acklington Station Flight
WL419 Meteor F.8, 13 Group HQ, RAF Ouston

(Roger Lindsay, Military Aviation Review, October 1979)

## Battle of Britain Display, 1959

Static Display:

TB252 Spitfire LFXVI, Gate Guard
TX171 Anson C19, RAF Acklington Station Flight
VM365 Anson C19, 13 Group CF, RAF Ouston
VS586 Anson T21, 13 Group CF, RAF Ouston
WG259 Valetta T3, 1 ANS, RAF Topcliffe
WJ776 Canberra B(I)6, 139 Squadron

WL419 Meteor T7, 13 Group CF, RAF Ouston

XD183 Whirlwind HAR4, 228 Squadron, RAF Acklington

XE582, XG237, and XG252 Hunter F.6s, 66 Squadron, RAF Acklington

XA824 Javelin FAW6, 29 Squadron, RAF Leuchars

XM355 Jet Provost T5, CFS, RAF Little Rissington

XF.874 Provost T.1, 1 FTS, RAF Linton-on-Ouse

XD875 Valiant B1, 207 Squadron, RAF Marham

VZ110 Vampire FB(T)5, 5 FTS, RAF Oakington

XH329 Vampire T.11

WJ947 Varsity T.1, 115 Squadron, RAF Tangmere

Static/ Flying Display:

WA733 Meteor T7 66 Squadron, RAF Acklington

WA909 Meteor F (TT) 8 66 Squadron, RAF Acklington

WB964 Slingsby Sedbergh TX1 (Glider) 642 FS, RAF Ouston

WK590 Chipmunk T.10, CNCS, Glider Tug for above

WK623 Chipmunk T.10, Glasgow UAS, Renfrew

WP213 Valiant B1, 18 Squadron, RAF Finningley

WS781 Meteor NF14, RAF Ouston

WV574, WV640, XF.889, and XF.894 Provost T.1 Display Team, 1 FTS, RAF Linton-on-Ouse

XD276 Scimitar F1, 800 Squadron, Ark Royal

XE519, XE521, XG153, XG154, XG226, XG253, XG255, XG256, and XG266 Hunter F.6s, 66 Squadron, RAF Acklington

XL620 Hunter T7, 66 Squadron, RAF Acklington

Flypast:

WF382, WJ920, and WL632 Varsity T.11, ANS, RAF Topcliffe

WZ459 Vampire T.11, 1 FTS, RAF Linton-on-Ouse

XG225, XG231, and XG238 Hunter F.6s, 92 Squadron, RAF Middleton St. George

XH437 Javelin T3, 33 Squadron, RAF Middleton St. George

XH715, XH716, XH718, XH719, XH720, XH721, XH786, XH790, XH835, XH836, XH838, and XH839 Javelin FAW7s, 33 Squadron, RAF Midlleton St. George

XJ430 Whirlwind HAR4, 228 Squadron A-Flight, RAF Acklington

XA938 Victor B1, 10 Squadron, RAF Cottesmore

XH481 Vulcan B1, 101 Squadron

Douglas Destroyer (RB-66B), 47 Bomb Wing, USAF

62992 F-100 and 2 other F-100s of the 20 TF, USAF

(Compiled by Jim Jobe)

# Battle of Britain Display, 1962

Static Display:

TB252 Spitfire LFXVI, Gate Guardian

G-ALPK Dragon Rapide

G-ARCZ D31 Turbulent

KF.314 Harvard T2B, A and AEE, Boscombe Down

TX226 Anson C19, FTCCF

TX232 Anson C19, 23 Group Communications Group

WF125 Sea Prince C1, RNAS Lossiemouth

WG260 Valetta T3, RAFC Cranwell

WG465 Chipmunk T.10, 13 Group, RAF Ouston

WJ728 Canberra B2, 231 OCU, RAF Bassingbourne

WK815 Meteor F.8, APS, RAF Sylt

WR971 Shackleton MR3, 120 Squadron, RAF Kinloss

WT485 Canberra T4, 231 OCU, RAF Bassingbourne

WW425 Provost T.1, 6 FTS RAF Acklington

WZ515 Vampire T.11, 8 FTS, RAF Swinderby

XF.420 Hunter F.6, 92 Squadron.

XH694 Javelin FAW6, RAF Exhibition Flight, RAF Bicester

XP634 Jet Provost T4, 6 FTS, RAF Acklington

XR441 Sea Heron, 781 Squadron,

XR654, XR656, XR664, and XR666 Jet Provost T4s, 6 FTS, RAF Acklington

57-0547 T.33A, RAF Wethersfield

XM... Gnat T.1, RAF

Flying Display:

PM631 Spitfire PRXIX, Battle of Britain Memorial Flight, RAF Coltishall

RA685 Lincoln B2, 151 Squadron, RAF Watton

TA634 Mosquito TT35, 3 CAACU, Exeter

WE188, WJ870, and WT489, XH584 Canberra T4s, Display Team, 231 OCU, RAF Bassingbourne

WJ815 Canberra PR7, 58 Squadron, RAF Wyton

WJ890, WJ892, and WL634 Varsity T.1s, RAFFC, RAF Manby

WL796 Shackleton MR2C, 204 Squadron, RAF Ballykelly

WZ404 Valiant B(PR)K1, 207 Squadron, RAF Marham

XA898 Vulcan B1, 230 OCU, RAF Waddington

XA932 Victor B1—unit not known

XD184 Whirlwind HAR4, 228 Squadron, RAF Acklington

XD217, XD219, XD220, and XD224 Scimitar F1s, 736 Squadron, RNAS Lossiemouth

XE975 Vampire T.11, 8 FTS, RAF Swinderby

XF.892 Provost T.1, 6 FTS, RAF Acklington

XM970 Lightning T4, Lightning CS, RAF Middleton St. George.

XN404 Britannia C2, 99/511 Squadron

XN605 Jet Provost T4., 6 FTS (solo display), RAF Acklington

XN603, XP638, and XP662 Jet Provost T4 Display Team, 6 FTS, RAF Acklington

XN850 Argosy C1, 114 Squadron, OCU, RAF Benson

XR395 Comet C4, 216 Squadron, RAF Lyneham

(Compiled by Jim Jobe)

## Battle of Britain Display, 16 September 1967

Static Display:

XS610 Andover C1, 47 Squadron

WJ339 Hastings C2, 24 Squadron, RAF Colerne

XG274 Hunter F.6, 4 FTS, RAF Valley

XF.418 Hunter F.6, 229 OCU, RAF Chivenor

XS765, and XS766 Basset CC1s, Northern Communications Squadron, RAF Topcliffe

XD165, and XJ729 Whirlwind HAR10s, A-Flight 202 Squadron, RAF Acklington

XR511 Wessex HC2, 72 Squadron, RAF Odiham

XS732 Dominie T.1, CAW, RAF Strubby

XD550 Vampire T.11, 3 FTS, RAF Leeming

WF383 Varsity T.1, 115 Squadron, RAF Watton

XP503 Gnat T.1, 4 FTS, RAF Valley

XF.509 Shackleton MR3, 203 Squadron, RAF Balleykelly.

XB287 Beverley C1, 47 Squadron, RAF Abingdon

WZ849 Chipmunk T.10, AEF Ouston

WT488 Canberra T4, 98 Squadron

XL474 Gannet AEW3, 849 Squadron, RNAS Brawdy

61605 T33, USAF

120227 Heinkel 162

Flying Display:

XS789 Andover CC2, RAF

VP971 Devon C2, RAF SSC

XR499 Wessex HC2, 72 Squadron, RAF Odiham

XS918 Lightning, 23 Squadron

WG555 Shackleton MR2, 204 Squadron, RAF Ballykelly

WE195 Canberra T4, 231 OCU

XR953 Gnat T.1, 4 FTS, RAF Valley

XS918 Lightning F.6, 11 Squadron

Four Lightnings, 23 Squadron, RAF Leuchars

XV166 Buccaneer S2, 736 Squadron.

XM603 Vulcan B.2, RAF

XE857 Vampire T.11, 1 FTS

XL479 Gannet AEW3, 849 Squadron

XS736 Dominie T.1, CAW

WD496 Hastings C2, A and AEE, Boscombe Down

WD310, and WG465 Chipmunk T.10s, RAF

XN187 Sedbergh Glider

XM491 Britannia C1, RAF

10564, 10571, 10573, 69212, 10563, and 10595 F-5As, 338 Squadron, Royal Norwegian Air Force.

6 FTS Aircraft on Airfield:

Jet Provost T3s—XN556, XN596, XN578, XN492, XN581, XM468, XN594, XN551, XM467, XM417, XM474, XM402, XM407, XN509, XM416 plus five unidentified aircraft.

Jet Provost T4s—XP636, XR646, X585, XP676, XS182, XP683, XR643, XR644, XR649, XR656, XR659, XR660, XR660, XR663, XR666, XR675, XR680, XS180, XR706 plus two unidentified aircraft.

(Compiled by Brian Jones and Air Britain)

# Bibliography

The National Archives, Kew

RAF Acklington—7 Armament Training Station, Air 29/544
RAF Acklington, Operations Record Book, 1939–1945, Air 28/17
RAF Acklington, Operations Record Book, 1946–1950, Air 28/971
RAF Acklington, Operations Record Book, 1951–1957, Air 28/1451
RAF Acklington, Armament Practice Station, 1946–1950, Air 29/1296
RAF Acklington, Armament Practice Station, 1951–1956, Air 29/2369
RAF Acklington, Operations Record Book, 1961, Air 28/1711
RAF Acklington, 6 FTS Operations Record Book, 1961–1965, Air 29/3510
RAF Acklington, 6 FTS Operations Record Book, 1964–1965, Air 29/3512
RAFAcklington, 6 FTS Operations Record Book, 1967, Air 29/3806
RAF Acklington, 6 FTS Operations Record Book, 1968, Air 29/3807
RAF Acklington, Operations Record Book, 1968–1969, Air 28/171
1630 Anti-aircraft Co-operation Flight, Air 29/880
6 Anti-aircraft Practice Camp, RAF Regiment, Air 29/ 439
59 OTU Operations Record Book, Air 29/684
25 Squadron Operations Record Book, Air 27/387
29 Squadron Operations Record Book, Air 27/274
32 Squadron Operations Record Book, Air 27/360
43 Squadron Operations Record Book, Air 27/441
46 Squadron Operations Record Book, Air 27/460
56 Squadron Operations Record Book, Air 27/531
72 Squadron Operations Record Book, Air 27/624
79 Squadron Operations Record Book, Air 27/664
111 Squadron Operations Record Book, Air 50/43
130 Squadron Operations Record Book, Air 27/937, Air 27/938
141 Squadron Operations Record Book, Air 27/970
152 Squadron Operations Record Book Air 27/1025
164 Squadron Operations Record Book Air 27/1085
198 Squadron Operations Record Book Air 27/1170

219 Squadron Operations Record Book Air 27/1360

222 Squadron Operations Record Book Air 27/1372

258 Squadron Operations Record Book Air 27/1530

266 Squadron Operations Record Book Air 27/1559

315 Squadron Operations Record Book Air 27/1699

316 Squadron Operations Record Book Air 27/1704, Air 27/1705

317 Squadron Operations Record Book Air 27/1706

322 Squadron Operations Record Book Air 27/1716

349 Squadron Operations Record Book Air 27/1744

350 Squadron Operations Record Book Air 27/1745

406 Squadron Operations Record Book Air 27/1791

409 Squadron Operations Record Book Air 27/1801

410 Squadron Operations Record Book Air 27/1802

607 Squadron Operations Record Book Air 27/2093

609 Squadron Operations Record Book Air 27/2102

## Books

Anon., *416 Squadron History* (Ontario: The Hangar Bookshelf, 1984)

Beedle, J., *The Fighting Cocks: 43 (Fighter) Squadron 1916–2009* (Barnsley: Pen and Sword Books Ltd, second revised edition, 1985)

Bragg, M., *RDF.1* (Paisley: Hawkhead Publishing, 2002)

Brandon, L., *Night Flyer: Pioneering Airborne Electronic Warfare with 100 Group Mosquitoes* (Manchester: Crecy Publishing Limited, 1961, reprinted 2010)

Brew, A., *The Defiant File*, (Tunbridge Wells: Air Britain (Historians) Ltd, 1996)

Chorlton, M., *Airfields of North-East England in the Second World War* (Newbury: Countryside Books, 2005)

Clark, P., *Where the Hills Meet the Sky: A Guide to Wartime Air Crashes in the Cheviot Hills* (Northumberland: Glen Graphics, second edition, 1997)

Cummings, C., *Last Take-Off: A Record of RAF Aircraft Losses 1950-1953* (Northamptonshire: Nimbus Publishing, 2000).

Davis, C. R., *Almost Forgotten: The Search for Aviation Accidents in Northumberland*, (Stroud: Amberley Publishing, 2012)

Docherty, T., *Swift to Battle: No. 72 Fighter Squadron in Action, Vol. 1 1937–1942* (Barnsley: Pen and Sword Books Ltd, 2009)

Dixon, R., *607 Squadron: A Shade of Blue* (Wolf's Nick Publishing, 2012)

Dobinson, C., *Fields of Deception: Britain's Bombing Decoys of the Second World War* (London: Methuen Publishing Ltd, 2000); *AA Command, Britain's Anti-Aircraft Defences of the Second World War* (London: Methuen Publishing Ltd, 2001)

Delve, K., *The Source Book of the RAF* (Shrewsbury: Airlife Publishing Ltd, 1994)

Ferguson, A. P., *Beware, Beware: The History of 611 (West Lancashire) Squadron, Royal Auxiliary Air Force* (Reading: Airfield Publications, 2004)

Francis, P., *British Military Airfield Architecture: From Airships to the Jet Age* (Somerset: Patrick Stephens Ltd, 1996)

Franks, N., and O'Connor, M., *Number One in War and Peace: The History of No. 1 Squadron 1912–2000* (London: Grub Street, 2000)

Gray, R., Corbett, J., Shipley, J., and Anderson, N., *Air Crash Northumberland: Planes, Pilots, Reasons, Recoveries* (Newbury: Countryside Books, 2008)

Hall, I., *Zeppelins over the North-East: Airship Raids of WWI* (Alnwick: Wanney Books, 2013); *Relics of War: A Guide to the 20th Century Military Remains in the Northumberland Landscape* (Alnwick: Wanney Books, 2013)

Halley, J. J., *The Role of the Fighter in Air Warfare* (Windsor: Profile Publications, 1978)

Jefford, C. G., Wg Cdr MBE BA RAF (ret'd), *RAF Squadrons: A Comprehensive Record of the Movement and Equipment of All RAF Squadrons and their Antecedents* (Marlborough: The Crowood Press Ltd, 2001)

Johnstone, S., Air Vice-Marshal, *Enemy in the Sky* (London: William Kimber & Co. Ltd, 1976)

Jubelin, A., Rear Admiral, *The Flying Sailor* (London: Hurst and Blackett, 1953)

Mahon, M., (ed.), *Nighthawk! A History of 409 (Night Fighter) Squadron* (Courtenay: E. W. Bickle Ltd, 1978)

Mason, F. K., *The Hawker Hurricane: An Illustrated History* (Manchester: Crecy Publishing Ltd, 2001)

Mason, P. D., *Nicolson VC: the full and authorised biography of James Brindley Nicolson* (Kent: Geerings of Ashford Ltd, 1991); *The Story of 25 Squadron: Royal Air Force* (Kent: Air Britain (Historians) Ltd, 2001)

Matusiak, W., Gretzyngier, R., and Wisniewski, P., *315 Squadron* (Poland: Stratus, 2004)

McKinstry, L., *Spitfire: Portrait of a Legend* (London: John Murray Ltd, 2007)

Nelson, K. J., *Spitfire RCW: The Wartime Exploits of Wg Cdr Royce Clifford Wilkinson OBE, DFM & Bar, C. de G. (France)* (Canada: The Author and Western Canada Distributors Ltd, 1994)

Norman, B., *Luftwaffe Losses over Northumberland & Durham 1939–1945: Broken Eagles 2* (Barnsley: Pen and Sword Books Ltd, 2002); *Luftwaffe over the North: Episodes in an Air War* (London: Leo Cooper, 1993)

Rippon, B., *The Amble Branch* (Southampton: Kestrel Railway Books, 2007)

Rolls, W. T. DFC, DFM, AE, *Spitfire Attack* (London: William Kimber & Co. Ltd, 1987)

Sands, R. P. D., Fg Off., *Treble One: The Story of 111 Squadron Royal Air Force* (Essex: North Weald, 1957)

Saunders, A., *No. 43 "Fighting Cocks" Squadron* (Oxford: Osprey Publishing, 2003)

Stewart, E., *RAF Acklington* (Northumberland: Amble Social History Group, 2002)

Smith, D. J., *Action Stations No. 7: Military Airfields of Scotland, the North-East and Northern Ireland* (Cambridge: Patrick Stephens Ltd, 1983); *Britain's Military Airfields 1939–1945* (Wellingborough: Patrick Stephens Ltd, 1989)

Taylor, L., *Luftwaffe over Scotland* (Caithness: Whittles Publishing, 2010)

Thetford, O., *Aircraft of the Royal Air Force since 1918* (London: Putnam Aeronautical Books, ninth edition, 1995)

Thomas, A., *Gloster Gladiator Aces, Osprey Aircraft of the Aces 44* (Oxford: Osprey Publishing, 2002)

Townsend, P., *Time and Chance: An Autobiography* (London: William Collins & Sons Co. Ltd, 1978); *Duel in the Dark: A Fighter Pilot's Story of the Blitz* (London: Arrow Books Ltd, 1986)

Sturtivant, R., ISO with Hamlin, J., *Flying Training and Support Units since 1912* (Kent: Air Britain (Historians) Ltd, 2007)

Walton, D., *Northumberland Aviation Diary: Aviation Incidents from 1790–1999*, (Northumberland: Norav Publications, 1999); *Northumberland Aviation Diary Supplement: Aviation Incidents from 1790–2005* (Northumberland: Norav Publications, 1999)

Wheatley, L., *An Erksome War* (Devon: Merlin Books Ltd, 1991)

Wills, H., *Pillboxes: A Study of UK Defences, 1940*, (London: Leo Cooper, 1985)

Ziegler, F. H., *The Story of 609 Squadron: Under the White Rose* (Manchester: Crecy Publishing, 1993)

## Magazines

'Blackburn', 'The Aerial Defence of the North-East during the Great War', November 553–Nov 557, *Air North, The North-East Branch of Air Britain (Historians)*, Vol. 39, No. 11, November 1999.

Carrott, G., 'Sheen's Third off the Northumberland Coast–The Coquet Island Ju 88', March 1941, Nos 561–562, *Air North, The North-east Branch of Air Britain (Historians)*, Vol. 40, No. 11, November 2000; 'The Saga of the Red Cross Heinkel, 1st July, 1940', August 382-August 383, *Air North, The North-East Branch of Air Britain (Historians)* Ltd., Vol. 40, No. 8, August 2000; 'The Kirknewton Twelve', May 263–May 265, *Air North, The North-East Branch of Air Britain*, Vol. 42, No. 5, May 2002; 'RAF Morpeth: Postscript', Aug 407–414, *Air North, The North-East Branch of Air Britain*, Vol. 43, No. 8, August 2003; 'The History of Boulmer Aerodrome', Mar 151–155, *Air North, The North-East Branch of Air Britain (Historians)*, Vol. 44, No. 3, March, 2004.

Fairless, M., 'The Wessex Era at Acklington', October 509–510, *Air North, The North-EastBranch of Air Britain (Historians)* Vol. 40, No. 10, October 2000.

Fairless, M., '6 FTS and the Provost T.1', August 416–419, Vol. 43, No. 8, August 2003.

Howarth, P., 'Defending the Peace: Fighter Command Airfield Development 1946–1960, Part 3', pp. 127–140, *Airfield Review*, No. 117, December 2007.

Linsay, R., 'Battle of Britain 14.9.57', pp. 14–15, *Military Aviation Review*, October 1979.

Lowry, B., 'Airfield Defences' pp. 139–140, *Airfield Review*, No. 92, October 2001.

Nesbit, R., 'The Flight of Rudolf Hess: Part 1', pp. 572–575, *Aeroplane Monthly*, Vol. 14, No. 11, November 1986.

'Spitfire 70: The A-Z of Mitchell's Wonder', *Flypast Special*, Key Publishing Ltd., Stamford.

## Internet Sites

British Newspaper Archive.
Flightarchive.
Hansard.
Acklington Village.
North-East War Diary.